Mama, I Am Yet Still Alive

Mama, I Am Yet Still Alive

A Composite Diary of 1863 in the Confederacy

As seen by the soldiers, farmers, clerks, nurses, sailors, farm girls, merchants, surgeons, riverboatmen, chaplains and wives.

Jeff Toalson, editor

iUniverse, Inc.
Bloomington

Mama, I Am Yet Still Alive
A Composite Diary of 1863 in the Confederacy

iUniverse books may be ordered through booksellers or by contacting:

iUniverse
1663 Liberty Drive
Bloomington, IN 47403
www.iuniverse.com
1-800-Authors (1-800-288-4677)

ISBN: 978-1-4697-5316-4 (sc)
ISBN: 978-1-4697-5317-1 (e)

Printed in the United States of America

iUniverse rev. date: 2/15/2012

To my parents

Glen and Jessie Toalson

A lifetime of thanks for your lessons in honesty, integrity, character, friendship and love.

The Butternut Series:

Dedicated to preserving the true history of the ordinary Confederate soldiers and civilians, by using their voices, which are so eloquently recorded in their diaries, letters and journals.

Books by Jeff Toalson

Butternut Series:

No Soap, No Pay, Diarrhea, Dysentery & Desertion
A Composite Diary of the Last 16 Months of
the Confederacy from 1864 to 1865

Send Me a Pair of Old Boots & Kiss My Little Girls
The Civil War Letters of Richard and Mary Watkins, 1861-1865

Mama, I Am Yet Still Alive
A Composite Diary of 1863 in the Confederacy

Contents

Introduction

No finer historians have emerged from the War Between the States than the common soldiers and civilians. Their 'voices' provide an intimate, personal view that is devoid of posturing. These marvelous writers recorded their thoughts in their letters, diaries and journals. The writings of farmers, nurses, riverboatmen, clerks, chaplains, sailors, common soldiers, nuns, farm girls, merchants, surgeons and wives relate a much different story than the correspondence of generals and politicians.

Most books about the conflict deal with campaigns, battles, strategy, politics and generalship. There are very few books that focus on the common soldiers, the civilians, and the impact of the war on their lives. The magic of their phrasing and the simple power of their words captured me ten years ago while working on my first book; I am still held by their spell. Private Charles Thomas of the 56th Virginia cemented that magic when I found this note he penned to his wife on January 13, 1863:

> "... *I washed my old shirt and draws yestady. My old pant is verry nasty and my ass is out and these is all I have got ...*" [1]

Is there anything else to say? Twenty six evocative words ... How could I begin to describe the situation as well as Charles has detailed it to his wife?

Many of these documents have significant spelling errors and problems with grammar and punctuation. But, as with Private Thomas, there is no difficulty comprehending his uniform difficulties because "*my old pant is verry nasty and my ass is out* ..." One can understand how I have become very partial to using letters, diaries and journals to present a picture of the war. This is especially true if the letters are not modified or embellished before publication.

Sometimes you find a treasure. Sometimes the treasure finds you. The treasure, in this case, was twenty huge file drawers filled with unpublished diaries, letters and journals in the archives of the United Daughters of the Confederacy in Richmond, Virginia. Mrs. Hilda Bradberry showed me these files in 2008 and told me, *"Ladies of the UDC have been sending in originals, transcriptions and photocopies of their ancestors' writings since 1958."* She knew I was almost ready to publish *Send Me a Pair of Old Boots & Kiss My Little Girls – The Civil War Letters of Richard and Mary Watkins, 1861-1865.* Hilda knew that there were hundreds of amazing 'voices' hiding in those file cabinets waiting for someone to help them tell their story. She chose me.

No Soap, No Pay, Diarrhea, Dysentery & Desertion used the "voices" of common soldiers and civilians to tell the story of the last 16 months of the Confederacy. Now I had a treasure trove of documents to use to tell the story of 1863. In August of 2011 I finished the files. What I found is almost beyond belief. I am awed by the simple power of their writing. Their 'voices' will capture you as you read the selections I have chosen for this book.

I found wonderful letters from daughters, sisters, sweethearts and grandmothers in addition to letters from nurses, teachers and farm wives. Letters from women are a significant addition because their letters went to the front and seldom came home. They were used for campfires or toilet paper and were lost to history. The women's letters add depth and complete the story by providing us with a picture of life at home. They are the perfect complement to the soldier's letters.

> Miss. Kate Blount, a farm girl near Woodville, Mississippi, writes, "We have a hundred sick soldiers here and all public buildings are occupied. They say we must take five hundred ..."

> Mrs. Mary Edmondson of Phillips County, Arkansas, notes, "All our efforts to procure salt have failed thus far. Our hogs are eating up our small supply of corn fast. What shall we do?"
>
> Miss. Elizabeth Sikes of Sikes Ville, Florida, in a letter to her brother pens, "... fish aplenty in the old Suwannee and I live handy to them.... They are a great help whare meat is scarce."
>
> Mrs. Margarette Harris writes her husband from Paris, Texas, that they, "have escaped all the diseases that this unfortunate village is infested with ... from smallpox, down to mumps."

I hope you find this composite diary of 1863 in the Confederacy interesting and thought provoking. It should open vistas to a side of the war with which you may not be familiar. As in all wars, it is the civilians and the common soldiers who suffer. Glory is hard to find amidst lice, dysentery, starvation and death. Hope does survive, as do many of these writers, and hope is just about all they will have when 1863 draws to a close.

Editor's Notes

It is my belief that documents lose their historical flavor, and their magical feeling, if the spelling, punctuation or wording is modified. In many cases, because of the scarcity of paper, writers did not use paragraphs. You will be reading the letters as they wrote them. I will not be creating paragraphs, correcting spelling or changing punctuation.

Many of these writers had unusual habits for using both periods and capital letters. This type of sentence structure is normal: *Mr Anderson was planting potatoes ... I inquired about the pigs Bro Edwin gave you ... we are going to see Mother W on saturday.* Periods are typically used at the end of sentences and seem optional in other situations. Some of the writers whom you meet, and Mr. Jacob R. Hildebrand in particular, leave gaps after each thought rather than using a period.

Quite often our writers spelled a person's name or a place incorrectly. I will put the correct spelling in brackets. *We are near Vixburg [Vicksburg] camped on the Aszoo [Yazoo] river. Gen Pemburton [Pemberton] is at Vixburg.*

Certain abbreviations are used on a regular basis: Yr Aff [Your Affectionate], Gen and Genl [General], &c[etc], CH & CoHo [Courthouse] are the most common. You will see consistent misspellings of recognizable words and phrases and these will not be changed: Troope, comlads [comrades], rashuns [rations], provishun [provisions], git, tolrable, enuf, sevrel, perty tite [pretty tight], prey for us, close [clothes], and ber footid [bare footed] are some key examples. You will be amazed at all the ways there are to spell diarrhea and mosquito.

There are terms like "a quire of paper" and a "bad case of bilious fever" which I will explain in editor's notes at the end of the letter in which the term first appears.

Those readers who are familiar with my editing style know that I use [...] to indicate that I have left out text before or after other text.... *We were payed off today ... am going to save my money ... I have two good pare of pants ... & a pare of large horse leather boots."*

I have tried to stay true to the style of the writers and have sometimes wished that my computer would quit trying to correct what I am typing. It will automatically turn befel to befell and saturday to Saturday. It is necessary to go back and correct the computer.

It is my pleasure to offer you these remarkable 'voices.'

January, 1863

As the cold New Year dawns on the Murfreesboro battlefield, the temperatures are below freezing and frost is on the clothing of the wounded and dead Union and Confederate soldiers. Captain Robert Smith of the 2nd Tennessee Infantry writes, "*Last night was very cold, and many a wounded soldier was frozen to death this morning.*" The battle at Murfreesboro, Tennessee, ends the fighting of 1862 and is the opening battle of 1863.

1862, at times, seemed to offer great hope to the Confederate cause. They still held Vicksburg, Chattanooga and Richmond. Their armies had achieved quite a few military successes. Grant had been turned back at Chickasaw Bluffs, Burnside had been defeated at Fredericksburg, and Bragg had pounded the Union army on the last day of the year at Murfreesboro. 1863 will be the critical year for the Confederacy in its quest to achieve independence.

On January 1st General Magruder recaptures the city and port of Galveston for the Confederacy. It will remain an open Confederate port for the balance of the conflict and provide blockade runners a port for delivering supplies to the Trans-Mississippi area of Texas, Arkansas and Louisiana.

Arkansas Post, 40 miles up the Arkansas River from the Mississippi River, surrenders to Union forces on January 11th with the loss of 4,791 men and significant quantities of weapons, stores and munitions.

Mr. D. A. St. Clair, proprietor and editor of the *Wytheville Dispatch*, informs his readers on January 13th of the sinking of the USS *Monitor* off Cape Hatteras, *"The famous Ercission* [Ericsson] *iron-clad steamer, called the Monitor, has fought her last fight.... she put to sea the other day to measure strength with Old Neptune, who brought one of his fierce Hatteras ruffies to bear upon her and ... she had to give up the ghost. Down she went ... into Davy Jone's Locker, and with her went down 32* [16] *of her crew...."* [1]

On January 20th General Burnside attempts to turn General Lee's left flank in what becomes the infamous "Mud March." By the 24th the Union forces are back in their camps facing Lee across the Rappahannock. On January 25th General Hooker replaces General Burnside as commander of the Army of the Potomac.

Inflation has reduced the value of the Confederate dollar to about 35 cents versus the U. S. Dollar. Prices of many staples have risen sharply and key items such as salt and cotton cards are becoming not only more expensive but more difficult to obtain.

Lt. Theophilus Perry of the 28th Texas Cavalry writes his wife from Pine Bluff, Arkansas, *"My life is miserable on account of our separation. Oh God! that, this War would close, and all could return to our homes & families."* His is a universal sentiment that is shared by soldiers in butternut and in blue.

January, 1863

January 1, 1863
Murfreesboro, Tennessee

Captain Robert D. Smith
Co. B – 2nd Tennessee Infantry

"The new year opened this morning ... Last night was very cold, and many a wounded soldier was frozen to death this morning.... Last night our troops took all the wounded with in reach and laid them in rows on the ground, both friend and foe ... They made fires between each row to prevent the poor fellows from freezing ... our troops kept up the fires all night." [2]

- - - - -

January 1, 1863
Murfreesboro, Tennessee

Private Theodore F. Harris
Co. C – 8th Tennessee Infantry

"We ... fought the battle of Murfreesboro.... I can scarcly picture our hard ships up to this time. provisions was scarce and bear [bare] for clothing. Some of us went along without shoes feet bleeding suffering from cold etc. In this engagement at Murfreesboro our Regiment went in with 600 men come out with 200, we sustained a heavy loss charging a battery across an open field, but we captured the battery alright, of course Bragg lost. Nothing more could be expected of Mr. Know all ..." [3]

- - - - -

January 1, 1863
Murfreesboro, Tennessee

Private W. E. Preston
Co. G – 33rd Alabama Infantry

"The burning of inferior powder caused our guns to choke and I think all had exchanged their Enfields for Springfields on the battle fields ... We had also exchanged our cedar canteen [for] block tin, oval shaped Yankee canteen and those who [had] not picked up a U. S. blanket, good black hat, blue overcoats or shelter tent could usually buy cheap … of men who had more than one." [4]

- - - - -

January 1, 1863
Fredericksburg, Virginia

Private Nimrod Newton Nash
Co. I – 13th Mississippi Infantry

"Dear Mollie
… We are going on piquet again to night…. have had a dull Christmast except one day we got plenty of apple brandy at thirty dollars pr gallon…. Some think [Longstreet] is going to give the most deserving furloughs - … if that is so your man will come in for one; now wont that bee fine for me to come home and see your big fat self. If you are smoking I wont stay with you long as light …

Newton" [5]

- - - - -

January 1, 1863
Halifax County, North Carolina

Mrs. Catherine Edmondston
Farm wife

" … I indulged in the now unwanted luxury of a Pudding, for with sugar at 87 ½ to $100 a lb, and with so many calls upon us as we have, I do not think it is right to visit the sugar barrel every day …" [6]

- - - - -

January 1, 1863
Rome, Georgia

Mr. R. S. Norton
Merchant

"This is the day President Lincoln says the Negroes shall be free. Everything is quiet, the hireing of servants going on, and at an advance of full 25% over last year …" [7]

- - - - -

January 1, 1863
Camp near Fredericksburg, Virginia

Corporal James Kibler
Co. F – 10th Virginia Infantry

"we Were Paid off yesterday. The confederacy paid us off, up to the Very Day. They owed us for two Month. I Drew $26.00. I think I shall send [home] some twenty Dollars." [8]

- - - - -

January 2, 1863
Fredericksburg, Virginia

1st Sergeant Henry S. Figures
Co. F – 4th Alabama Infantry

"My Dear Ma
Isaac Gill got here this morning. he said he had a letter & a pair of boots for me but they were stolen from him at the hotel in Richmond, He lost a suit of clothes for Jack Byrns & something for almost all the boys. I am very sorry you know as it is the second pair of boots that have been sent for me. Do not send anymore for fear that they will get lost. I am well and have been so ever since we left Maryland....

I expect we will all get furloughs in a week or two. Col. Bowles told me yesterday that Gen Law said that he would have them for the regiment in that time. I dont know how many will be allowed to go from each company but I suppose about fifteen or twenty, in that case we will have to draw a number to go If I dont I will buy some one of the boys. We had a very dull Christmas here, some of the regt were drunk ... but not a drop went down my throat.... Tell Pa that my promotion has not come yet. Tell Otey that I have bought that little rifle from Pres Drake for him. I gave him Twenty five dollars for it. When I come home I will bring it to him & learn him how to shoot ...

Has Mary Alexander got back from Georgia, if she has ... give my love to her ... Ask sister if she has ever heard from Annie Brown my old sweetheart.... I must close. So good bye.
Your eff son
Henry S Figures" [9]

- - - - -

Description of the Confederate Soldier — Private Carlton McCarthy
Richmond Howitzers

"Reduced to a minimum the private soldier consisted of one man, one hat, one jacket, one shirt, one pair of pants, one pair of drawers, one pair of shoes and one pair of socks. His baggage was one blanket, one rubber blanket, and one haversack. The haversack contained smoking tobacco and a pipe and generally a small piece of soap, with temporary additions of apples, persimmons, blackberries and other commodities as he could pick up on the march.

Common white shirts and drawers proved the best … (for) the common private. The infantry … carried their caps and cartridges in their pockets. Canteens … were discarded. A good strong tin cup was better … easier to fill at a well … and serviceable as a boiler for making coffee.

(Each soldiers) one blanket and one rubber cloth were rolled together lengthwise, with the rubber cloth outside, tying the ends together and throwing the loop over the left shoulder … the (tied) ends hanging under the right arm." [10]

- - - - -

Undated — Private Evan S. Larmer
Co. B – 25th Virginia Cavalry

"we had very scanty rashens & porley closed the only close I got my dear old Mother sent me. Som of my comlads were almost ber footed & raged close … at times we suffered greatly." [11]

- - - - -

Undated — Private W. E. Preston
Co. G – 33rd Alabama Infantry

"A dogfly is made of cotton sheating about five feet square, with buttons and button holes on three sides, each weighed about one and a half or two lbs.

Three men slept together, each had a fly, they button two flys together, stretch it across a ridge pole, close up the North or back end with the third fly so it is a tent with the front end open." [12]

- - - - -

January 2, 1863
Richmond, Virginia

Private Marion H. Fitzpatrick
Co. K – 45th Georgia Infantry

"General Hospital No. 20
Richmond, Va.
Jan. 2nd, 1863

Dear Amanda,
I write to you again to let you know how I am getting along. My wound is improving fast, and I think it will soon be entirely well so that I can rejoin my Reg …

… You also wrote that your cards [cotton cards] were nearly worn out. This I am sorry for, as it cannot be easily remedied. Cards are worth $25.00 a pair here, but I hope they are cheaper there. But you must get them when yours wear out no matter what the price …

… May God bless you. Write soon.
Your husband,
M. H. Fitzpatrick"

(ed: Cotton cards were rectangular wooden paddles with hundreds of metal teeth, about a half inch long, mounted on one side. The "cards" were used to separate and align the fibers of cotton prior to spinning. Wool cards were used for accomplishing the same task with sheep's wool.)

(ed: Marion received a 30 day furlough on January 18. He rejoined his unit near Guinea Station, Virginia on February 18. This would be the first of only two furloughs he would receive during the war.) [13]

- - - - -

January 3, 1863 | Exemption Committee Petition
Polk County, North Carolina | Mrs. Violet Johnson & neighbors

"To the Exemption Committee
Dear Sirs

The undersigned wives or Sisters of the Soldiers of this immediate Section of Said County: Proposes respectfully to Showeth unto your Honors, our very great dependence upon Mr. G. W. Rhodes, and his Mill. We are all living within a Mile + a half of the said Mill, and Nearer to it than any other Mill, besides we are all poor + a large majority of us have no other way of toteing our grain to Mill than packing it upon our Shoulders; Now if we were deprived of this friend and convenience, the Most of us will be necessitated to pack our grain a cross a very high + rugged mountain to other mills; Your Honors will please consider the premises … [and] confer a lasting favor + benefit upon your humble petitioners by detailing Mr. G. W. Rhodes to remain at home … as Miller of a grist mill on Mill Creek …"

Violet Johnson
Harriet Panter
Elmina Phillips
Rebecca Goodson
Jane Rhodes
S. A. Thompson
Caroline Newman
Imanda Buly" [14]

(ed: The ladies were successful. A 60 day exemption was granted and the initial exemption was followed by further exemptions. The last exemption in the file was a 60 day exemption dated May 19, 1864. Mr. Rhodes was able to provide services, based on the above petition, till at least mid July 1864. It was noted that he would often provide milling services for free to assist the families while their husbands and brothers were off in the army.)

- - - - -

January 3, 1863
Murfreesboro, Tennessee

Private William T. Charles
Goldthwaite's Alabama Artillery

" ... of all the nights I ever passed through, before or since, this Saturday night ... was the most terrible. The following night may have been colder ... But on this Saturday night – no man who was there, and lived to get through it will ever forget it.... we left Murfreesboro at about 7.30 OC [o'clock] in a pouring rain. I was riding next to the lead in our gun ... The wagon train, of course, had gone on in front, and the turn pike, from incessant rain and the excessive travel of marching and counter marching of the army with artillery as well as wagons, was "cut up" until it was worse than no road at all. There was so much suffering that night among the infantry, that really in as much as it was possible for human nature to forget their own troubles ... we, of the artillery, forgot ours. The riders were mounted, though it was colder riding, and the cannoneers were allowed at very bad places in the road, to "mount" the limber chests and caissons, though it was all the horses could do to pull them. But the poor infantry, many with worn out shoes – alas, many with no shoes at all! – the rough, uneven stones cut their feet until they bled. – many gave out; dropped down by the way side to die, - probably to freeze to death!

All night long we marched through the rain.... just about daylight on this gloomy Sunday morning, when we had halted for a few moments for some purpose, "Enoch," the body servant ... of Lieut. Fitzpatrick, came up to me as I sat listlessly on my horse, and slyly touching the canteen by his side said in a low tone of voice: "Mr. Charles don't you want a drink of Tennessee Whisky?" "Great Scott!" I cried, brightening up in a second; "how much?" for I knew he had it for sale. He produced a "cap-box" – one of those tin boxes intended to contain 250 waterproof caps – and which would hold a good sized wine glass full, and replied, "a dollar a drink." I had just one five dollar bill in my pocket – Handing him that ... I said, "Give me the canteen." He did so, and turning it up to my mouth I drank ... and I have often said to him since ... , "Enoch, I believe you saved my life on that Sunday morning on the retreat from Murfreesboro to Estelle Springs." [15]

- - - - -

January 2 and 3, 1863
Chattanooga, Tennessee

Miss. Kate Cummings
Hospital Matron

" ... A battle was fought at Murfreesboro on the 31st... The weather is very cold, and I shudder to think what our men have had to suffer on the battlefield. Our hospital is filled with wounded. Mrs. Williamson and myself are not able to do any thing for them....

The wounded kept coming in last night [January 2] ... Every corner of the hospital is filled with patients, and the attendants had to give up their beds for them.... Many have to be carried from the ambulances, as they are unable to walk. We have sent off a great many to-day, to make room for others.... Bread, beef, and coffee are all we have to give them; they are thankful for that. Our cooks have been up for two or three nights in succession; the surgeons and nurses the same.... " [16]

(ed: Kate is the hospital matron, or head nurse, and Mrs. Williamson is the assistant matron. The Confederate government passed an act to allow the employment of women in the hospitals on September 27, 1862. Matrons were provided a salary of $40 per month and assistant matrons were paid $35. Kate will spend the entire war providing services for the Army of Tennessee..) [17]

- - - - -

Undated
Knoxville, Tennessee

Private Stokley Acuff
26th Tennessee Infantry

"I was wounded in [my] first battle [Murfreesboro] I maid my way to Knoxville was signed to the hospittle and then was sent home ... never able for service any more." [18]

- - - - -

January 3, 1863
Sulphur Springs, North Carolina

Mrs. Cornelia Henry
Farm wife

"Saturday – Mr. Henry went to Ashville this morning, staid all day. Got a bolt of shirting, had to give 75 cts. pr. yard. Done up some lard today & made sausage meat. Sam cutting up the hogs. Killed none today.... I helped to make the sausage & I made myself a pair of shoes today. They fit very neatly. The children have got no shoes." [19]

(ed: Sulphur Springs is located in what is currently West Asheville, North Carolina. Cornelia always refers to her husband, William L. Henry, as Mr. Henry or Mr. H. The Negroes began the winter hog butchering on January 1 and will butcher the last of 100 hogs on January 20.)

- - - - -

January 4, 1863
Murfreesboro, Tennessee

Private John Jackman
Co. B – 9th Kentucky Infantry

"Up before daylight: The Dr. having a spare horse, I was to ride. We mounted just at daylight, and rode off through a pelting rain. All had left before the dawn. We overtook our regiment 5 miles from town, on the Manchester pike, acting as rear guard. Being mounted, Col. H. sent me ahead to turn back an ordnance wagon. The road was a perfect "loblolly", and in riding by the infantry, sometimes I would splatter mud on them, and often expected to be bayonetted.... camped near Manchester. Not having been on horseback for so long, this ride of 30 miles tired me almost as much as if I had walked." [20]

- - - - -

January 4, 1863
Murfreesboro, Tennessee

Captain Robert D. Smith
Co. B – 2nd Tennessee Infantry

" ... We held all the Battle ground up to the time we left and I cannot understand why our Generals decided to retreat." [21]

- - - - -

January 4, 1863
Little Rock, Arkansas

Captain Elijah P. Petty
Co. F – 17th Texas Infantry

"My Dear Ella
... It rained in torrents yesterday and the roads are miserable ... This has been the pleasantest winter so far that I ever saw ... it is well for the poor soldier that the weather is good.... I have about 60 men including officers in camp some 3 or more unfit for duty – At Austin I have about 7 and at Little Rock about 6 or 7 more. The balance of the company are back in Texas on one pretence or another. Some sick and most of them playing Opossum.... My love to all for the present. Good bye.
Yours ever
E P Petty" [22]

- - - - -

January 4, 1863
near Vicksburg, Mississippi

Private Grant Taylor
Co. G – 40th Alabama Infantry

"Beloved wife and children,
... We landed at Vicksburg last Tuesday night about dark and started here at ten o'clock that night. We are 7 or eight miles north of Vicksburg on the edge of the Miss swamp. We left every thing at Vicksburg except what clothes we have on and one blanket. We lie out at night and take all kinds of weather. It's rained a lots in the last 36 hours and we had to wrapt up in our blankets and take it. Night before last I lay on two rails with a jug for a heading. I slept pretty well although it rained heavily the most of the night. My blanket kept me nearly dry.... only get one meal a day. It is pretty rough but we all stand it finely.

... You must do the best you can with your affairs. I am too far off to give advice. Surely Pap will advize you. I think if you can you had better get more than 50 bu of corn.

Give my best respects to all … Kiss the children for me and believe your true one, as ever.
Grant

I received your ambrotype [photograph]. How sweet and natural it looks." [23]

(ed: On January 8 Grant advised Malinda, "You had better buy more than 50 bu corn. Let it cost what it may. It is cheaper now than it ever will be again." Grant is sure it will take more than 50 bushels to support the animals and family until the next crop is harvested.)

- - - - -

January 4, 1863 — Mrs. Catherine Edmondston
Halifax County, North Carolina — Farm wife

"The *Alabama* … has captured a California Steamer. Got no gold … Instead of destroying her, however, he bonded her in the sum of $125,000 & her cargo & freight for $135,000 to be paid to the Confederate Authorities within thirty days after the establishment of the independence of the Confederacy. I fear me that bond will not be redeemed…. " [24]

- - - - -

January 5, 1863 — Captain Griffin Frost
Gratiot Prison, St. Louis, Missouri — Co. A – 2nd Missouri Infantry

"There are now about 800 prisoners in Gratiot, and more coming in every day … We are allowed only two meals per day … Some two or three hundred eat at a time, and the tin plates and cups are never washed from the first to the last table. For breakfast we have one-fifth of a loaf of baker's bread, a small portion of bacon, and a cup of stuff they call coffee. For dinner the same amount of bread, a hunk of beef, and a pint of water the beef was boiled in … sometimes a couple of boiled potatoes – all portioned [eaten] with the hands; knives, forks and spoons not being allowed." [25]

(ed: Gratiot Prison is the former McDowell Medical Hospital, located on Gratiot Street in downtown St. Louis, and it has been converted from a hospital to a prison.)

- - - - -

January 5, 1863 — Reverend Samuel R. Houston
Union, Virginia — Presbyterian Minister

"Jeans $2, linsey $2, flannel $3. The dresses of my little girls cost $18 to $25 apiece, and the servant girl's living dress about $15." [26]

(ed: Linsey is a coarse fabric which is a blend of cotton and wool.)

- - - - -

January 6, 1863 — Mr. R. S. Norton
Rome, Georgia — Merchant

"This is sale day … The sale of Estate property was unusually large, and particularly so for negroes which sold unusually high …

Boys from 9 to 14 sold from $800 to $1400; women as high as $1500, men up to $1600. Cash." [27]

- - - - -

January 7, 1863 — Miss. Emmie Robbins
St. Louis, Missouri — Resident

"My darling brother
… I had a very pleasant New Years. I kept the house open and received between forty and fifty calls…. many were the toasts that were drunk to absent brothers, lovers and friends in Dixie.
… Ned I wish you would try and get me a button from all of the Southern states. I want to have a bracelet made of them …

I remain your devoted

Sister" [28]

(ed: Ned is 1st Sgt. Edward Robbins of the Landis Missouri Light Artillery. In late 1863 he will transfer from the Landis Artillery to a regiment of Texas Cavalry.)

- - - - -

January 8, 1863
Pine Bluff, Arkansas

Captain Elijah P. Petty
Co. F – 17th Texas Infantry

"My Dear Wife
… We are away out here in the woods away from every body and every thing. The water is bad and at some distance off. The wood is good and abundant. The ground where the camps are situated is pretty good but swampy around. What they want with us here is beyond my imagination to fix up … I send $2 to buy Van a pig. He shall be even with the other children.
Yours truly
E P Petty" [29]

(ed: On the 4th Elijah had written to his daughter, Ella. This letter is to his wife, Margaret. They have three sons; Frank, Don and Van. All of the children have their own pig except for the youngest. Now, Van will get to raise his own pig.)

- - - - -

January 8, 1863
Tedford's Ferry, Arkansas

Sergeant W. W. Heartsill
Co. F – 2nd Texas Cavalry

"We have THREE CRACKERS each, issued to us, nothing for our horses. this is all we have had to eat since breakfast." [30]

(ed: Hardtacks are of course the crackers W. W. was issued. The Confederate soldier more normally had cornbread to go with his fatback. When they did have hardtacks they would cook them in the fatback grease to soften them and they called them "Mucks.")

- - - - -

January 9, 1863
Danville, Virginia

Reverend James Carmichael
Chaplain of the Post

"A. W. Sanders, Esq.
Charleston, S. C.

Dear Sir,
It is my painful duty to announce to you the death of your brother Corporal Henry J. Sanders, Comp. H … Hampton Legion. He died of typhoid fever, was calm and rational to the last, perfectly willing to die, and I am sure was prepared for the change. I enclose you a list of his effect, and a self-explanatory printed form which must be sworn and subscribed before a Justice by a witness and yourself, and then the Clerk of Court must certify … that the Justice is a Magistrate. Do this and return to me by mail, and I will send them by Southern Express to your address at yr. risk.

Your brother requested on his death bed that you should have all his effect. I buried him, and would advise you to remove his remains at once, if you contemplate doing so at all.
Respectfully

James Carmichael
Chaplain of the Post" [31]

(ed: Reverend Carmichael received Mr. Sander's paperwork on January 19 and shipped a box with clothes, money (less box and freight cost), pipe and knife. He advised in a note with the shipment that the grave was marked with "a durable wood headboard in military cemetery with name, co, regt & date of death." Mr. Sanders confirmed receipt of the box on January 30th.)

(ed: "Typhoid fever is an acute, highly infectious disease caused by the typhoid bacillus, Salmonella typhosa, transmitted by contaminated food or water and characterized by red rashes, high fever, bronchitis and intestinal hemorrhaging.") [32]

- - - - -

January 9, 1863	Captain David Pierson
Snyder's Mill, Mississippi	3rd Louisiana Infantry

ORDNANCE RECEIPT

"Received [______________________] this 9 day of Jany 1863 of Capt. S. S. [________] Ord Off Hebert Brig Maury Div the following ordnance and ordnance stores:

	Condition
28 Cart Boxes	Good
37 Cap Boxes	..
30 Waist Belts	..
48 Haversacks	..
38 Canteens	..
43 Canteen Straps	..
1040 Enfield Cartridges	..
390 Miss. Cartridges	..
1360 Perc Caps	..

David Pierson
Capt Commdg 3rd La Regt" [33]

(ed: Most of these items are self explanatory. The Enfield rifle and the Mississippi rifle took different cartridges but the same percussion cap. When possible, units tried to have all of the same type of rifle but that was not always possible. The cap boxes held the percussion caps which were placed where the hammer would strike when the trigger was pulled. The percussion cap would discharge the cartridge which had been loaded down the muzzle.)

- - - - -

January, 1863
near Franklin, Virginia

Private John W. Calton
Co. I – 56th N. Carolina Infantry

"Dear Brother and Sister
... we marched from Franklin down her about fore miles in a blinding snowstorm ... bin on aforced march ever Sance ... tell you I am all most wore out my feet & legs Swell like an old brok down [____] ... I march all day & Just eat a small pice of raw bacon without bread & I get along very well on it ... " [34]

- - - - -

January 9, 1863
Wytheville, Virginia

Wytheville Dispatch

"LOCAL ITEMS

Soldiers at the Depot – We are informed that the wounded and sick soldiers at the Depot are suffering from want of proper attention. They need food of proper quality, and careful nurses. We hope our citizens will make arrangements to add to their comforts.

Small Pox – One District of our County (the 4th) is still affected with this terrible scourge. There are, we understand, fifty cases in the hospital. Three deaths have occurred." [35]

(ed: The paper was published semi-weekly. Normally this occurred on Wednesday and Saturday but sometimes the issues came out on Tuesday and Friday. Subscription for 6 months was $2.50 and for 3 months was $1.50. Individual copies sold for ten cents.)

- - - - -

January 10, 1863
near Fredericksburg, Virginia

Private John H. Corwin
Co. D – 5th Alabama Infantry

" … The boys are still after squirrels. If they ever show themselves they are as good as dead … Commenced raining today about eleven o'clock and continued all day and rendered every thing extremely disagreeable. Our fly leaked in several places but happily I had my oil-cloths with me and kept my blankets dry." [36]

- - - - -

January 10, 1863
near Fredericksburg, Virginia

Private Samuel Pickens
Co. D – 5th Alabama Infantry

"… a barrel of Apples that cost in Rich.[mond] about $20. sold up at the army for $164 – what swindling. Every thing is immensely high now. In Rich. Coffee is $5.50 lb. & Sulpher $1.00 to 1.10. Salt has been $2.50 lb. but I'm happy to hear has fallen to 40 cts. You cant [buy] a pr. Boots for less than $50…. Caval. horses are very high tho not as high as they were last Summer. They sold in Rich. at 5 & 6 hundred dollars…. There is no telling what thing will come to if the war continues much longer - & the Gov cont. issue half mill. daily in Treas. notes." [37]

- - - - -

January 10, 1863
Sulphur Springs, North Carolina

Mrs. Cornelia Henry
Farm wife

"Saturday – Rained nearly all day. Mr. Henry in the house nearly all day…. Abbe Parker was buried yesterday. She died Wednesday morning…. The vaccine matter has done very finely in the children's arms. Jinnie made sausage meat today & washed a little for the children. Tena finished the lard today. Atheline not well." [38]

(ed: The children have all had the smallpox vaccination. Sometimes smallpox is called variola. Varioloid refers to a milder form of smallpox in someone who has already had smallpox or who has had the vaccination.)

(ed: Jinnie, Tena and Atheline are negroes owned by William and Cornelia.)

- - - - -

Ambulance Corps
Army of Northern Virginia

Dr. Thomas F. Wood
HQ – 3rd N. Carolina Infantry

"The rule ... was that two, two-mule or two-horse ambulances were allotted to each regiment. The ambulances were plain spring wagons without cushions, the bedding for the wounded men being such straw or hay as the driver was able to collect ... These ambulances were under the control of the medical officers of the regiment – The ambulance corps consisted of twenty men – two from each company. The men were selected ... because of physical strength and personal courage ... Each regiment was allowed a hospital cook and a medical knapsack bearer." [39]

(ed: Dr. Wood later noted that the medical knapsack for the field surgeon contained, "lint, bandages, sponges, tourniquets, four splints, chloroform, morphine, and a pint of alcoholic stimulants.") [40]

- - - - -

Undated
Cleveland, Tennessee

Private William J. McLarrin
19th Tennessee Infantry

"... and there at [Murfreesboro] I was wounded in the left leg and sent to the hospital in Cleveland Tenn and lay in hospital untill I was able to be moved they sent me up to Athens and Bob Clack met me there with a wagon with a bed in it and took me home ... I have been a cripple ever since the wound would never heal ..." [41]

(ed: William continued to have problems with his leg following the war. In 1905 he had to have the leg amputated.)

- - - - -

January 11, 1863
Richmond, Virginia

Mr. John B. Jones
Clerk – War Department

"The enemy's gun boats (two) came up the York River last week, and destroyed an oyster boat. Beyond the deprivation of oysters, pigs and poultry, we care little for these incursions." [42]

- - - - -

January 11 & 12, 1863
Arkansas Post, Arkansas

Private Benjamin Seaton
Co. G – 10th Texas Infantry

"Sunday 11th – at 8 A.M. the fireing commencd again and kept up vary study all day and a 10 A.M. small arms commencd and was kept up untell 4 P.M. when the white flag was run up on our wright wich we was vary sory to sea but nevertheless it was so so we were orderd to stack arms and was marched down to the river bank and a strong guard placed around us fer the knight. We are prisners of war.

Monday 12th – we lay thar on the bank untell late in eaving when we went on one of ther boats to start to Yankadom. I was vary sick fer several days on the boat – no correct time of anything will be ceapt [kept]. We went up the Missippi River to St Louisville some 600 miles by water and thar our officers were taken from us and sent to Camp Chace in Ohio near Columbus and the privets went up to Aulton some 50 miles and thar taken the cars to Chicago to Camp Douglas som 250 miles by railrode. Arived thar on the 28th – vary cold and snowing – servare cold weather. The troops suffered a grate deale – it made a grate meny sick and caused a grate many deaths in the command. We cold git no correct news while we remained thar – we wer treated tolerable well about as well as we cold exspect prisners of war to be treated." [43]

(ed: Camp Chase was a major prisoner of war camp near Columbus, Ohio. From Alton, Illinois the privates were sent to Camp Douglas, in Chicago, which was the largest prison camp in the Union prison system.)

(ed: Benjamin uses a lot of very interesting phonetic spelling of his words but is quite consistent. It is quite interesting in the last paragraph when "could" and "cold" are both spelled "cold.")

- - - - -

January 12, 1863
Arkansas Post, Arkansas

Captain Samuel T. Foster
Co. H – 24th Texas Cavalry

"It is reported this morning that we are to go on board one of the steamers, and go to Vicksburg to be exchanged, for surenough we are prisoners of war. *Prisoners of war* – Those are terrible words.... By 9 O'Clock AM we commence to go aboard an old steamboat called the *John J. Roe* a name never to be forgotten by those that went on board of her that day ... After we all get on board, Col Wilkes informs us that we lost 68 men in the fight, killed and wounded.... We get under way in the evening going down to Vicksburg to be exchanged ... We get to the mouth of the Ark river and stop in the Miss river among a lot of coal barges – where our boat takes on coal - ... Next morning ... one steamer whistles ... then starts up the Miss. river and we after it ... Vicksburg is down the river and we are going up the river. All speculation and ...guess work ...

The next day after we start up the river it commences to snow, the first we have seen this winter – It is very cold no fires no clothes no blankets – or at least not enough – I saved one Mexican blanket but it has several bullet holes in it – " [44]

(ed: The 24th Texas is dismounted cavalry. They will serve the entire war as infantry. Most of the war they will serve as part of General Patrick Cleburne's Division in the Army of Tennessee.)

(ed: 10 days after boarding the John J. Roe *they will reach St. Louis. From St. Louis their journey will take them to Vincennes, Cincinnati and finally Columbus, Ohio where they will be confined in Camp Chase. In the spring they will be transferred to Ft. Delaware and from there they will journey to Ft. Monroe and finally City Point, Va. for exchange in early May. Vicksburg and Aiken's*

Landing near City Point were the two prisoner exchange points as established by the Dix-Hill Cartel of July 22, 1862. However, General Grant was trying to capture Vicksburg and these POW's would provide instant reinforcements for the defense of the city. Therefore, these troops spent almost 4 months in captivity and were exchanged in Virginia.) [45]

- - - - -

January 12, 1863
Arkansas Post, Arkansas

Sergeant W. W. Heartsill
Co. F – 2nd Texas Cavalry

" ... we are all supplied with a liberal breakfast composed entirely of river water, and of course cannot complain. At 10 o'clk we receive the same for dinner that we got for breakfast, which is a very extravagant bill of fare. In the evening the "Rangers" are transferred to the Str *Sam Gatey*, and at sunset we receive a good supply of fat bacon and hard tack, WHICH IS THE ONLY FOOD THAT WE HAVE HAD FOR EIGHTY FOUR HOURS." [46]

(ed: The Sam Gatey *will go upriver in company with the* John J. Roe *and other ships transporting prisoners. Officers will be sent to Camp Chase and the enlisted men in the 2nd Texas Cavalry will be split between Camp Douglas in Chicago and Camp Butler in Springfield, Illinois.)*

- - - - -

January 13, 1863
Meherrin, Virginia

Mrs. Mary Watkins
Farm wife

"My dear Husband
Purnall Dickinson is here and starts back to the army tomorrow so I will write and send this letter by him ... we persuaded him to stay until Wednesday hoping that we might find a servant to send with your horse.... Mr. Anderson [overseer] ... sent a bucket of the fresh meat and a bucket of very good sausages Saturday evening.... The last hogs weighed 1088 lbs. Mr Anderson has just measured up the new corn and finds that he has 125 barrels to begin the year with after fattening the hogs ...

… Nannie Watkins [sister-in-law in Granville, NC] is very low with typhoid fever, has bleeding at the nose, a great deal of very bad symptoms…. Brother Nat has been with her a fortnight. Mama has a good many sick negroes here. Dr. Eggleston was here yesterday … Patience he thinks will go off in consumption like the other women we have lost here…. Write me soon whether to send Purnall or not [with your horse] …Minnies mouth is still very sore her limbs and back are covered with sores too….
Good bye
Your own
Mary" [47]

(ed: Mary is living at her Mama's farm which borders the northern boundary of the Watkin's farm. She walks or rides over several times a week to review farm operations with the overseer. Mary did not like living alone with her two little girls, Emmie & Minnie, so she moved to Mrs. Dupuy's farm to live with her mother and sisters.)

(ed: Patience [a slave] has tuberculosis which was called consumption in the 1860s.)

- - - - -

January 13, 1863
Bellevue, Louisiana

Private William H. King
Co. B – 28th Louisiana Infantry

"Three Texas travelers staid with us last night & informed us that flour was worth $50.00 per hundred lbs.; pork, 20 to 25 cents per pound; corn 1 to $2.00 per bushel; salt, 10 to $12.00 per bushel. Indeed, speculation is rife every where. Two years ago had one predicted that salt at this time would be worth 10 or $12.00 per bushel & other things in proportion, he would have been as non compos mentis [mentally incompetent]. So the world goes." [48]

(ed: Three days later, in his journal, William noted, "Ate 'snowbread' today for my first. It is splendid, & is made by mixing the snow with dry meal & baking in a quick oven.")

- - - - -

January 14, 1863
Camp near "Guinia" Station, Va.

Private Charles W. Thomas
Co. B – 56th Virginia Infantry

"My Dear Wife
... Mary, I have good news to rite you. I got in a application last monday for a furlough. It went through all the big mens hands except our commanding General and they ware a little something rong. It want rote exactly rite but it is fixed now and I hope I will be with you in 8 or 10 days if old Gen Lee will only assined it. If I get it through, it want be but for 12 days ... I washed my old shirt and draws yestady. My old pant is verry nasty and my ass is out and these is all I have got but I hope I will soon be where I can get some from you ... You must excuse mistakes and bad riting ... fare well for the present.
C. W. Thomas" [49]

(ed: Charles and Mary live in Mechlenburg County, Virginia so the transit time is fairly short. This is especially true if the 56th is near Richmond at the time leave is granted.)

- - - - -

January 14, 1863
Grenada, Mississippi

4th Sergeant Robert Elliott
Co. E – 35th Alabama Infantry

"Rain all night and now the wind is blowing very hard our tent shakes ... I am so tired of rain but still thankful that we are not on the march exposed to the rain & mud ... we have 2 men sick in our tent to day It is very bad to be sick in a tent lying on the ground.... Johnson & Spotswood are out in the rain atrying to cook some bread Bob Wilson is agrowling because ... the ground in the tent is right Wet & the tent is leaking what a time we will have to night heard to day that we would have peace in 10 days but I expect it will be apeace of bread & beef which we would like to have now ... in Piny grove camp near Grenada Miss" [50]

- - - - -

January 14, 1863
Richmond, Virginia

Mr. John B. Jones
Clerk – War Department

"Some 4000 more negroes have been called for to work on the fortifications near Richmond. I believe 10,000 are at work now." [51]

- - - - -

January 15, 1863
Camp near Fredericksburg, Virginia

Corporal Tally Simpson
Co. A – 3rd S. Carolina Infantry

"Dear Home Folks
We have been living finely since we received the box. We have had several blackberry pies and lots of crab lanterns. We are waiting for one to get thoroughly cooked before dinner is brought in. The peach and apple butter is very fine indeed, and you can't imagine how we enjoy it….
Your affect son & bro
T. N. Simpson

… Howdy to all the negros. Lewis begs to be remembered to all the black ones and his family." [52]

(ed: Although well educated and from a fairly wealthy family, Tally will not rise above the rank of corporal. He does have a slave, Lewis, who has accompanied him to the front to be a cook and servant.)

- - - - -

January 18, 1863
Marshall, Texas

Mrs. Harriet Perry
Farm wife

"My dear Husband:
… I am doing very well, with the exception of a bad cold. When my baby was eight days old, I sat up all day & wrote to you & Mother. I was remarkably well I thought & so did Aunt Betsy, but that was too much for me. I was taken that night in violent pain, Aunt Betsy had to steam & sweat me, give me hot

ginger drams &c after I got easy I had a shaking ague. I took quinine & it did not return fortunately for me it threw me back several days.... my baby will be four weeks old next Wednesday – he [Theophilus] is the finest & best boy you every saw, sleeps all day & all night – Aunt Betsy says, tell you, he would not be good if you were here, you would spoil him - ... he is so much like the Perry's – he is not at all like my family – he resembles your family as strikingly as Daughter does mine – he is very much like your Father & your sweet self ... he is very fat & large – I give the greatest quantity of milk as much again as I did before. he nurses a great deal & my breast are always full, often painful, though I have had no trouble with them as I did before....

I killed my hogs on the 30th of Dec. Aunt Betsy attended to it for me – the six hogs weighted 1231 pounds, averaging 206, lacked one pound of averaging 207 – three of them weighted over two-hundred, the blue one weighed 240 long sanded 215, white wild one 210, little black 190, big black 198, little sanded 188 – they were about fourteen months old ...

... Daughter & Theophilus & I send you a thousand kisses May God bless you ... is the prayer of your loving wife.
Harriet Perry" [53]

(ed: Ague is a fever that is accompanied by chills and sweats and fits of shivering.)

(ed: This is Harriet's second letter to Lt. Theophilus Perry since the birth of their son. Their daughter, Martha, now has a little brother. Lt. Perry serves in Company F of the 28th Texas Cavalry. They will serve most of the war as "dismounted cavalry," or infantry, due to the inability of the government to provide adequate feed and forage for their horses.)

- - - - -

January 18, 1863
Richmond, Virginia

Mr. John B. Jones
Clerk – War Department

"Calico, which could once be bought for 12 ½ cts. per yard, is now selling at $2.25, and a ladies dress of calico costs her about $30.00.... All other dry goods are held in the same proportion. Common tallow candles are $1.25 per pound; soap $1.00; hams $1.00; oppossum $3.00; turkeys $4 to $11; sugar, brown $1.00; molasses $3.00 per gallon; potatoes $6.00 per bushel etc." [54]

- - - - -

January 18, 1863 | Private Bryant Folsom
Martinsburg, Virginia | Co. C – 26th Georgia Infantry

"... Dear Sister [Miss. Lucy Johnson] we got here yesterday evening & we wrested today and I have just washed my shirt & drawers just gave them a cold water wrench ..." [55]

(ed: Bryant is married to Nancy Johnson Folsom and Miss. Lucy is his wife's sister. It is normal in correspondence of this era for everyone to be noted as Sister Lucy, Brother William & Cousin Joe. Unless you know the family members it can be very difficult to determine exact relationships.)

- - - - -

January 20, 1863 | Major David Pierson
Snyder's Mill, Mississippi | 3rd Louisiana Infantry

"Dear Pa,

We are still encamped on the Yazoo River about 14 miles from Vicksburg and decidedly the muddiest place I have ever lived.... The mud is so bad that we have been compelled to agree to a harsh law ... no one shall go inside the tent with his shoes on.... As to eating, we fare sumptuously just now ... We get pork, potatoes, butter, and chickens from the farmers in the area at reasonable prices....

Yours Affect'ly
D. Pierson" [56]

(ed: It is much easier for the officers to supplement their diet by purchasing goods from the local farmers. A private is only paid $11 per month and the army normally runs two months behind in payments.)

- - - - -

Importance of Salt

"The per capita consumption of salt in the antebellum South had been about 50 pounds per year, it being used chiefly in diet, preserving, and the tanning of hides. The prewar South purchased most of their salt from the North and from England." One must question why with their thousands of miles of coastal shoreline the South did not have hundreds of sea-water salt plants. "North Carolina had three sea-water salt plants; One in the Currituck Sound, another near Morehead City, and the longest surviving works near Wilmington. These were run by private manufacturers under contract. Virginia had an extensive salt work near Saltville and these works even supplied some "300,000 bushels per year under contract to North Carolina." Significant quantities of salt were required by the provisions contractors to preserve the huge quantities of salt pork and salt beef needed to feed the military of the Confederacy." [57]

- - - - -

January 23, 1863
Gratiot Prison, St. Louis, Missouri

Captain Griffin Frost
Co. A – 2nd Missouri Infantry

"Did not get to see my wife today. She went to the Provost's office and tried again to obtain a permit, but was denied; the best thing she could do was to write me a note, informing me of her unsuccessful efforts, and that she would leave St. Louis to-night on the one o'clock train. May God protect her in her mid-night journey." [58]

- - - - -

January 23, 1863
Grenda, Mississippi

Mr. W. Goodman, President
Mississippi Central R.R. Co.

"Hon. J. A. Seddon
Secretary of War, Richmond;

Dear Sir: I find it almost impossible ... to keep our road and it's equipment in repair ... One half of our engines are now useless for the want of materials to repair them; our cars are in a dilapidated condition ... our rails on our road have been permanently injured by our own army and that of the enemy ... Unless we can procure articles necessary for the repairs of our road and equipment, I do not see how our road is to be kept in running order.... I desire to import articles of immediate necessity ... I desire permission to be granted to this company to export cotton ... and that such cotton shall have safe conduct through the Confederate lines. It will require ... $500,000 to put our road and it's equipments in as good repair as it was one year ago." [59]

(ed: What is unsaid is that the cotton would be "exported to Memphis, Tennessee" where it would be sold to Union merchants, to be shipped to Union mills, and to be paid for in U. S. dollars. With these monies Mr. Goodman could purchase needed materials. Some of these materials would come from Union merchants and some would come through the blockade from Europe.)

- - - - -

January 24, 1863
Camp near Vicksburg, Mississippi

Private Charles T. Shelton
Botetourt Artillery

"My dear Father
Let me congratulate you, I received a letter from Hallie a few days ago in which she informed me of the advent of my little sister of whose coming I have had not the slightest suspicion until ... a letter from Billy about Xmas. I have often heard you say that you did not want to hear any more babies cry at Roseneath but I am willing to bet two to one that you are today the proudest man in Louisa County.... Tell Ma she had better give the baby to Hallie as she already has seven daughters.

... I do hope some change will soon take place in order that we may get out of Miss. I never saw such a climate in my life and am afraid that it will go hard with us Virginians to remain here during the summer. It rains here almost incessantly, and the mud in these low grounds is in a good many places knee deep. I do not exajurate at all when I say that we have three rainy days to one clear one. This portion of the army is a great deal worse fed than any I suppose in the confederacy. One of the butchers told me that frequently they had to lift up the cattle brought here for beef. I know they are poorer than I ever saw your cattle in the spring after an unusually hard winter. I had no idea before I was a soldier that a man could stand so much or live so well with so few of the luxuries of life. Hard as our fare is I am as fat and healthy as I ever was in my life but I am very much afraid of the fever and ague I therefore am anxious to get away from Miss. Now with best love for the girls & Ma with a kiss for baby I am with much love and affection
Your son,
Charles" [60]

(ed: The Botetourt Artillery is from Botetourt County, Virginia. Charles is a long way from home but he is willing to bet his father is one "of the proudest men in Louisa County," Virginia.)

- - - - -

January 26, 1863 — *Columbia*
Cargo Manifest — J. Burroughs – Master

"about 259 tons out of St. George's, Bermuda to Nassau

157 bales, 260 cases, 1 cask, 100 pigs lead, 50 bundles steel rod, 35 cases brandy, 1 case merchandise, 1 cask brushes." [61]

(ed: Mr. John Bourne, the Commercial Agent in Bermuda for the Confederate government, maintained records of cargo on blockade runners bound for Wilmington and Charleston. The manifest showed a false destination. The cargo manifests that I will list each month are all bound for Wilmington. It is the cargo contents that tell the story.)

- - - - -

January 27, 1863
Grenada, Mississippi

Private Robert C. Dunlap
Landis Missouri Light Artillery

"Left our warm & comfortable cabbins & struck out in the cold & mud for Grenada. Arrived there by sundown with part of the battery; but not without the greatest difficulty. The mud being so deep the horses often stall, fall & mire down & then the Sargeant would command cannoniers to the wheels & then we would have to plunge into the mud & help out. One of the Caissons & the baggage waggons did not get in; consequently we had to endure the "bleak northwesters" without tents or blankets & without sleep. However this was no new thing; but to have something rare I got slightly inebriated ... for the first time in my life. I was not alone in being intoxicated on first rate peach brandy." [62]

(ed: Robert is a 23 year old private from Dekalb, Missouri – a small town near St. Joseph. He enlisted in 1861 and in March of 1862 joined the battery of Missouri artillery commanded by Captain Landis.)

- - - - -

January 29, 1863
Shelbyville, Tennessee

Captain James P. Douglas
Douglas's Texas Artillery

"Dear Sallie
... If you will give me your word for it that you will write me a letter on the first day of each month and as many more as are convenient, I will give you my word that I will write to you on the same day and as often otherwise as I have anything interesting to write.... What say you to such a bargain?" [63]

(ed: Sallie is his sweetheart and would you believe that he even has one of the guns in his battery nicknamed "Sallie." James and Sallie will be married in late March, 1864 when he is home on furlough.)

- - - - -

January 30, 1863 Corporal Tally Simpson
Camp near Fredericksburg, Virginia Co. A – 3rd S. Carolina Infantry

"My very dear Sister
The last week ... has been an extremely severe one.... it commenced snowing and never ceased till the earth was nearly knee deep with its spotless flakes. I suppose its depth averaged ten or twelve inches.... Nothing is being done.... Snow balling has been indulged in more this time than I ever saw before....

The next morning was clear and calm, the snow in fine kilter for making cartridges, and the fight was renewed. In this battle the 2nd and 3rd joined forces, conquered the 7th, and then joined it to their strength and made a powerful attack on the 15th. It was driven out of camp and completely demoralized.... The eyes of our leaders, Capt John Nace, Adj't Pope, & others, were directed by this time to the reduction of the 8th. This regt was situated upon a hill. By going directly in front to the attack we would have to ascend a steep slope, giving them every advantage. But by a skillful maneuver, a part of our forces made a desperate assault upon their right flank and drove them back. The main part of our army then attacked them furiously in front ... and carried the hill and the victory was complete. So you see the "3rd" has been with the victors from the beginning.
... Give my love to all ... Write soon to
Your ever affec bro
T. N. Simpson" [64]

- - - - -

Undated – Late January, 1863 Colonel Edward T. H. Warren
Camp near Fredericksburg, Virginia 10th Virginia Infantry

" ... had 383 [men] present, 313 fit for duty, 16 sick, 37 on extra duty and 17 under arrest.... [The regiment is missing] 151 officers and men absent sick, 18 officers and men absent with leave, 29 men absent without leave, and 169 deserters." [65]

- - - - -

January 30, 1863
Camp Mill, Arkansas

Captain Elijah P. Petty
Co. F – 17th Texas Infantry

"Dear Wife
… There is no news here today. Our Commissary Department here has been trying to starve us out but I hope they won't succeed. We have for a week been living on poor beef (dog meat) & corn bread and a very small quantity of meat at that. I can't eat the meat so I have been living on bread and water…. the men have spent half their wage provisioning themselves … It is hard for a private to serve for $11 per month and buy his own clothes and board himself. It is becomeing unbearable and the men will not submit much longer…. Take care of my little ones … Kiss them all for Pa …
Yours truly
E P Petty

P.S. I bought a Cook Book which I will send you as soon as I can." [66]

(ed: In his January 31 letter Elijah notes, "I am good, well, weigh 135 pounds in good & cheerful spirits – my Company about 55 men may be more.")

- - - - -

January 30, 1863
Newtown, Virginia

Miss. Kate Sperry
Winchester refugee & nurse

"Mrs. Sturman and Miss Ellie Barnes, together with myself in capacity of driver, tried Winchester. As usual, had no difficulty in getting in – arrived at home – all well. Did our shopping, and after much persuasion [with Provost Marshall] got a guard to take us through the lines. The Provost Marshall wrote an order, I read it, that we should be examined and not be permitted to return until loyal [to the Union]. At the last picket stand, the Yanks made us get out of the buggy and took us in an old house which was a perfect shell – they tote out all the wood-work to burn in the cellar in an old fireplace. It looked more like the *infernal regions* than a shelter for human beings. There they compelled us to take off our bonnets and wrappings – our pockets searched and shoes turned upside down to see if we had any letters – as though we'd be guilty of such foolhardiness to carry letters unless we had a pass. I'm thankful we escaped a complete disrobing – I never saw Mrs. Sturman as angry in my life. I firmly believe that if we hadn't made such a fuss, and if there hadn't been one gentleman in the crowd, we'd have been more roughly dealt with.... I've had my dose of Yanks and the next time I go to Winchester, I'll stay." [67]

(ed: Kate is 19 years old. Her father was a Winchester merchant who joined the Confederate quartermaster corps. With the departure of her father, Kate lived with her Aunt Wardy, her two younger sisters, and her step-mother in her grandfather's house. She took some empty ledgers from her father's store and in July of 1861 began what would be a 4 year, four ledger diary of life during the conflict.)

- - - - -

January 30, 1863
Springfield, Illinois

Sergeant W. W. Heartsill
Co. F – 2nd Texas Cavalry

"We find ourselves on the Chicago, Alton and St. Louis Railroad. We are off through several little towns and at 9 o'clk p m; we halt within two miles of Springfield ... the guards collected up lots of rails and soon there is a string of fire from one end of the train to the other." [68]

- - - - -

January, 1863

Blockade Running

"Union blockade efforts focused on the key southern ports. By 1863 blockade runners were limited to using the ports of Wilmington, Charleston, Mobile, and Galveston, with a small trade carried on at St. Marks, Florida. For the most part, vessels coming out of Bermuda ran to Wilmington, while steamers from Nassau employed both Wilmington and Charleston. The majority of supplies landed at Charleston and Wilmington were shipped by rail to Augusta (Georgia), the main depot for the Western armies, or Richmond (Virginia), the Eastern depot. Goods coming to Mobile were usually sent by rail to Augusta or via riverboat to Selma. Cargo bound to St. Marks, Mobile, and Galveston normally came out of Havana." [69]

- - - - -

January 30, 1863	Lt. Theophilus Perry
Q. M. Depot, Pine Bluff, Arkansas	Co. F – 28th Texas Cavalry

"Dear Wife: I send this letter by Capt. Jessup ... who has been ordered back to Texas for the purpose of buying Beef cattle. The mails have been very irregular of late, on account of high waters. Dr. Cade Ass. Surgeon ... arrived here yesterday ... he was 3 weeks coming from Shreveport ... all on account of high water.... My life is miserable on account of our separation. Oh God! that, this War would close, and all could return to our homes & families....

My Fingers are now cold & numb. Kiss the children for me every day. Tell Daughter to kiss little Brother for Papa. Let her hold the baby some every day for Papa. Tell her Papa says so. I wish I had something to send to you & Sugar Lumpy. Some day I will bring myself.

... What are negroes worth What can my little places be sold for in Confederate money It may be that I can sell my little place near Marshall for 1500 or 2000 in Confederate money. At any rate every thing has advanced for 2 or 300 pr.cent. I think if I was home I could make some good arrangements. But you must consult Papa in every thing. Your Fond & Loving Husband Theophilus Perry" [70]

- - - - -

January 30, 1863	2nd Lt. Noah B. Feagin
Hamilton's Crossing, Virginia	Co. B – 15th Alabama Infantry

"Dear Sisters
... We have been transferred from Trimbles brigade to Laws which is composed of Alabamians, altogether.... I am pleased at the change, but I hate to leave our old brigade and division. We had fought together in so many battles and had won such a name ... We are now in Hoods division, Longstreets Corps, out from under Stonewall entirely, no doubt it is better for our health.... But still, there is something which throws a damper over the mind when we reflect & think of being entirely [separated] from our esteemed General's command. Every soldier

of Jackson's Corps when asked what command we belong boastingly says, "Stone-walls." The soldiers under him think they are better, tougher, braver than any other soldiers, can stand more hardships, march faster and farther, go barefooted oftener … out fight, whip oftener … capture more … tear up more railroad and ride on it less … than any other soldiers….

We have had a considerable snow here. It now lies on the ground 10 and 12 inches deep…. The Texas brigade came over and whipped the 47th and 48th Alabama … our regt…. went to their relief but … they turned traitor and pitched on us, whipped us and captured our flag and took us prisoner. We likewise turned traitor and … about three thousand in number, marched upon and attacked the South Carolina brigade … routed them, captured their Colonel … little blood was shed, quite a chilling engagement … I will report the casualties in my next letter….

Let me hear from you soon. There is no chance of a furlough now. Tell my sweetheart howdy. Kiss her for me.
Your true and affectionate brother
NBF" [71]

- - - - -

Mushroom Poisoning *Mackenzie's 5000 Receipts*

"Remedies – Give the patient immediately three grains of tartar emetic, twenty-five or thirty of ipecacuanha, and an ounce of salts, dissolved in a glass of water, one third to be taken every fifteen minutes, until he vomits freely. Then purge with castor oil. If there is great pain in the belly, apply leeches, blisters, &c." [72]

(ed: Most homes, if the residents could read, had at least one book of home remedies to provide guidance in medical situations and also in areas as varied as tanning, gardening, farriery, pickling, bees and agriculture. Books such as The Cottage Physician, The Confederate Receipt Book, *and* Mackenzie's Five Thousand Receipts in all the Useful and Domestic Acts *were on hand to provide knowledge on a wide variety of subjects.)*

- - - - -

February, 1863

The calm of winter descends over the armies. The armies move into winter camps and grant furloughs to the men to go home to visit their families. Private Joshua Callaway writes, *"I am now … housed up in my tent by the fire. You have no idea of the amount of comfort it adds to our condition to have chimneys to our tents…."*

Private Milton Barrett of the 18th Georgia Infantry writes his brother from Fredericksburg, *"i dont see any probability of pice … we git short rashons but can do very wel on them…."* Major David Pierson of the 3rd Louisiana writing from Mississippi notes, *"We now draw ½ lb. of pork to the man pr. week and potatoes and peas also once a week…."* From Port Hudson, Louisiana, Private John Robison tells his wife, *"Nothing fit to eat. Corn bread and beef and the beef is dried on foot. I never eat sutch beef before …"*

The Confederate Commissary Department is having a difficult time procuring and supplying the needs of the military commands. In large parts of Georgia, which have been ravaged by drought, the farmers are unable to make their crop support payments and the Governor sends letters to the Confederate Government seeking understanding and assistance.

General Grant sends forces up the Yazoo River to see if he can approach Vicksburg from the north or perhaps move past the northern approaches and attack from the northeast. All is quiet in Tennessee and Virginia as the opposing armies rest in their winter camps.

Cornelius Vanderbilt is busy acquiring eastern railroads as he begins to build his railroad empire. Boss Tweed is constructing the base for his political machine in New York.

Diarrhea, dysentery, camp fever and typhoid make their appearances in the winter camps. Sanitation is an ongoing challenge and the close confinement of large numbers of men always causes problems. The men complain about diarrhea and dysentery, but the disease they fear most is smallpox. They never fail to mention if someone in the camp gets smallpox and is moved to the "pest hospital."

Despite the short rations and camp discomforts, the men prefer winter camps to summer campaigns. The opportunity for furloughs and a break from marching and fighting is welcomed. Fresh recruits are arriving, wounded comrades are returning and weapons, clothing and equipment are being resupplied. Spring will come soon enough and the armies will be mended and readied for the next campaign.

February, 1863

February 1, 1863
near Woodville, Mississippi

Miss. Kate T. Blount
23 year old farm girl

"My dear Cousin Robby, ... Do you remember five years ago today? ... I was arriving in Wilmington [North Carolina].... Since then how much have we suffered ... When will this state of things end? We have seen and heard of so much misery my heart is sick. They are daily expecting an attack on Port Hudson and have sent away all the sick soldiers. They have established a hospital in Woodville. We have a hundred sick soldiers here and all public buildings are occupied. They say we must take five hundred.... There are no contagious diseases among the sick at present ... We have every reason to trust in Vicksburg, but Port Hudson has never been tried.... Many predict that by spring hostilities will cease ... I dare not venture a thought." [1]

(ed: Kate's letter is addressed to Lt. Robert Calder, Co. B – 2nd North Carolina Infantry. She is writing from Glenco, the family farm near the town of Woodville.)

- - - - -

February 1, 1863
Shelbyville, Tennessee

Lt. Joshua K. Callaway
Co. K – 28th Alabama Infantry

"Mrs D. Callaway
... I am now, like every body else, housed up in my tent by the fire. You have no idea of the amount of comfort it adds to our condition to have chimneys to our tents.... Our huts are built by setting puncheons on the ground and letting [them] come together at the top on a ridge pole ... like the rafters of a house; and then throwing dirt all over it. The ends are stopped up in the same

way leaving a space wide enough for a chimney and a door. The chimney, in order to extend above the top of the hut, must be a little higher than my head....
Josh" [2]

(ed: Joshua uses formal salutations and almost never opens with "Dear Dulcinea." Joshua is a former mail carrier and teacher. He is 27 years old and they have a daughter Amelia (1858) and a son Joseph (1862). Joshua enlisted in March of 1862 shortly after Joseph was born.)

- - - - -

Undated
Abbeyville, South Carolina

Mrs. Alice Ball Duvall
Refugee from Virginia

"Things were getting scarce. Our shoes were giving out and there wasn't any way of getting any more. So I took heavy cloth of old pants and coats, and made the top of the shoes. Then bound the edges with some heavy binding, cut four or five pieces for the soles, left one of the soles for the bottom piece then dipped the middle pieces in tallow and pitch, and put a piece of clean cloth on top and bottom of the sole. Bound it all round, then whipped the binding together, turned it on the wrong side, and sewed it with wax thread, which formed the shoe, having the sole nearly an inch thick." [3]

- - - - -

February 3, 1863
Mobile, Alabama

Miss. Kate Cummings
Hospital Matron

"Provisions are higher still. I have been not a little amused at the novel lights we have; instead of oil and candles, nature has bountifully supplied us with illuminators in our pitch pine knots. We have a little oil which we keep for special occasions....

Although there is a great deal of speculating, and people growing wealthy, still it seems a much greater boast to be poor than rich. Every one has a story of how hard it is for him to live.... I have been trying to get some servants to go back with me, and also a few ladies. I have succeeded in getting one of the latter. We expect to leave in a few days [to return to the Chattanooga hospitals].... "[4]

- - - - -

Report of Confederate Purchases in Europe
by
Major Caleb Huse, C. S. Purchasing Agent

"Colonel John Gorgas, the Chief of Ordnance for the Confederacy, received a capitulation of purchases from Major Huse in early 1863. This was a total of completed shipments, goods enroute, and goods purchased awaiting shipment. The report covered his purchasing activities from his arrival in 1861. However, the vast majority of this activity was in 1862. Huse based himself in London and most of his purchasing activity was in England, Belgium and Austria. On February 3, 1863 the report was forwarded by Colonel Gorgas to the Confederate Secretary of War. Highlighted below are just some of the items and quantities purchased for the Confederacy:

70,989	Long Enfield Rifles	40,240	Gun Slings
27,000	Austrian Rifles	34,655	Knapsacks
21,040	British Muskets	74,006	Boots (pairs)
9,715	Short Enfield Rifles	62,025	Blankets
2,020	Brunswick Rifles	6,703	Shirts
354	Carbine Enfield Rifles	16,178	Cavalry Sabres
32	Bronze Austrian Cannon	18,000	Shells
10,000	Shrapnel Shells for same	4,000	Canteen Straps
46	Sets of armorer's tools	78,520	Yards of cloth
36	Sets of saddler's tools	17,894	Yards of flannel
19	Sets of farrier's tools	81,406	Bayonet Scabbards

129	Cannons – Including 6 Rifled Blakely cannon
357,000	Pounds of cannon powder
94,600	Pounds of musket powder
32,000	Pounds of rifle powder
170,724	pairs of socks
10,100,000	Percussion caps

and many other items" [5]

- - - - -

February 4, 1863
near Goldsboro, North Carolina

Private Louis Leon
Co. C – 1st N. Carolina Infantry

" ... We then fixed our bed in the snow and stole fodder for a bed and rails to make fire. We took snow, put it in our kettles, and made coffee. When I say coffee, I mean Confederate coffee – parched corn – that is our coffee. Ate our corn bread and bacon and retired to our couches and slept as good if not better than Abe Lincoln." [6]

- - - - -

February 5, 1863
Sulphur Springs, North Carolina

Mrs. Cornelia Henry
Farm wife

"Thursday – This morning there is the deepest snow I ever seen or ever want to see again. It is about 16 or 18 inches deep when it is not drifted. Everything is shut up now, a complete blockade.... One of Dillard Love's negroes is waiting here till the snow leaves a little. He is a white nigger. We have done nothing today but sit by the fire. I finished Sam's pants.... I had the chickens caught & put in the hen house cellar & chaff house. The turkeys have not been out of the trees today.... I am so sorry for our poor soldiers if they have such weather as we have. May God temper the winds to the shorn lamb is my prayer." [7]

(ed: In a Friday note Cornelia adds, "nearly impassible for a horse ... Tis dreadful on the stock. We have a yearling choked on straw. I expect it will be dead by

morning. We have had three nannie goats to die this winter & our lambs have nearly half died…")

- - - - -

February 5, 1863 Mrs. Catherine Edmondston
Halifax County, North Carolina Farm wife

"Patrick commenced yesterday filling the Ice House, a work which has gone on steadily all day in spite of the Rain. The snow thaws rapidly but as the ice is thick Patrick thinks if he can get it in the Ice House that it will create an atomosphere for itself and freeze again." [8]

(ed: Catherine will refer to husband, Patrick Edmondston, as both Mr E and Patrick.)

- - - - -

February 7, 1863 Sergeant W. W. Heartsill
Camp Butler - Springfield, Illinois Co. F – 2nd Texas Cavalry

"One week in Camp Butler, and we can sum up the results of the brutal treatment as follows: THIRTY have died and TWO HUNDRED have taken the oath." [9]

- - - - -

February 8, 1863 Mrs. Harriet Perry
Marshall, Texas Farm wife

"My own darling Husband: It will be seven months to-morrow since you left your little home & family … it has been a long dreary & sad time … To-morrow is also the anniversary of our marriage –

We are all well at present – except myself – I rise every morning with a dull heavy headache … The piles are troubling me very much, sometimes I am in pain enough to keep me from sleeping ... I have a very good baby indeed, he grows rapidly & is as large now as Mattie was at six months ...

I hate to tell you, but I am on the eve of breaking up [housekeeping].... I see no likelihood of the wars ending & I am afraid to stay here alone & I cannot have any thing done at all – Billie Hinton says he will hire Sam, Rufus & Jane & I thought I would let him have them –

... I have sold my turkeys & ducks, $1.50 for the Goblers & $1.00 for the hens, $1.00 for the drake, .50 cts for the ducks – I have been selling butter at thirty cents a pound & eggs at twenty five cents a dozen - ...

I have paid Dr. Young our medical account for the years of 1861 & 62 – it was $90.50 but Sam had worked for him to the amount of $22.00, which brought it down to $68.50. I have paid our little account at Bludsworth & also at Swartz – I paid for having the buggy mended ... Husband I shall endeaver to manage the best I can, so that when you return our circumstances will be more easy than now...

... Good-bye – Accept a thousand kisses from me & our little jewels – Farewell my darling, farewell –
Harriet" [10]

(ed: Harriet and the children will move in with Mr. Perry, her father-in law. They will rent out their slaves to create additional income. Harriet is selling most of their livestock, especially the birds, and using the monies to clear small debts like Mr. Bludsworth at the local grocery in Marshall. Consolidating households was very common during the war.)

- - - - -

Consumption and Importation of Salt

"The adjutant general of Alabama calculated that with a population of some 9,000,000 people the Confederacy needed 300,000,000 pounds of salt per year. Prior to the war the United States was importing 12,000,000 bushels of salt per year or some 600,000,000 pounds. This was happening despite the fact that no country on the globe was richer in salines than the United States. New Orleans alone saw salt imports on an annual basis of some 100,000,000 pounds. The southern states were the ultimate importers and for the English it was the perfect ballast on inbound ships coming to southern ports to load cargos of cotton. People cannot eat 50 pounds of salt per year so what drives this per capita consumption? The logical answer is the curing of meats. More than 200,000,000 pounds of salt per year is needed in the Confederacy to cure pork, beef, mule, fish, and fowl. The combination of smoking and salt curing is the only way to preserve meats. Salt was also used in the pickling of fruits and vegetables." [11]

- - - - -

February 8, 1863
Camp Timmon near Vicksburg

Private Grant Taylor
Co. G – 40th Alabama Infantry

"Beloved wife and children,
I will try to write a few lines at last. I am very weak yet. This is 25 days since I was taken sick and yet I am not able to sit up but very little yet. I had the Typhoid fever for 18 days. I have had no fever for 7 days and yet I mend very slowly. But I hope if I get no backset I will get well now. I hope and pray that these few lines may reach you and the dear children in the best of health.... Several in our com[pany] are sick.... If I could have got off to a hospital I intended to send for you but here in camps there is no place for you to stay and there is not a private house that I know of in 2 miles of this place.

... There is no chance to get a furlough ... Kiss the dear children ...
Grant" [12]

- - - - -

February 9, 1863
Union, Virginia

Reverend Samuel Houston
Presbyterian Minister

"Sugar selling at $1.... Direct tax of one per cent on every man with above $1000 property." [13]

- - - - -

Undated

Private William G. Allen
5th Tennessee Cavalry

"... we furnished our own horses and arms our arms was a shot gun or Colt Piston [pistol] ... our saddels poor. we soon captured better guns and saddels – the western horse was no good to a Tenn or Kentucky cavalry man they wanted medium size horses. keen and active." [14]

- - - - -

February 10, 1863
Chattanooga, Tennessee

Miss. Kate Cummings
Hospital Matron

"Arrived at Chattanooga at 7 A. M. Left Mobile on the 5th, by steamer to Montgomery. Captain Finnegan was very kind to myself and Miss Groom, who was with me. He did not charge us for our passage ...

The Alabama River is formed of the Coosa and Tallapoosa rivers, which unite some ten miles north of Montgomery. It then flows west to Selma, below which point it is very tortuous, flowing south-west until it unites with the Tombigbee, forth-five miles north of Mobile. The river formed by this confluence is the Mobile, which empties into the Mobile Bay. It is three hundred miles in extent, and is navigable for large boats. Along its banks are immense cotton plantations. In peace times hundreds of thousands of bales of cotton pass down this river yearly, to be transported from thence to all parts of the world." [15]

- - - - -

February 10, 1863
Blackwater Bridge, Virginia

Surgeon David Wade
27th Virginia Cavalry Battalion

"Dear John
Gen Pryor told me that by writing to some one in Richmond I could get cloth enough for a uniform suit from the Q. M. Department – If you can

possibly do so I would be much obliged as I need one very badly. And also cloth for overcoat – as I unfortunately burnt mine so badly in the fire, that I can't wear it.... I authorize you to put my name to any requisition necessary to get it....

Our wounded are all doing well. Our friends are all well. Write me soon ... We don't wish the cloth sent here but let me know as soon as purchased & the cost &c & then will send money.
Yrs truly,
DWade

Written by camp fire I hope you can read it." [16]

(ed: The soldiers would heat their clothing over the fire to force the lice to the surface where they could kill or remove them. Sometimes the uniforms got too hot and caught fire. It was a delicate task that took skill and patience.)

- - - - -

Undated — Private W. R. H. Matthews
Tennessee River crossing — 9th Battalion. Tennessee Cavalry

"One of the triing incidents was fording of the Tenn river by our command during a frequent rain had to cross shales led by a guide each man keeping his horse noze to the preceeding horses tail. the line in form like a verry erregular waim fince watter mostly to saddle skirts a few feet either side depth to 10 to 20 feet.... Cathey's horse just before me fell ... my horse did the same wetting us all over our clothes froze stiff on us before we got to the bank we had to march ten miles in sleet and rain in that condition and camp." [17]

- - - - -

February 11, 1863
Vicksburg, Mississippi

Private Nathan D. Foreman
Co. H – 40th Alabama Infantry

"Dear Wife ... You need not uneasy yourself about my deserting. I hope I am made of better material than that ... I have no stamps ... but I will try to get some soon.

You must take care of your self and your boys.... I am going to write something you must not let anyone see but yourself. When you go to write the word could you spell cod. You must notice how I spell it could and not cod .. . if anyone else was to get holt of your letter they would make fun of it. I do not want you to think hard of me for writing to you about it.... I want you to write whether your vaccination took or not. We have got shed of the small pox in this Regt. and I hope we will keep clear of it.

I do not see any chance for me to get home soon. You must do the best you can ... I hope and trust to God that I will live to enjoy your presense in peace once more and that we may be permitted to raise our children....
Yours truly
Nathan" [18]

(ed: Nathan is killed at Vicksburg. In the late summer of 1863 his wife gives birth to their final son and she names him Nathan.)

- - - - -

February 12, 1863
Vicksburg, Mississippi

Private William J. Bowers
Co. E – Waul's Texas Legion

"Dear Cousin
... I avale myself of this opportunity of answering your welcome letter of the 2nd January.... Your letter found us all in good health. Your brothers are both able for duty. They have improved very fast for the last month ... We have been ordered and moved 18 miles below Vicksburg.... The women and children have been ordered out of the city.

The Yanks ordered the surrender of the city a few days ago and our Generals told them that if they wanted it to come and take it or that was my information.... They will have to fight soon or leave on account of deserters in the Yanks army. There has been a great many deserters and coming over we met a great many between here and Granada. They say they are leaving as fast as they can get away.... I am very tired of the camps ... demoralizing places ... There is but few Christians in our Battalion ... I remain yours most truly.
W J Bowers" [19]

(ed: "Dear Cousin" is Miss. Mattie Nunn and she is William's sweetheart. He is serving in the same company as two of her brothers. They are all from Washington City, Texas . Mattie and William will get married following the war.)

- - - - -

February 12, 1863
Gratiot Prison, St. Louis, Missouri

Captain Griffin Frost
Co. A – 2nd Missouri Infantry

"I learned today that my brother Dan Frost is a Colonel in the Federal army, and his son a Major...." [20]

(ed: The Frost family is from Ohio. Griffin's parents, and most of his siblings, still live in Ohio.)

- - - - -

February 12, 1863
Fredericksburg, Virginia

Private Milton Barrett
Co. A – 18th Georgia Infantry

"Dear Brother and Sister ... i am well ... everything is stil a long the line, nothing of note occurred since i last wrote.

Our regiment has just come off picket. We stood clos together and cold talk to each other, then when the officers were not present we exchanged papers and barter tobacco for coffee. The way we managed this is with a small boat, with sail set it will go over by itself then they send back in return the same way. Some of our boys went over and staid a while. The Yankees would let us know when to come back....

... we have had a sever snow storm but night be fore last thar came a warm rain and it all melted. Today is a pleasant day.

... i dont see any probability of pice ... Our army never was in better fix for fighting than they ar now. The health of the army is excellent.... We ar all making out tolrable wel; we git short rashons but can do very wel on them. They ar paying us five dollars a month for to make up for our rashons...." [21]

(ed: Milton is older than the normal Confederate private. Milton is 35 and his brother Lawrence is 31. Most privates in the army are 17 to 26. Milton is semi-literate. All of Milton's letters, except this one, contain phonetic spellings, non-capitalizations and other assorted errors. The original of this letter is missing and only the corrected transcription is available. Using the other letters in the collection I have tried to return this letter, as close as possible, to his original style.)

- - - - -

February 13, 1863 *Wytheville Dispatch*
Wytheville, Virginia

"WANTED
A substitute to take service in the 2nd Va cavalry. Horse and equipments furnished A liberal price paid. For further particulars apply at this office.

HOPS HOPS
1000 POUNDS of Hops wanted, for which I will pay the highest cash prices or exchange for copperas.

C. COLLIAN" [22]

- - - - -

February 13, 1863
Vicksburg, Mississippi

Private Grant Taylor
Co. G – 40th Alabama Infantry

"Beloved wife and children,
... my health is improving ... Tomorrow it will be one month since I was taken sick.... I have just received your affectionate letter of February 6th ... It seems your hogs were very small for 2 years old.... I think you had better plant a few acres of your best land in corn....

I see some of the papers are pretty confi[dent] that peace will be mad[e] some time this year ... But I do not believe but very little I see in the papers. Deserters from the Yanks come over the river to Vicksburg nearly every day. Some on rafts some in skiffs and one came across on a log. They say they are heartily tired of the war ... As soon as they come they are paroled and sent home.... Kiss the dear children for me and believe me your loving husband and father, as ever,
Grant" [23]

- - - - -

February 13, 1863
Richmond, Virginia

Mrs. Judith McGuire
Nurse

"I sent over to the market this morning for partridges and eggs ... gave 75 cents apiece for the one, and $1.50 per dozen for the other. I am afraid that our currency is rapidly depreciating ..." [24]

- - - - -

February 13, 1863
Wytheville, Virginia

Wytheville Dispatch

"FRESH GOODS RECEIVED THIS DAY

500 Yds MUSSLIN de Lain, Calico &c
20 Men's and Boy's Hats and Caps
100 Boxes Gun Caps

50 Pairs Mens Army Boots & Shoes
50 Pairs Gloves and Gauntlets
150 Army over Shirts
20 dozen Cotton and Silk Handkfs,

Together with a full supply of Groceries and Fancy Goods, which I will sell as low as the times will admit for cash or trade.

J. P. KAVENAGH" [25]

- - - - -

February 14, 1863
Rome, Georgia

Mr. R. S. Norton
Merchant

"… There was a sale of Property belonging to an Estate (Cash). Bacon sold for 72 cts; Lard, 65 cts; Corn, $3.35; Peas, $3.25; Fodder, $10 (per bundles, and small); Cotton seed, 72 cts; Sugar, 90 cts per lb." [26]

- - - - -

February 15, 1863
Sulphur Springs, North Carolina

Mrs. Cornelia Henry
Farm wife

"Sunday – I washed the children last night & put their clean clothes on & then darned some stocking of Willie's and a pair of Zona's. They wear their stockings very fast…. I will stop now as I want some apples, walnuts & peach leather. The [dried] apples will soon be gone. Mr. Henry is sitting here teaching Willie to talk & mawking me…. Mr. Henry and I read after dinner. I read a good deal in the bible. I will soon go to bed as Willie is sleepy & I am tired of doing nothing." [27]

- - - - -

February 17, 1863
Richmond, Virginia

Colonel Robert Kean
Confederate Bureau of War

"The most alarming feature of our condition by far is the failure of means of subsistence. The Commissary General gets more and more gloomy and complains heavily of department commanders robbing the little stores he is able to scrape together for the future." [28]

(ed: Robert Kean works directly for the Secretary of War and is chief of the Confederate Bureau of War. He will serve under George Wythe Randolph, James A. Seddon, and Gen. John C. Breckinridge during the conflict.)

- - - - -

February 17, 1863
Lake City, Florida

Mr. E. W. Jones
Railroad Conductor

"Dear Brother,
… Eliza has just recovered from a severe attack of Bilious fever and is still sick…. Eliza will leave here on the 23rd of this month for Savannah … I send by Eliza a present to you of a Maynard Rifle with cartridges & caps already for shooting they are fine guns and will shoot 500 yards using the sights according to distances. They are fine for deer shooting … Eliza will show you how to use the gun…. If I live to see it over [war] I shall quit Rail Roading. I go to steamboating as I have a fine offer …" [29]

(ed: Bilious means pertaining to or characterized by gastric distress caused by sluggishness of the liver or gall bladder.) [30]

- - - - -

February 17, 1863
Camp near Fredericksburg, Virginia

Private William R. Stillwell
Co. F – 53rd Georgia Infantry

"There is eight inches of snow here … Gen. Longstreet and his Adjt had a fight with snow balls. The General charged him and took him prisoner." [31]

- - - - -

February 18, 1863 Mrs. Harriet Perry
Harrison County, Texas Farm wife

"My dear Husband: ... Little Theophilus sleeps with me. I know *now* what it is to have a good baby. it is not unusual for him to sleep all night without waking ... he grows very fast & is a fine baby. sometimes he sleeps three & four hours in the day at a time – I wish you could see him – Mattie is very fond of him & talks to him a great deal – he was eight weeks old yesterday ...

... Your father [Levin Perry] has sold three thousand bushels of corn at two dollars to a Government Agent, he paid him the money – he says he thinks he can sell two thousand bushels more, but is waiting for a better price.

... Write often, I wont complain of you any more you did well last month, but do better, it will only please me more – I have rec'd 4 letters written last month – Good-bye – Good-bye my good Husband ...Devotedly your wife Harriet" [32]

(ed: Harriet has now taken up housekeeping at her father-in-law's farm. In addition to the pants and drawers she promised in an earlier letter, she also sent a few candles, a little coffee, a towel, and a wash cloth. She is knitting a pair of suspenders which she will "send soon.")

- - - - -

Undated Private Robert M. McAlister
Co. G – 11th Tennessee Cavalry

"The experance of a Calvery Man is some what complicated. Hear to day. There to morrow. Most all ways on the go. Either running to or from the foe ..." [33]

- - - - -

February 18, 1863
Snyder's Mill, Mississippi

Major David Pierson
3rd Louisiana Infantry

" ... we have been living better for the last week than we were previously. We now draw ½ lb. of pork to the man pr. week and potatoes and peas also once a week... " [34]

- - - - -

February 18, 1863
Weatherford, Texas

Mrs. Mary J. Cheek
Farm wife

"My Dear, It was the greatest joy that I received a letter from you some days ago, just the day before I got it the news come that you were all killed or taken prisoner, and that your Captain was killed, you can never imagine my feelings on hearing that awful news, for then I never expected to hear from you again, I had not received a letter for nearly three weeks, and was afraid ... I do not get my mail regular at all, I scarcely ever get my papers ... I'll tell you when I heard you were killed or taken prisoner, it made my blood boil for revenge and I felt like if it was only in my power I would go and have it if I lost my own life in the attempt, sometimes I long to be a man, so that I could go and help you fight the infernal Yankees I do think I would love to kill them, for they have caused us women so much trouble ... O plague on the Yankees, I wish they were all dead and in heaven, a great many think peace will be restored this spring, but I have no hope for it as long as old Lincoln is in office ... no news of importance ... every thing is so high us poor women don't stand much chance but thank fortune I am not obliged to buy very much of anything except cotton and wool the last cotton brought in is selling at 40 cents but I think it will be cheaper as soon as grass rises, wool has been selling at one dollar per pound but I think it will not be worth more than 50 cts at shearing time, flour is still ten dol per hundred, corn meal three dollars per bushel I have let a few bushels of corn go for corn next fall I got and a half for one bushel now, I think I have plenty ... Your Pa passed here about five weeks ago on his way to see Julia and has not returned, he bought one of Margaret's young horses for one hundred dollars, I dont know whether she had any more to sell or not if she has I will try to buy one, I have no need of the money you sent and have not spent a cent of it yet, though I will have the taxes to pay in a short time, I have in all about eighty dollars, I have not sold my yarn yet but expect to get about fifty dollars for it ... You must not risk your money by mail ... I have also heard that you have lost all your clothes ... do not allow yourself to suffer any uneasiness about us at home I wish I knew you were doing half as well, Uncle Tomy True send his best respects to you and say ... kill the Yankees, Mrs True also sends her respects, May God bless you and bring you home soon, Your wife Mary Cheek" [35]

(ed: Mary's husband, T. F. Cheek, is serving in Captain Ball's Company in the 8th Texas Cavalry in Walker's Division and they are currently operating is Louisiana.)

- - - - -

February 18, 1863 Honorable Joe E. Brown
Milledgeville, Georgia Governor of Georgia

"His Excellency Jefferson Davis:
Owing to the drought last summer a large part of Cherokee, Ga., did not make a support. Corn now worth $3 a bushel, and soldier's families suffering.... The little supplies in the hands of a few is being seized by Confederate officers, leaving none to distribute to those likely to starve. If this continues the rebellion in that section will grow, and soldiers in service will desert to go to the relief of their suffering families. This conduct of your officers is worthy of your attention and I beg you to stop it without delay. Plenty of corn can be bought in Southwestern Georgia, and the railroads are at the command of the Confederate officers. Please order them to get supplies for the army from that section.
I beg an immediate reply." [36]

(ed: Confederate quartermasters are impressing crops in a portion of Georgia that was ravaged by drought in 1862 and has been unable to provide its crop tithes. The Governor of Georgia deems this unacceptable and is appealing for help.)

- - - - -

February 18, 1863
Richmond, Virginia

Mr. John B. Jones
Clerk – War Department

"All the necessaries of life in the city are still going up higher in price. Butter, $3 per pound; beef, $1; bacon, $1.25; sausage meat, $1; and even liver is selling at 50 cents per pound.

By degrees, quite perceptible , we are approaching the condition of famine.... " [37]

- - - - -

February 19, 1863
Stuarts Farm, Virginia

Sergeant Levin Gayles
Co. G – 9th Virginia Infantry

"camped at Stuarts Farme five miles from Richmond up to our ankles in water all night never saw it raine harder ... cant get our fires to burne. It is harde times ... No sleep tonight again." [38]

- - - - -

February 19, 1863
Camp Mills, Arkansas

Captain Elijah P. Petty
Co. F – 17th Texas Infantry

"Dear Daughter
... We are still at Camp Mills but will perhaps move a short distance tomorrow to try and better our condition for we are now in a perfect swamp. Cant go ten steps from your tent without getting in the mud & water.... it has rained 2 or 3 times a week and some times oftener. To day it is clear and a regular March wind is blowing. It reminds me of spring and doesn't seem right that the people should be in such strife butchering each other like savages but they should be at home farming. I am in fine health. Weighed last Sunday 141 ½ pounds, and I have no doubt but would weight more now.... I think I am now acclimated to Arkansas ...

... Negroes are awful high here and the present state of affairs does not lessen the price in the least ... There is verry little prospect here of a crop as nearly all the negroes have been run off....
Your affectionate father
E P Petty" [39]

- - - - -

February 19, 1863
"Culpeper Coho," Virginia

Captain Richard Watkins
Co. K – 3rd Virginia Cavalry

"My darling Mary
Here we are snowed up. Snow from six to eight inches deep yesterday. not quite so deep this morning, the roads without bottoms, our horses standing in mortar. Ourselves in soak, surrounded by melting snow.... Quite a gay time Miss Purnall. Wish you could ... take a squint at your old man as he pens these lines, see him sitting down on a little pile of wet straw surrounded by damp blankets & wet saddles ... with a pair of saddle bags in his lap for his writing desk.... Last night I dreamed that I applied for a furlough & wrote to old Genl Rob E Lee that I had not been blessed with a furlough or indulgence since last February but that old Genl sent it back with a note that he had not had one since the war commenced. Ha Ha Ha! Twas all but a dream." [40]

- - - - -

February 19, 1863
Guinea Station, Virginia

Captain Ruben A. Pierson
Co. C – 9th Louisiana Infantry

"Dear Father

... I am in tolerable good health. I have had chills this month ... We have had one case of small pox in the company ... It has not spread any yet ... Not even my messmates have taken it though they slept in the same tent with him till after he had broke out. I was in the tent and saw him ... the splotches are much larger than measles but look very similar. The whole of our company has been vaccinated ..." [41]

(ed: "Smallpox was a scary disease because no one could be certain that their vaccination had been done properly or if the vaccine material had been contaminated. Quite often the Confederate soldiers got abnormal reactions and they were never sure if it related to their own poor nutrition or contaminated vaccine.") [42]

- - - - -

February 20, 1863
Vicksburg, Mississippi

Private William J. Bowers
Co. E – Waul's Texas Legion

"Dear Father and Sister, ... We are camped 18 miles below Vicksburg. The Yanks commenced bombarding Vicksburg on the morning of the 18th ... we got news from this last night, they have not done any damage ... killed 5 mules and 1 cow.... The peace convention was to meet in Frankfort, Kentucky on the 18th ... then we can judge better whether the war will end this spring ... the Lord grant that it may for the soldiers are all sick and tired of it.... So farewell, Father, Mother, Brothers and Sisters
William J Bowers" [43]

- - - - -

Age of Soldiers in Companies A & D – 16th Georgia Infantry

"Age in 1860	No. of Men	Age in 1860	No. of Men
11	1	29	4
13	1	30	1
14	3	31	3
15	12	32	6
16	5	33	2
17	8	34	2
18	14	35	2
19	8	36	7
20	16	38	2
21	10	39	1

“Age in 1860	No. of Men	Age in 1860	No. of Men
22	6	40	3
23	8	43	1
24	9	45	2
25	12	47	1
26	11	49	1
27	5	52	1” [44]
28	5		

(ed: 176 of the 270 men who served in these two Companies were found in the 1860 census report. The 11 to 14 year olds probably did not join the unit till 1863 or 1864 when they would have been 15-18 years old. Most Confederate soldiers were in the 18-26 year old group in almost all Companies. Of the total 270 men 187 enlisted in 1861 when the units were formed, 58 in 1862, 20 in 1863 and 3 in 1864. 23 recruits were added as a result of draft age expansions in 1863 (ages 18-45) and 1864 (ages 17-50).)

- - - - -

February 20, 1863 — Mrs. Catherine Edmondston
Halifax County, North Carolina — Farm wife

“Planted Irish potatoes here at Looking Glass. Walked for the first time in some weeks with Mr E. Went to the river. The low grounds are full of water, in fact it is running out at the Lower breaks but still rising steadily. The land & negroes are soon to undergo a valuation by State Assessors for the purpose of Taxation. I wish they could see it [the land] now.” [45]

(ed: They have two homes on their land. The river bottom home is called Looking Glass and their home on the high ground is called Hascosea. These two plantations have a total of almost 1900 acres and the Edmondston’s own 88 slaves. Catherine and Patrick will spend the majority of the spring, summer and fall at Hascosea.)

- - - - -

February 20, 1863
Port Hudson, Louisiana

Private John W. Robison
Sparkman's Tennessee Artillery

"Josephine … I have nothing strange to right. Times is verry hard. Nothing fit to eat. Corn bread and beef and the beef is dried on foot. I never eat sutch beef before … Kiss the children for me …" [46]

(ed: Sometimes this unit was also called the Maury Light Artillery.)

- - - - -

February 21, 1863
Camps near "Fredricksburg," Virginia

Sergeant Benjamin F. Porter
Co. E – 11th Alabama Infantry

"Dear Ma, I received a letter from you & Sister bearing date of Jan. 26th on yesterday eavning…. I have no news of interest …

The army remains in the vicinity of Fredricksburg. Our Regt. is on Picquet every three days. Our poste is on the bank of the River & the Yanks on the other. We sometimes trade with them or exchange news paper. I hope we will not have to fight any more though we do not no what a whipping is.

… We wer payed off today. I received $68.00, 4 months pay…. I am going to save my money to defray my expenses Home if I should be so fortunate as to get to go. [furlough]

My health is good. I have plenty of good cloths … I have two good pare of pants 2 drawers 4 shirts one jacket 3 pare of socks … & a pare of large horse leather Boots.

… My haire is I believe a little darker, my whiskers are as red as blood & about three inches … Prey for me, I beseech you. Prey for your affectionate son.
B. F. Porter" [47]

- - - - -

February 21, 1863
Chattanooga, Tennessee

Miss. Kate Cummings
Hospital Matron

"We have three white girls, who have come from Mobile, as laundresses. I can not but wonder at some persons, these ware times. We gave these girls a very nice room. The beds in them were new, but hospital style, like what we have ourselves. They told me if they could not get better they would not stay. I begged them to give it a trial, and I would endeavor to improve matters. It is so difficult to get servants, that we are thankful to do any thing for them. We have men as *laundresses*, as well as in other capacities; but their help is very uncertain, as not a day passes without an order from General Bragg "to send all men to the front." [48]

(ed: Dr. B. M. Wible sent a note to Dr. Stout on March 21 and noted, "it is impossible to procure laundresses at 12 dollars per month, and I am obliged to require nurses to perform laundry duty … ") [49]

- - - - -

February 23, 1863
Meherrin, Virginia

Mrs. Mary Watkins
Farm wife

"My dear Mr Watkins
I must thank you for the nice present you sent of shoes, spools, cotton, buttons, pins &c. The shoes are very nice and fit me exactly … I have not received a letter from you for more than a week …" [50]

- - - - -

February 24, 1863
Jefferson, North Carolina

Captain Samuel P. Wagg
Co. A - 26th N. Carolina Infantry

"Dear John
I will write you a short note to night as I expect to leave home in a day or two for my command, and may not have the chance to write again soon. I have written to you once since I come home and have been looking for an answer

but have not received it…. I dont know when I can come again. Pa received a letter from Alf to night as well. The Regt is at Goldsboro now. I have enlisted six men I think I have done well considering how things are now…. I will write again when I get to camp. Give my love to Sister Vin.
Your brother
S. P. Wagg" [51]

(ed: John Wagg is Sam's brother and he is the Methodist minister of the Hillsville Church in Asheville, North Carolina. Sam has been home on a furlough recruiting men for Company A.)

- - - - -

February 25, 1863 Lt. Jesse P. Bates
Camp near Shelbyville, Tennessee Co. G – 9th Texas Infantry

"My dear wife I take this opportunity of writing you a few lines to let you know I am well … I have not received a letter from you in a long time. The last I got from you was dated the 12th of Aug…. I have sent you ($560) five hundred and sixty dollars and now I send you ($140) one hundred and forty dollars by Capt. Hopkins provided he gets off. If he don't get off, I will not send it till a better opportunity.

… This winter has not been very cold, but the last two months has been very wet and muddy and it is now thundering since raining. Tell James Hooten's wife that he is well. All of our neighbors boys is well …

My love, I want you to be as contented as you can and try and prevent those speculators and swindlers from getting you[r] money nothing. What money I send you … try to spend it to the best advantage … Try to buy some good stock that will increase and grow… Tell Frank and Sarah … to be good little children and to mind ma and help her work and if there is any chance to send them to school…." [52]

(ed: Jesse and his wife, the former Susan Ann Nicks, are both from Hickman County, Tennessee and most of their families and relatives are still in Tennessee. They moved west and live in Hopkins County, Texas. Jesse is encouraging Susan to use the extra money to buy sheep, chicken, or horses.)

- - - - -

February, 1863
Jefferson Cty., Arkansas

Lt. Theophilus Perry
Co. F – 28th Texas Cavalry

"Dear Harriet: … I send Sugar Lumpy [Mattie] a great sheet of paper filled with pictures of animals…. I shall be able to send you several hundred dollars when I am paid up my wages. Use it freely for whatever you need my dear. Georgia [John A.] Harris can give you a great deal of news about me. Go over to see him & wife. I will conclude by stating that my heart is with you Sugar Lumpy & in the cradle of the Baby. I desire to go home above all things.
Your Husband
Theophilus Perry" [53]

- - - - -

February 25, 1863
Jefferson, North Carolina

Mrs. Mollie W. Windle
Farm wife

"Dear Brother [John Wagg – Methodist Minister]
… After supper Mr. Windle and I were sitting by the fire talking about Sam [Wagg] when who should step in but him you can guess how I acted for I cant tell he is looking very well … and is a fine looking man as I ever saw…. I shall not see him any more until he starts for his company he will leave Jefferson Sunday I tremble for his fate for he is very wicked he swearz and drinks he does not drink much but you know when it is touched at all there is great danger … I want you to warn him and oh! Pray for him hourly …
Your sister
Mollie" [54]

- - - - -

February 25, 1863 Captain Tod Carter
Tullahoma, Tennessee Co. H – 20th Tennessee Infantry

"Our army is again in good fighting trim, and the ranks rapidly filling up by the influx of absentees. I suppose it is better clothed, equipped and fed than ever before. The country is bountifully supplied with game, but the boys are forbidden to shoot, for fear of hitting some General's aide. These sweet smelling, kid-glovely, band boxey, tea cakey … exquisities are as plentiful as gnats … But you must not construe my expression into any reflection upon the usefulness of this necessary appendage of our Gypsy-life. It is true they dangle a dress sword gracefully, run handsome horses … and smile most daintily at the ladies, yet it is not less true they can tell ragged, weather beaten fellows that foots it with a gun and heavy knapsack, exactly where he ought to be. You can … appreciate … their usefulness, and the necessity … to protect them from the weather and the disagreeable inconvenience of camp life, and to guard against the rudeness of bringing them in contact with unmannerly soldiers, and everything calculated to grate harshly upon their tender sensibilities." [55]

(ed: Tod wrote under the pen name of "Mint Julep" and sent regular correspondence to the "Chattanooga Daily Rebel" to share with their readership. This was too clever to leave out of the collection.)

- - - - -

February 26, 1863 Corporal Tally Simpson
Fredericksburg, Virginia Co. A – 3rd S. Carolina Infantry

"I am now in my tent, sitting by a blazing, cheerful fire, the very sight of which makes me feel as if I would like to be at home for while to enjoy its luxuries. Everything is very scarce in camp and the surrounding country. It is as hard living now as I have ever experienced – a little bacon and flour with a little sugar and rice occasionally – I never hungered for beef as badly before. A morsel of old cow would taste as good as "ginger bread." We bought two gallons of buttermilk today ($1.50 per gal) and made our dinner upon milk and bread and bacon gravy." [56]

- - - - -

February 26, 1863
Near Kinston, North Carolina

Private Louis Leon
Co. C – 1st N. Carolina Infantry

"Two men out of our regiment were whipped for desertion. They were undressed all but pants and shoes, tied to a post, and each given thirty lashes on their bare backs." [57]

- - - - -

February 27, 1863
Fayetteville, North Carolina

Private O. Goddin
Co. D -51st N. Carolina Infantry

"Gov Vance
Dr Sir
Please pardon the liberty which a poor soldier takes in thus addressing you as when he volunteered he left a wife with four children to go to fight for his country. He cheerfully made the sacrifices thinking that the Govt. would protect his family, and keep them from starvation. In this he has been disappointed for the Govt. has made a distinction between the rich man (who had something to fight for) and the poor man who fights for that he will never have. The exemption of the owners of 20 negroes & the allowing of substitutes clearly proves it.... By taking too many men from the farms they have not left enough to cultivate the land thus making a scarcity of provisions and this with unrestrained speculation [by rich, exempted land owners] has put provisions up in this market as follows Meal $4 to 5 per Bus, flour $50 to 60 per Brl, Lard 70 cents per lb by the brl, Bacon 75 cents per lb by the load and everything else in proportion.

Now Govr. do tell me how we poor soldiers who are fighting for the "rich mans negro" can support our families at $11 per month? How can the poor live? ...

I am fearful we will have a revolution unless something is done as the majority of our soldiers are poor men with families who say they are tired of the rich mans war and the poor mans fight, they wish to get to their families ... There is great dissatisfaction in the army and as a mans first duty is to provide for his own household the soldiers wont be imposed upon much longer....

I would also request in behalf of the soldiers generally ... for you to instruct our representative in Congress to introduce a resolution as follows. That all single young men now occupying salaried positions as Clerks Conductors or Messengers in the Depts of Govt & State & Rail Road & Express Cos. be discharged immediately & sent into the services and their places filled by married men and men of families who are competent to fill the positions.

Such a move ... would fill our ranks with a very large no. of young active men who have no one dependent upon them for a support and who are shirking service.... Our soldiers cant understand why so many young magistrates are permitted to remain at home and especially so many militia officers there being no militia and two sets of officers.
Respy your obt svt
O. Goddin" [58]

(ed: The Confederate Government passed a tax law on April 24, 1863 that required each farmer, after subtracting a specified personal use & replanting reserve from his grain and livestock, to provide 10% of the remaining for government use to feed the armies. However an additional tithe to support indigent soldier's families was left to individual counties and states.) [59]

(ed: "The Confederate Exemption Act of October 11, 1862 exempted one white male, either owner or overseer, on every plantation with 20 slaves or more. Overseer exemption was later modified but, for purposes of farm production and slave control, it was never ended." The Exemption Act also made classes of workers exempt to keep the "home front operating" with some efficiency: teachers, tanners, apothecaries, justices of the peace, government clerks, train engineers, and various types of factory workers. Many connected, well-to-do men quickly switched to these occupations.) [60]

- - - - -

February 27, 1863
banks of Amite River, Mississippi

4th Sergeant Robert Elliott
Co. E – 35th Alabama Infantry

" … we will rest until there is some provisions brought to us from Clinton I have eaten up the last of rations which was only a small peace of Bacon & some sour corn bread … sent Jones out foraging got Potatoes Bacon & we had a nice supper Fried meat Potatoes meal Coffe & some nice corn bread & we eat heartaly & we were hungry it is now dark so good night." [61]

- - - - -

February 27, 1863
Camp Butler – Springfield, Illinois

Sergeant W. W. Heartsill
Co. F – 2nd Texas Cavalry

"Nearly every day one from our Barrack dies; … men in good health one day; take sick and in two days are in the dead-house, the number of deaths now run up to about ONE HUNDRED AND TWENTY FIVE." [62]

(ed: On April 7 the men of Company F will depart by train heading east, they will then transfer to a ship for transport to Aiken's Landing near City Point, Virginia for exchange. W. W. Heartsill will be exchanged on April 15.)

- - - - -

Coffee

Mackenzie's 5000 Receipts

"It is allowed that coffee promotes digestion … dispelling flatulency, removing dizziness of the head, attenuating viscid humours, increasing the circulation of the blood, and consequently perspiration; but if it drank too strong, it affects the nerves, occasions watchfulness, and tremors of the hands; … Turkey coffee is greatly preferable in flavour to that of the West Indies. Drank, only in the quantity of one dish, after dinner, to promote digestion, it answers best without either sugar or milk; but if taken at other times it should have both …" [63]

- - - - -

March, 1863

On March 3rd the U. S. Congress grants President Lincoln the right to suspend Habeas Corpus.

Union attempts to attack and subdue Vicksburg via the Yazoo River fail. In mid-March an effort to use Steele's Bayou as a route for taking Vicksburg also fails. Private George Crosby of the 59th Tennessee Infantry is moved from the Yazoo down to a levy below Vicksburg, "*for weeks & all so down in swamps in Company with cotton mouth snakes, alligators, Gallinixens, moscetoes, lizards, ...*" From Vicksburg Sergeant James Drake of the 42nd Alabama Infantry writes his wife, "*there ant any enemy in site ... tho I keep harty I have the bowel complaint ...*"

The Territory of Idaho is approved by the U. S. Congress.

Soldiers returning from furlough bring two key items back to their messmates: boxes of provisions and letters. Private Milton Barrett of the 18th Georgia Infantry writes, "*Some of our boys has just come from home and brong 17 large boxes of provishon.... two moar started home on furlows. we draw to see who would go first. i come out blank a gain.... two will go ever month tel we all git off.*"

On March 23rd the Confederate States authorizes the issuance of their 6th series of Confederate monetary notes. The 5th series had been authorized in early December, 1862. Some $140,000,000 has been printed and issued in the past 4 months. The 6th issue authorizes the printing of over $50,000,000 per month starting in April, 1863. The government wants to issue more bonds and reduce the money in circulation. The citizens continue to demand more currency which just feeds the inflation.

Sergeant John Beaton of the 9th Virginia Infantry, from camp near Petersburg, Virginia, thanks his sister for, *"the things you sent ... and very much obliged to you for them.... If you can conveniently get a black slouch hat ... I would like it very much, these little caps are anything else but comfortable in rain or snowy weather the water runs down my neck ..."*

There is a great deal of fishing, trapping of birds, and collecting of wild onions and bee hives as the troops augment the meager rations provided by the Confederate Commissary Department.

Spring is just around the corner. What lies in store for the Confederate soldiers and civilians?

March, 1863

March 1, 1863
"In Camps near Richmond"

Private Michael L. Hambrick
Co. A – 10th Bttn. Georgia Infantry

"Dear Sister
I now take the opportunity of riteing you a few lines … John Mims got here fryday he sed you stayed at his house the nite before he left … I have sent two pens home an I have sent money to pay the postage tell the war ends and I want you to rite how you are getting on …" [1]

- - - - -

March 2, 1863
Louisville, Mississippi

Masonic Lodge 75

"Resolutions
Louisville March 2nd 1863 To the W Master, Wardens and Brethren of Louisville Lodge No 75;

The undersigned committee appointed to dispose of the Carpet belonging to this Lodge for the benefit of destitute Soldiers – submit the following report, to wit,

That the said Committee had said carpet cut up in proper size for blankets, and hemmed and sent to Grenada & then & there disposed of the same on the first & second days of Feby last by donating them to those who appeared to be the most needy in the 20th Mis regmit, a list of names of those who received the same with the letter of the Co. – are herewith submitted …

Wm Whiles	G	J A Bevill	C	W L Miller	D
J W Ward	G	J P Bevill	C	W C Baber	D
T B Futrill	G	Henry Spear	C	J P Hughes	D
S M Massey	G	W Roach	C	J O Tyler	D
L Dawkins	G	W C Obannon	C	C C Calloway	D
J E Rawland	G	J H Smith	E	G W Castle	D
J N Porter	G	T O Finally	E	B F Black	D
T J Ivy	G	D Mahaney	H	A Powers	D
J Mitchell	G	M S Fitzgerald	H	S L Hyde	D
E T Graham	G	T L Finally	H	John Connor	D
A Roach	G	J B Graham	H	J H Castle	D
C P Burk	H	J M Miles	H	Thos Brown	H” [2]
T C Creed	H	John Jackson	H”		

- - - - -

March 2, 1863 SOLDIER JIM
Atlanta Southern Confederacy 8th Georgia Infantry

“We are all now encamped on a very dry oak ridge surrounded by springs and small streams. Our late camp was about two miles away … located in a pine swamp … we were almost up to our eyes in mud and water. A few nights ago … we were filed out into the woods [here] to camp. Soon we gathered pine tops and spread upon the ground, on which [we] laid our wearied limbs, and covering with our blankets, slept soundly … while a heavy snow fell, which buried us all, and the weight … woke us about 3 A. M. A slight raising up of our heads, however, soon convinced us that the best policy was to be perfectly still till day, which we did.” [3]

(ed: This letter from SOLDIER JIM was published in the Atlanta Southern Confederacy *on March 8, 1863. Many of the Southern newspapers, rather than send staff to cover events, used various soldiers who mailed them accounts from the field. They used a variety of pen-names. Some regular contributors to the Atlanta paper were: DIXIE, CIRCUIT JUDGE, TIVOLI, POTOMAC and X.)*

- - - - -

March 3, 1863
Gratiot Prison, St. Louis, Missouri

Captain Griffin Frost
Co. A – 2nd Missouri Infantry

"The small-pox has broken out among the prisoners, two cases to-day, taken to the small-pox hospital. One hundred and forty prisoners were notified to leave tomorrow; destination unknown …" [4]

(ed: The prisoners were being sent east to Washington to be exchanged. Most of the eastern exchanges took place at Aiken's Landing near City Point, Virginia.)

- - - - -

March 3, 1863
Maury County, Tennessee

Mrs. Josephine Robison
Farm Wife

"My dear beloved husband
… Wee are all well … John your Father is going to leave us. I do not know what will become of me and your little children for he is all that I have to look to for assistance but I will try to do the best I can. Oh that you was with me tonight. I think sometimes that I have not got a friend on earth…. I never ly down at night but wat I think where is my loved one tonight." [5]

(ed: It appears, from reading the correspondence, that John's father has been forced into the army as a substitute to honor a debt. John, in future letters, notes that he is trying to get his dad transferred to the Maury Light Artillery because infantry life is too difficult for a man of his age.)

- - - - -

March 4, 1863
Camp near Fredericksburg, Virginia

Private William R. Stillwell
Co. F – 53rd Georgia Infantry

"I draw one pound of meat to last six days. Beef sausage $1.50 lb. Sweet potatoes 50 ct. lb. cow peas 85 ct. quart … " [6]

- - - - -

March 4, 1863
Pine Bluff, Arkansas

Captain Elijah P. Petty
Co. F – 17th Texas Infantry

"My dear Wife
I am still here at work in the Court Martial. We are getting along pretty well. Have disposed of 8 cases up to this time. The other Court Martial have sentenced 4 men to be shot.... I am hard hearted enough to want to see a military execution ... They are to be shot for desertion. It has become a military necessity to shoot some body for this offense as an example to prevent the disintegration of our Army...." [7]

- - - - -

March 5, 1863
Guinea Station, Virginia

Private Marion H. Fitzpatrick
Co. K – 45th Georgia Infantry

"Amanda, ... I have washed once since I got back, I got my clothes clean with but little trouble because I had soap. I do not mind washing atall now. One of my overshirts have commenced wearing out already. I patched it good the other day. " [8]

- - - - -

March 5, 1863
Camp near Petersburg, Virginia

Sergeant George W. Bradley
Co. E – 2nd S. Carolina Rifles

"My dear companion,
... I am in good health at present, hoping these few hurried lines ... find you and the baby ... doing well.... I am sorry to hear of Mr. McWhorter's daughter and Mr. Jerry Hunt's wife being dead. There is a great sickness in that district. I hope the health of the people may be better.
George" [9]

- - - - -

March 6, 1863
Huntsville, Alabama

General Gideon Pillow
HQ Conscript Bureau
Army of Tennessee

"To Planters of Lauderdale, Lawrence & Franklin Counties

Your position is endangered by the raids of enemy cavalry. Wherever they go they sieze all the negroes they can find. Our army has 2,000 veteran soldiers driving teams. We want to hire negro teamsters to relieve these soldiers and restore them to the ranks.... All the negroes you hire to the army will thus be saved to their owners, while at the same time the army is more able to defend and protect the country. I have made the same requirement of the slave owners of Maury, Giles and Lincoln Counties, Tenn., and of Madison, Limestone and Morgan Counties, Ala., and I now call upon you.... I send Captain McIver, assistant quartermaster, with contracts ... the terms of the contract, you will see, are liberal, and in everything protect your rights." [10]

(ed: As the Confederacy searches for more ways to bolster manpower in the ranks, they hire negroes from their owners as mechanics, teamsters, nurses, orderlies and for a variety of support jobs. This hiring frees men for slots in the artillery and infantry.)

- - - - -

March 7, 1863
Goldsboro, North Carolina

Captain Samuel P. Wagg
Co. A - 26th N. Carolina Infantry

"Dear John
... I have written to you ½ dozen times since I received any letter from you, now I thought you were a better boy than to treat me so.... I think since you married you have become lazy, you dont care for any boddy but Vin. well I dont blame you much you ought to remember your unfortunate brother one that cant afford a wife.... My company is in splendid health and spirits. I am 180 lbs of man myself I am very fleshy, I have a very sore mouth with that exception I am enjoy the best of health.... We are not very comfortably situated we have no tents and are in a country where we have to burn pine

wood the men are smoked perfectly black … John I want you to write to me.
Dont be so mean
Your broth
S. P. Wagg" [11]

- - - - -

March 7, 1863
Doughtys Hill, Texas

Mr. John W. Trotter
Overseer

"Dear Brother [John W. Robison]
… I am very badly crippled up [shot in the shoulder], have but little use of my right arm, though can make a living if Linkon does not take our negroes away. I am at this time overseeing for a man who is in the army … I am nearly half done planting corn … and am getting along finely concidering the emence quantity of rain …" [12]

(ed: John Trotter and John Robison are brothers-in-law.)

- - - - -

March 7, 1863
Richmond, Virginia

Colonel Robert Kean
Confederate Bureau of War

"Flour in the city is $30; the butchers are closing their stalls – meat at $1.25 per pound. Farmers are making preparations for only so much corn as will suffice for their own use. They resent the Secretary's schedule prices which are often 50% below the market … The army will be starved, and famine will ensue in the cities … The merchants of this city whose flour was impressed on the 5th inst. have determined to obtain injunctions from the state courts. If the judges grant them, the Government has to elect between a total abandonment of the policy … or the disregard of the authority of the process of the courts …

I recently made a rough calculation to compare the present currency with a sound one in the matter of my household expenses. The result is that my salary of $3000 will go about as far as $700 would in 1860. Then, flour $28 against $7, tea $15 or $1.25, Bacon $1.25 or 20 cents, fresh meats $1.00 or 8 to 10 cents, wood $15 per cord or $3 to $4, ... and other things in proportion. A coat costs $120, calico $2.50, unbleached cotton $1.00, bleached $2 to $2.50, linen $7, etc." [13]

- - - - -

March 8, 1863 — Lt. Theophilus Perry
White Sulphur Springs, Arkansas — Co. F – 28th Texas Cavalry

"Dear Harriet ... My overhaul pantaloons have been objects of unusual admiration. They have been of inestimable value to me during the severe weather to which I have been exposed. At one time in January the weather was so cold, that I was compelled to put on my whole wardrobe ... I put on three pair of socks, two pair of drawers, two pair of pants, and the overhauls on over them. With all this protection I [still] suffered exceedingly with cold, during our retreat ... towards Pine Bluff after the Post [Arkansas Post] was taken. My boots froze on my feet and boot to my stirrup....

... I send you Five Hundred dollars by Billy [Hargrove]. I think it will be enough to pay all of my little debts.... Hire out the negroes for whatever they will fetch. Send Sam to Shreveport to work....
Kiss Sugar Lumpy & Theophilus ...
Your Husband Theophilus Perry" [14]

- - - - -

March 9, 1863 — Captain Griffin Frost
Gratiot Prison, St. Louis, Missouri — Co. A – 2nd Missouri Infantry

"Received a box from my wife today, containing a lot of butter, some peach, tomato, and blackberry preserves, two bottles of catsup, and a fine large ham. Had to have a fresh introduction; have not seen such delicacies for so long we had become strangers." [15]

- - - - -

March 10, 1863 | Miss Kate Cummings
Chattanooga, Tennessee | Hospital Matron

March 10, 1863
Chattanooga, Tennessee

Miss Kate Cummings
Hospital Matron

"The great trouble about hospitals is the sameness of the diet, in the morning we have batter-cakes made of the mush left from the previous meal, rice, and stale bread, … hash made out of the soup-meat, toast, mush, milk, tea, coffee, and beefsteak. Our batter-cakes never have eggs in them; they have a little flour and soda, and are very nice. For dinner we have beef and chicken soup, potatoes, rice, dried fruit … For each meal we have what is called special diet, for the worst cases sometimes, as is specially ordered by the surgeons, and others whatever we can get the patient to eat; it generally consists of light diet, such as chicken and beef-tea, arrowroot, sago, boiled milk thickened with flour, milk, tea, and toast. We get a good deal of milk and eggs now. For supper we have dried fruit, toast, tea, and coffee." [16]

(ed: Arrowroot is a tropical American plant (Maranta arundinacea) whose root produces an edible starch. In earlier times it was used to draw the poison from arrow wounds.) [17]

- - - - -

March 10, 1863
Richmond, Virginia

Mr. Charles Palmer
Commission & Ship Agent

" … Today leaf [tobacco] is $10 higher than the sales of last week and it is impossible to say what a Southern article of manufacture will get to. If whiskey is to be an example rising from 20 cents to $60 per gallon…." [18]

- - - - -

March 11, 1863
Tullahoma, Tennessee

Private Joseph A. Rogers
Acting Assistant Surgeon
28th Tennessee Infantry

"Dear Papa
I concluded ... to write a few line they have me well except that I have the Diarrhea to some extent I hope to get over it soon ... Please send me the hat the first chance I was pleased very much with the shoes I would like to have a pair of pants and a pair of socks ... I am anxious to hear from you all." [19]

(ed: Although a private in Company B, he is on detached duty as the "Acting Assistant Surgeon" for the Regiment. Because Joseph was a first course medical student, he is not qualified to be the "Assistant Surgeon" but he has started his schooling and certainly has some training and the potential skill.)

- - - - -

March 11, 1863
Fredericksburg, Virginia

Private Milton Barrett
Co. A – 18th Georgia Infantry

"Dear Brother and sister
... So far i have met with the good luck to git such things tolrable easy. Some of our boys has jest come from home and brong 17 large boxes of provishon. one of my messmates was fortinate enuf to git a large box of ham sausage and butter and other sweetmeats. So we have had a fine breakfast and has enuf to do us sevrel days. two moar started home on furlows. we draw to see who would go first. i come out blank a gain. i can not tel when i wil git to go home. two will go ever month tel we all git off.

... Times is a shuting in perty tite hear, meat is a giting perty carse [pretty scarce], we git ¼ of a pound per day, beef has plade [played] out. we git a little sugar that use to sweetin our tea with, we ar tolrable wel...." [20]

- - - - -

March 11, 1863	Mr. John B. Jones
Richmond, Virginia	Clerk – War Department

"Gold sells at $5 in Confederate states notes for one; U. S. Treasury notes are at a premium here of $2.50. Even the notes of our State banks are at 60 per cent premium over Confederate notes. This is bad for Mr. Memminger. An abler financier would have worked out a different result." [21]

- - - - -

Real Estate Owned by the Men of
Companies A & D – 16th Georgia Infantry

"$ Value of Real Property	No. of Men	$ Value of Real Property	No. of Men
0	70	3000-3499	11
1-499	24	3500-3999	3
500-999	25	4000-4499	2
1000-1499	14	4500-4999	3
1500-1999	8	5000-5499	2
2000-2499	3	5500-8999	1
2500-2999	6	9000-10000	4" [22]

(ed: This provides solid evidence that for Madison County, Georgia it was a poor man's fight. Of the 176 soldiers in the data base, 70 did not own any property. 66% owned less than $1000 of real property. A search of the personal property records, which list slaves, shows that 117 of these men did not own slaves. 66% of these soldiers did not own a slave. They did not own any land, many were still quite young, and they could not afford nor did they have any use for a slave.)

- - - - -

Ages at Enlistment
Botetourt County, Virginia

Botetourt Light Artillery

"Age	#	Age	#	Age	#
17	6	26	5	35	1
18	26	27	9	36	1
19	13	28	9	38	3
20	9	29	4	39	3
21	14	30	1	40	1
22	12	31	2	41	1
23	8	32	4	43	1
24	11	33	2	57	1" [23]
25	8	34	3"		

(ed: These were the enlistment ages shown for 153 of the 326 men who served in the Botetourt Light Artillery during the war. Infantry units normally had the youngest ages and cavalry units normally had the older ages. Because CSA cavalrymen provided their own horses the younger men who did not yet have any property, real or otherwise, could not afford to be in the cavalry.)

- - - - -

March 12, 1863
Lafayette, Louisiana

Mrs. Francis McCutcheon
Farm wife

"Dear Cicero:
... Pat is ... one of the wildest, worst little scamps you ever saw and I believe gets worse every day, though I think I can straighten her with a few good switchings. Lalla & Fannie are not so far behind in badness.... I returned the salt long since & will pay my debts when I can get money ... The old chimney has most smoked my eyes out today & they pain me so I will have to stop writing. The children are all asleep ... Write very soon
Your affectionate
Frank

PS – Lalla sends her love & kisses and her doll sends love & if you kill any Yankees to send her a yankee cap." [24]

- - - - -

March 13, 1863 — Private John W. Calton
4 mi E of Wilmington, North Carolina — Co. I – 56th N. Carolina Infantry

"Dear Brother [Thomas Calton]

… I and som of the Boys went down to the sound yesterday and got a boat and went a cross the sound over to the Beach and took a look at the Atlantic Ocean whitch was a buteful seen to look upon for one that never had seen it. the sound is about tow miles wide you ought to come down and take a look … and get preey sea shells and get a mess of fish and oisters … I will close by saying to you to give my love to all of my Friends so I remains your Brother till death
JW Calton" [25]

- - - - -

March 15, 1863 — Private Marion H. Fitzpatrick
Guinea Station, Virginia — Co. K – 45th Georgia Infantry

"Dear Amanda,
I shall try to write you a few lines this morning. I am sorry to say to you that I am quite sick and I have been ever since last Monday night. I have got the mumps, and I think some kind of fever with them. I have had high fever and sick stomach nearly all the time. I tried to throw up one night and fainted and they had to carry me in the tent. I think I am getting better now. I can eat a little and sit up a good part of the time but I am so weak. The Dr. done nothing for me, said he had no medicine…." [26]

(ed: Mumps (Rubula inflans) is an acute, inflammatory, contagious disease of especially the parotid glands and sometimes the pancreas, ovaries or testes. It is caused by a virus.) [27]

- - - - -

Remedy for Chill & Fever

Undated

Captain John W. Taylor
Co. B – 1st N. Carolina Artillery

"Take one teaspoon of Spiritt turpentine & mix with yolk of one egg. Give 1/3rd morning, 1/3rd noon, 1/3rd at night the day before and the day you expect the chill." [28]

- - - - -

March 15, 1863
Fredericksburg, Virginia

Sergeant Benjamin F. Porter
Co. E – 11th Alabama Infantry

"Dear Ma, … I hope Mr. Davis will be joined throughout the Confederate States in preying for peace. God grant that it may be a universialy carryed out. Peace and independence is what we want & we must have it…. I have suffered greately though I am very well fixed now. Three of us has dug a hole in the side of a hill & built a house three logs high built a chimney to it & covered with apiece of a tent. It is a warm as a house…. Ma, I have ruined my blue socks. The last big snow I got my feet wet & when I went to dry them I burnt both the bottoms out. But I have more … I must go and detail my men for piquet from ten to fifteen men every two days, so I will close. Write soon to your son,
B. F. Porter" [29]

- - - - -

March 15, 1863
Shelbyville, Tennessee

Lt. Joshua K. Callaway
Co. K – 28th Alabama Infantry

"My Dear Wife,

… I have just eaten a very hearty breakfast of Biscuit, eggs and meat. I went out foraging yesterday and only got one dozen hen eggs and half a dozen

goose eggs and 7 pounds of soap for all of which I paid $3. I also bought me a fine coverlet for $10.00. The filling is blue and the warp is white. I bought a blanket the other day for $4.00, a good heavy blanket.... I will now stop for a prayer meeting ...
JK" [30]

- - - - -

March, 1863 | Private George W. Crosby
Vicksburg, Mississippi | Co. I – 59th Tennessee Infantry

" ... we then got orders to move over near Aszoo [Yazoo] river. here remaind for a short time... then come fun we was on picket on the levy below Vicksburg for weeks & all so down in swamps in Company with cotton mouth snakes, alligators, Gallinixens, moscetoes, lizards ... " [31]

(ed: Gallinipper is a large flying insect, mosquito like, that bites. Gallinixen is a colloquialism for a large flying insect that stings or bites.)

- - - - -

March 16, 1863 | Major David Pierson
Snyder's Mill, Mississippi | 3rd Louisiana Infantry

"My Dear Sister,
... Provisions are very scarce and some days the boys get nothing to eat but bread ... If I had a few cows and a dozen hens, I would not desire a handsomer fortune. Butter is worth 2 dol. a pound, & eggs, 2 dol. pr. dozen. What do you think of it? ... I have just got me a fine uniform from Mobile. I wish you could see it. I think it very pretty.
Write soon.

Affectionately yours
D Pierson" [32]

- - - - -

March 16, 1863 Private Mial H. Gammon
Vicksburg, Mississippi Co. C – 56th Georgia Infantry

"Dear wife & children. I seat myself to write you a few lines. I am not well. I am so weak and nuvers I cant write hardly at all … I hope this may find you & my sweet little children well…. I have been sick going on three weeks … I have been weakening down all the time till I can't walk fifty yards without resting .. . Dear I have fell away till I have no idea that you would know me if you could see me. I weighted 158 & 165 when was at home. Now I dont think I would weigh 120. Dear I can't get nothing here that I can eat…. I bought one dozen bisquets and one pound of butter except that I have not eat as much as I could hold in my hand in two weeks…. I had to give one dollar & fifty cents for my bisquets and two dollars for the pound of butter & hard beging to get them at that. The people here don't pretend to work … depend on making their living by speculating on soldiers…. Kiss the babies for me. Farewell." [33]

(ed: Mial was captured & exchanged when Vicksburg surrendered in July. In late November, 1863 he was captured in the battles around Chattanooga and sent to Rock Island Prison in Illinois. He died March 8, 1864 from Rubeola [Measles]. Mial is buried in grave #850 in the Rock Island Prison Cemetery.)

(ed: Measles is an acute contagious virus marked by red spotted skin eruptions. Roseola is a rose colored skin rash. Scarlet fever is an acute contagious disease marked by scarlet skin eruptions and high fever. In the 1860s these were collectively known as the "eruptive diseases.")

- - - - -

March 17, 1863 *Wytheville Dispatch*
Wytheville, Virginia

"LOCAL ITEMS

Burglary – The store-house of Mr. Stephen S. Crockett was entered on Friday night last, and robbed of a large quantity of money and valuable goods. A slave from Tazewell County, & a free negro woman Sophy – a notorious thief and evil doer – were arrested and have confessed their guilt. We hope an example will be set, in this case, that will not be lost." [34]

- - - - -

March 17, 1863
Bayou Teche, Louisiana

Private William H. King
Co. B – 28th Louisiana Infantry

"Some of us have just paid $1.00 per lb. for lard.... We are forced to fight in defense of the [vendors] rights & property for $11.00 per month, we are not furnished with the rations necessary to sustain life in a healthy condition & our only chance is to purchase them at ruinous prices." [35]

- - - - -

March 20, 1863
Camp Winder, Virginia

2nd Lt. George D. Buswell
Co. H – 33rd Virginia Infantry

"Dear Cousin [Miss. Bettie Hite]
... It is now 2 o ck P.M. & has been snowing nearly all the time since day light though the snow is not very deep. If I were in Page [County] now & there were as much snow there I think I would sleigh some person.... I guess I am entitled to a furlough next. I do not know when I will get one. I think they have quit granting furloughs for this winter....

You, in your letter spoke of a very nice valentine you received two years ago and accuse me of sending it. I guess I had as well acknowledge that I sent it how did you find it out? ...
GDB" [36]

- - - - -

March 21, 1863 Mr. Carter Coupland
Mobile, Alabama Riverboatman

"My dear Mother
I did not go up on the Boat this Trip – as I did not feel very well, having had a chill or two & some slight high fever – But I feel all right today having had Dr. Ketchum [________] of me - & the few days rest I will get will benefit me amazingly – Do not be at all uneasy for I am doing first rate & should not have mentioned that I had been unwell except that several Greensboro people came down with me & went up on the Boat & I am afraid they might report me sick –

I got a long & aff letter from Brother this morning written Feby 16th – They have all been Sick since you left but were well when he wrote. – Oh! How I wish they could get out of Yankee Land! There is nothing of interest here – Everybody expecting to Starve – Provisions are enormously High – Flour $80.00 a Barrel. Beef from 50 to 54c for lb Turkeys 6 to 7 $ apiece - & every thing else in proportion – God bless you my darling Mother. I must say farewell – I long to see you, but don't hasten your visit on my account – I have written to Hattie Several times lately – but have not heard a word from her … Write to me soon
Your Aff Son
Carter" [37]

(ed: Carter's brother is living in Williamsburg, Virginia which is controlled by the Yankee troops. Carter's mother (Mrs. Juliana Dorsey) spends very little time in Williamsburg. She is a refugee living with relatives and friends in various areas including Greensboro and Mobile. Carter works on riverboats which carry cargo, passengers and troops between Mobile and Selma, Alabama.)

- - - - -

March 21, 1863 | Miss. Pattie Watkins
Prince Edward County, Virginia | Farm girl

My Dear Sister
… Mr Redd … has had a great deal of sickness in his family this winter. We all dread the whooping cough very much some of the negro children are very sick with it …

Brother Dick is home now. He had a twenty day furlough. He was in a charge a few days before he came home & lost another horse though he got a very good one in exchange. They were on a scout, it was during the last snow, & were ordered to charge on the Yankees, which they met in a large force. He was commanding a squadron (2 companies) … his horse ran up in some brush … and fell throwing Dick over his head into a very large mud hole. He gathered himself & looked for his horse. He had run on a head & gone to the Yankees…. Gen. Fitz Lee gave him a beautiful iron gray Yankee horse with an elegant army saddle & two yankee blankets new that were almost as good as his own … He was wringing wet … & as they were twenty or thirty miles from camp & his feet were almost frozen.
Pattie" [38]

(ed: Capt. Richard Watkins was thrown from his horse during a skirmish at Hartwood Church, Virginia.)

- - - - -

March 22, 1863 | Colonel Robert Kean
Richmond, Virginia | Confederate Bureau of War

"A warm sun today is thawing the snow with wonderful rapidity. In 24 hours the nine to ten inch [snow] had been reduced to three and by night four-fifths of the fall will be gone. High water and deep mud will be the consequences … " [39]

- - - - -

March 22, 1863
Richmond, Virginia

Mr. John B. Jones
Clerk – War Department

"... Corn meal is selling at from $6 to $8 per bushel. Chickens $5 each. Turkeys $20. Turnip greens $3 per bushel. Bad bacon $1.50 per pound. Bread 20 cts. per loaf. Flour $38 per barrel, - and other things in proportion." [40]

- - - - -

March 22, 1863
Fredericksburg, Virginia

Private Nimrod Newton Nash
Co. I – 13th Mississippi Infantry

"Dearest One
... I have suffered a good deal with cold; but strange to say my bowels have not troubled me since we parted.... I am very much reduced in flesh ... [but] am as lively as a cricket." [41]

- - - - -

March 23, 1863
Atlantic Ocean

John M. Kell, Exec. Officer
C. S. Cruiser *Alabama*

"On the moring of the 23rd of March we made two captures, the *Morning Star* of Boston and the *Kingfisher* of Fair Haven, Massachusetts. We released the first on ransom bond and burned the latter. She was a little whaler ... Two days after burning the *Kingfisher* we made two captures, the *Charles Hill* and the *Nova*, both of Boston bound for Liverpool. We took 40 tons of coal and a half dozen recruits from those ships and burned them both." [42]

- - - - -

March 23, 1863	CSA Congress authorizes a 6th series of Confederate monetary notes

"The demand for currency increased and so did further inflation. The Act of March 23, 1863 authorized the sixth issue of Confederate currency. The $5 to $100 notes could be issued in monthly amounts not to exceed a total of $50,000,000. Plus the 50 cent, $l and $2 could be printed for a maximum series total of $15,000,000. The notes could be funded into 6% bonds in their first 12 months. If not funded they were payable, without interest, 2 years after a treaty of peace.

The following amounts were printed of the 6th Issue and dated April 6, 1863:

$ 5	$ 38,728,000
$ 10	$ 74,208,000
$ 20	$ 88,560,000
$ 50	$ 116,200,000
$ 100	$ 193,160,000
$ .50, $1, $2	$ 15,000,000
Total	$ 525,856,000

The fifty cent notes were engraved and printed by Archer & Dale of Richmond. The engraving for all of the other notes was done by Keatinge & Ball of Columbia, South Carolina and the designs were similar to the December 2, 1862 fifth issue. The firms of B. Duncan, J. T. Paterson & Co., and Evans & Cogswell had contracts to assist with the printing of denominations up to $20. Keatinge and Ball printed all of the $50 and $100 notes." [43]

- - - - -

March 23, 1863
Camp near Petersburg, Virginia

Sergeant John Beaton
Co. G – 9th Virginia Infantry

"Dear Sister
... I received the things you sent ... and am very much obliged to you for them. The shoes are rather thin, the snow soaks through them very soon. We have had an unusual quantity of that this winter. For the last four days we have had to travel through it nearly 15 inches deep. A pair of heavy boots would have been a great deal better. If you can conveniently get a black slouch hat ... I would like it very much, these little caps are anything else but comfortable in rain or snowy weather the water runs down my neck ... being wet is something I am used to ...

You would have laughed to have seen great grown men Saturday with their traps and dead falls catching birds. We were very successful, the mess I am in caught quite a number. We made a large pot pie which was very nice....

I have been right busy lately, being the first sergeant of the company. I have all the business to do and am now fixing up my rolls and have to give an account of every man ... It is a sad duty writing dead opposite so many names ...
I remain your affectionate brother
John K Beaton" [44]

- - - - -

March 23, 1863
Shelbyville, Tennessee

Asst. Surgeon J. J. Callaway
9th Georgia Infantry Battalion

"I certify that I have carefully examined Lieutenant I. J. Meadows of Co. B, 9th Geo. Battalion of Infantry, C. S. Army, and find him laboring under a chronic disease of the lungs (Chronic Bronchitis) and Chronic Diarrhea in consequence of which he is, in my opinion, unfit for performing military service. His lungs have been effected with disease for several years and he has had diarrhea for the past eighteen months, and both diseases have been much aggravated by the exposure of camp life. As I do not believe he will ever again be fit for service, I respectfully recommend that his resignation of office be accepted." [45]

(ed: This was the medical endorsement that went along with Lt. Meadow's resignation paperwork.)

- - - - -

March 24, 1863 Mrs. Harriet Perry
"Spring Hill" – Harrison Cty., Texas Farm wife

"My dear good Husband: Cousin Billie Hargrove reached here last Friday ... I was overjoyed to get your sweet long letter.... Your father tries to tease me, he says I read your letters all day ...

... I have paid *all* our little debts ... I paid Dr Sears ... $92 – I also paid Dr Elim Johnston five dollars for visits to Rufus when the horse kicked him ... I had no idea you would be able to send me so much. You have done well ... Your Father laughed and asked me where you got so much, but said he did not wonder you had been handling quires of it ... he said he reconed it was what fell off the table ... I exceedingly regret that Norflet [slave/servant] has left you – we have heard nothing of him but I hope he will make his appearance at home soon, though I fear he will try to get to the Fed.

... Accept a thousand kisses from me & the children – I kiss them every day for you – devotedly Your wife
Harriet" [46]

- - - - -

1863 Sergeant James T. Drake
Vicksburg, Mississippi Co. E – 42nd Alabama Infantry

"Dear Companion, I again seat myself to drop you a few lines ... there ant any enemy in site at this time ... I don't know how long wee will sta here nor where we will go ... I want you to send me 2 par of pants having good thick

coten … I don't know when I shall git the chance to go home … you must manige the best you can … They have detached me as a Rear Guard. I don't have much to do … I want you let me know how you managed about salt and how many hogs you had to kill for meat and how the hogs come on … I want to no whether you have got that money I sent you or not and how much you receved … I hant got many dimes to by tobacco with now … tho I keep harty I have the bowel complaint every once and awhile …
Your loving husband …
James T Drake" [47]

- - - - -

March 25, 1863 Major M. S. Temple
Saltville, Virginia M. S. Temple Company

"Hon Joseph E. Brown
Governor of Georgia
… The great demand for salt for the Confederate States, and the State of Virginia, was such, that nearly all available transportation on the Va. & Tenn. R. R. was appropriated to the benefit of those interests, in hauling wood and salt, they demanded preference in every instance over all other states.

I have sent from this place to Bristol, since the first of January, only 8 carloads of salt … My principal difficulty is transportation … The Confederate States pay for their salt at this time $2.50 per bushel…." [48]

(ed: The Salt Works are way behind in the contract with the State of Georgia. They have requested that Georgia provide them with railcars, locomotives and perhaps even the railroad crews to collect the salt for delivery to Georgia. They have offered to negotiate terms based on the ability of Georgia to provide train and crew support to the operation. They have also proposed a renegotiation of the salt price due to the rising costs of production and transportation.)

- - - - -

March 25, 1863
Winkley's Bluffs, Mississippi

Private Robert C. Dunlap
Landis Missouri Light Artillery

"We have been living on very slim rations for a few days. part of the time nothing but corn bread & not enough of that. The fault is undoubtedly on the part of the Commissary. Bees are numerous, there being scarcely a day but what the boys find four or five bee trees. Consequently our camp flows with [_____] & honey." [49]

(ed: Winkley's Bluffs commands the mouth of the Big Black river where it enters the Mississippi. The battery "is planted" on the bluff with a splendid view of the Big Black, the Mississippi and the "country round.")

- - - - -

Undated
Army of Northern Virginia

Lt. Colonel R. A. Hardaway
2nd Corps Artillery Staff

"Artillery – Table of Fire
U. S. 3" Rifles & 10 lb Parrotts, 7.16 charge, 10 lb shot

Elevation	Range	Fuse Time
0 degree	380 yards	1.27
1	645	1.75
2	1000	2.7
3	1300	4.0
4	1525	4.7
5	1835	6.0
6	2100	7.2
7	2325	8.5" [50]

(ed: Tables of fire allowed the gun captain to set the proper fuse time for the charge, type of shot, and gun elevation to have the shell explode in a timely manner in relation to the target.)

- - - - -

March 26, 1863
Milledgeville, Georgia

Honorable Joseph E. Brown
Governor of Georgia

" ... we could now turn out about 100 pairs of cotton cards per day if there was on hand a supply of wire ... I have made an engagement with Messrs. Russell Bro. & Co., of Dalton for the manufacture of wire and have sent an officer to make contact with certain importers ... It is not easy to estimate the exact cost of making a pair of cards with the present difficulty of getting leather and wire. It cannot ... fall below four dollars at this time...." [51]

(ed: The State had purchased 5 machines for manufacturing cotton cards. They have already produced 1,177 pairs and are now sitting idle because there is no wire.)

- - - - -

March 28, 1863
Camp near Shelbyville, Tennessee

Lt. Jesse P. Bates
Co. G – 9th Texas Infantry

"Dear wife, ... J. M. Lindly has been back 12 or 15 days, but he never brought the clothes up with him. He left them with Rowland and Tanner and the letters you sent to me by him are in the boxes. James Ferrell has got back and he saw the clothes in Montgomery, Ala.... The health of our company is very good ... Father was up here about the 10th of this month. He said all the folks was well. I have heard nothing of late from your mother ... March 31st – I have received your letter of the 21st of Dec. and was very glad to hear from you once more and to hear that you and the children was well. I got the things you sent to me.... I need white shirts worse than anything else. I am sorry that you have had bad luck with your cows and I am also sorry Confederate money is valued so little in Texas ...

You say that you have no more paper to write on, I will send you some and I want you to write to me as often as you can ... Farewell my love for the present.
Jesse P Bates" [52]

- - - - -

March 28, 1863 Mrs. Sue Watkins Redd
Prince Edward County, Virginia Farm wife

"My dear Brother [Sgt. Nathaniel Watkins]
I have been wanting to write you for a long time but first one thing & then another had to be done and letter writing has always been put off … We are just through with one of the worst spells of weather we have had during this remarkably bad, wet winter; today is a real March day, almost the first fair windy day this month. Crops and gardens very backward. Mr. Redd has not commenced sowing oats yet, and I have done very little in my garden, have a fine pea patch 3 or 4 inches tall and a good many onions, thats all. Lambs, chickens &c all froze in the long snow storm … I was very glad to hear you had gotten another furlough … We saw very little of Dick while he was a home, was truly glad he was not in that battle…. We are in the midst of the whooping cough, about 20 negroes with it, and all 5 of our children … 36 in all have it …
Your aff Sister
S. Watkins Redd" [53]

(ed: Nathaniel is a Sergeant in the King & Queen Heavy Artillery which is stationed at Drewry's Bluff, Virginia. In 1864 they will be reorganized as the 34th Virginia Infantry.)

(ed: "Whooping cough is an infectious disease involving inflammation of the mucous membranes of the nose and throat and is characterized by spasms of coughing interspersed with deep, noisy inspiration [raspy attemps to breathe air in]." It was normally most fatal to the young and old segments of the population.) [54]

- - - - -

March 28, 1863 Mrs. Catherine Edmondston
Halifax County, North Carolina Farm wife

"River very high and still rising. Went out yesterday with Patrick in the canoe, the water smooth as a lake. He shot several partridges and Musk Rats…. " [55]

- - - - -

March 30, 1863
Fredericksburg, Virginia

Corporal Tally Simpson
Co. A – 3rd S. Carolina Infantry

"Dear Ma
… We are all doing remarkably well at present in the way of health. Provisions are very scarce. We drew some tough cow meat yesterday and "sorter chewed" at it this morning but had to swallow it before it was comfortably masticated to save teeth. Sam & Miles Pickens came over to our brigade on Friday … Miles is a warm friend of mine, next to a brother…. Miles brought me a fine mess of potatoes and dried fruit.

31st /63
This morning the ground is covered with snow to the depth of two or three inches. The weather is still bad, and may continue so a day or two. It commenced snowing last night, and I enjoyed it finely. Tis said that Kershaw's [Brigade] [has] the finest minstrel band in these parts, and I am inclined to believe it. No news. My love to all.
T. N. Simpson" [56]

- - - - -

March 30 & 31, 1863
Richmond, Virginia

Mr. John B. Jones
Clerk, War Department

"I am spading up my little garden, and hope to raise a few vegetables to eke out a miserable subsistence for my family….

March 31st – Another stride of the grim specter, and corn meal is selling for $17 per bushel. Coal at $20.50 per ton, and wood at $30 per cord…. Common tallow candles are selling at $1 per pound." [57]

- - - - -

Shoeing Horses in Winter *Mackenzie's 5000 Receipts*

"In Canada, where winter is never of less duration than 5 months, they shoe their horses in the following manner, which serves for the whole winter; - The smith fixes a small piece of steel on the fore part of each shoe, not tempered too hard, which turns up about a ¼ of an inch, in the shape of a horse's lancet; the same to the hinder part of the shoe, turned up a little higher than the fore-part, tempered in the same manner. In going up a hill, the fore-part gives a purchase that assists the horse, and in going down prevents him sliding forwards." [58]

- - - - -

April, 1863

On the farms it is time for spring planting. In the armies the winter camps are broken. Plans have been made and it is time for the campaigning to begin in earnest.

The Surgeon General of the Confederacy is concerned about the lack of vegetables and greens in the diet of the soldiers and issues orders for the medical directors to procure a variety of vegetables, wild onions, lamb's quarters, watercress and other greens to promote the health of the soldiers and avoid scurvy.

On April 2nd, women in the city of Richmond riot over food prices and the lack of availability of foodstuffs. Private Milton Barrett of the 18th Georgia Infantry writes from Fredericksburg, *"a bout one thousand women arm ther self with axes and clubs … and march in to the citty and broak open stoers grocers and comassary's took what every tha wanted …"* Confederate currency is depreciating; soldiers in their letters home are encouraging wives to pay their debts and buy horses, sheep, chickens and timbered property rather than hold Confederate currency.

Large religious revivals are held in the camps and thousands of men are baptized and join various faiths.

General Lee sends Longstreet's Corps into southeastern Virginia to lay siege to the city of Suffolk and to assist the Confederate Commissary Department in collecting supplies and grains and other foodstuffs from the farms of southeastern Virginia and northeastern North Carolina. This reduces Lee's forces facing the Union army of General Hooker by nearly half. General Hooker is planning a rapid move up the Rappahannock River and then a quick move southward to turn General Lee's left flank. Hooker puts his army in motion on April 27th.

To distract attention from his army near Vicksburg, Mississippi, General Grant sends Colonel Benjamin Grierson on a cavalry raid in mid-April. Grierson departs LaGrange, Tennessee, on April 17th and cuts a path of destruction, burning railroad bridges, depots and warehouses, all the way to Baton Rouge, Louisiana, which he reaches on May 2nd. This distracts Generals Pemberton and Johnston who send portions of their commands in pursuit. At the same time, Grant runs his fleet of gunboats and transports down the Mississippi River, past the defenses of Vicksburg, while his army marches south on the Arkansas side of the river. On April 30th his forces start crossing into Mississippi, south of Vicksburg, at Bruinsburg. His final drive to capture Vicksburg has begun.

Private William Corson of the 3rd Virginia Cavalry writes his sweetheart on April 4th, *"We are faring badly now I tell you. Men only get one fourth rations and horses are starving."* The Confederacy needs a more structured way to acquire meat and grains. On April 24th the Confederate Congress passes a 10 percent tax on produce to meet the supply needs of the armies. Farmers will be assessed and will pay their 10 percent tax in grains and meats, on a regular basis, in each county. The Commissary Department will coordinate the collection and distribution of the produce.

The days of furloughs and winter camps are over. Spring has arrived, the roads are drying, the armies are moving and death is riding on the April breezes.

April, 1863

Early April, 1863
Harrison County, Texas

Mrs. Harriet Perry
Farm wife

"... I think we have every promise of a good fruit year. the peach & plum trees are just in full bloom & I hope the cold is all gone – Your Mother speaks of drying a great many peaches for the soldiers ... I am sure you shall have as many as you want, if I have to cut every one with my own hands.... Daniel sold my lard, 55 pounds, at 40 cents – Your Mother got a dollar for her butter & $1.75 for turkey hens – I will do whatever you say about selling our places ... " [1]

- - - - -

April 1, 1863
Guiney Station, Virginia

Surgeon Harvey Black
"Hospital 2 ANV Corps"

"My dear Wife
I rcd your letter of the 27th on yesterday, and if my letters cheer you up when you are sick, I am willing to write you any day....

... A sutler at the Depot was found selling liquor and his goods were confiscated and turned most over to me. We got two barrels of spiced ginger cakes, 2 brls of Berlin sausage ... , 1 barrel Rice, bag of peaches, 11 jars of pickles, box tobacco, box candy, 20 Galls. Brandy, box soda, & all that he had would probably sell for $2000.... I gave most of the eatables to the small pox patients ... " [2]

(ed: The 2nd Corps Hospital had been created by Dr. Hunter McGuire in December of 1862 and Dr. Black was appointed Head Surgeon. The Hospital was a separate

entity from the regimental, brigade & division hospitals. Dr. Black had a staff of 4 surgeons, 4 stewards, 8 cooks, 31 nurses, 4 washers, 2 druggists, 1 agent and 1 ward master. This Corp Hospital served half of Lee's Army of Northern Virginia.) [3]

(ed: "Hospital 2 ANV Corps" is the way Surgeon Black designated his command.)

- - - - -

April 1, 1863
Richmond, Virginia

Samuel P. Moore
Surgeon-General, C.S.A.

"Medical directors will direct medical officers … to have collected for the use of the sick … threatened with scurvy daily supplies of … native edible plants and herbs growing in the vicinity of the camp, viz: Wild mustard, water cresses, wild garlic or onion, sassafras, lambs-quarters, sorrel, pokeweed, artichoke, plume of dandelion (bleached), garden parsely, pepper grass, wild yam." [4]

- - - - -

April 1, 1863
Halifax County, North Carolina

Mrs. Catherine Edmondston
Farm wife

" … Prices are fearfully high even for depreciated currency, which … is indisputable. – Lard 1.25, Bacon 6.00 & upward, Flour $30 per barrel, Tea $7 per lb, sugar $1.12 ½ to 1.25 per lb, boots $50 a pr, Long cloth $2 to 2.25 a yard, Cotton Card $50 for two pair, I think salt considered cheap at $25 per bu, butter $2 per lb …" [5]

- - - - -

April 1, 1863
Fredericksburg, Virginia

Private Nimrod Newton Nash
Co. I – 13th Mississippi Infantry

" … Our company bought two seins yesterday verry large. think we will get plenty of fish now One company in the 17th [Mississippi] caught over 700 at one drag. Gen. Barksdale has given us permission to fish as much as we want." [6]

- - - - -

April 1, 1863
Paris, Texas

Mrs. Margarette A. Harris
St. Clair Cty., Missouri refugee

"My darling husband: … I do hope it will soon be warm again so that we can raise something to eat. Am so sick of bacon and bread and nothing but barley to drink! … Mr. Wells …, died and four of his children; none but his wife and one child living. He and one of his children were buried in the same coffin…. the small pox is said to be in town…. I feel more lonesome than when you were absent before …" [7]

(ed: Edward E. Harris is the surgeon attached to the 1st Missouri Infantry in Frost's Brigade.)

- - - - -

April 2, 1863
Gratiot Prison, St. Louis, Missouri

Captain Griffin Frost
Co. A – 2nd Missouri Infantry

"Four hundred and eighty-four prisoners left today, on exchange, for City Point, Va…. Had a letter from a married sister in Ohio, advising me to take the Oath and be a good Union man. Will study on it awhile first…. " [8]

- - - - -

April 2, 1863
Camp near Fredericksburg, Virginia

Private Samuel Pickens
Co. D – 5th Alabama Infantry

"Surg. Gen … has issued orders to Commissar. To exert them selves to procure Pease potatoes &c … pickles, crout, & dried fruit for Soldiers. They have neglected them very much - satisfied with … flour & Bacon alone. Surg. orderd detail be sent every morng. fr. every Co. to […] vegetables – such as wild Onions, lambs[…] Water crests &c &c. & the Commis […] nets & catch fish. Plenty of shad in Rappah[annock]. now…. " [9]

(ed: The Surgeon is concerned with many soldiers exhibiting signs of scurvy. Clear signs are " bleeding of the gums, teeth loose, spots of various colors on the skin …" The suggested treatment was to "Remove the patient to a new and healthy situation … give him plenty of fresh vegetables such as spinnage, lettuce, beets, carrots, and scurvy-grass." The wild onions, watercress, & other vegetables that Pvt. Pickens mentions would fulfill these needs.) [10]

- - - - -

April 2, 1863 — Mrs. Judith McGuire
Ashland, Virginia — Nurse

"We were shocked … to hear of the riot which occurred in Richmond today. A mob, principally of women, appeared in the streets, attacking the stores. Their object seemed to be to get anything they could; dry goods, shoes, brooms, meat, glassware, jewelry, … I fear that the poor suffer very much; meal selling today at $16 per bushel." [11]

- - - - -

April 4, 1863 — Private William Corson
Culpeper C. H., Virginia — Co. G – 3rd Virginia Cavalry

"My Dear Jennie,

… We are faring badly now I tell you. Men only get one fourth rations and horses are starving. They are only allowed 8 pounds of corn and 1 ½ pounds of hay in 24 hours…. The weather here is quite cold, but the roads are quite good…. We do not expect to remain here long…. In haste.
Your William" [12]

(ed: William is writing to his sweetheart Jennie. Following the war, they will be married in 1866.)

- - - - -

April 4, 1863 Dr. Thomas F. Wood
Morton's Ford, Virginia HQ – 3rd N. Carolina Infantry

"My Dear Mother:
... I enjoyed a cup of tea at dinner hugely. I had some corn bread and nice raw pork, and with an appetite sharpened with exposure and exercise, who would want a better meal? ... We are getting one ration a day ... one pound of meal, four ounces of meat, with occasionally a little sugar and molasses. This is really insufficient rations.... " [13]

- - - - -

April 5, 1963 Mrs. Harriet Perry
"Spring Hill" – Harrison Cty., Texas Farm wife

"My dear absent Husband: ... Your Father told me laughingly to tell you if he had known when he gave the secession vote, it would put flour so far away, he should have considered a long time ... we have been entirely without for five or six weeks. we have fatty cakes for supper & muffin for breakfast – that I think is very good ... Your Father has about twenty [bushels] of wheat ... he is going to send to the mill this week.... Your Mother sent forty pounds of butter [to Shreveport] to sell.... Are you ever coming home? ...

We hear no war news – Great things will be expected of your army now that you have Genls Smith & Price to command it – I hope they will not take you further off....
Harriet
Accept a thousand kisses & a heart full of love – Good-bye – Good-bye – " [14]

(ed: Harriet is making reference to General Edmund Kirby Smith and General Sterling Price.)

- - - - -

April 5, 1863
Meherrin, Virginia

Mrs. Mary Watkins
Farm wife

"My dear, precious Husband
It is Sunday night and I am sitting by a cozy little fire … Thinking about someone who is away in the army … and imagining him sitting on the floor of his tent before a good warm fire with his head reposing comfortably on his saddle or roll of blankets taking an evening nap … I wish I had a pair of wings and could fly down close by you without anybodys seeing me I comb your hair whilst you are asleep. I do want to see you so bad, I mean to borrow some tonight and go to see you in my dreams any how …
Your own
Mary" [15]

- - - - -

April 5, 1863
Camp Magnolia
Port Hudson, Louisiana

4th Sergeant Robert Elliott
Co. E – 35th Alabama Infantry

"Just one year this day that I took leave of my Dear Mary & the children to leave for the army … I am thankful to the ruler of all things that he has spared me … " [16]

- - - - -

April 6, 1863
Richmond, Virginia

Mr. John B. Jones
Clerk – War Department

"The rails of the York River Railroad are being removed to day toward Danville, in view of securing a connection with the N. C. Central Road." [17]

(ed: The Confederacy does not have the manufacturing capability to produce railroad rails. Therefore they are tearing up designated lines to build and repair roads elsewhere. The York River road runs from Richmond to West Point on the York River. With the Union navy in control of the York this line serves no

useful purpose. Compounding problem is the fact that Southern railroads were constructed in one of 7 different gauges. Therefore the lines cannot interconnect and rolling stock on one line, being of a different gauge, is not able to travel on another.)

- - - - -

April 6, 1863
Milledgeville, Georgia

Honorable Joseph E. Brown
Governor of Georgia

"To the General Assembly:

... Again, there is a class of rich speculators who remain at home preying like vultures upon the vitals of society, determined to make money at every hazard, who turn a deaf ear to the cries of soldiers' families ... If laws are passed against extortion, they find means of evading them. If necessaries of life can be monopolized and sold to the poor at famine prices, they are ready to engage in it. If contributions are asked to clothe the naked soldier or feed his hungry children, they close their purses and turn away.... To make money and accumulate wealth is ... the only object of their lives...." [18]

- - - - -

April 7, 1863
Shelbyville, Tennessee

Lt. Joshua K. Callaway
Co. K – 28th Alabama Infantry

"My Dear Love, ... You ought to see me. I have shaved off some whiskers, trimmed my hair, had that old tooth pulled out and washed my face; now if I had a hat I'd be fine looking, but this old cap has got to be the ugliest thing I ever saw....

I am sorry to hear of your losing the smoke house.... Kiss the children and pray for me ...
JKC" [19]

- - - - -

April 8, 1863
Camp near Shelbyville, Tennessee

Lt. Jesse P. Bates
Co. G – 9th Texas Infantry

"Dear and beloved companion, … I have wrote to you to try and buy some stock that would grow and you said it was a hard matter to buy mares or any other stocks and if you cannot buy stock, I want you to buy land or land certificates or a young negro … If you can buy a good piece of timbered land any where near to home so that it will be in reach of home to haul timber … buy it for it will not pay to keep money lying up to no purpose….

I will send you more money as soon as I draw … I will send a sheet [of paper] in each letter that I send to you … So I remain your affectionate husband and companion until death.
Jesse P Bates" [20]

- - - - -

April 9, 1863
Camp Allenton, Texas

Private James Lewis
Co. C – Baylor's Texas Cavalry

"Dear [Mary]
… we put in our names for two shirts and a hat to be drawn in a few days. I will be much pleased to get a hat … I don't know what to think of the ware. the future looks dark to me. I dred a famine more than the ware for the Federals calculates to starve us in subjection and if the Confederacy fails to raise a good crop we are gave up …" [21]

- - - - -

April 10, 1863
Fredericksburg, Virginia

Corporal Tally Simpson
Co. A – 3rd S. Carolina Infantry

"My dear Sister
… I tell you we are pushed for something to eat. Our rations, which should have lasted till this evening, gave out yesterday at noon. I borrowed meat for

my yesterday's meal at dinner and have not smelt any since. I had dry bread without grease or soda, and a little coffee for breakfast …

I was on guard or picket night before last and spent a very pleasant time indeed. A Mississippian had a small boat about three inches deep and two feet long, with rudder and sails affixed and every thing in trim. We took it down to the river, waved our hand [at the Yanks], and received the same signal in return. We than laded her with papers and sent her across. She landed safely and was sent back with a cargo of coffee. The officer of the day is very strict with them [the Yanks] and whenever he is about, they have to keep close…. it looks strange that we [are] so friendly at one time, when in the next moment we may be attempting to draw each other's life blood….

The revival still continues, and several hundred of Barksdale's men [Mississippi troops] have been converted, and many more are still anxious about their soul's salvation. I saw, the other day, about twelve young men baptized in Baptist faith.

… I am about getting out of soap … I gave one dollar for four sheets of paper like this and four envelopes…. Give my love to all …
Your affec bro
T. N. Simpson" [22]

- - - - -

April 11, 1863
Pine Bluff, Arkansas

Lt. Theophilus Perry
Co. F – 28th Texas Cavalry

"Dear Harriett, … Sell our Buggy if possible for what it will bring and use the money to pay debts with it. Be sure to do it. It has become too small for our family. I reckon it will bring two hundred dollars. It is the best buggy I ever saw. I am trying to buy another horse up here. They are very high I shall have to give three or four hundred dollars I reckon.

I have heard nothing from Norfleet, & am confident that he has gone to the federals. I can do very well without a servant as busy as I am in a mess where there are many… If I get in a mess where there is none I shall send for Sam or Rufus. A negro is invaluable in the Army. An officer has to live like a hog without one. I think I would like to have Rufus any way. Has he ever had the measles or whooping cough?

… Tell Sugar lumpy that Papa will bring her candy when he comes. Tell her to dry some peaches for Papa this summer, to send to him in the War. I have been pleased to hear from your people in Carolina.

I would like above all things to be able to send you to Carolina to see them. Live in hope. I shall do so after awhile. Good night my dear Wife….
Your Husband
Theophilus Perry" [23]

(ed: Theophilus continues to advise Harriet to try to sell their two pieces of land in Marshall and other items, such as the buggy, to pay off all of their small debts. He feels that it will be impossible to survive, after the war, if they have debt. The declining value of the Confederate currency only increases his concern.)

- - - - -

April 11, 1863 — Colonel Robert Kean
Richmond, Virginia — Confederate Bureau of War

"On Saturday the 11th, General Longstreet crossed [the Blackwater] in force at Franklin and … invested Suffolk to the Nansemond river. The object of the expedition is to forage for his army in the unexhausted and productive country between the James and the [Albemarle] Sound, especially on the Chowan. He was anxious the *Richmond* should go down and co-operate with him by holding the mouth of the Nansemond. If this were done he could probably capture the force in Suffolk…. The *Richmond* is such a stupid failure, drawing fourteen feet of water [so] that she cannot go up and down the river … and as she can only steam at about three knots, being worthless as a ram …" [24]

(ed: The C. S. Richmond, *like many other Confederate ironclads and rams, drew too much water and had an undependable and underpowered engine which reduced her to a moored or anchored armored battery.)*

- - - - -

April 11, 1863 — 4th Sergeant Robert Elliott
near Jackson, Mississippi — Co. E – 35th Alabama Infantry

"I took a notion to go to town & having procured me a pass I set out for the City which I soon reached & of all the tall prices for things I never seen every thing I seen was six dollars & fine got completely wore out on walking looking & disgusted with the prices & started for our Camp…." [25]

- - - - -

April 12, 1863 — Private Charles W. Thomas
Washington, North Carolina — Co. B – 56th Virginia Infantry

"My Dear Wife
… We only gets one quarter of a pound of meat and that is tainty at times. We gets bread enough to make out with…. Everything is scarce down here…. Ned Kidd is sick at the hospittle up beyond Golesburg [Goldsboro] … Mary I hope you have got rid of your diptharia. I ware verry sorry to hear that you had it … I remain your devoted husband untell death … C. W. Thomas" [26]

- - - - -

April 12, 1863 — Mrs. Catherine Edmondston
Halifax County, North Carolina — Farm wife

"Sunday – Came brother to see us. He tells us that the riot in Richmond was more serious than we supposed, 20,000 persons being assembled in the streets … But I do not see that they attacked the right places for food. Shoe stores & dry goods establishments will not satisfy the cravings of hunger …" [27]

- - - - -

April 12, 1863
Richmond, Virginia

Mr. John B. Jones
Clerk – War Department

"Our members of Congress get salaries of $2750. A cobbler (free negro) who mends shoes for my family, told me yesterday that he earned $10 per day, or $3000 per annum.

A pair of pantaloons now costs $40; boots $60; and so on." [28]

- - - - -

April 13, 1863
near Woodville, Mississippi

Miss. Kate T. Blount
23 year old farm girl

"My dearest Robbie - … The sick soldiers are so well treated in Woodville that Gen. Gaidner countermanded his orders for them to move and the hospital is still here. About three weeks since two cases of small pox appeared, but the surgeons by using every precaution prevented it from spreading … I must tell you of our frolic last Friday. Some of the gentlemen gave a picnic about six miles from town and we had a fine time. It is the first time I have participated in amusement since the war commenced…. We danced all day and … till eleven o'clock that night. I nearly wore my feet out to say nothing of my shoes, but the pleasure proved sufficient to repay me for all damages … " [29]

- - - - -

April 14, 1863
Fredericksburg, Virginia

Private Milton Barrett
Co. A – 18th Georgia Infantry

"Dear Brother and sister
… Some ten days ago a grate visit took place at Richmond. a bout one thousand women arm ther self with axes and clubs and firearms and march in to the citty and broak open stoers grocers and comassary's took what every tha wanted in spite of milatary or sivel authority. Jeff Davis got among them

to make a speech But could not stop them ... Our newpapers have bin very cearful not to say anything a bout it But i see the yankees have got a full history of it ... The fack is to wel known to be disputed that we ar a runing short of suplyes and if what we have on hand will do tel the new crop come in and thar is a sefishent suplies of grain made tha will be meat for the cattle nor hogs is not in the country, we git no beef now and not quite half rashons of bacon and somes times it is spoilt so we cant eat it. we git a plenty of flout. The cearsity [scarcity] of provishons is cosing a grate deal of uneasiness a mong the soldiers. the yankees cant whip us only by starving us out.

... hopeing to hear from you soon. i am your loving Brother
Milton Barrett" [30]

("The so called bread riot occurred in Richmond on April 2. Food shortages in urban areas and elsewhere in the South were periodically acute. This riot was put down after intervention by President Davis and local police and militia.") [31]

- - - - -

April 14, 1863
Richmond, Virginia

Mr. William M. Wadley
Assistant Adjutant General

"A report was forwarded to the Confederate Secretary of War, James A. Seddon, on the number of engines (locomotives) and cars needed by various Southern railroads, after 2 years of war, to bring their rolling stock back to normal levels. The shortages were as follows:

Railroad Company	Engines needed	Cars needed
Richmond & Danville. Southside	2	50
Virginia & Tennessee	4	50
E Tenn & Va. E Tenn & Ga.	4 or 5	75
Nashville & Chattanooga		50
Richmond & Fredericksburg		5
Petersburg		50

Railroad Company	Engines needed	Cars needed
Wilmington & Weldon	4	100
Wilmington & Manchester	1	100
North Carolina	4	100
Charlotte & South Carolina	2	50
Northeastern	2	25
Southwestern		50" [32]

(ed: The above numbers reflect the major railroad companies in the report. In total the report listed 31 engines and 930 cars as the quantity needed to restore the railroads to their prewar operating levels. This reflects a shortage of about 25%. Considering the limited means of repair, and the impossibility of manufacturing new engines and cars, it is surprising that conditions are this good.)

\- - - - -

Mid April, 1863
near Fredericksburg, Virginia

Sergeant W. R. Montgomery
1st Georgia Sharpshooters

"My Dear Aunt Frank
... we have a new Gen in command of our army & say his name is *General Starvation* & I think for once they are about right, for we only get 4 ounces of bacon & one small pound of flour & sometimes a little salt." [33]

\- - - - -

April 15, 1863
Ashland, Virginia

Mrs. Judith McGuire
Nurse

"Spent yesterday in the hospital. I am particularly interested in two very ill men. One is a youth of seventeen ... sinking with consumption ... His name is Stansberry, and he's from Baltimore." [34]

(ed: Judith's diary noted that Stansberry died on the 16th from consumption [tuberculosis].)

- - - - -

April 15, 1863
Camp near Vicksburg

Sergeant Martin A. Hardin
59th Mounted Tennessee Infantry

"Dear Mary,
... Brother Joe writes that he will do anything for me he can in the way of getting me a substitute. I say to him to get me a man or boy that is sixteen years old that is well grown and healthy and he will be received. I think I will get a swap with a cavalryman in Captain Van Dykes company. If I succeed I don't want to pay so much for a man to take my place. But if Brother Joe makes a trade I will take him." [35]

(ed: Martin would like to get a substitute and remove himself from service or transfer to the cavalry. The infantry has the highest casualty rate so either option is better than staying in the infantry. When a substitute is hired the contract is not binding until the substitute has been accepted by the commanding officer of the company. Martin is in Company E of the 59th so the Captain in command of Co. E has final approval.)

- - - - -

April 16, 1863
Pine Bluff, Arkansas

Captain Elijah P. Petty
Co. F – 17th Texas Infantry

"My dear Wife
... I cant find any thing here to invest money in. Every thing here is enormously high. I have some surplus money on hand that I saved to come home on. Now I dont need it and will send it to you. Dont press the collection of your debts now – let them stand for present. If any body offers to pay how ever dont refuse. We have staked our all on the issue of the Confederacy and lets sink or swim with it....

... I have no news. Multiplied kisses to my brats & respect to friends. Yours etc
E P Petty" [36]

- - - - -

April 16, 1863
Camp near Guinea Station, Va.

Lt. John C. Allen
Co. A – 13th Georgia Infantry

"Miss Disa Darden
Sister ... I have no news that will interest you We are lying on the Rapahahanock Very Still at this Time I do not [know] how long we will remain so. Summer is Near At hand And The Summer Campaign will open soon. The enemy is just on the Opposite side of the River ... At times we Converse With Them ... they are Tired of the War....

They is a Great Deal of fish Caught on the River At this time they are Principaly What they Call the North Carolina Shad they are Very good to eat Some of them are very large Weigh from 3 to 5 Pounds.... We put them in hot ashes and let them remain for a Short Time take them out and Salt them and they are very Nise. We use Ashes instead of Lard. we have Lerned to economise and I recon not Soldgiers only but Citizens Combined Throughout the hole South.

Disa these lines leave me in Good health ... this is my last until I hear from you Good by
J C Allen" [37]

- - - - -

April 16, 1863
Shelbyville, Tennessee

Corporal J. T. Forrest
Co. E – 1st Georgia Infantry

"Dear Wife ... I am well at this time ... I want to hear from you oftener ... We are getting along very (well) in camp. We get tolerable plenty to eat. Our meat is usually bacon. Sometime pork and some beef and corn meal last Friday.... This company will draw money today but I will not get mine yet. They say it won't be many days till the whole battalion will draw. L. B. Hemby, T. R. Summers, Bill Given and Bob Given has all run away.... Tell Eli to cut a pair of half soles for my boots and send them to me ... Well Margaret when you write again write whether Susan can plow the mare or not ... Kiss Jimmy for me. Bless his little heart.... " [38]

- - - - -

April 17, 1863
Guinea Station, Virginia

Private Marion H. Fitzpatrick
Co. K – 45th Georgia Infantry

"Dear Amanda,
... The last letter I wrote home was ... about 10 days ago. I have been very sick since then with the bloody flux. I suffered a great deal but it did not last but three days, but I have had the diareah ever since, which I suppose is nothing amiss as it would not do to stop it too suddenly.... There are a good many cases of bloody flux in the Reg. and some of them very serious, among which is Orderly Hatcher here in our tent. I do not think he will live long ...
Your husband,
M. H. Fitzpatrick" [39]

(ed: Flux is another term for dysentery. The combination of diarrhea and dysentery was the number one killing disease during the conflict. Bad water and poor sanitation created the perfect climate for bacterial infection in the digestive tract. Bloody flux or bloody dysentery means that the walls of the intestine are breaking down and bleeding. The soldier is becoming dehydrated and is also having difficulty processing or gaining any nutrients from the food. There was no medical cure in the 1860s.)

(ed: Mackenzie recommends: "As the dysentery or bloody flux is almost always ... connected with considerable inflammation, it will be proper, in most cases, to bleed the patient ... Whether it be thought prudent to bleed or not, repeated doses of castor oil ... and blisters to the belly, should never be omitted. If there is much vomiting at the commencement, the stomach and bowels may be cleansed by barley or rice water taken by mouth ... As soon as this is effected, give a grain or two of solid opium; if it be rejected, 80 or 90 drops of laudanum in a table-spoonful of chicken broth ... Clysters of the same articles [a castor oil enema], with the addition of an ounce of olive oil and twenty drops of laudanum may be injected daily...") [40]

- - - - -

April 17, 1863
Camp Skull Creek, Texas

Private James Lewis
Co. C – Baylor's Texas Cavalry

"Dear Wife ... I have to eat course corn bred and poor beef, pirncitably. Sometimes get something diferent by buying it at a high price." [41]

- - - - -

April 18, 1863
James Island, South Carolina

Private Charles P. Segler
Co. H – 2nd S. Carolina Artillery

"Dear Father an mother ... I am tolerubly wel ... I have had the chil an fever.... It is gitting very sickly hier with the chil an fever [Charleston] ... Tha sa we wil move over to town before long. The doctor ses it wil not doo to sta on this island too year. we have drew a shirt and a pair of shoes a pece ... I recon you hav hird of the yankees atacting fort sumter ... Tha sa we sunk one of the best iron clads the yankees had.... So I hav no thing more at present ... I reamin youse affectionect son ontil deth ... C. P. Segler" [42]

- - - - -

April 19, 1863
Sulphur Springs, North Carolina

Mrs. Cornelia Henry
Farm wife

"Sunday – Six weeks has passed since I wrote in you, my dear old journal. I have been confined in that time & got up again to health. My babe [Gustavus Adolphos] was born 8th March at 23 minutes after 8 o'clock in the morning. A fine healthy boy.... He is like the most of children, loves nursing. The children think a great deal of it.... Aunt Patsey staid with me till the babe was nearly a week old.... I was confined upstairs & did not get down till the babe was two weeks old. We have had a great deal of company for the last six weeks.... My babe weighed eight lbs. before it was dressed & 13 ¾ lbs. when it was a month old...." [43]

- - - - -

April 19, 1863
Deer Creek, Mississippi

Private Grant Taylor
Co. G – 40th Alabama Infantry

"Dear wife,
... There has been a heap of rain here of late and last night there was an awful storm. It blew down many of our tents. I burnt up all your letters just before I started on this last tramp for fear they would fall into the hands of others than myself. Paper is from 2 to 4 dollars per quire in Vicksburg and I am out of money and only have one sheet of paper left. I will have to make my letters short until I can get more paper.

... We have a hard time over here taking all kinds of weather, marching sometimes day and night, and some of the time from shoe mouth to half leg deep in mud, yet the men are in better health than usual. We get plenty of meat and bread to eat....

You must excuse this scrappy letter as I can get no other paper not having seen my knapsack since we came over here. But I expect it will come up tomorrow.
... Give my best love to all ...
G Taylor" [44]

(ed: A quire of paper is 24 sheets. It is actually 1/20 of a ream which should be 25 sheets but the stationers sell as a quire of 24. This gives them a few sheets as samples and also covers for the possibility of a few sheets in the ream being damaged.)

- - - - -

April 19, 1863
Near Fredericksburg, Virginia

Private Samuel Pickens
Co. D – 5th Alabama Infantry

"Had a miserable night of it after chill went off, a hot followed & lasted a long time. I took off my jacket & threw the cover off till I cooled off some. It seemed the longest night to me I had ever seen. This morng. Dr. Hill came around to see me & gave me a blue mass pill....

April 20 … Walkd down to Dr. Hills & got dose Salts wh. took in Red pepper tea, & 12 Grs. Quinine which I made into 3 pills & took during the day … I had the good fortune to miss my chill [during] night … " [45]

(ed: Blue mass is a pill made of pulverized chalk and mercury. The mercury is supposed to act as a purgative/laxative to help clear your system.)

- - - - -

April 20, 1863	___ T. F. C _______
Camp near Pine Bluff, Arkansas	Young's Regiment

"Dear Mary,

For fear of arousing your jealousy I will mak an explaination that I aught to have made before now. On all fools day I amused the boys and myself by writing Aprils fools for them to send to their sweet hearts some of which were sent off in my handwriting to Parker, you may chance to see some of these and think once of them thoughts too loud (for me) you spoke of in your last letter. But me assure you that my fidelity still remains unshaken towards you. that however high I go up on bubys and legs that women of loose character continually follow the army throwing around me all of their silken wiles. still I never have had any desire to wrong you are break my sacred vows made in holy wedlock.
Yours Affectionally
TFC" [46]

(ed: The manuscript folder and the letter provide no more information than "T.F.C. in Young's Regiment." More research of the Trans-Mississippi commands is required to perhaps identify T.F.C.)

- - - - -

April 21, 1863
Suffolk, Virginia

Captain Thomas Goree
ADC, 1st Corp Staff, ANV

"Dear Sis Frank:
... We have driven the enemy into their stronghold & fortifications at Suffolk where we wish to keep them until we get the corn & bacon from the adjoining counties, of both which there are great quantities. It is thought that in the three counties in N. Carolina ... there can be obtained a sufficiency of bacon to supply our own & Genl. Lee's army for two months.... " [47]

(ed: Thomas is on General James Longstreet's staff where he is serving as an aide de camp. General Longstreet commands the First Corp in Lee's Army of Northern Virginia.)

- - - - -

April 22, 1863
Meherrin, Virginia

Mrs. Mary Watkins
Farm wife

"My Darling Husband
... I had better send your horse by Willie Booker who starts out next Monday ... Will send your brown pants as soon as I can ... I was surprised yesterday by a bundle containing two neat, pretty calicoes. I need not tell you ... how much I thank you ...

Minnie is getting along well with the whooping cough and Emmie has not taken it yet.

Minnie is about the most headstrong, obstinate child that I ever saw ... I have to whip her nearly every day. She and Emmie have two little kittens which Minnie tortures half to death. She ... pours water on them and squeezes them and kisses and rocks them by turns ... Mr. James Daniel has lost his youngest child [typhus fever] and several negroes with it and his three other daughters were down with it. Lucy they thought would not recover. Mary Graham (the one who died) was taken sick Saturday and died Sunday and a good many cases died in three hours.... Dr Wilson said ... he did not know what to do

for it. It [the typhus] was brought from Weldon [North Carolina] by the hands which were sent to work on the fortifications there; 90 out of 100 who went from neighborhood have died with it. I reckon Bro Nat feels very anxious about his little family.... I want to see you too bad. Good bye
Your own
Mary" [48]

(ed: The government had conscripted 100 slaves in Granville County, North Carolina for work near Weldon. They all contracted typhus and were returned to Granville County immediately. All of them made it back to their farms before 90 died and spread the typhus throughout the county. It was either a flea borne or lice borne typhus and the majority of the victims died in less than 24 hours.) [49]

(ed: Typhus can be several forms of an infectious disease caused by the microorganisms of the genus Rickettsia. The disease is characterized by severe headache, sustained high fever, delirium and red rashes.) [50]

- - - - -

April 22, 1863 — Private Grant Taylor
Issaquena County, Mississippi — Co. G – 40th Alabama Infantry

"Beloved wife & children,
I am well this morning except cold ... I received your welcome letter yesterday dated the 9th....

... How much money have you on hand now I am trying to quit using tobacco in order to save some money but I do not believe I can do it. But I will try. We will be paid 2 months wages to-day. They will then be behind nearly 4 months but I suppose they cannot get any more to pay us now. I gave 1 dollar for 2 or three pounds of soap the other day and the same for a pair of socks.

... Tell all howdy for me and kiss the dear children for me and believe me ever your true and loving husband,
Grant" [51]

(ed: Nothing speaks to the problems of the Confederate government more than their struggles to feed and pay their soldiers. The soldiers need their meager salary to help with needed foodstuffs and also to send some monies to family at home. A private gets $11 per month. Grant is hoping, today, to get $22 of the $66 that the government owes him.)

- - - - -

April 23, 1863 — Private John Jackman
Beech Grove, Tennessee — Co. B – 9th Kentucky Infantry

"Broke up camp at Manchester & marched to Beech Grove, 12 miles toward Murfreesboro. Camped in a clover field. The hills about here remind me of Kentucky. They are covered with such pastures and beautiful groves of beech trees, which are now leaving-out. Spring-time is again coming over the hills … Beech Grove, in other days, had a country grocery and post office; there is a nice church, which is still used as a place of worship." [52]

- - - - -

April 24, 1863 — Captain Griffin Frost
Philadelphia, Pennsylvania — Co. A – 2nd Missouri Infantry

" … We went on board the steamer *Major Reybold*, laid at the quay about an hour and left for Fort Delaware, situated on an island sixty miles below Philadelphia, which we reached a little after dark, where we were conducted to our quarters, where we met several old Gratiot acquaintances who left St. Louis before us." [53]

- - - - -

April 24, 1863 — Corporal Tally Simpson
Fredericksburg, Virginia — Co. A – 3rd S. Carolina Infantry

"My dear Aunt
… We are still living hard. Tho it may appear to you to be very serious, still it would make you laugh to see us sitting around our daily meal of sop and

bread. Sometimes we don't have more than three little slices of bacon for six men, and I can eat a half pound of bacon in one meal. The other day there was one biscuit left, and the boys actually drew straws for half of it. We went down in the field yesterday and dug a mess of wild onions, which we ate for supper as a substitute for meat. I understand that we are to get a half pound of bacon very soon. I trust this may be so." [54]

- - - - -

April 24, 1863	2nd Lt. George D. Buswell
Camp Winder, Virginia	Co. H – 33rd Virginia Infantry

"Dear Sister,
Your interesting letter was received a few days ago. Although I date this at Camp Winder we are not at exactly the place we have been all winter. On Monday last we moved camp about a mile farther down the road to the river.... The move was recommended by the Brigade Surgeon. Our present camp is in a field, wood & water handy.

We passed a pleasant day yesterday as you may imagine when I tell you that whilst it was raining pretty hard and we were all closed up in our tents many in their beds ...

... I wrote a letter to Pappa by Jack Johnston also sent my Knapsack boots & 3 pairs socks by him. I sent my Ambrotype by Hamilton Keyser I suppose he has sent it home by this time I had it taken at Guiney's Station, it cost ($8.00) Eight dollars.

I am still enjoying very good health most of the company are well. You know I am always glad to hear from you.
Your Affectionate brother
G. D. Buswell" [55]

(ed: In a 4/27 letter George notes that "Capt. Orrich, our Commissary Sgt., Dr. Flin & myself were below Port Royal to day in search of Shad. We got (7) seven very fine ones apiece ... " He also noted that General Lee had increased the limit

of officers personal baggage from 50 pounds to 150 pounds "so we have concluded to have our mess-chest brought back." More importantly he states, "I think I can keep two pairs [of pants] with me at least for awhile.")

- - - - -

April 24, 1863	Mrs. Cornelia Henry
Sulphur Springs, North Carolina	Farm wife

"Friday – Mail brought no news of importance. The conscripts are called out to 40. Oh! if Mr. Henry should have to go, I don't see how I could ever stay here. I hope he may not have to go. He is the best of husbands & then so kind to the children, so patient. Life would be a blank to me without he was near me. The conscripts have to be examined next week in Asheville. I pray he may not have to go.... " [56]

(ed: On the 25th Cornelia noted, "I bought 8 lbs. of honey yesterday of old Jim Case. It is not very nice. Gave a lb. of bacon for a lb. of honey. Bacon is selling at 75 per pound. Corn from 4 to $6 a bu. & flour 25 cts. per lb. Dear living to those who have to buy.")

- - - - -

April 24, 1863	Captain Reuben Pierson
Fredericksburg, Virginia	Co. C – 9th Louisiana Infantry

"Dear Aunt
... I am in very good health as usual. Our fare is only tolerable good. We have ¼ pound of bacon and one pound of flour per day to each man.... Most of the boys make light bread with their flour and there is quite a spirit of rivalry among them as to who shall excel in the art.... I must say that many of them beak as nice bread as I ever saw any where. We draw peas, rice & sugar occasionally ... About once a month we draw a mess of beef sometimes fresh & at others pickled.... I had a fine mess of white shad this morning but they are very dear & consequently we cannot afford them very often...." [57]

- - - - -

April 25, 1863
Suffolk, Virginia

Sergeant John Beaton
Co. G – 9th Virginia Infantry

"Dear Sister ... We have had rain every day since we have been here. I have not been dry in a month. My musket, my only friend, I have to keep dry consequently that gets the largest share of my blanket. This paper will testify [water stained] to how dry we have been ... None of us have a shift of clothes. Our fancy goods are scarce. I have the last sheet of paper in the company. We are traveling light – besides our warlike implements we have nothing but our blankets, haversacks and canteens. This kind of life suits me. I enjoy better health than I ever did ... We are now in a swamp where water only ankle deep is called a dry place. We throw down two tiers of rails and sleep as well as if we were on beds of down ... I don't know how I should feel to sit down at a table and eat a meal, and then go regularly to bed, it would be strange indeed ... I came near forgetting to say I received one pair of socks from you for which I am very much obliged. Accept my love for yourself ... John K. Beaton" [58]

- - - - -

April 25, 1863
Warrenton, Mississippi

Lt. Calvin M. Smith
Co. D – 31st Tennessee Infantry

"... slept some last night the muesquetoes was very troubulsome will get under the blanket of which I was covered up head & foot and sing cozzen in my ears ... Indeed we have declared war against them. Snakes of which there are hundreds here of all kinds and sizes. The boys have been trying to catch fish but failed today." [59]

(ed: Cozen means to deceive by a petty trick or fraud. Perhaps Calvin is saying that the "muesquetoes" would sing in his ear to try to trick him into removing the blanket to let even more in. Regardless, mosquitoes, fleas, ticks and chiggers drove the soldiers to distraction.)

- - - - -

April 26, 1863
Ft. Delaware Prison

Captain Griffin Frost
Co. A – 2nd Missouri Infantry

"St. Louis and Springfield [Missouri] are paradises compared with this, all are complaining of hunger. Do not know what we would have done if it had not been for a barrel of oysters we were allowed to purchase from an oyster boat. We relished them as only such poor hungry devils could." [60]

(ed: Griffin reached City Point, Va. on May 2; Petersburg, Va. on May 5; Demopolis, Alabama on May 11; Brandon, Mississippi on May 14; returned to Demopolis and spent a month in an exchange camp and hospital May 17 to June 18; finally crossed the Mississippi and returned to the Trans-Mississippi Department on July 1 at Helena, Arkansas.)

- - - - -

April 29, 1863
Ashville, North Carolina

Petition to Rev. John Wagg
Methodist Minister

"Revd J. D. Wagg
Sir The time has come when all young men Should act in defense of their country, when the ministry Should be laid aside for the musket; and as you are a young man, able in our opinion, to take your place in ranks by the side of your fellow countrymen, we respectfully ask you to resign your position as minister of the Hillsville Church, and Volunteer in the defense of the country, we feel assured that you (from your past course) have patriotism enough to comply with our request,
Hopeing you will comply, we
Remain Very Respectfully
Your Obedient Serv'ts" [61]

(ed: This undated petition was signed by 45 male members of the congregation. On April 29, 1863 a military exemption was requested by Revd. J. D. Wagg by reason of him " being a Minister of the Gospel." This exemption was approved on Sept. 19th by Capt. D. C. Pearson, Enrolling Officer, 10th District. Quite often the local pastors rotate in volunteering their services as chaplain for various local

units. However, there is nothing in the correspondence to indicate that this option was even considered.)

- - - - -

April 30, 1863 Coffee Substitute Greensboro *Patriot*

"Like every other family ... where the blockade rendered coffee so scarce ... my wife began to cast about for a substitute, and we tried ... Okra seed. Mrs. Cloud had some washed and dried, preparatory for parching. We used about the same quantity by weight ... that we had formerly done of coffee. It was carefully parched and the coffee made in the usual way, when we found it almost exactly like coffee in color, very pleasantly tasted and entirely agreeable. All other substitutes were laid aside, and the Okra has been used in my family for the last eighteen months ... I can say in all candor ... I should have no preference, at 10 cents per pound between Okra and Coffee. When well made ... it is delicate and finely flavored, entirely wholesome, of a rich golden color, and in all respects equal to the best Java coffee, except the Coffee flavor, which may be imparted to it, if preferred, by grinding with the baked Okra seed, ten or twelve grains of baked Coffee, for each meal ... nor has it any perceptible effects upon the nervous system, through which medium headache is often produced by Coffee, in ... females especially." [62]

- - - - -

April 30, 1863 Miss. Kate Sperry
Winchester, Virginia Nurse

"Today's my birthday – 20 years old – already begin to feel antiquated – if I keep on I'll be an old maid – Whew. That'll be charming." [63]

- - - - -

April 30, 1863 William Culpepper
Petersburg, Virginia

"the Poplar Lawn Hospital
Mrs. Susan Hambrick
... your sun Michael Hambrick is at the Popularlawn Hospital very sick indeed ... he is in abad condishion an no proaspect of his getting eny beter ... i am sorry for eny poar salger that is in his condiishion toda the dr is giving him medicin ..." [64]

(ed: William Culpepper is not listed as a member of the 10th Battalion of Georgia Infantry. Perhaps he was an orderly at the hospital. Records show that Michael died of typhoid fever on the same day as this letter was written to his mother.)

- - - - -

Treatment for Worms *Mackenzie's 5000 Receipts*

"Intolerable itching at the ... fundament, ... hardness in the belly, gradual emaciation, colic, and sometimes convulsions [are symptoms]. The white thread worm resembles a small piece of white thread, and is usually found near the fundament [anus], at the lower end of the guts, where it produces a contraction of the parts, and a most intolerable itching. Clysters [enemas] of lime water will frequently bring whole nests of them away, and procure instant relief. The tincture of aloes ... is by far the best remedy known, for not only this, but the round worm.

Tape worms inhabit the whole of the internal canal and frequently defies all our efforts to get him out ... Large does of spirits of turpentine, from one to two ounces in barley water, have been advantageous ... large quantities of gruel, or barley water, should be used with it, in order to prevent its irritating the stomach and kidneys.... Repeated purges with calomel is as effectual remedy for worms as we have ..." [65]

- - - - -

May, 1863

General Lee moves quickly to counter the thrust of General Hooker and 73,000 Union troops threatening his left flank near Chancellorsville, Virginia. He leaves General Early and 10,000 men to hold General Sedgewick's 40,000 men at bay at Fredericksburg and takes 43,000 men to meet Hooker. Lee determines to hold Hooker near the Chancellor House with 17,000 men, while he sends General Jackson on a long flanking march with 26,000 men. Late in the day on May 2nd Jackson's men tear into the Union right flank and roll it back for miles. Fighting continues on May 3rd while Early is holding Sedgewick at Fredericksburg and Salem Church. In a brilliant display of calculated daring and generalship Lee has roundly defeated yet another Union general. The victory is expensive with the loss of more than 11,000 men killed or wounded at Chancellorsville plus the losses at Fredericksburg and Salem Church.

From Fredericksburg on May 7th, Private Talley Simpson of the 3rd South Carolina Infantry writes, *"Never did troops fight better than ours or worse than the Yankees ... Our boys swept over their lines like a hurricane ..."*

On May 10th General Stonewall Jackson dies as a result of the accidental wounds he had suffered at the hands of his own men on the evening of May 2nd at Chancellorsville.

Confederate General Pemberton, headquartered in Vicksburg, Mississippi, is going to receive the same type of lesson in daring and maneuvering that

General Hooker has received. On May 1st General Grant takes Port Gibson, Mississippi, on May 5th he captures Grand Gulf and then moves rapidly eastward and inland. Cutting off his own supply lines he wins a battle at Raymond on May 12th. On May 14th he captures Jackson, the capital of Mississippi, brushing aside the forces of General Johnston. Grant then turns westward toward Vicksburg, winning battles at Champions Hill and Big Black River and, on May 17th has General Pemberton pinned in Vicksburg. He assaults the Confederate lines in major attacks on May 19th and May 22nd but suffers bloody repulses. While Grant constructs his siege lines around Vicksburg, the citizens of Vicksburg dig elaborate caves and move underground to survive the constant bombardment of the Union fleet and mortar barges on the river and the artillery from the Union trenches surrounding the rest of the city. The soldiers and citizens quickly realize that it will not be long until horses, mules, pigeons, rats, cats and dogs become their only food.

Gold is discovered in Montana and overnight the town of Virginia City blossoms.

Citizens with Southern sympathies are being banished from St. Louis, Missouri.

In Louisiana General Nathaniel Banks attacks Port Hudson and fails. While Grant tightens his lines around Vicksburg, Banks lays siege to this other key Confederate stronghold on the Mississippi.

The sugar growing regions of Louisiana are all now controlled by Union forces. The only sugar producing region in the Confederacy still under Confederate control is a small area of Texas. Sugar becomes a scarce commodity for the balance of the war. Limited quantities come in through the blockade, but most citizens turn to molasses and other substitutes.

May, 1863

May 1, 1863
Sikes Ville, Florida

Miss. Elizabeth Sikes
Farm girl

"My dear Brother,
...Time are hard. Bacon and lard are fifty cents per lb. corn for one to four dollars per Bus., salt from 3 to 5 dollars per Bu at the Bay. Fish aplenty in the old Suwannee and I live handy to them. I can go and catch a mess when ever I want to ... They are a great help whare meat is scarce." [1]

- - - - -

May 2, 1863
Chancellorsville, Virginia

2nd Lt. David Champion
Co. G – 14th Georgia Infantry

" ... We reached here [the exposed right flank of the Union army] about 4:30 in the afternoon and the enemy were completely unaware of our approach.... we suddenly raise the "rebel yell" and charged down the Plank Road. It was as sudden and unexpected as a flash of lightning from a clear sky. Even the wild game fled, startled at our onrush. Parts of the enemy lines were driven in two miles before dark and hundreds of men and quantities of supplies were captured. We were very hungry after an all-days march, so I cut a canteen and haversack from a dead Yankee and was sitting on a log enjoying a sumptuous meal, when a Minnie ball sang right by my head ... I moved to a less conspicuous place and kept on eating." [2]

- - - - -

May 3, 1863
Chancellorsville, Virginia

Private William F. Maiden
Co. B – 48th Virginia Infantry

"[General] Jackson was a great believer in prayer. When he was expecting a fight next day … he spent the night before [in prayer] when this was the case the boys would note it and say boys we will have a fight tomorrow Jackson is praying." [3]

(ed: William noted that he was "shot down" on May 3rd and "carried" to the same place as his wounded General, "Guina Station.")

- - - - -

May 5, 1863
"Tally Hatchie Co.," Mississippi

Private William J. Bowers
Co. E – Waul's Texas Legion

"Dear Cousin,
… I am alive though I have had a very hard spell of inflammation of the brain and spinal infection and was out of my head for 14 days … I have not yet got able for duty … I think that I will get stout again soon…. though I have suffered greatly with my head, there was a great many who died with the same disease….

I have delayed writing some time on account of the river being blockaded, though I thought that I would risk it … I will be very sorry if the[y] cut off communication … I am in hopes that they will become satisfied that they cannot subjugate the South and go home…. I would be very glad to see you all and enjoy peace and harmony…. Farewell for present.
W J Bowers" [4]

- - - - -

May 5, 1863
Hospital – Vicksburg, Mississippi

Private Charles T. Shelton
Botetourt Artillery

"Dear Father:
Before this reaches you you will have learned the result of the battle of Bayou Pierre how our small force held ten times their number in check all day. Our

battery suffered severely – we lost four of our guns. I send a list of killed & wounded. I was slightly wounded in right hand & therefore have to write with my left. I thank God that I escaped with my life. My best love to all.
Affectionately your son
Charles T. Shelton" [5]

- - - - -

May 6, 1863
Richmond, Virginia

Colonel Robert Kean
Confederate Bureau of War

"Prisoners and wounded have come in in large numbers. Dr. Carrington, medical director here, told me last night he had received 8000 of our wounded, and that Dr. Guild, medical director of General Lee's army, had informed him there were 2000 yet to come." [6]

- - - - -

May 6, 1863
Middleville, Virginia

Sergeant Levin Gayles
Co. G – 9th Virginia Infantry

" ... have to march to Middleville before we can get any rations. It is harde to have to march 22 miles with out and carry all you have to cover with and the[n] make your bed on the ground ... hardships of a poor olde Soldier in Bob Lees Army." [7]

- - - - -

May 6, 1863
Chancellorsville, Virginia

Private Leroy W. Cox
Carrington's Battery
Virginia Light Artillery

"... The next morning [after Stonewall Jackson was wounded] General Stuart was put in command ... We resumed the attack bright & early. Our infantry charged the breastworks near Chancellor's house two or three times but there was a big lot of enemy in the woods on the left and they would shoot our men out … General Stuart came back to where we were located … we had two or three rifle cannon. He ordered us to fire on the woods … we were presently ordered to change our firing a little bit … a young artillery officer standing in his stirrups cried, "You've got it, kid! Give it to them!" We loaded 50 shots and shot into the woods … the woods caught fire … The General … ordered us to hitch our guns and go to the front … we rumbled ahead and took the breastworks, dropped in front of them. We opened with double canister and there was a big execution…. I was No 1 at the gun…. we then changed to single charge of canister and then to shrapnel and then we fired second and one-half bullets … I was really in the thick of that encounter." [8]

(ed: Private Cox also noted that, "Gen. Stuart would call this a charge of artillery on infantry which was a rare thing in battle.")

- - - - -

May 6, 1863
Washington City, D. C.

Private Samuel Pickens
Co. D - 5th Alabama Infantry

"Pr[i]soner of War –
Cliffburne Barracks
Washington City, D. C.
Care Col. C. M. Alexander

Jno. Chrisitian wrote home a list of Prisoners fr. our Co. Up pretty early this morning & out being counted & divided into squads of 50 & given charge of one our Sergts. to draw rations together. There are 5 rooms in our building & 10 cooks in each detailed fr. amg. Prisoners to do cooking & we go up by squads & as each man name is called he draws his 4 crak[crackers] slice meat & cup coffee…. confusion this morning. as not know how much wd. take to feed us Rebels. 740 in no…. Went round to sutlers & got orang. app. & Pies…." [9]

- - - - -

May 7, 1863
Fredericksburg, Virginia

Corporal Tally Simpson
Co. A – 3rd S. Carolina Infantry

"Dear Pa
Ere this reaches home, you will have heard, ... of our passing safely through the series of battles which have been fought since the last letter I mailed. Oh how grateful I am to an over-ruling Providence for thus mercifully protecting us, and my prayers have been repeatedly offered at the throne of grace ...

... Never did troops fight better than ours or worse than the Yankees. We met with almost uninterrupted success from beginning to end. Our boys swept over their lines like a hurricane and as resistless as the billows of the sea. The artillery did admirable execution, and on the whole tis considered the most brilliant victory of the war. The superior generalship of the gallant Lee has completely checked the mad career of the Federal general and sent him limping and howling back to his den on the other side of the Rappahannock River.

... I am as dirty as a hog. I have lost all my clothes and have none to put on till these are washed. My shoes are out, and my feet are so sore that I can scarcely walk. We have no tents, and the weather is as cold and rainy as any in the winter time. I must say this much – we have been well fed.... Genl Lee say his infantry can never be whipped....
... Your affect son
T. N. Simpson

I send a likeness of McClellan and a one dollar greenback. The bill has a photograph of old Abe on it. I send them home as curiosities." [10]

- - - - -

May 7, 1863
Big Black, Mississippi

4th Sergeant Robert Elliott
Co. E – 35th Alabama Infantry

"Rested very well last night was very uneasy about my knapsack heard that all of our bagage had gone on to V. Burg & it was thought probably would be lost & in a soldiers knapsack is his all & if he looses that it hurts him as much as if a rich man looses his whole crop of cotton ... "[11]

- - - - -

May 8, 1863
Prison – Washington City, D. C.

Private Samuel Pickens
Co. D – 5th Alabama Infantry

"For Brkt, crkers, small slice meat, mouthful frid Ir. Potato & cup coffee, Dinner Light brd. beans & rice boiled together. Supper Light brd. & Spoonful molassas & Coffee. Bef[ore] Dinner went round trying buy tin cup & at house where Yanks eatg dinner 1 gave me cup & told pay what I wishd. Had scarcely any silver & gave him $1.00 Confed. looked at it as curiosity & seemed surprised I offerd so much - & returnd it saying it wd. be useful to me when return home & no use to him ... He filled it with soup & gave me bread & seemed to be careful that no officer saw it. I thanked him and told him if he should ever be in South under same circumsts. I'd be glad to do him any favor.... The soldiers disposed to treat us well – much better than we wd. treat them in Richmd: but that is natural for we consider them invaders trying to subjug. & rob of everythg. we hold dear on earth. While many of them are only in army for a living ... Markd cup & will try take care of it.... "[12]

- - - - -

Undated, 1863
Winston County, Mississippi

Mrs. Nancy C. Wallace Porter
Farm Wife

In her notebook Nancy listed the clothing she made and sent to Thomas D. Wallace and James R. Wallace, her brothers, who both served in Mississippi infantry regiments.

"Close made for T. D. Wallace ...

2 flanel shirts
1 per flannel drawers
2 per of socks

2 per of pants geans
1 wiscat

Close made for J. R. Wallace …
1 geans coats
1 per pants
1 wescoat
1 per gloves
2 blankets" [13]

- - - - -

May, 1863 — Dr. Thomas F. Wood
Chancellorsville, Virginia — HQ – 3rd N. Carolina Infantry

"My duties as Assistant Surgeon were to go along with the Regiment on the field, and dress the wounds of the men as they fell out and came to the rear…. in stopping to dress wounds we got pretty well to the rear … My ambulance man carried a canteen of whiskey and one of water. We had sponges, bandages, ligatures, and necessary medicines – usually morphine and opium. Surgical instruments were scarce … That it was not every Assistant Surgeon who had a pocket case, so that having none myself, I secured [over time] a very poor one…. " [14]

(ed: Thomas performed his first battlefield amputation on Sunday at Chancellorsville with the assistance of 2 hospital stewards. He removed an arm just below the shoulder joint. Thomas noted, "This was my real introduction to surgery and a trying one it was …" The patient survived and they met again many years later. Thomas did not recognize the man but the man told Thomas, "I remember you … You removed my arm at Chancellorsville.")

- - - - -

May 8, 1863
Guinea's Station, Virginia

Sergeant Micajah D. Martin
Co. D – 2nd Georgia Infantry

"Dear Father and Mother:
... About two o'clock [on May 2] rations were brought to us. They consisted of biscuit, ham and sugar. We drew for three days. I got 20 biscuits, three-fourths of a pound of bacon, and one pound of sugar. I had to get two haversacks to hold all my provisions ...

... Sunday, the 3rd of May ... We were formed in line of battle, and advanced ... Although I was not hit, I was very near it.... I mentioned about having two haversacks on; a shell whistled by me, cutting them both off. It carried one of them at least forty feet behind me, while my biscuits, bacon and sugar was scattered around promiscuously. Several of the boys were struck by the biscuits, and more than one thought he was wounded. I had to rely on the generosity of my friends for the next two days for something to eat." [15]

- - - - -

May 8, 1863
Hamilton's Crossing, Virginia

2nd Lt. George D. Buswell
Co. H – 33rd Virginia Infantry

"Dear Bro,
... One or two of the boys of our company got behind & did not get in the fight [Chancellorsville]. Those that were in did very well.... We captured ... 15 or 20 pieces of artillery a great many small arms, knapsacks, canteens, blankets, gum clothes &c it is rumored that Hokeer [Hooker] was wounded by a piece of a brickbat knocked from Chancellors house (a suitable weapon for him to be killed with) ..." [16]

(ed: In a diary entry dated May 10th George noted, "Today we were pained by the melancholy news of the death of our heroic & beloved leader Lieut. Gen. Jackson. He died this evening about 3 pm ...")

- - - - -

May 8, 1863 Mrs. Cornelia Henry
Sulphur Springs, North Carolina Farm wife

"Friday – We have had another victory near Fredericksburg Va. Gen. Jackson had an arm broke. We lost one Gen., killed, Paxton & Gen. A. P. Hill & Heath [Heth] were wounded. I have not seen the casualties yet. The loss on our side not so great as on the yanks. Oh that they could see the error of their ways & turn from this wickedness before too late. I would ask thy blessings Oh Ruler on high on us as a nation, give our soldiers courage & endow our rulers with wisdom from on high.... grant us a speedy peace on honorable terms is my prayer Oh! most merciful God." [17]

- - - - -

May 9, 1863 Private Grant Taylor
Vicksburg, Mississippi Co. G – 40th Alabama Infantry

"Beloved wife and children,
I embrace the present moment to pen you a few line. I am tolerable well. I have the diarrhea some but not enough to stop me from duty. I hope these line may reach you all well. I received a letter from you day before yesterday dated 23d and one yesterday with 2 in it dated 26 and 30th of April. I was glad to get them but sorry to hear of the boys' sickness. I do hope they have got well.

... I do not need any clothes of any sort yet and if I can draw from the government I shall not draw any more from home.... I have had to leave my overcoat and one blanket behind. I do not expect ever to see them any more.... Capt. Lofton has ... resigned his office on the account of rheumatism. He has got one letter for you but I expect to send this by mail as he has as many letters [from Company G] as he can carry.

... It is a little after sunrise and I must close and eat my breakfast and get ready to march. We got here yesterday. I feel very sore from marching.

Continue in prayer for me.... Kiss the children for me and believe me your true one as ever,
Grant" [18]

(ed: This is Grant's last letter before the surrender of Vicksburg on July 4, 1863. He was then paroled and returned to Pickens County, Alabama to await exchange on August 23, 1863. The officers and men, reluctantly, began reporting to Demopolis, Alabama to reform Company G the first week of October. Grant, a paroled prisoner of war, spent the majority of July, August and September on his farm with Malinda and the children.)

- - - - -

May 9, 1863 Miss. Kate Sperry
Winchester, Virginia Nurse

"Saturday – This morning the whole of the Yankee Army above us came back – they had been up as far as New Market – they arrested every boy and citizen here in town – searched all the houses except this – suppose the reason we escaped was there were three search parties and each one thought the other had done it. I stood on the pavement and blazed away at them – whereupon one of them said I was pretty strong and spunky but had made a d___d poor selection in holding up for Secesh – we called them everything. We've had glorious news – our Army has whipped Hooker all to pieces at Chancellorsville and the Yankees are almost disconsolate ... It's reported that General Jackson is wounded – some say has lost his left arm, but I hope that's incorrect." [19]

- - - - -

May 9, 1863 *Wytheville Dispatch*
Wytheville, Virginia

"SUGAR SUGAR

Just to hand a consignment of Four Thousand pounds nice Brown Sugar, call before it is all gone.

JNO W PAULETT" [20]

- - - - -

May 10, 1863
Hanover Junction, Virginia

Captain Samuel P. Wagg
Co. A - 26th N. Carolina Infantry

" ... John perhaps you would like to know how my men are accupied to day (Sunday) Well I can sit in my tent and count 12 streatched upon the grass asleep. I see several seated a short distance from me, talking of the defeat of Old Jo Hooker and the victory Lee gained [Chancellorsville]. I see some ... are cooking their rations, notwithstanding the sun is shining very wearm. some are gone to the river fishing, and I see two of them reading their bibles. Lts Gentry and Duvall are asleep in my tent and from their looks are dreaming pleasant dreams....

John I have no news later than you have. It is reported that Gen Lee's wife is going to apply for a divorce. Do you want to know the cause? She dont like it because the Gen has been running after a Hooker. Do you blame her? ...

We have very little duty to do. nothing but to guard two bridges. It is reported that Lee is going to cross the river and attack Hooker if he does we will be in front.

John I wish you would write often to me
Your brother
S. P. Wagg" [21]

- - - - -

Undated – early May, 1863
Chancellorsville, Virginia

Lt. Green B. Samuels
Co. F – 10th Virginia Infantry

"I am sick unto death with this awful war and were it honorable to leave the service I would not think any sacrifice too great that would restore me to your loving arms." [22]

- - - - -

May 10, 1863 Mrs. Margarette A. Harris
Paris, Texas St. Clair Cty., Missouri refugee

"… Have excaped all the diseases that this unfortunate little village is infested with … from smallpox, down to mumps … I have had the children vaccinated but do not know wheither the vaccine was good or not; they had pretty large sores on their arms …" [23]

- - - - -

May 10, 1863 Mrs. Mary Watkins
Meherrin, Virginia Farm wife

"My own dear Husband
… Emmie and I have just been walking in the garden and Emmie is completely carried away with the beautiful flowers. I never saw a child so fond of flowers. Whenever I go out to walk she begs me to bring her wildflowers and sit and talks to them by the hour…. Emmie has worn out three prs of shoes this winter and is getting through her fourth pair right rapidly…. Mr. Tom Anderson [overseer] called … the day after he wrote you, his leaf tobacco came in order and he had taken it all down and bulked it nicely and would prize it as soon as he could. He had finished making his potatoe hills and would finish hilling up tobacco and be ready to go weeding corn Monday. The commissioners were at our house Thursday and impressed 250 to 300 lbs of bacon …
Your loving
Mary" [24]

- - - - -

May 11, 1863 Mrs. Susan E. Scott
Lake Creek, Texas Farm wife

"Dear Husband I received two letters from you yesterday dated 22nd and 29th of April. I had despaired of hearing … you had gone to La…. I know that I write every week and will continue to write … whether you answer them or not.... I have had another severe spell of toothache my face is just beginning to look like a humans again ... I have not been well for three weeks and look like a skeleton except my face which is fat I weighed yesterday one hundred and fifteen pounds last time I weighed on some steel yards I weighed a hundred and 40. I feel so anxious to have an appetite so I can give milk for the baby ... Maria [slave] was bit by a rattlesnake last Monday ... she has been the most swelled sight I ever saw she was bit on her little toe ... the swelling extended to her shoulder ... I was sure she would die ... but she is a great deal better and can sit up and eat the swelling is now confined to her foot and leg ... spirits of turpentine relieved her gave her to drink and rubbed her with it.... Our corn is very good in the field near the house ... I have not seen the lower field since it has been worked ... they will get done scraping cotton thursday ... They are pressing negroes in Grimes & have not been here yet ... You must come home ... the children and I want to see you so bad ... Yours, Susan" [25]

- - - - -

May 11, 1863
Hamilton's Crossing, Virginia

Captain James Carrington
Charlottesville Light Artillery

"Mrs. McCoy
Dear Madame
I wrote several days ago but everything has been in so much confusion here. I fear the letter was not sent and therefore deem it proper to again announce that your son was very seriously wounded in the recent engagement at Chancellorsville [May 3] while he was conscientiously discharging his duty in a most manly way. I sympathize most deeply with you in this sad affliction.... I most correctly hope he will speedily recover. He was sent from this place to Richmond and I hope before this letter reaches you he will be safely at home. If so please give him my deepest sympathy.
Very respectfully,
James Carrington
Captain Charlottesville Battery"

(ed: Sgt. William K. McCoy was wounded when a shell he was carrying exploded in his hands. He was cutting the fuse. His face was burned, his hands were burned,

several fingers broken and three fingers were partially missing. He had a deep wound in his right inner thigh and a large, deep wound in the right inner arm below the shoulder. He was evacuated to the Baptist Female Institute Hospital in Richmond. He was transferred to the private home of Mr. Roger Martin, a family friend, whose property was about one mile from the hospital. Dr. Bolton gave William morphine to ease his pain. William died on Tuesday, May 19th with his nephew at his bedside.) [26]

- - - - -

Undated May, 1863
Trenton, Louisiana

Captain Elijah P. Petty
Co. F – 17th Texas Infantry

"My dear Wife
... all the Sugar growing portion of Louisiana is now in the hands of the feds. Texas now has the only sugar region in Confederate Lands. We are nearly ruined on the Sugar question and if you hav'nt laid in enough you had better haste on the subject. Sugar will be out of reach soon ... So buy if you have to pay a big price for it. Also buy some molasses a barrell at least....

... Our communication with the east is almost entirely cut off. What is done is by chance. So you see that by Yankee persistency and ingenuity that although checked yet they continue to encroach upon our borders and contract our limits.

... A thousand kisses for you & them. Write as often as possible.
Your's truly
E P Petty" [27]

(ed: In June Captain Petty will be wounded at the battle of Milliken's Bend. His shoulder wound will be minor but he will be furloughed home to recover. On August 11, 1863 Elijah will depart Bastrop, Texas to rejoin his command.) [28]

- - - - -

May 12, 1863 Mrs. Cornelia Henry
Sulphur Springs, North Carolina Farm wife

"... I took the toothache after dinner, not very badly. The baby's ear still runs, smells rather offensive. I hope it may not injure his hearing but I greatly fear it will. Willie still wheezes some. The other two little ones very well.... " [29]

- - - - -

May 13, 1863 Mrs. Emily Howe Dupuy
Prince Edward County, Virginia Farm wife

"May 14th – No false alarm at all my dear son [Richard H. Watkins], for about midnight Mary gave birth to a fine _____ Oh you are hoping it is a son but our Heavenly Father knows what is best, it is a daughter ... The mother bore the trial well, & is quite comfortable this morning... You never saw happier children than Emmie & Minnie were this morning upon being introduced to their little sister.... Mary sends love and says don't be uneasy about her.
Your mother [in-law]
E. H. Dupuy" [30]

- - - - -

May 13, 1863 Corporal Benjamin Freeman
Richmond, Virginia Co. K – 44th N. Carolina Infantry

"Dear Farther and Mother
I this evening take the opportunity of writing you a few line to inform you that I am well and getting on well as common General Jackson is dead he was shot in the arm and it had to be amputated ... Our Regiment had to hold an escort ... over General Jackson's corpse.... There has been a great many Yankees through this place – the las week from Fredricksburg. We had a great many wounded soldiers The hospitals are full of them poor fillows Wheet looks splendid here the finest clour ... I hope it will not be but a

few days before I get my Furlo ugh … I will come to a close I am your son until Death
Cpl Benjamin H. Freeman" [31]

(ed: Benjamin has a unique writing style. He always spells father as farther. He generally does not use periods but just leaves a space. It is fairly easy to figure out his words such as las [last], clour [color], wheet [wheat], fillows [fellows] and polk [pork]. Benjamin has a wonderful voice.)

- - - - -

May 14, 1863	Captain Weldon E. Davis
Camp near Fredericksburg, Virginia	Co. B – 30th N. Carolina Infantry

"Ma
… We left the battlefield Wednesday the 6th inst, about 3 o'clock in the evening and stopping to rest. A good part of the day the rain was falling almost as hard as I ever saw it, and the mud was almost half leg deep …

Our regiment has 29 killed and about 125 wounded … We were in the hottest of the fight for nearly four hours … Their [Yankee] dead lay scattered through the woods for over 200 yards….

If I had known the fighting was going to end Sunday evening I could have saved sugar and coffee enough to have lasted me a month or two. We got some of the nicest soap you ever saw, and many of the boys supplied themselves with writing paper for some time to come. I didn't even save a cotton shirt, as many as there were and as bad as I needed them.

But for the hard rain – we could have almost ruined the Yankee army. Our army formed three sides of a square and the river the forth side. The Yankees were in there and the shot and shell from our artillery could meet in the center. We have everything ready to begin upon them Tuesday, when the rain fell in torrents as to break it up and that night they skedaddled across the river …
As ever, your affectionate son, Weldon" [32]

- - - - -

May 14, 1863
Vicksburg, Mississippi

Lt. Calvin M. Smith
Co. D – 31st Tennessee Infantry

"… We are accumulating large amounts of provisions and forage at Vicksburg with the intention of holding that place at all hazzards." [33]

- - - - -

May 14, 1863
James River near Richmond, Virginia

Mr. George R. Wood
Barge boatman

"Henry [Richards] [negro crewman] would gather all the driftwood which we had the privilege to carry to the amount of two cords which brought us $12 profit. Each trip we often brought corn and doubled our money. One day a fisherman left his seine with us and we caught 120 shad in two tides. We sold eighty for $1.00 each, Confederate money, and salted forty for home. We often made extra money and would be greeted with loving smiles through tears when I gave it to mother. I only kept a few dollars for tobacco … " [34]

- - - - -

May 14, 1863
Macon, Georgia

Macon Daily Telegraph

NEW DENTISTRY OFFICE
Over Harris & Dense's – Cherry St.

"Having had long experience and being universally successful in inserting teeth, on gold or other material, and having a good stock of Jones & White's Teeth on hand, for beauty, durability and workmanship, my work will be entirely satisfactory.

Unsound teeth treated, filled with gold or skillfully extracted.

JOHN M. LUNQUEST
of Charleston, late of Griffin, Ga." [35]

- - - - -

May 16, 1863
Orange C. H., Virginia

Private William Corson
Co. G – 3rd Virginia Cavalry

"My Dear Jennie,
... I went all through the counties of Rhappahanock, Fauquier and Louden, and fared sumptuously. The citizens were delighted to see us and gave us everything that was good to eat and drink free of charge. On our return we had to keep in the mountains and traveled over the roughest country I ever saw. Got in among the Dutch Quakers and had a big fight with the women. We impressed their horses and they came down on us like a thousand of brick on a rotten pumpkin. I hung a big fat gal and in the scuffle knocked a dutch-churn down, crippled a cat, and nearly drowned the baby in Butter-milk....
Your devoted lover
Wm C Corson" [36]

- - - - -

May 17, 1863
Big Black River, Mississippi

Private John Dennis
Co. D – 43rd Tennessee Infantry

"On May 16 [17] went in to battle of Big Black and had to fall back and to fall back inside the ditches by Vixburg and then it was one continuel [...] of guns and canon 47 day and nights our rations was just one little bisket a day and the same amount of pea or rice bread and a little cow meat that was so pore that they coulnt git up when we eat up all the pore cows we then began on the sore backed mules ..." [37]

- - - - -

May 18, 1863
Vicksburg, Mississippi

Private George W. Crosby
Co. I – 59th Tennessee Infantry

" ... this being the 18th of May, the Ball opened, cannonading opened on land & on the water at intervals, musketry – hear we faced cannon & musketry for 47 days & knights on short rations, pea meal for bread, with bugs in peas, then came Rice full of weevil, then came poore Buff [beef], then last meat was mule, next come starvation all of supplys, bad as it was, all give out, ..." [38]

- - - - -

May 18, 1863
Little Rock, Arkansas

Dr. William McPheeters
Price's Division

"General [Sterling Price],
On the 15th Inst. we visited and carefully inspected each regiment ...

The ground ... is well selected, high, sufficiently shaded, and to all appearances healthy. In Gen. McRae's Brigade the tents are regularly ... arranged, and sufficiently remote from each other as to admit of being properly policed ... Sinks [latrines] are prepared and regularly used both for the reception of the offal accumulating in cooking, and other purposes. Each company is divided into messes of ten ... This ... is common to the entire Division....

There are however ... no Hospital tents, no other arrangements for isolating the sick ... There is also a scarcity of water ... It is obvious to remark that a sufficient supply of water, not only for drinking and cooking purposes, but also for washing the clothes and keeping the persons of the soldiers clean is essential to the health of the army....

There seems to be some hesitation on the part of regimental surgeons in sending their seriously sick to the General Hospital.... the severe and protracted cases ... can be better cared for and their dietetic and other wants speedily met in the General Hospital.... an order covering these cases might have a salutary effect.
Very Respectfully
W M McPheeters
Surgeon & Med. Insp." [39]

- - - - -

May 18, 1863
Chattanooga, Tennessee

Miss. Kate Cummings
Hospital Matron

"The papers are filled with accounts of raids which have taken place all over the Confederacy. Mississippi and North Alabama have suffered from these horrible scourges. The raiders burn houses and destroy provisions of all kinds, and I am told they have positive orders to destroy all farming implements. This is the way they think they will make us submit – ruin the country, and starve us.... There is no doubt we will have great suffering, but it will be of short duration.... "[40]

- - - - -

May 18, 1863
Columbia, South Carolina

Mr. William L. Henry
Farmer

"My Dear Dinah [Cornelia Henry]
I will start home in the morning. Sold Bacon at $1. Mr. Lopez will try to get some hands and will write.

I have bought a knife apiece for the children. Please speak to them of Papa and the knives with string holes.

... I eat green peas yesterday. I saw strawberries but did not relish them.

You see the certificate. I send it so as to stop the sale of bacon or any other disposition.

... Tell old man Cagle narry a pound of coffee for sale in Columbia that I can find. Stores have checked striped county domestic at $2.00. How do you like it? Flour is selling at $12 ½ ...

Nothing to write. I will fill with wishing myself home to enjoy things that are not on this side of home nor no place else. I will bring you and Willie a negro girl from Grand Papa. Hope to stay at home when I come "a few days." Love

to the children and to their Mother my highest esteem & purest love. I close by subscribing my name as your lover.
Bill" [41]

(ed: William has contracted with the Confederate government for the sale of 5307 pounds of bacon at $1 per pound. He mailed a copy of the sale receipt to Cornelia to stop her from selling any bacon to other potential buyers.)

- - - - -

May 20, 1863 Private Robert C. Dunlap
Vicksburg, Mississippi Landis Missouri Light Artillery

"There is not a safe place inside the intrenchments as the land batteries & sharpshooters are playing on us all the time & Porter shelling the city & camp with his mortar fleet. The citizens most all have caves dug in the hillsides, in which they shelter from the missiles. We again worked until late in the night throwing up dirt on our redoubt." [42]

(ed: Porter is the Union naval commander David D. Porter. His gunboats and mortar fleet keep up a steady shelling of the city and the defenses during May and June.)

- - - - -

May 20, 1863 Mr. John B. Jones
Richmond, Virginia Clerk – War Department

"Butter is worth $4 per pound. A sheep is worth $50. A cow $500.

May 21st - ... Strawberries were selling in the market this morning at $4 for less than a pint. Coal $25 per load, and wood $30 per cord." [43]

- - - - -

May 21, 1863
Port Hudson, Louisiana

Private Melmon M. Butts
Maury Artillery

"[Sent] to Port Hudson … then hard times began built fortification bressworks magazines … we could get sugar and molasses siege began we were fighting for 48 days and nights captured on 8 July 1863 … " [44]

(ed: Melmon was sent to prison at Camp Morton, Indiana near Indianapolis.)

- - - - -

May 21, 1863
Richmond, Virginia

Sergeant Benjamin F. Porter
Co. E – 11th Alabama Infantry

"Winder Hospital, Ward 35
… Fearing you have not received my first letter … I write, though with pains from my wounds. I am able to go where … feel disposed. Eat all I can get & am … mischievous as you ever saw me.

… I expect you have heard of the mourning … of the death of our brave General Jackson. He was shot by our own men. It is beyond all doubt. We all lament his loss.

Sister I will have my ambrotype … & send it to you the first opportunity. I am not able to ware my jacket … my wound is one inch & a half below the shoulder joint on the back part of … arm….

I hope you all will prey for me. I am sick & sore … I prey but my prayers are very feeble …
Benj. F. Porter" [45]

(ed: Benjamin was wounded in the right shoulder at Salem Church on May 3, 1863. He was sent to Chimborazo in Richmond, transferred to Winder Hospital and on June 13th he was transferred to Danville General in Danville, Virginia. He was discharged and returned to duty on July 29, 1863.) [46]

(ed: Benjamin wrote his sister a note on May 23rd and noted, "A revival of relig[ion] Is going on in this hospital it reminded me of our meetings at home. The meetings will continue & I expect to go every opertunity.") [47]

- - - - -

May 21, 1863
Strasburg, Virginia

Miss. Kate Sperry
Winchester refugee

"Mrs. Morris came out from Winchester – she's been nursing some of our wounded that were left in Winchester when our men left last December – has been sick herself – she describes the situation of the people in Winchester as horrible – so many sick. I haven't heard for over a week from home. She got out without taking the oath because she was matron of our hospital and all summer attended to some Yankees also." [48]

- - - - -

Undated
Port Hudson, Louisiana

Private Elijah Thompson Hassell
Co. B – 50th Tennessee Infantry

"While we were at Port Hudson we fared very well. The Yanks attacked with gun boats and we set one on fire with hot shot, and she went down. when went from Hudson to Jackson Miss there I went to the hospittle … with stone in my bladder and I was sent from there to old Marion Miss and there I staid about four months and past stones from my bladder as rough a cucklebururs …" [49]

- - - - -

May 21, 1863
15 miles south of Columbia, Tennessee

Captain James C. Bates
Co. H – 9th Texas Cavalry

"My Dear Ma:
… I bought another horse today one of the finest and most beautiful dapples I ever saw.… I tell you I paid 600$ for him. Any kind of ordinary horse is worth 300$ here – and almost impossible to get.… " [50]

- - - - -

May 22, 1863
Camp Paxton, Virginia

2nd Lt. George D. Buswell
Co. H – 33rd Virginia Infantry

"Dear Father,
... Capt. Shuler & myself were in Fredricksburg Wednesday the town is very much riddled but few families living in it. The Yanks are encamped on the opposite side & very near the river.

This Brigade has contributed for the erection of a tomb over Gen. Jackson's grave. It is said Mrs. Jackson says nothing shall be put over his grave unless it is done by this Brig. I think the Brigade will raise ($6,000) Six thousand dollars for it This Regt. gave about ($800) eight hundred & some who are absent I am confident will give something. I gave ($20) twenty dollars which together with the amt. I paid for the pants I sent by you has reduced my 'pile' that I will have to ask you to send me $25 or $30 by the first safe opportunity....
Your Affectionate Son – Geo. D. Buswell" [51]

- - - - -

May 22, 1863
Vicksburg, Mississippi

Mrs. Dora R. Miller
Resident

"Clothing cannot be washed or anything else done.... At all the caves I could see from my high perch, people were sitting, eating their poor suppers at the cave doors, ready to plunge in again. As the first shell again flew they dived, and not a human being was visible.

... The cellar is so damp and musty the bedding has to be carried out and laid in the sun every day ... The confinement is dreadful.... " [52]

(ed: Dora is the young wife of a lawyer. They came to Vicksburg from Arkansas. There is no legal work in town and now they are trapped and they "are cut off from the world." Dora, daily, records events and thoughts in her diary.)

- - - - -

May 22, 1863
Okolena, Mississippi

Mr. Samuel Robbins
Refugee from St. Louis

"Dear Son
I have been banished from St. Louis … with many other citizens we arrived at this place last night.… Em [sister] has gone to Kentucky with Miss Sue Wollfolk to spend the summer.… Terror reigns supreme in St. Louis and they are trying to subjugate all the Southern people.…

Your Father in love
Saml" [53]

- - - - -

May 23, 1863
Campti, Louisiana

Lt. Theophilus Perry
Co. F – 28th Texas Cavalry

"Dear Harriet: We arrived here early yesterday morning.… I have a strong notion of sending for Rufus. He is small but I can make him be of great service to me I think. Has he had the measles?

I have been using Billy Hargroves boy Guy; but will have to give him up as soon as Billy Returns, and am liable to be deprived of the use of a Negro at any time. There is one thing sure, I will not cook for myself, if I have to pay fifty dollars a month just for cooking. I was once without a servant for two weeks, during the sickness of Norfleet, and I liked to have perished to death …

Have my overcoat bound around the edges for use next fall & winter. I do not need my pantaloons at present … Be sure to have my boots made large enough. No 8 ½ is best, but 9 rather than smaller than 8 ½. Direct me a letter to Shreveport. We have a mail ride that will go there every week for us.

… The Sun is now rising; Breakfast is announced & every thing about ready to move, so I must close.
Your fond Loving Husband Theophilus Perry" [54]

- - - - -

May 23, 1863
Fredericksburg, Virginia

Captain Andrew J. McBride
Co. E – 10th Georgia Infantry

"Friend Jake: … There are some interesting occurrences along our lines – some of them tender and melancholy, others ludicrous and amusing. A short time ago a Federal band came down to the river and played Yankee Doodle; when it had concluded the Yankees cheered loudly; they then played Dixie which caused our boys to cheer as loud; they then played Home Sweet Home, when a universal shout went up from both sides. A pleasant episode in a soldiers' life …

The other day a fine horse came down to the river of the Federal side, jumped into the river and swam to an island about half way across. The Federals called him by whistling, &c; but our boys neighed like a horse, when the horse jumped in and swam to our side. Both sides seemed to enjoy it finely." [55]

- - - - -

May 24, 1863
Fredericksburg, Virginia

Corporal Tally Simpson
Co. A – 3rd S. Carolina Infantry

"Dear Sister
… All is quiet here…. Our quarters were inspected by Genl McLaws in person on yesterday. Each mess was formed in front of its tent as the Genl came round. We have a beautiful camp ground and the streets and tents were as clean as brooms could make them, and I feel satisfied the Genl was highly pleased with the appearance of things.

Preaching still continues daily, and the soldiers are constantly connecting themselves with the church. There will be communion service today at 11 o'clock, and I trust we may all be benefited by it.

… Remember me kindly to all friends and write soon to
Your ever affect bro
Taliaferro Simpson" [56]

- - - - -

late May, 1863
Vicksburg, Mississippi

Lt. Charles S. O. Rice
Co. M – 7th Tennessee Cavalry

" … rations for man and beast would be scarce … how hungry we became … had bread of meal and peas mixed, when cooked meal was done peas were still undone … meat was almost a thing of the past … some of the boys indulged in the rare dish of rodent, well cooked in a hollow log and that without taking off his epidermis…. I did not indulge … in a few days we had better meat … one of our mules [killed] … cut a bucket full of steaks from sd. dead mule and we all joined in … made jerked meat from what was left over … fed our horses on mulberry leaves and the long moss which hung from the trees." [57]

- - - - -

May 24, 1863
Vicksburg, Mississippi

Miss. Lucy McRae
Merchant's daughter

"[Our cave] had four entrances, dug in the form of arched hallways, coming to a common center, at which point was dug a room which was curtained off. In this cave my mother took refuge with her three young children, my father having such an aversion for a cave that he would not enter one…. Mother took pillows, comforts, provisions and clothing into the cave with her. There were about two hundred persons in this cave, mostly women and children …" [58]

- - - - -

May 24, 1863
Shelbyville, Tennessee

Captain James P. Douglas
Douglas's Texas Artillery

"The health of the army is very good…. Our men are well clothed and our commissary department is as good as could be expected, though our fare is rough, amounting to little more than meat and cornbread." [59]

- - - - -

May 25, 1863
enroute to Chattanooga, Tennessee

Private John Jackman
Co. B – 9th Kentucky Infantry

"The train ran away with the engineer, while coming down the mountain, this side of Tunnel. The grade is steep and 7 miles long, and we ran the 7 miles in 4 minutes and a half. I was sitting on a camp stool in the center of the car and could hardly keep my seat. The moon was just sinking behind the mountains, and as I watched it, as it were, skipping from crag to crag, I thought farewell "old moon." I'll never see you again! We thought every moment the car would be dashed in pieces against the rocks, or be pitched off some of the cliffs and ground into dust. At last the train was stopped, and word came forward that the hindmost car, on which was company "C", had smashed up, or was missing at least. We all expected to find the last men killed, or badly hurt, and our surgeons started back to find them. I went back also. The car flew to pieces just as the train was at the bottom of the grade. No two pieces of it were left together; but fortunately, though some of the boys were hurt, not a man was killed, or a limb broken. One little fellow, that was on top of the car, was thrown clear over the telegraph wire, into a bramble of briars, receiving no worse injury than being "powerfully" scratched." [60]

- - - - -

May 25, 1863
Vicksburg, Mississippi

Lt. Calvin M. Smith
Co. D – 31st Tennessee Infantry

"... Today they sent in another flag of truce [to bury Union dead] ... All hostilities cease. Our soldiers and the Yankies got together and joked ... Yankie account is that they lost 6000 killed ... the [Yankies] are hunting the dead that having been wounded would crawl into the brush and die, some have been lying 10 days, and I could smell them ¼ of a mile or more, they were thrown into rough holes and covered over." [61]

- - - - -

May 25, 1863
"Camped on Rap Ane River", Virginia

Corporal Ellis Creed Sharp
Co. E – 4th Texas Infantry

"Dear Sister:
... I cannot tell what is going to be done here. The Yankees may fight us again hear but they are fools if they do....

When I first joined the company at Waco there was 11 in my mess and too besides myself is all that is in the company now and to of us have been wounded. I am in hopes this thing will soon close that I may return home." [62]

- - - - -

May 26, 1863
Richmond, Virginia

Colonel Robert Kean
Confederate Bureau of War

"Colonel [Briscoe G.] Baldwin, chief of ordnance, Army of Northern Virginia reports 26,000 small arms taken from the battlefields above Fredericksburg and counted, besides small lots still coming in and such as regiments keep in their wagons as a reserve: 13 cannon, 9 caissons, 4 battery wagons, 2 forges etc. He deducts 10,000 as our own muskets. Majors Venable and Talcott [aides on Gen. Lee's staff] think this excessive since many of our men exchange on the fields, and ... our wounded ... bring their arms off with them." [63]

(ed: A major source of arms for the Confederate armies are the collected weapons from battlefields. They are forwarded to various armories such as Tredegar in Richmond and the Fayetteville Arsenal in North Carolina to be repaired and refurbished and then are returned to the ordnance supply system.)

- - - - -

May 26, 1863
Rome, Georgia

Mr. R. S. Norton
Merchant

"Gold [in Richmond] selling at 6.00, Silver, 5.50; Sterling Bills, $6.25 ... Here in Rome, a good common Buggy Horse sells for $350 to $400, a common Cow for $75 to 100; Cotton Yarn, 15 cts pr Bunch of 5 lb." [64]

- - - - -

May 27, 1863
camp near Fredericksburg, Virginia

Private Bryant Folsom
Co. C – 26th Georgia Infantry

"... Nancy I will give you A statement of ourrshings [our rations] & how mutch money I have drawed ... we get 1 lbs of flour to the man A day & half pound of meat sometimes we draw A little shugar & A few peas ... I have only got sixety four dollars know and only fifeen eying to mee." [65]

- - - - -

May 30, 1863

Private Amos T. Johnson
Co. K - 49th N. Carolina Infantry

"Mr Govner Vance I hierd a substitute March the 22 1862 and had him sowin in for the war and he is in survice yet in the 53 Regt in company C under Captain Joseph Ritchenson an is sound and Dos his part of survice in the war But he is under 40 and tha have arrested me on it and Brought Mee to camp holms and in tends to keep mee in survice and tha ar going to send Mee to the 49 Regt of NC. T. and some men tells me wher A Man Put in A substitute Bee fore the Conscript Law Past he is exempt that told mee when I Put him in survice I was Clear for the war and now tha tha Brought Mee A way from my farm and ef tha keep Mee my farm is lost and My wife is not able to work at this time and she wont Bee soon and I think I have don My Part to wards this war for it cost mee all the Money I had in hand and I cant Drill not with out suffering from it verry much for I have hurna on the left side verry bad and I think my farm would doo more god than I can doo in the war and I want you to write me wheather my substitute Clears mee or not or wheather you think I ought to Bee clear or not Sow I Remain yours and Co write soon as you get this Direct your letter to Camp Holms
Amos T. Johnson" [66]

(ed: In September of 1862 the upper end of the draft age was extended to 45. "Many substitutes were now included within the age limits. The War Department ruled that principals were now liable for service once their substitutes had been

enrolled. The public hostility toward this action would eventually lead the Confederate Congress on January 5, 1864 to end all substitution and draft the principals." This would lead to legal challenges but the position of the Congress was upheld by the courts.) [67]

- - - - -

May 30, 1863
Vicksburg, Mississippi

Mrs. Dora R. Miller
Resident

" ... so tired of corn bread, which I never liked, that I eat it with tears in my eyes.... We are lucky to get a quart of milk daily from a family near who have a cow they hourly expect to be killed. I send five dollars to market each morning, and it buys a small piece of mule meat." [68]

- - - - -

May 31, 1863
Fredericksburg, Virginia

Corporal James M. Amos
Co. L – 21st N. Carolina Infantry

"Camp near fredericks burg va
May the 31st 63
Dear father I must seat myself this evening to try to write you a few lines ... I was very glad to hear from you all and hear you was all a bout this leaves me very poly [poorly] but better than I have been I have not bin well since the fight [Chancellorsville] and I am a feared I never will be a sound man any more ... I have no good humor to write times is hard ... I must bring this letter to a close for my hand is so weak and trimbly. I can't write farther ... I remain your affectionate son til death good by.
James M. Amos" [69]

- - - - -

May 31, 1863
near Kinston, North Carolina

Private John D. A. Brown
Co. B – 46th N. Carolina Infantry

"...North Carolina Camp near the gum swamp Dear wife I drope you few lins to let you know that am not well I took a chill yestday morning it lasted too hour on me then I took a hie fever and through up gall I am able to be up today I work the brest works ... and fri night I stood gard and it rain a little and I got damp ... I hope when thes few lins coms to hand that thay find yous all well doing well our mess has had plenty to eat ...Dear wife I sent you a few lins by Monroe Peller and 15 dollars no fight exspect heare but that may be Pickets fight the yankee coms evry once and while from new burn thay come about 25 mils ... and pluder and burn houses the yankee burnt lot of houses below Kinston ...thare is little talk of our brigage going to Virginia but I dont kno wether it is so or not ... Dear wife I must bring my letter to a close at the present time this day week ago I left you and too Dear children perhaps I may never see you my Dear wife and children on earth no more oh remember me in this trubsum time remember me in prayer ... I Remain you husband untill Death J D A Brown" [70]

(ed: John had just returned from a furlough with Sarah and their children last week. He will probably not have another chance to see them until the winter of 1863-1864. Most furloughs are granted in the winter months when the armies are in winter camp and not campaigning.)

- - - - -

Cider Vinegar

Mackenzie's 5000 Receipts

"The poorest sort of cider will serve for vinegar, in managing which proceed thus. – First draw off the cider into a cask that has had vinegar in it before; then put some of the apples that have been pressed into it, set the whole in the sun, and in a week or 9 days it may be drawn off into another cask. – This is good table vinegar.

Vinegar from the refuse of fruits – Take the skins of raisins after they have been used in making wine, and pour three times their own quantity of boiling water on them; stir them well about and then set the cask in a warm place, close covered, and the liqueur, in a week, when drawn off from its sediment, put into another cask, and well bunged down, will be a good vinegar for the table."[71]

- - - - -

June, 1863

General Lee is positioned to build on the Chancellorsville victory and move the campaign into Union territory. With the loss of General Stonewall Jackson, he deems it best to break his army into three corps. General Longstreet retains his 1st Corps and Generals Richard Ewell and A. P. Hill are promoted and given command of the 2nd and 3rd Corps respectively. On June 3rd Lee puts his armies in motion westward and northward toward Williamsport, Maryland, and beyond.

The largest cavalry battle ever fought on the North American continent occurs at Brandy Station, Virginia, on June 9th when the Union cavalry, under General Pleasanton, surprises the Confederate forces of General J. E. B. Stuart. The Confederates regroup and Pleasanton falls back toward Fredericksburg.

On June 14th Lee's infantry units are crossing the Potomac River. On June 19th Private Samuel Pickens and his fellow soldiers of the 5th Alabama Infantry begin to cross the river. Samuel notes that, "*The water was just above the knees ... Almost all the men were denuded of pants & drawers, & cut a rather odd figure.*" The army moves rapidly through Maryland and spreads out toward key towns in south central Pennsylvania. Lee's soldiers send all sorts of descriptions of the beautiful Dutch farms and the bountiful crops homeward to their loved ones in their June letters.

Union General Grant tightens his siege lines around General Pemberton and the defenders of Vicksburg. The only safe place inside the Confederate lines, for both soldiers and civilians, is underground. The bombardment of the city never stops. Rations are getting short and on June 18th Private Robert Dunlap of the Landis Battery of Missouri Light Artillery writes, "*Rations per man ¼ lb flour, ¼ lb bacon, ¼ lb rice. About enough to keep a man alive.*" Miss. Lucy McRae, from her quarters in a cave, describes meals of rat and sweet potato coffee. How long before starvation leads to the fall of Vicksburg?

The C.S. Cruiser *Alabama* is capturing and sinking Union merchant ships east of Brazil in the South Atlantic. On June 20th she captures the Bark *Conrad.* The Confederates arm her using captured weapons, crew her with selected men from the *Alabama,* then christen her the C.S. Cruiser *Tuscaloosa* and double their potential to wreak havoc on Union merchant shipping.

General Rosecrans and his Union army in central Tennessee outwit and outmaneuver Confederate General Bragg and the Confederate Army of Tennessee. By the first week of July, Bragg is in Chattanooga and all of central and middle Tennessee is under Union control.

As the month comes to an end, General Lee is beginning to consolidate his forces near Cashtown, Pennsylvania. Late on the 30th one of his divisions, under General Henry Heth, starts moving toward a small town named Gettysburg.

June, 1863

June 2, 1863
Richmond, Virginia

Mr. John B. Jones
Clerk – War Department

"A circular from the Bureau of Conscription to the commandants of conscripts says, the Assistant Secretary of War (Judge Campbell) suggests that overseers and managers on farms be disturbed as little as possible just at this time, for the benefit of the crops. But what good will crops do, if we be subjugated in the mean time? I thought every man was needed … on the field of battle." [1]

- - - - -

June 3, 1863
Jackson, Mississippi

Private John Jackman
Co. B – 9th Kentucky Infantry

"We had a good place to bathe, in Pearl river. The boys caught a great many fish out of the lake and river. One way of catching them was rather novel: Two men would go into the lake, when the water was not very deep, and hold a blanket spread out, down close to the water, then others would commence lashing the water about, making it muddy, and the fish would commence skipping above the surface of the lake, and fall on the blanket, thus being caught by the hundreds." [2]

- - - - -

June 3, 1863
Camp Paxton, Virginia

2nd Lt. George D. Buswell
Co. H – 33rd Virginia Infantry

"Dear Father & Mother,
… we were ordered to quietly prepare to move; to cook all the rations on hand, 3 days, strike tents, and load the wagons. I of course do not know

which way we will go, perhaps toward Culpepper Court House. I would not mind a moderate march through a cherry country now, as I suppose they will soon be ripe....

Lieut.. Gen. Ewell has taken command of the 2nd Army Corps composed of Early's (formerly Ewell's) Johnson's and Rhode's (formerly D. H. Hill's Division). A. P. Hill's division is taken out of the corps....

You will perhaps see in the Richmond papers ... that our Brig. will be hereafter known officially as the "Stonewall Brigade."... I should not be much surprised if we cross the Rappahannock.
Your Affectionate son, Geo. D. Buswell

P.S.... send me $25 or $30 in money by the first safe opportunity. Mr. Coffman brought me my watch. GDB" [3]

- - - - -

June 3, 1863
camp near Fredericksburg, Virginia

Private Bryant Folsom
Co. C – 26th Georgia Infantry

"... My Dear Wife I thought when I left home I would not shave off my beard til I returned back home & it has bin so mutch longer than I espected I shaved my face off clean ..." [4]

- - - - -

June 4, 1863
Camp near Yazoo City, Mississippi

Lt. Jesse P. Bates
Co. B – 9th Texas Infantry

"Dear wife, ... we left Shelbyville 3 weeks ago last Sunday and came to Jackson on cars ... then we come here 4 days ago....We are about 65 miles from Vicksburg. I expect there will be a great battle fought in this state ... We are in Walker's Division ... We are getting a powerful army down here now ... The last letter I got from you was date the 24th of Feb. The chance to send letters is bad at this time.... We are in very hilley country at this time and the water is bad and all we get to eat now is poor beef and corn bread, but I hope we will soon fare better; so soon as the wheat is gathered and ground. The corn crop looks very promising ... The health of the army is tolerable good ... but I fear the effects of bad water ...

I am out of money and have been for a month and I do not know when I will draw any more. There is 3 months wages due me. I want you to pay everything we owe ... I think that before a great while our money will be worth more than it is now.

... The guns are booming down the river. I must close.... So farewell for present my loved ones.
Jesse P Bates" [5]

- - - - -

Economy in the use of Salt Dr. E. F. Porcher

"Coal consists mainly of the carbon in wood, which in burning forms a very drying heat. Most of our readers are familiar with the usual process of barbecuing large pieces of meat over coals. If such meat were too high above the coal-fire to roast, it would soon dry. When dry, a very little salt and smoking will keep it indefinitely. Like cured bacon, it should be packed in tight casks, and kept in a dry room.

After one kills hogs, if he is short of salt, let him get the water out of the meat by drying it over burning coals as soon as possible, first rubbing it with a little salt. Shade trees around a meat-house are injurious by creating dampness. Dry meat with a coal fire after it is smoked. You may dislike to have meat so dry as it is suggested, but your own observation will tell you that the driest hams generally keep best. Certainly sweet, dry bacon is far better than moist, tainted bacon, and our aim is simply to show how meat may be cured and long kept with a trifle of salt, when war has rendered the latter scarce and expensive." [6]

(ed: Salt was becoming scarce in the Confederacy by the end of 1861. Now in 1863 the scarcity is very serious. Dr. Porcher has been released from his regular medical duties and his job is to publish articles telling the Southern folks how they can conserve resources and still accomplish tasks. He also spends a great deal of his time on natural remedies and herbal replacements for products. This can range from quinine substitutes and coffee substitutes to the very mundane.)

- - - - -

June 5, 1863
South Quay, Virginia

Private Laban Mauldin
Co. A – 18th Georgia Infantry

"Dear friend, [Mr. Jesse McMahan]
I received your kind letter yesterday evening … Jesse, we are camped on black water river & we spend a grate portion of our time in fishing & other sport in the river which is veary amusing to soldiers.

I am truly glad to hear of such good prospects of fine crops this year, if ever we needed fine crops it is now, we must have subsistence from some where & if it isn't made in the Confederacy I don't know how we will get it…. I remain your true friend & well wisher.
L. Mauldin" [7]

- - - - -

June 5, 1863
Orange County, Virginia

Private George W. Davis
Co. K – 30th N. Carolina Infantry

"Ma
… We are now on the tramp, but where to I do not know…. We are now eight miles from the Rappidan … and about the same distance from Orange Courthouse…. Our brigade passed [the wagons] about an hour since … I saw Weldon and Tom … it is very dry up here and the dust rising from the roads in clouds.

... I went off this evening to graze mules ... I believe everyone is of the opinion that we are going to Pennsylvania.... We will start in the morning at 3 o'clock ... The wagons start before the troops in order to have time to graze the mules before the troops come up. Our mules are all in good order. The clover up here is excellent....
As ever, GWD" [8]

(ed: Both Weldon and Tom, his brothers, are in Company B of the 30th North Carolina. George is on detached duty as a teamster for the Brigade. The wagons start early before the troops and can halt in the afternoon to graze the mules while the Brigade catches up and goes into camp. Obviously the wagons can only lead when other infantry and cavalry are further in front and on the flanks securing the line of march.)

- - - - -

June 5, 1863 | *Cornubia*
Cargo Manifest | J. Burroughs – Master

"259 tons from St. George's, Bermuda to Nassau

100 boxes combustible material, 99 cases hardware, 101 boxes combustible material, 50 pigs lead, 111 boxes general merchandise, 63 cases general merchandise, 25 bales general merchandise, 5 carboys acid, 5 cases brandy, 3 ½ barrel borax, 30 coils telegraph wire, 100 barrels beef and pork, 40 boxes bacon, 70 barrels onions, 1 barrel potatoes." [9]

- - - - -

June 6, 1863 | Mrs. Cornelia Henry
Sulphur Springs, North Carolina | Farm wife

" ... I washed and cleaned all the children except the baby. Pinck has an ugly sore on his foot, 'tis getting better now. Mr. Henry gave Willie an emetic yesterday morning of ipacac. It made him vomit a good deal, yet has not stopped the rattling in his throat. He is giving him one this evening. I hope this one will do him good. We bathe his chest with spirits turpentine. The babe is growing finely…" [10]

- - - - -

June 6, 1863
Meherrin, Virginia

Mrs. Mary Watkins
Farm wife

"My dear Husband
… Mama is right unwell this morning, is in bed now. Lavallette is most always sick and Nannie and everybody else here have the whooping cough. The Doctor has just come to see one of the little negroes who is very ill with it. Mama has lost two negro children with it and there are two others that she thinks will die. Oh it is dreadful … it makes me right nervous to see the little negroes cough out in the yard. They … whoop and strangle and look as if they would die before they can get their breath…. Our negroes are beginning to whoop and I dread it mightily for those little babes over there. Old Uncle Frank sent me some snake oil root to put around my baby's neck, said he had put it around all the childrens necks over there and he knew it would not go so hard on them … June 11th – Mama lost another little negro with it last night … The babe is right fretful this morning and I must stop and take her.
Good bye Write often to
Your own
Mary" [11]

(ed: A total of 65 people at Mama's (Linden) and at the Watkin's (Oldham) had the whooping cough. All of the children, both White and Negro, and many of the older adults were sick. This was approximately 50% of the population of the two farms. Despite all the visits by the doctor, 8 of the Negro children died.)

- - - - -

Undated
Port Hudson, Louisiana

Private William H. Lucy
Co. G – 3rd Tennessee Infantry

"While at Fort Hudson, La. our provisions ran short had a drove of Texas steers and nothing to feed the steers so we laid a fence rail on the ground drove the steers over it and all that were able to step over the rail let them live all that were so weak they fell we killed them for beef We did this every day untill the whole drove had been eaten by us." [12]

(ed: Private Lucy was captured on May 12 at Raymond, Mississippi. He went to a POW camp in Memphis, on June 15 to Fort Morton, on June 22 shipped to Fort Delaware, and on September 20 shipped to Point Lookout. In April, 1864, after 11 months in prison, he took the Oath of Allegiance and was released from prison.)

- - - - -

June 7, 1863
Culpeper C. H., Virginia

Private Nimrod Newton Nash
Co. I – 13th Mississippi Infantry

"Dear Mollie
Our army is now on the moove for some place unknown to me.... the Yanks crossed over to try and get us to come back but Gen Lee is too smart to bee fooled by a Yanky.... I believe our army is going to the north ... have forty five men in our company.... God bless you my own sweet wife. your Newton" [13]

- - - - -

June 8, 1863
Camp near Culpeper, Virginia

Corporal Tally Simpson
Co. A – 3rd S. Carolina Infantry

"Dear Sister
A great movement is now on hand. Nearly all the army is here and is cooking up rations to move on. Lee is concentrating a very large army, and tis generally believed that he intends attacking the enemy and then march directly for Pennsylvania....

We have had some very hard marching to do, and there is no telling what is coming. We have orders to keep three days' rations in our haversacks at all times. So far I have stood the tramp remarkably well with the exception of sore feet. Genl Lee has issued some very stringent orders concerning straggling and leaving ranks &cc, all of which go to show that he intends making long and rapid marches.... I have no idea where we will meet the enemy....

... Harry had his daguerreotype taken the other day and would have me to sit with him. They are not good at all, but they show you how we look in the war....
Your affect bro
Tallie S" [14]

- - - - -

June 8, 1863
Vicksburg, Mississippi

Mrs. Margaret Lord
Minister's wife

"Imagine to yourself in the first place a good-sized parapet about 6 feet high, a path cut through and then the entrance to the cave – this is secured strongly with boards, it is dug the height of a man and about 40 feet under the hill.

It communicates with the other cave which is about the same length opening out on the other side of the hill – this gives us good circulation of air. In this cave we sleep and live literally under ground. I have a little closet dug for provisions, and niches for flowers, lights and books – inside. Just by the little walk is our eating table with an arbor over it, and back of that our fireplace and kitchen ... " [15]

- - - - -

June 10, 1863
Near Hamilton's Crossing, Virginia

Captain Samuel P. Wagg
Co. A - 26th N. Carolina Infantry

"Dear Brother John
... You will see from this that we are now a part of the army of the Rappohannock. We are 8 miles below Hamiltons Crossing. We came here

night before last stacked arms in the road and have been here since, we are near the banks of the river.... I am awful lazy I do nothing but lay in the shade eat crackers & Smoke good tobacco. Cigars are out of the question you know.... John I have my face badly poisoned. it gives me some pain and I fear it is going to be worse....

I will have to go on picket in a day or two ... I have been used to shooting at the yanks at the first sight but here we are more friendly. We talk back to them and exchange papers with them....
Your brother
S. P. Wagg" [16]

- - - - -

June, 1863
Hamilton's Crossing, Virginia

Dr. Thomas F. Wood
HQ – 3rd N. Carolina Infantry

"Dear Mary [sister]:
... I hope Ma is getting strong and hearty. The field certainly agrees with me now. When I came up here I weighted about 140 – now I weight 153 – more than I have ever weighted before. We are getting pretty good fare now. Everyday we have butter, milk, eggs, lettuce, asparagus, green tea & coffee etc. – always some of these things besides our regular army diet. Strawberries can't be bought here just now, but we get green peas & lima beans ... " [17]

- - - - -

June 10, 1863
Richmond, Virginia

Private John D. A. Brown
Co. B – 46th N. Carolina Infantry

"Dear wife I seate my self drop you few lins to let you know that I am well at the present time and I hope when thes few lins coms to hand that my find yous all well ... we left Kinston on the 7 day of June we got to Petersburg on 8 day of June and we marh from Petersburg to Richmond I com the mach better then I ever did ... I dont know how long we will stay heare at this place sum thinks we will go to Fredixburg sum thinks will stay roun Richmond we fare tarable I got plenty to eat ever since I left home the health in regiment is good better then I ever saw it we had to shoot one man in our regiment for runing way he was of God I saw him shoot thay shot him at Petersburg twelve men shot him thay put nine balls in him it look hard to see the poor man shot he has a wife and children no news of portance … I must close my letter … may god bless you all … is the prayer of you Dear husband John D A Brown to his Dear wife Sarah C Brown" [18]

- - - - -

June 11, 1863
near Benton, Mississippi

4th Sergeant Robert Elliott
Co. E – 35th Alabama Infantry

"… it was raining thundering & lightning & the ground all wet so there was no chance to sleep … got under a tree & made our bed down & slept very well … after reading 9 letters from home to day I felt a great deal better … I recon that we will remain here all day it is the worst place we ever Camped in nothing but a swamp full of some of the biggest snakes that I have ever seen in My life all we need now is a few aligaters to make the place interesting … " [19]

- - - - -

June 12, 1863
Camp near Culpeper, Virginia

2nd Lt. Sanford Branch
Co. A – 8th Georgia Infantry

"Dear Mother [Charlotte Branch]
… The calvary fight on Wednesday created a little excitement very little. Our division was under arms and march to within 3 miles of the Battle field [Brandy Station] were we lay in the sun all day and at night marched back to camp. You cannot imagine what a contemptable opinion the veteran infantry have of the calvary. This fight of Wednesday was the heavyest the calvary have ever had in Virginia. Our forces were completely surprised … After our men recovered … they fought pretty well and finally drove the Yanks across the river. Our loss 70 killed 200 wounds & about 150 prisoners. Enemy 100 dead

on the field, 80 wounds, prisoners in our hands & 350 prisoners. A Georgia Regt also captured 3 pces. artillery.

As I have no ink to write with I must stop. Remember me to all.
Affect. son
Sanford" [20]

- - - - -

June 12, 1863
Winchester, Virginia

Miss. Kate Sperry
Winchester Resident

"Jennie and I went to Middletown this morning. The mule stumbled and I fell almost over its head – recovered myself, however, when it fell down on the ground and I with it, bruising and skinning my knee right badly – it made me so mad – never fell off a horse before in my life and rode so much, but it wasn't my fault that the mule fell – tore my skirt badly – stopped at Mrs. Heater's to sew it up – after mending up, we mounted and came on through Middletown...." [21]

- - - - -

June 13, 1863
Raleigh, North Carolina

Mr. Jonathan Worth
State Treasurer

"To the Sheriffs and Tax Collectors of North Carolina:

Under the act of the Confederate Congress of the 23d March last, relating to the funding of Confederate Treasury notes, these fundable notes are divided into three classes:

1. Those dated prior to December 1st 1862.
2. Those dated between 1st December, 1862 and 6th April, 1863.
3. Those dated on or after 6th April, 1863.

The first is fundable in 7 per cent bonds until the 1st August next, after which they are not fundable at all.

The second class are also fundable in 7 per cent bonds until the 1st August next, after which they are fundable at 4 per cent.

The third class are fundable for one year from the first day of the month printed in red ink across the face of them in 6 per cent bonds, after which they are fundable at 4 per cent.

The faith of the Confederate government is pledged for the ultimate payment on all of these issues, and all of them are receivable in payment of taxes and other dues to the Confederate government at any time …

… you will abstain from collecting taxes in the old issue until the action of the Legislature [North Carolina] shall be known….

Until you receive further instructions, you are, therefore, advised to receive only in payment of State and county taxes, the Treasury notes of this State, the notes of all the Banks of this State, gold and silver coins, and the interest bearing Treasury notes of the Confederate States." [22]

(ed: The Confederate government would like to force people to buy bonds with their old currency and remove it from circulation. This did not work. People continued to use whatever issue of paper monies they had to buy goods. All currency continued to decline in value. Treasurer Worth is advising his tax collectors to follow the above policy until it is determined if the North Carolina legislature would support the funding law. As you will note, when reading other letters in this collection, there are merchants and individuals who are refusing to accept Confederate currency to pay debts.)

- - - - -

June 15, 1863
Bivouac near Widow Carter's

2nd Lt. George D. Buswell
Co. H – 33rd Virginia Infantry

"Dear Father& Mother:
I would have written before this but the wagons with my paper were not up with us … I also concluded to wait until we knew the result of our enterprise….

We are much pleased with our new Brigadier also with Gen. Ewell who goes on crutches and sometimes in a carriage.

I have a cold with a very bad cough, which I caught by getting wet & sleeping cold & wet Saturday night when I was on picket. I am something worse & am very hoarse since I waded a stream of water whilst charging the Yanks this morning. You will therefore please pardon this badly written letter for I feel quite badly & not at all like writing.... We have just drawn 2 days rations with orders to cook one. We may move from here this evening or tomorrow but I have no idea in what direction....

Capt. Hamp Keyser was here to day. I borrowed $20.00 of him & gave him an order on you for the amt. which you will please pay out of my money. There was no one from Page [County] killed to day; one Philip Loudabach very slightly wounded....
Your Affectionate son,
George" [23]

- - - - -

June 15, 1863
Winchester, Virginia

Miss. Kate Sperry
Resident

"Am safely home, and all well except Aunt Wardy. She's very ill with typhoid fever - ... The Yanks evacuated as quietly as possible about 3 o'clock this morning and we captured, killed and wounded at least 7,000, and old Milroy hadn't many more – he managed to make his escape, but we got all his stores – it's been a joyful day for us ... " [24]

- - - - -

June 17, 1863
Hayes, North Carolina

Mr. James C. Johnston
Plantation owner

"To His Honor
Governor Vance
Sir
It is with great reluctance that I again trespass on your time ... A letter date the 7th ins from Mr Henry J Fentrill my manager on my Roanoke farm near Halifax informs me that he is advised that he's liable to be called out as a conscript & unless I swear that I cannot procure a person over 45 yrs of age to supply his place.... and I am well satisfied that it would be utterly impossible to do so even if I had twelve months ... Beside Mr Fentrill is an infirm man ... being afflicted with piles ... and bleeding at the nose which exhaust him ... He has 300 negroes under his care and his nearest white neighbor is four or five miles off except one who is three. He manages these negroes well & keeps them in proper subjection but if he is taken away they would ... entirely demoralize the corn crop now growing & wheat now harvesting would be totally lost - Mr Fentrill has had management of my farm upwards of twelve years and the negroes are perfectly under his controul & obedient to his orders. Some shallow pated persons believe that any man can be an overseer and manage a farm & gang of negroes but from an experience of sixty years ... I have found four in all that time on whom I could rely. And in my opinion it requires more sense and talents to direct a large farm [with] a number of negroes than it does to be a short sighted Politician & statesman. The loss of my crop of corn & the wheat would be a serious one to me and not a small one to the quartermaster when he wanted supplies in the present scarcity.

The present year I sold the Confederate qr masters 2400 bus of corn & that was not more than one fourth of my usual crop ... The feeding of an army in my opinion is of as much importance as equipping it with arms for no men can fight without food ... the conscription list might be easily filled by ... do nothing office holders & their worthless assistants who scuttle into some insignificant office to protect them fr enrollment ...

… I beg the favor of you to have Mr Henry J Fentrill of Halifax Co exonerated from the conscription list…. With the highest & personal respect & great admiration of yr Administration.
Yrs
Ja. C. Johnston" [25]

(ed: Mr. Johnston makes an extended appeal to keep his "overseer exemption" for Henry Fentrill on his farm in Halifax County. While perhaps not exactly tactful he boldly states that, "it takes more sense and talent to be an overseer than a short sighted Politician." Would Governor Vance consider himself a politician? I was unable to find any record of a Henry J. Fentrill ever serving in the Confederate military.)

- - - - -

June 17, 1863 — Mrs. Catherine Edmondston
Halifax County, North Carolina — Farm wife

"Moon changed & no prospect of rain. The drought is getting alarming. The potatoes cannot be set out & the garden vegetables are burning up…. Have been busy with my Honey today. The yield is but poor & the comb dark … Making Walnut Catsup & Walnut Pickles … I have not made the first since '56 and my stock is now all gone." [26]

- - - - -

June 17, 1863 — Mrs. Annie Hileman
Lexington, Virginia — Resident

"Dear Cousin …
I was at Gen. Jackson's burying …Gen. J's body was embalmed in Richmond & brought to Lexington on the 14th and on the 15th he was buried. He lay in state at V.M.I…. He was removed to the Presbyterian Church, accompanied by the whole corps of cadets …

After Gen Jackson was buried the cadets fired three volleys of blank cartridges over our heads as the custom is for anyone buried with the honors of war. The grave was then covered with wreaths and flowers …" [27]

(ed: Portions of Jenkins Cavalry, who were in Lexington, along with the V.M.I. Corps of Cadets provided the honor guard for General Jackson.)

- - - - -

June 18, 1863 Private Robert C. Dunlap
Vicksburg, Mississippi Landis Missouri Light Artillery

"Rations per man ¼ lb flour, ¼ lb bacon, & ¼ lb rice. About enough to keep a man alive." [28]

- - - - -

June 19, 1863 2nd Lt. Sanford Branch
Camp on Shenandoah River, Virginia Co. A – 8th Georgia Infantry

"Dear Mother
… I have never experienced such warm oppressive weather. It seemed impossible to live, we have lost 20 out of 37 men, several of them very sick. Fortunatelly for me, my nose bleeds almost every day which I think saved me. yesterday forded the river at Millwood and were resting …

Arrived at the Gap [Snickers] about dark tired & wet to the skin. Made a shelter and slept all night. next morning crossed the river & took position in the Gap. even 50 thousand Yankeys could not dislodge us.

This valley is the land of Milk & Honey. Butter & cheese at 15 cents per lb & eggs 10 cents doz. Since first crossing have been continually on the move crossing & recrossing, sometimes with cloths on & sometimes off…. we have only to guard the Gaps of the Blue Ridge. if we do this, which is very easy, Hooker cannot get in the rear of Ewell …

Give my love to all … Have had but 1 mail in eight days and no letter in that. Write soon.
Your affect. son
Sanford" [29]

(ed: Lee's Army is starting northward toward Maryland and Pennsylvania. The 8th Georgia is on the right flank of Longstreet's First Corps and Ewell's Second Corps as they move northward using the Blue Ridge Mountains as a shield.)

- - - - -

June 19, 1863
Williamsport, Maryland

Private Samuel Pickens
Co. D – 5th Alabama Infantry

"This morning our Brigade waded the Potomac at Williamsport. Almost all the men were denuded of pants & drawers, & cut rather an odd figure. The river was about 200 yds. or probably wider. The water was just above the knees – swift & beautifully clear." [30]

- - - - -

June 19, 1863
Chattanooga, Tennessee

Miss. Kate Cummings
Hospital Matron
Newsom Hospital

"The erysipelas, which is infectious, is spreading. Two of the girls in the washhouse had their ears bored, and have it very badly, taken from washing the clothes, though they are never touched by them until they are put into a large boiler and well boiled. One of the girls is a perfect sight; her face is so swollen that her eyes are closed, and part of her hair has had to be cut off." [31]

(ed: Erysipelas is "an acute disorder of the skin and subcutaneous tissue caused by a streptococcus and marked by spreading inflammation." Mackenzie recommends, "bathing ... with laudanum or lead water, or dusting them with rye meal or wheat flour, are the best. The application of a blister will sometimes put an end to it.... Cold lemonade in liberal quantities ... tends powerfully to cure.") [32]

- - - - -

June 19, 1863
Vicksburg, Mississippi

Private Jesse H. Pepper
Co. B – 1st Miss. Light Artillery

" ... Ragin Price and Genl. Moore's Orderly Henry Barnes mortally wounded by the explosion of a shell, which they were trying to open for the powder.... Ragin lived 4 hours, Henry about 12. Both their skulls were broken ..." [33]

- - - - -

June 20, 1863
Sulphur Springs, North Carolina

Mrs. Cornelia Henry
Farm wife

" ... Nothing of importance going on. The militia is called out the first of Aug. & then my own dear husband will have to go. Oh! what will become of me & my little ones, God only knows. I wish I could see one ray of hope in the future. It would lighten my heart of a great load but I see not the faintest hope for my poor sinking heart to cling to. Oh God I beseech Thee to grant us an honorable peace before more blood is shed...." [34]

- - - - -

June 20, 1863
South Atlantic east of Brazil

John Kell - Exec. Officer
C. S. Cruiser *Alabama*

"On the 20th of June we captured the Bark *Conrad.* She was a pretty little vessel and Captain Semmes resolved to make a cruiser of her. We had captured and taken from the *Talisman* two rifled 12 pounders which we transferred to our cruiser. Acting Lieutenant Low was made Captain, Midshipman George StClair, first lieutenant, Adolph Marmelstein second lieutenant, and two young seamen watch officers, and we gave them ten men. Twenty rifles and half a dozen revolvers completed the armament. We called her the *Tuscaloosa* being the offspring of *Alabama*.... The youthful Captain and crew made sail on their cruise, our first appointed meeting to be at the Cape of Good Hope." [35]

(ed: Since May 25 the Alabama *had captured the* Gilderslieve *of New York, the* Justina *of Baltimore, the* Jabez Snow *of Bucksport, the* Amazonia *of Boston,*

and the Talisman *of New York. The* Justina *was bonded and the others were burned.)*

- - - - -

June 20, 1863 Mrs. Joephine Robison
Santa Fee, Tennessee Farm Wife

"My dear beloved husband
... I do not neede eny money now. I have drawed twenty dollars sence your Father went away and I have not spente any of the money that your Father give me.... I herde yesterday that soldiers wifes could send to Columbia and draw a half bushel of salt. That will helpe me out mightly. I have got a sow and six very nice shoats. I want to try to make my meate out of them nexte yea." [36]

- - - - -

June 21, 1863 Private Robert C. Dunlap
Vicksburg, Mississippi Landis Missouri Light Artillery

"Rations short. Beef selling at from $1 to $2 per lb, Bacon $2, Rice .50, pepper $8, soda $8, small biscuit .25 to .50 each, small pies at $1.25, milk $2 to $4, per gallon." [37]

- - - - -

June 21, 1863 Sergeant Benjamin F. Porter
Danville, Virginia Co. E – 11th Alabama Infantry

"Dear Ma, ... I left Richmond the 9th inst.
Danville is a prety little town about 140 miles from Richmond. My ward is so nice & clean compared with thoes of Richmond. Our matron is a Lady from Fredricksburg, a widow & a refuge. but a lovely woman almost like a mother to all the soldiers. I wish you could see her....

… my wound is nearly well & my health is very good. I am as fat as ever I was….
I remain your obedient & affectionate Son.
B. F. Porter” [38]

- - - - -

June 21, 1863 — Lt. Joshua K. Callaway
Shelbyville, Tennessee — Co. K – 28th Alabama Infantry

“My Dear Love, … 1 o’clock P. M. I have just eaten a very hearty dinner of lettuce, fried onions, rice pudding, dew berry pies and apple pies. Now I want to be at home to lie down & play with the children & talk with you. I wish you could have taken dinner with me….
Goodby My dear
JK” [39]

- - - - -

June 21, 1863 — Mrs. Dora R. Miller
Vicksburg, Mississippi — Resident

“ … the *Citizen* is printed on wallpaper; therefore has grown a little in size …

I had gone upstairs … to enjoy a rest on my bed and read the reliable items in the *Citizen* when a shell burst right outside the window in front of me. Pieces flew in, striking all round me, tearing down masses of plaster that came tumbling over me.

When H. rushed in I was crawling out of the plaster, digging it out of my eyes and hair. When he picked up beside my pillow a piece as large as a saucer, I realized my narrow escape. The window frame began to smoke, and we saw the house was on fire. He ran for a hatchet and I for water, and we put it out…. It has taken all the afternoon to get the plaster out of my hair, for my hands were rather shaky.” [40]

(ed: Dora uses “H.” in her diary to designate her husband, Anderson Miller.)

- - - - -

June 21, 1863
Vicksburg, Mississippi

Miss. Lucy McRae
Merchant's daughter

"Our provisions were becoming scarce, and the Louisiana soldiers were eating rats as a delicacy, while mules were occasionally being carved up to appease the appetite. Mother would not eat mule meat, but we children ate some, and it tasted right good, having been cooked nicely.... sweet potatoe coffee was relished by the adults." [41]

- - - - -

June 21, 1863
Shenandoah, Virginia

Private Nimrod Newton Nash
Co. I – 13th Mississippi Infantry

" ... the weather intencely hot, as hot as I ever saw in Miss. A great many fainted in the road with heat and several died from the same cause. I fainted on the way on day about two P. M.... I am so proud of my shirt, nice enough for any body. Some of the boys say they wist for a woman to send them nice shirts...." [42]

- - - - -

June 22, 1863
"banks of the Shannado ten miles of"
Winchester, Virginia

3rd Corporal Milton Barrett
Co. E – 3rd Battalion
Georgia Sharpshooters

"Dear Brother and sister, i take my pen in han to let you [know] that i am well. I was at Culpeper when I rote last. we have bin a marching every scence a round an thrue the blue ridge from place to place ... i have saw a grate many prisnors that our troops have captured within the last week.... we are in pershession [possession] of winchester and Martinsburg and harpers ferry and Maryland hights and Manassas Gap....

... we have had rain in abounce [abundance] and have lay the dust and the roads is very wet. we waided the river last night. it was up to our arms and it was with much difacult that we keep our provishons and powder dry. several of the boys fel down and got ther rashons and powder wet. we are a lying over hear to day a resting and i thought i would write you a few lines … it is thought that we will be the invaders be fore long….

I have not heard from Laurence in some time… we ar a giting a plenty to eat hear now and i dont think we will have much fighting to do this side of the Potomack. i will close for the present.
i am your loving Brother
Milton Barrett" [43]

(ed: On June 8, 1863 Milton was transferred from Company A of the 18th Georgia Infantry to Company E, Third Battalion, Georgia Sharpshooters. The Sharpshooters had been formed in May of 1863 and were commanded by Lt. Col. Nathan Hutchins, Jr. who had originally been in Company I of the 18th Georgia. The Sharpshooters would remain attached to Wofford's Brigade. Lawrence, Milton's brother, remained in Company I. At about this same time Milton was promoted to 3rd Corporal.)

- - - - -

June 22, 1863
Richmond, Virginia

Mr. John B. Jones
Clerk, War Department

"It is a difficult matter to subsist in the city now. Beef is $1 and bacon $1.65 per pound, and just at this time there are but few vegetables. Old potatoes are gone, and the new have not yet come. A single cabbage, merely the leaves, no head, sells for a dollar, and this suffices not for a dinner for my family.

My little garden has produced nothing yet …" [44]

- - - - -

June 23, 1863
Vicksburg, Mississippi

Private Robert C. Dunlap
Landis Missouri Light Artillery

"... My disease [flux] is growing worse on me. I will have to postpone my writing until I get better.

Immediately to the left & rear of our redoubt on the descent of the hill stood a stately oak pierced by thousands of minnies & by shot & shell on which a little mocking bird perched day after day during the siege & warbled its varied songs whilst the storm ... poured around & often the smoke ... shut it out from sight. Hour after hour have we sat & watched & heard it sing ... I would have given a fortune for that bird." [45]

(ed: When your dysentery has progressed to the point where you are discharging blood from your intestinal tract it is often called bloody flux. The terms flux and dysentery both described a serious condition much worse than diarrhea. Dysentery is an infection of the lower intestinal tract producing pain, fever, and severe diarrhea often including the passage of blood and mucus.) [46]

- - - - -

June 24, 1863
near Chambersburg, Pennsylvania

2nd Lt. George D. Buswell
Co. H – 33rd Virginia Infantry

"Dear Bro.:
As we have camped early today, I will appropriate the leisure moments I have to writing to you. We have gone back into the United States again, crossed Mason's & Dixon's line early this morning so we are one days march into Pa. We are within 1 mile & in sight of Chambersburg, Gen. Rhode's Division is in front of us....

When I wrote my last letter we had just crossed the river [Potomac]. Last Saturday we moved through Sharpsburg & camped just outside of town. Whilst we were laying there, we got some calicoes & other goods, but they were nearly up to Confederate prices. Calicoes were $1.00 per yard. I have enough for two shirts which I will send home by the first opportunity to be made. Surely the girls of Sharpsburg are as sour as vinegar & as ugly as any set of girls I ever saw. I do not think there is any danger that I or any of our boys will ever marry about Sharpsburg....

Yesterday evening Capt. S[hular] & myself went a short distance from camp & got a very good mess of cherries, we did not steal them, we asked the owner, an old man, for them, he told us to help ourselves & said he would have given us our supper but they had no bread baked, he said he was a rebel....

... perhaps we will go on toward Harrisburg which is 50 miles from here. There the Yanks have some state troops, their Militia were driven from here by Jenkin's Cavalry a few days ago. We do not regard the Militia at all." [47]

- - - - -

June 24, 1863
Vicksburg, Mississippi

Mrs. Mary Loughborough
Officer's wife

"A certain number of mules are killed each day by the commissaries and are issued to the men, all of whom prefer the fresh meat, though it be mule, to the bacon and salt rations that they have eaten for so long a time without change. There have already been some cases of scurvy. The soldiers have a horror of the disease.... [My husband] did not like to see me eating mule until I was obliged to ..." [48]

- - - - -

June 25, 1863
Vicksburg, Mississippi

Private Jesse H. Pepper
Co. B – 1st Miss. Light Artillery

" ... Our rations are reduced from 9 oz. of rice flour & flour to 7. The result is suffering." [49]

- - - - -

June 25-26, 1863
Vicksburg, Mississippi

2nd Lt. William R. McCrary
Co. I – 43rd Mississippi Infantry

" … Our rations are rapidly giving out. The men are weak from lack of food and desponding…. Heard some of the fatest mules were driven to the butcher pen yesterday so we are not starved out while the mules last. Some of the soldiers are cooking and eating cane and various kinds of weeds." [50]

- - - - -

June 26, 1863
State of "Peansylvinia"

Private Charles W. Thomas
Co. B – 56th Virginia Infantry

"My Dear I will drop you a few lines to night … to let you hear from me. This leaves me a little unwell. I have a very bad coal. My throat is verry sore … well I have got me a par of pants and a par of shoes and if you see any way to send me some socks you must … for I will nead them…. I am just out of Mariland today…. fairwell, god bless you … CWT" [51]

- - - - -

June 26, 1863
Williamsport, Maryland

Corporal Tally Simpson
Co. A – 3rd S. Carolina Infantry

"Dear Sister
The reason I have not written home since we crossed the Blue Ridge is simply because we have been marching nearly all the time…. The morning we left the top of the mountain was one of the worst I ever saw. The rain fell in torrents, and the mud was thick and deep. But we soon discovered to our extreme delight that we were fast descending from a rainy region to one of sunshine….

Having arrived at the foot of the mountain, we waded the Shenandoah River. It was high and rising fast. It took me nearly up to my arm pits and was so swift that it came near washing me down with the current. Several were carried down and picked up by those who were riding horses….

Yes, we are again in Maryland, and I trust that ere we return, the grand object for which we came shall be accomplished, and we my all soon return to our homes in peace.... Our army is strong and in fine spirits ...

... Our rations are getting a little short again. We drew beef last night and only got a ¼ of a pound to the man. I ate my day's ration at one mouthful – not one meal, but one mouthful....
Your affect bro
T. N. Simpson" [52]

- - - - -

June 26, 1863 Private Samuel Pickens
Shippensburg, Pennsylvania Co. D – 5th Alabama Infantry

"We had a very disagreeable march this morning to Shippensburg. It rained last night & nearly all day to-day. The road was very wet & sloppy.... We were quartered in a large barn ... There were a great many cherries & one large tree of black hearts which were the finest I ever tasted. A good many hens were about the barn but they soon disappeared. Some few were paid for by men who happened to have a little U. S. currency.... They issued whiskey & sugar to us, and Tean Nutting & I made a very nice egg-nog with milk in it.... we enjoyed it hugely. John then came with the chicken stew & other nice things & we made a hearty supper." [53]

- - - - -

June 28, 1863 Mr. F. W. Shober
Salisbury, North Carolina Citizen

"His Excellency Z. B. Vance,
My dear Sir –
I have been requested, in behalf of citizens of this County, whose slaves are now said to be at work on fortifications in Wilmington to represent to your Excellency that the term of service for which their slaves were taken expired some two weeks ago, but that they are still held by military authorities

in Wilmington and are likely to be held for an indefinite period, unless your Excellency will interpose for their restoration to their owners at once. The harvest is now approaching & this labor will be needed greatly. One gentleman told me today, that he has promised to cut wheat for several widows & wives of soldiers in the neighborhood, but that he will be unable … unless his slaves are returned … These instances are common …

A gentleman, who was sent down to Wilmington last week, for the purpose of bring back the negroes from this County, has returned home without them … this Gentleman infers that they intend to retain them indefinitely. He says also that these negroes are not employed on fortifications, but are doing odd jobs about Wilmington such as cleaning up the public streets &c.

I therefore would beg you Excellency, in behalf of our people, to interpose for the immediate return of these slaves to their homes.
I remain your very truly
F. E. Shober" [54]

(ed: Counties were regularly given quotas to provide a quantity of slaves for a set period of time to build fortifications, railroads, etc. The County normally hired a local person to accompany the slaves during this period to act as an overseer not only of their work but specifically of their welfare. Governor Vance on the back of this letter noted, "I have preemptorily ordered the negroes to be returned by harvest, and Gen. Whiting has promised to comply.")

- - - - -

Undated
Vicksburg, Mississippi

Private J. P. Funk
Co. G – 43rd Tennessee Infantry

"My bedfellow had his left jaw shattered by a minnie ball at Vicksburg … we slept in the open, had no tents, eat when we had anything to eat …" [55]

- - - - -

June 28, 1863
Chambersburg, Pennsylvania

2nd Lt. Sanford Branch
Co. A – 8th Georgia Infantry

"Dear Mother:
… we are in the Union again…. This is really the land of plentitude, the whole country appears to be one broad field of grain. Wheat, rye, barley and oats are the sold products of the soil. The people are all of Dutch descent, and of course, are mean and cowardly. Thus far, we have inflicted no damage to private property, except in foraging horses, cattle and commissary stores.

In passing through Chambersburg the women were right saucy … The Division [Hood's] is resting here today and resuming the march tomorrow. I don't know when I will get an opportunity of sending this off but hope it will be soon. Love to all.
Your affect. son,
Sanford" [56]

(ed: Sanford will be wounded in the left breast, through the lung, during Longstreet's assault on the Union left during the afternoon of July 2, 1863, at Gettysburg. Sanford was considered too critical to move and was left behind. Dr. Thomas A. Means, Surgeon of the 11th Georgia, chose to stay with the wounded men of Anderson's Brigade.) [57]

- - - - -

June 28, 1863
Chambersburg, Pennsylvania

Corporal Tally Simpson
Co. A – 3rd S. Carolina Infantry

"My dear Aunt
… I am in Yankeedom … The country is the most beautiful I ever beheld, and the wheat and corn crops are magnificent. All the fields are covered with beautiful green grass and clover, two and three feet high, and burdened with a rich growth of wheat, mostly bearded wheat, and fine fields of young corn are seen every where.

The country is very thickly settled, and each farmer, whether rich or poor, has a fine barn or granary as large [and] some handsomer than, the hotels in Pendleton. They are fine livers, and during this season of the year, they luxuriate upon all kinds of vegetables, rich milk and butter, honey, poultry, and in fact every thing that is tempting to one's appetite….

… The most of the soldiers seem to harbor a terrific spirit of revenge and steal and pillage in the most sinful manner. They take poultry, hogs, vegetables, fruit, honey, and any and every thing they can lay their hands upon. Last night Wofford's Brigade of this div[ision] stole so much that they could not carry what rations they drew from the commissary…. I have not nor will I take one thing in such a manner … my conscience will not permit me to take that which is necessary for the sustenance of women and children.

… I send you some cherry seed which you must plant. The fruit is the large white cherry, as large if not larger than a partridge egg and the finest I ever saw. I hope you may get some of them to come up and grow.

Hoping to hear from you soon I remain
Your ever affect nephew
T. N. Simpson" [58]

- - - - -

June 29, 1863
Carlisle, Pennsylvania

Dr. Thomas F. Wood
HQ – 3rd N. Carolina Infantry

"My dear Parents,
… Everyone remarks on the odd appearance of the magnificent barns in this country, built near houses very inferior to them. Every field here is groaning under the burden of immense crops, which we are in hopes to eat. Fruit with the exception of cherries is still green … Gooseberries and currants are just turning. Quinces, pears and such fruit … is quite plenty…. The towns we passed through furnished us abundant stores, except shoes and clothes. Many of our men are barefooted …" [59]

- - - - -

June 29, 1863 Private Hezekia L. Hamilton
Camp Hardee – Savannah, Georgia Co. E – 30th Georgia Infantry

"Dear Mother
... I have been at work on a steam boat a blockading the river between Thunderbolt and Savannah and I expect to work at it next week if I keep well. It is hard work but we have hands enough to tote anny treetop. We can hall but one load a day and the tide has to be up ... It was my choice to work on it because I don't like to stand guard." [60]

- - - - -

Late June, 1863 Private Newton Camper
Southern Pennsylvania Co. D – 11th Virginia Infantry

" ... the army was in Pennsylvania, moving slowly and halting frequently, which circumstances gave the men time to straggle off after provisions. While Co. D was passing a farm house a member whom we shall call H espied a patch of onions and having a weakness for that vegetable, soon cleared the fence and was proceeding to help himself, when the landlady swooped down on him with a broom and made him beat a hasty retreat. He now went to the barn and gave chase to some chickens and ducks. Again were his hopes destined to be dashed to the ground. In anticipation of this kind of marauding, two girls had been stationed there with sticks; and while H was making desperate efforts to lay hands on a fleeing pullet, one of these girls belabored him over the back till he was glad to escape, minus the pullet and amid the laughter of his comrades. Our friend could face bullets and cannon balls, but when it came to running the gauntlet of these Dutch farm girls armed with heavy stick, bent on defending their property, he was satisfied afterwards to be excused." [61]

- - - - -

Dysentery and bilious disorders *Mackenzie's 5000 Receipts*

"The medical qualities of pulverized charcoal are daily developing themselves. In addition to its value in bilious disorders, two ounces of the charcoal, boiled in a pint of fresh milk, may be taken in doses of a wine-glassful, by adults, every two hours, in the most obstinate dysentery, until relief is imparted, which has not failed to be the effect in almost every instance. It is harmless, and the experiment may be safely tried. Charcoal made from maple wood is the fittest for this purpose." [62]

- - - - -

July, 1863

The first four days of July see the largest battle of the war at Gettysburg and the surrender of Vicksburg in the face of starvation. General Lee loses over 22,638 men killed or wounded and another 5,425 missing. Lee has lost basically 30 percent of his army in three days. Among those losses are many generals, colonels, majors and captains who have formed the leadership core of his army. The replacement of manpower is becoming a critical issue for the Confederacy, and the replacement of competent commanders at the company, regiment, brigade and division level is becoming daunting, if not impossible.

General Pemberton surrenders Vicksburg to General Grant on July 4th. Not only are 27,000 Confederate soldiers captured and paroled, but large quantities of artillery, rifles, ammunition and military supplies are also lost. The captured men will not return to the Confederate armies until late in 1863 per the terms of their paroles. The munitions and supplies are lost forever. On the 8th of July Port Hudson, Louisisana, is surrendered, and the Union forces gain total control of the Mississippi River. The eastern Confederacy is now cut off from the Trans-Mississippi states of Texas, Arkansas and Louisiana.

The Federal Enrollment Act of March 3rd, 1863 becomes active, and on July 11th the Provost Marshall draws the initial names of those to be drafted. Draft riots break out in New York City on the 13th and 14th. Mobs wreck the draft office, the Second Avenue armory and then begin looting liquor stores, dry goods stores and jewelry stores. Property damage is in the millions of dollars. Perhaps as many as 1,000 people are killed including a number of negroes who are chased and attacked by the mobs. A colored orphanage is set afire and the rioters cheer. Troops from the Army of the Potomac, at Gettysburg, are dispatched by train, and the city returns to a nervous normal by July 18th. [1]

General Lee and his Army of Northern Virginia return to Virginia soil by mid-July. He begins repairing the damage to his army. The wounded flood the hospitals in the Shenandoah Valley and as quickly as possible they are transferred to larger facilities in Richmond and Lynchburg.

General Bragg and his Army of Tennessee accomplish nothing for the Confederate cause and are now camped around Chattanooga, cautiously watching the Union soldiers of General Rosecrans.

Camp Letterman has been built on the Wolf farm, one mile east of Gettysburg on the York road. Initially there are over 20,000 wounded Union and Confederate soldiers being treated by Union medical personnel and some Confederate doctors and surgeons who stay with their men. Winter will be approaching before the last of the wounded can be transferred from Camp Letterman to other hospitals in Maryland, Pennsylvania, Delaware and New York.

July, 1863

July 1, 1863
Tullahoma, Tennessee

Sergeant Robert Watson
Co. K – 7th Florida Infantry

" … marched all day through mud ankle deep and the hottest sun I ever saw in my life. Many men fainted, and some were sun struck, several of them died.… thought that I should faint several times but we were on a retreat and must get out of the way of the Yankees or be taken prisoners." [2]

- - - - -

July 1, 1863
Gettysburg, Pennsylvania

Private Samuel Pickens
Co. D – 5th Alabama Infantry

"Left camp this morning at 6:30 A. M. & marched 7 miles on the Chambersburg road to Middletown, where we turned to the left on the Gettysburg road. As we approached the town we heard the cannonading & formed a line of battle about 2 miles off & advanced upon the Yankees. Our Regt. was on the left of the Brigade & as it moved forward it made a partial right wheel & thus kept us at a double quick march all the time; & as it was an excessively hot day & we were going through wheat fields & ploughed ground & over fences, it almost killed us. I was perfectly exhausted & never suffered so from heat & fatigue in my life. A good many fell out of ranks being completely broken down & some fainted. We halted & lay down for some time at a fence … Our Regt. then went forward … We were under heavy fire from the front & a cross fire from the left & pretty soon had to fall back … Oh! what terrible work has been done to-day. The loss in our Brig. was very heavy – particularly in our Regt. I was much affected on learning that my warm friend & mess-mate Tean [George] Nutting had been mortally wounded & died … on the field. He was at his post with the colors." [3]

- - - - -

July 1, 1863 Lt. Colonel Hillery Moseley
Gettysburg, Pennsylvania 42nd Mississippi Infantry

"Arriving at the hospital four miles in our rear – began early to display fruits of the terrible conflict going on in front. Ambulance after ambulance arriving day and night with the mangled and mutilated forms.... soon strewn thick around [the surgeons] are the amputated limbs ... so much pain, suffering, and death....

The surgeons continued the work incessantly until the morning of the 4th without having finished the work ... Orders had been received the night previous to have the wounded made speedily ready to send forward to Winchester.... We left many fellows too badly wounded to risk ... transportation." [4]

(ed: Hillery was wounded in the foot near the railroad cut on McPherson's Ridge. The 42nd Mississippi sustained the second highest casualty rate of any Confederate regiment engaged at Gettysburg. They lost 60 men killed and 205 men wounded. Only the 26th North Carolina had greater casualties.) [5]

- - - - -

July 3, 1863 Sergeant Levin K. Gayles
Gettysburg, Pennsylvania Co. G – 9th Virginia Infantry

"On the moring of the 3 caled up at three Oh clock in the morning and started for the Field of Battle and formed ... in front of Cemetary Hill and the enemy are in our front verry plaine.... we have been tolde what to do that is to Charge that Hill and take those cannon.... At one Oh clock our bateries opened fire on the enemy works and after two hours shelling we charged the works and tak a section of them and hold them 20 minutes and the the first thing I knew they had me hemed up and carried me to the rear where I remained until 12 Oh clock at night then we started to Westminester ..." [6]

(ed: The 9th Virginia is in Armistead's Brigade which went over the wall near Cushing's Battery on Cemetery Ridge. Many of the men, including Levin, were surrounded and captured. From Westminster, Maryland he was shipped to Baltimore and then on to Fort Delaware Prison, on Pea Patch Island, in the Delaware River, south of Wilmington.)

- - - - -

July 3, 1863
Gettysburg, Pennsylvania

Private Joseph P. Bashaw
Co. I – 7th Tennessee Infantry

" ... were in the third days battle – I was in the great charge, and was wounded close to the rock fence, but got back without being captured that day." [7]

- - - - -

July 3, 1863
Gettysburg, Pennsylvania

Private Henry P. Blakely
Co. F – 14th S. Carolina Infantry

"I lost my right leg below the knee at Gettysburg ... amputated on my birthday 3rd July. Sent to hospital from Gettysburg to Davids Island, New York sent to City Point [for exchange] from there then to Petersburg then home." [8]

- - - - -

July 3, 1863
Gettysburg, Pennsylvania

2nd Lt. David Champion
Co. G – 14th Georgia Infantry

"On the whole, I think, to me, this was the most miserable day of the war. On every side rose the shrieks of wounded and dying men and the pitiful neighing of horses. Lying on our guns the night, we were kept awake by cries of help from the wounded between the lines." [9]

- - - - -

July 3, 1863
Gettysburg, Pennsylvania

2nd Lt. George D. Buswell
Co. H – 33rd Virginia Infantry

"Fri. 3rd – Slept a little this morning before light. The 33rd Regt. opened the fight at this point before daylight & sunrise. When we had fired all our ammunition we were relieved by the 4th Regt. We had hard fighting here nearly all day, in which our Brig. suffered severely. Our Co. lost 4 killed, 17 wounded, 3 mortally. The killed are – 1st Sgt. Menifee, 2nd Sgt. Rosenberger, Pvts. Wm. Jenkins & Haley Morris. Mortally wounded, John P. Hite, Wm. Purdam & David Morris.... We failed to carry the works in front of us. We fell back after midnight, were not followed by the Yankees. Our Company went into the fight with 36 men, had 21 killed & wounded, 4 of them slightly, returned to the Company for duty in a day or two." [10]

(ed: Co. H, and the Stonewall Brigade, are becoming ghosts of their former selves. When the 4 slightly wounded returned to Co. H, their strength would be 19 men. The Confederacy is nearing the tipping point. They are struggling to replace the losses from battle and disease. Co. H mirrors the larger problem.)

- - - - -

July 3, 1863
Ashland, Virginia

Mrs. Judith McGuire
Nurse

"The scarcity of blank-books, and the very high prices, make them unattainable ... therefore I ... begin another volume of my Diary on some nice wrapping paper ... and though not very pleasant to write on, yet it is one of the least of my privations." [11]

- - - - -

July 3, 1863
Vicksburg, Mississippi

Private Robert C. Dunlap
Landis Missouri Light Artillery

"A flag of truce was sent out – the purpose being it was thought to capitulate terms of surrender, as the rations were reported to have give out. Mule beef was issued to the troops, which tasted very well to a hungry man." [12]

- - - - -

July 4, 1863
Gettysburg, Pennsylvania

Private Louis Leon
Co. C – 1st N. Carolina Infantry

"No fighting to-day, but we are burying the dead. They have been lying on the field in the sun since the first day's fight; it being dusty and hot, the dead smell terribly." [13]

- - - - -

July 4, 1863
Fort Morgan, Alabama

Lt. Colonel James Williams
21st Alabama Infantry

"Dear Lizzy
... I had a violent head-ache and nausea which kept me in bed all day [yesterday] – I feel quite fresh this morning.... Mosquitos and fleas are rampant here – the bar [sandbar] protects me from the first but the fleas worry me not a little....
Williams" [14]

(ed: Fort Morgan is one of two forts that protect the entrance to Mobile Bay. The 21st Alabama Infantry is assigned to the forces defending the fort.)

- - - - -

July 4, 1863
Vicksburg, Mississippi

The Daily Citizen
Final "Wallpaper" Edition

"Two days bring about great changes. The banner of the Union floats over Vicksburg. Gen. Grant has "caught the rabbit." He has dined in Vicksburg, and he did bring his dinner with him. The *Citizen* lives to see it. For the last time it appears on "Wall paper." No more will it eulogize the luxury of mule meat and friccaseed kitten – urge Southern warriors to such diet nevermore. This is the last wall-paper edition, and is, excepting this note, from the types as we found them. It will be valuable hereafter as a curiosity." [15]

(ed: The final "wallpaper edition" is one page with news from July 2nd and July 3rd with the above final note in the lower right hand corner. The piece of wallpaper measures 11 x 17 and is a light tan color on the newspaper side. The wallpaper side is a lighter tan with a pattern of dots, five pointed stars that look like "jacks," and circles around the stars.)

- - - - -

July, 1863
Retreat from Gettysburg

Private William P. Holland
Co. G – 11th Virginia Infantry

"I was not at the battle … but several miles off, and heard the cannon firing from where I was. I was along on the retreat…. It rained a great deal during the time of this retreat. The Yankees followed but didn't com very close often…. it was thought that General Kemper, who was severely wounded, was dead … so a coffin was made for him. As he kept on living … the coffin was thrown aside in a clover field … it was so muddy that several of us tried to get on the coffin for a sleeping place. Major Green secured it, and … stretched out on it and went to sleep.

Some Yankee cavalry attacked a part of the wagon train in the streets of Williamsport [Maryland] … when I rode along there a little later, I saw many dead Yankees. The Potomac was a good deal flushed, and when I went across the mule I rode nearly had to swim…." [16]

- - - - -

July 5, 1863
9 miles north of
Chambersburg, Pennsylvania

Captain Richard Watkins
Co. K – 3rd Virginia Cavalry

"My Dear Dear Mary
I know you feel concerned about me not having heard from me for such a length of time…. My company has dwindled to about 10 or 15 the horses of the rest having completely broken down. Have lost as yet no members of my company & only two wounded … Last night we marched the entire

night in a hard rain.... Have unsaddled our horses only for two nights of the fortnight.... My health strange to say continues good though ... much exhausted from fatigue. I feel that my preservation is owing entirely to the goodness and mercy of God.... From present appearances I think that our Army is falling back and will probably recross the Potomac ... I still think it is a very bad policy for us to attempt an invasion of the North but our great men are wiser than I & much more courageous.... Much very much love to all. May God take care of you my own Dear one. Good bye Yr Richard" [17]

- - - - -

July 5, 1863 — Lt. Colonel Hillery Moseley
Greencastle, Pennsylvania — 42nd Mississippi Infantry

"Ten o'clock, Sunday, the 5th, found us so far safe at Greencastle, 14 miles distant from Williamsport. We were near this point attacked by a small body of cavalry, taking possession of a section of artillery and about 40 wagons. Our cavalry soon assembled and took all that we had lost except our artillery horse. We were soon again all right and on our way tho still dogged by the watchful enemy. We arrived in Williamsport early in the evening, found our rations destroyed, and the river booming. We were making good use of the ferry boat, crossing the wounded ... we crossed about three o'clock [a.m.]. Got near Martinburg, from a kind, good family, some bread and milk, and had our wounds dressed." [18]

- - - - -

July 5, 1863 — Mr. R. S. Norton
Rome, Georgia — Merchant

" ... The Prices of Goods and property of all Kinds is still increasing ... Horses $400 ea to $600; Cows $100 to $300." [19]

(ed: If you look at Mr. Norton's entry from May 26 you will see that the upper end of prices for horses and cows were $400 and $100 respectively. Only 5 weeks later those prices are now the low end.)

- - - - -

July, 1863
South of Gettysburg, Pennsylvania

Private Joseph P. Bashaw
Co. I – 7th Tennessee Infantry

" … the Yankee cavalry run on us, and took 40 or 50 wagons loaded with wounded … I was one of them … they carried us to Marsburg, PA that night … next morning they took all that could walk, and sent them to prison; those that could not walk were paroled and left in the old college.

The citizens fed us for about a week, then the Yankees came along and carried us to Philadelphia and after one night took us to Chester, PA to one of their hospitals where we fared just like their soldiers." [20]

- - - - -

July 6, 1863
Vicksburg, Mississippi

Captain B. F. McPherson
Provost Marshall

"Vicksburg, Mississippi, July 6 A. D. 1863

To All Whom it may Concern, Know Ye That
I B. F. McPherson a Capt. & Provost Marshall of Genl. Pemberton's Corp, C.S.A., being a Prisoner of War, in the hands of the United States Forces, in virtue of the capitulation of the City of Vicksburg and its Garrison, by Lieut. Gen. John C. Pemberton, C.S.A., Commanding, on the 4th day of July, 1863, do in pursuance of the terms of said capitulation, give this my solemn parole under oath –

That I will not take up arms against the United States, nor serve in any military, police or constabulary force in any Fort, Garrison, or field work held by the Confederate States of America, against the United States of America, nor as guard of prisons, depots, or stores, nor discharge any duties usually performed by soldiers against the United States of America until duly exchanged by the proper authorities.

B. F. McPherson, Capt. & Prov. Marshall
Of Lt. Gen. Pemberton's Corp

Sworn to and subscribed before me at Vicksburg, Miss. This 6th day of July, 1863.

C. [__________], Capt. 101st Regt. Ill. Vol. and Parolling Officer" [21]

- - - - -

July 6, 1863
Vicksburg, Mississippi

Private William T. Alexander
Co. B – 30th Alabama Infantry

" … we were beseiged for 47 days lived 47 days on 10 days rations. Ate Mule Meat & went half naked and on July 3, 1863, surrendered to Genl Grand & was paroled after being fed by the federals ten days … " [22]

- - - - -

July 7, 1863
Ft. Morgan, Alabama

Lt. Colonel James Williams
21st Alabama Infantry

"Dear Lizzy
I have nothing important to write – all feel very sorely the loss of Vicksburg which we learn by telegraph … I may possibly go to the city [Mobile] next Thursday but can't tell yet … Col. Powell's horse was struck by lightning last night – no-body hurt. Your letter and package came –
Goodbye
Williams" [23]

(ed: Lizzy is renting residence in a private home in Mobile with their son, George Dixon, who was born in May of 1863.)

- - - - -

July 8, 1863
Sulphur Springs, North Carolina

Mrs. Cornelia Henry
Farm wife

"I made Charlie's pants today & began Hanes'. I made the pies for dinner of rasberries. The hands are cutting wheat. It is very fine. We have rain nearly every day. The June apples are ripening fast." [24]

(ed: In her July 1st entry Cornelia noted, "I made an apron for myself this evening of an old gingham dress. I have had ten years & cut another out of it. I had it before we were married. It is worse for wear.")

- - - - -

July 8, 1863
38 miles west of Helena, Arkansas

Captain Griffin Frost
Co. A – 2nd Missouri Infantry

"Yesterday was a hard day on soldiers, they were not able to travel over 10 miles, the roads were horrid – mud knee deep in places. This is a wild rough country … The men were nearly worn out, had been wading through mud and water … This Arkansas is delightful country, always a favorite of mine." [25]

- - - - -

July 8, 1863
Hagerstown, Maryland

Captain Weldon Davis
Co. B – 30th N. Carolina Infantry

"… our wagon train went to the rear for a place of safety, but went too far, and a few Yankee cavalry made a dash on them, run off the Guard, and destroyed thirty or forty and carried off a few others. Our baggage wagon was among those destroyed, so I have lost all my clothes again…." [26]

- - - - -

July 9, 1863
Fort Delaware, Delaware

2nd Lt. James H. Wentworth
Co. D – 5th Florida Infantry

"We only get 2 meals a day consisting of one slice of dingy light bread and a small slice of fresh beef boiled in dirty water … The island is about two feet below the surface of the bay around which there is a levy thrown up to keep the water off and there is a moat about 30 ft. wide on the inside of the levy in which the men wash their clothes and bodies … [the water has] a green scum … and innumerable maggots working in it and that is the place they get the water to make our bread and boil our meat. Such filth is enough to kill us all." [27]

- - - - -

July 10, 1863
Burke County, North Carolina

Thirty Five Citizens

"To Governor Z. B. Vance.
We the undersigned Citizens of Burke would most respectfully petition you to grant a special exemption under the late militia law to John P. Janes a citizen of said County, for the reason that we feel that his services are indispensible in the neighborhood … He is the only mechanic in the neighborhood – he makes looms, bed-steads, trays, chairs, tables, chests, stocks, scythes, plows &c &c – He is almost constantly engaged in the above work & during the present summer he has only worked upon his farm about three days…. he has been engaged in work of the above description for the last ten or twelve years, and that said Janes works now for the same prices which he charged in times of peace. We would also represent that Mr. Janes an one other person in our neighborhood are the only persons who make coffins … We feel that it will be a great loss … for him to be taken from us. He is about 43 years of age & has a wife & ten children the youngest of which is about 10 months old – his oldest a son not 19 years of age, has been in the army as a volunteer for more than six months – For the reasons set forth we trust that your Excellency will deem it proper to cause Mr. Janes to be exempted from the service …
[Thirty-five signees]" [28]

- - - - -

July 10, 1863
Helena, Arkansas

Dr. William McPheeters
Price's Division

"The supplies promised by Dr. Castleberry or rather a portion of them came out today including a hogshead of ice, which is very acceptable as the weather is very hot. Received a communication from Dr. Beaumont at Trenton in charge of wounded sent over there and replied to it. [I] took quinine and blue mass, feeling symptoms of intermittent fever. Seven of our wounded have died up to this date." [29]

(ed: Dr. Castleberry, a Union doctor in Helena, has sent some medical supplies through the lines to assist Dr. McPheeters and his staff. It is not uncommon for Union and Confederate medical staffs to share supplies since they are both caring for wounded of the opposing army.)

- - - - -

July 12, 1863
Delhi, Louisiana

Captain Theophilus Perry
Co. F – 28th Texas Cavalry

"Dear Harriet: ... The people are much discouraged about the fall of Vicksburg. It is the necessary reaction of overweaning confidence. Every day I live I have less and less respect for people. I was prepared for the fall of Vicksburg and had not brought myself to think it was a vital point...." [30]

(ed: Captain Phil Brown of Company F died of a pistol wound in early July, and Theophilus was promoted to Captain of Company F on July 5, 1863.)

- - - - -

July 12, 1863
Danville, Virginia

Sergeant Benjamin F. Porter
Co. E – 11th Alabama Infantry

"Gen'l Host. No 7, Ward 2nd
Dear Ma, I regret to hear of the fall of Vicksburge. I fear that our homes in Ala. are in danger.... I have had too chills. The last one prooved to be a conjestive chill of the slight order. The chill was attended by a severe pain in the small of the back.... I thought I was near my end ...

My pen & ink are given out, so I will take my pencil.... I hear some of hour boys have been killed in the late battle of Gettys Burge, Pensylvania.... My wound is well, but I have not got the youse of it [shoulder] as I had first.... It will not be long before I start to my Regt....
Benj. F. Porter" [31]

- - - - -

July 13, 1863
Fort Morgan, Alabama

Lt. Colonel James Williams
21st Alabama Infantry

"Dear Lizzy
All quiet as usual – two or three blockade running steamers are out and as many blockaders are absent from the fleet: whether they are in chase or only cruising on suspicion we don't know ...

... visitors to the Fort ... are not permitted to enter and ramble about at pleasure ... we do all regret one thing and that is the ... exhibition of pretty ankles – not to mention legs – which the dear ladies furnished us in climbing up and down the steep steps to the ramparts.
Williams" [32]

- - - - -

July 13, 1863
Zollicoffer, Tennessee

Sergeant Robert Watson
Co. K – 7th Florida Infantry

"I went into the country to buy provisions and after walking about 6 miles and inquiring at every house that I passed I finally bought 16 onions for $2.00 …" [33]

- - - - -

July 14, 1863
Williamsport, Maryland

Private Samuel Pickens
Co. D – 5th Alabama Infantry

"The Potomac being swollen, was very wide & was over waist deep. The water felt cool when we first entered it, but afterwards very pleasant. We waded two & two side by side, holding on to each other in order to resist the current better & be more steady. There were orders for the men to hang their cartridge-boxes around their necks, but a great many failed to do it & there was a considerable amount of ammunition damaged & destroyed by getting wet. Our clothes, blankets (partly) & haversacks all got wet, which increased our load and made it very disagreeable marching after crossing. The banks were muddy & … steep & slippery that it was difficult to scuffle up … David Barnum & several others went out & killed two hogs. We broiled the meat at the fire & ate one for supper…." [34]

- - - - -

July 14, 1863
St. George's, Bermuda

Major Smith Stansbury
C. S. Ordnance Department

"Major Caleb Huse
Major: … We are in urgent want of Saltpeter to keep our powder works in Augusta, Ga. in operation.

The capacity of the Mills is to produce five thousand pounds per working diem of ten hours, or ten or twelve thousand pounds working day and night, and this could be nearly doubled by certain improvements.

The supplies of Saltpeter are from 1st Running the Blockade, 2nd The limestone caves of Va., Tenn., etc 3rd The Nitre Beds –

… the importance of having always on hand largely of this material cannot be overestimated.

We are also in need of percussion caps and it would be well to send over four or five million as soon as possible…. " [35]

(ed: Major Stansbury is the commanding officer of the C. S. Ordnance Department in Bermuda. He works closely with Mr. John Bourne, the C. S. Commercial Agent, to coordinate shipments of various supplies to Wilmington and Charleston. Major Caleb Huse is the C. S. Purchasing Agent in Europe. Huse concentrates his efforts in England, Belgium and Austria and is headquartered in England.)

(ed: The requirements for saltpeter and lead were critical. Virtually every blockade runner carried some portion of the cargo in one or both of these products. From 11-1-63 through 12-8-64 a total of 1,933,000 pounds of saltpeter and 1,507,000 pounds of lead were brought into various southern ports on blockade runners.) [36]

- - - - -

July 14, 1863
north of Martinsburg, Virginia

Private Louis Leon
Co. C – 1st N. Carolina Infantry

"These roads are so bad that it is hard to trudge along. I stuck in the mud several times and lost one shoe in a mud hole, but of course took it out again. One consolation we have got, it is raining so hard that the mud is washed off our clothing, therefore they were not soiled too bad…. We are now, thank God, on Confederate soil, but oh, how many of our dear comrades have we left behind." [37]

- - - - -

July 14, 1863
Winder Hospital, Richmond, Virginia

Sergeant F. M. Ross
Co. I – 13th Mississippi Infantry

"Dear Sister Mollie
I have to perform the sad task of writing the death of your poor Newton [Pvt. Nimrod N. Nash] to you he was killed on the 2nd of July … in a charge on one of the enemies batteries near sundown … Our Co. carried 46 guns into the fight and had 33 men killed and wounded and 3 missing … Gen Barksdale and Col. Carter were killed … Newtons body was buried the next morning … Charles was not in the fight he had been left in Va sick …" [38]

- - - - -

July 16, 1863
Near Winchester, Virginia

Private W. K. Hadaway
Co. F – 24th Georgia Infantry

"Dear Companion
… I received a leter from you las night. It was such a kine and lovly leter & had bin so long since I had a leter from you I could not read it with dry eyes. Martha I am 12 mils of Winchester whear I was when I rote last tho I hav bin in Marilen [Maryland] & rambled & seen many things since…. I have to cook for the company and cold not rite [could not write] the arma [army] is fallin back & we don't think we gand [gained] enything by the Marilen trip. We hav capereda [captured] gret meny horses beeves & Yeankes … but lost a great meny men … Martha I am afred [afraid] the Confredsay will sune be stobe up [soon be stove up]. I have heard Vixburg is taken … we are all woren out tho we ar restin now … I remane your best fren." [39]

(ed: This simple letter by Private Hadaway to his "companion" Martha is so touching and poignant. His descriptions and wording are truly magical and almost haunting in their simplicity.)

- - - - -

July 17, 1863 Corporal Tally Simpson
Bunker's Hill, Virginia Co. A – 3rd S. Carolina Infantry

"Dear Sister
The night we left Hagerstown [Maryland] was the worst I ever saw. The mud was almost knee deep and about as thick as corn meal batter. We waded through it like horses, and such a squashing you never heard. I believe I had over fifteen or twenty pounds of mud clinging to my shoes and pants. Poor Harry stuck to it like a man. His shoes gave out completely, and he was compelled to go barefooted. Marching over those turnpikes nearly ruined his feet. But fortunately yesterday, while coming through Martinsburg, he bought an old pair of shoes. They were too short and he cut the toes off, and it looked funny to see him trudging along in the mud with his toes sticking about an inch or two out of his shoes.

... I can't imagine where we are bound for. Some think we will remain above Winchester for some time, others think we are bound for Richmond. I think our movements will depend entirely upon the movements of the enemy.

... Hoping to hear from you soon I remain
Your affec bro
Taliaferro Simpson

Lewis was a little sick yesterday, but is much better today. Sends his love to his family and to all the negros generally." [40]

(ed: Tally, although an enlisted man, is from a fairly affluent family and has a servant that travels with him and does his cooking and other chores. This is far more common for the officers but is not an uncommon situation in the ranks.)

- - - - -

July 17, 1863 Captain Theophilus Perry
Trenton, Louisiana Co. F – 28th Texas Cavalry

"Dear Harriet: ... Our Division is on the west side of the Washita once more....

I am in my company. I get on tolerably well. There is a good deal of sickness here. Some chills and fever. There are not many violent cases, but much complaint. We have all been debilitated by the swamps.... I think I feel better now than I did while on horseback. Walking seems to agree with me....

I have received your letter of the 7th. I am grieved to hear of the death of my little Brother Joseph Henry. I lament with Mother. I know she feels heart broken....

Tell daughter to write me another letter. I will be glad to get a letter from her. I carry your Picture and daughters in my side coat pocket all the time, and sleep with head on them at night....

... Do not send me a servant until I send for him. Have him ready to come though. Send me some Pound Cakes the first chance. Farewell. Kiss the children. My love to all ...
Your Affectionate Husband
Theophilus Perry" [41]

- - - - -

July 17, 1863
Retreat from Jackson, Mississippi

Private John Jackman
Co. B – 9th Kentucky Infantry

"Last night, 16th, at 12 o'clock, fell in silently, and moved through the city, across the pontoon bridge over Pearl river, and marched out on the Brandon road. We were the last troops to cross the river; and the brigade moved in such good order, that it excited the admiration of the commanding Gen'l. It has covered so many retreats, the boys know just how things have to be done. When daylight came, we were 4 miles from the city. Marched 14 miles during the day, and bivouacked 2 miles east of Brandon. A very hot day, and dusty marching. All the troops having to move on the same road, we were delayed greatly." [42]

- - - - -

July 17, 1863
Richmond, Virginia

Mr. John B. Jones
Clerk – War Department

"... we are in a half starving condition. I have lost twenty pounds, and my wife and children are emaciated to some extent....

To-day, for the second time, ten dollars in Confederate notes are given for one in gold; and no doubt, under our recent disasters, the depreciation will increase." [43]

- - - - -

July 17, 1863
near Tyner's Station, Tennessee

Sergeant W. W. Heartsill
Co. F – 2nd Texas Cavalry

"My mess had a rare treat for our dinner to day; in the shape of a nice LARGE BLACKBERRY PIE ..." [44]

- - - - -

July 17, 1863
Macon, Georgia

Macon Daily Telegraph

AUCTION SALES
by
J. B. SMITH & CO.

"Will be sold at the CourtHouse THIS DAY, at the usual hours of sale, several likely Negroes, men and women, 44 ½ shares of Lanier House Stock, a lot of very fine Furniture, consisting of Mahogany Marble Top Bureaus, Wash Stands, Wardrobe, Chairs, Bedsteads &c. A fine new Buggy, one Rockaway. Also 7 milch Cows and 1 dry will be sold on Wednesday.

J. B. Smith & Co., Auctioneers" [45]

- - - - -

July 18, 1863 | Private I. Norval Baker
1 mile south of the Potomac River | Co. F – 18th Virginia Cavalry

"Our regiment was about the last to cross the river, we went in camp about a mile or so south of the river with orders to unsaddle our horses. Our horses backs were raw with ulcers one and two inches deep and full of maggots. The green flies had put up a big job on us, our blankets were full of maggots and rotten, our saddles had from a pint to a quart of maggots in them and we had to run them out with hot water and soap and it [will be] months before the horses backs [are]cured." [46]

(ed: Mackenzie recommends, "Mix with one quart of water, a table spoonful of the spirits of turpentine, and as much of the sublimate powder as will lie upon a shilling. Shake them well together, and cork it up in a bottle, with a quill through the cork, so that the liquid may come out of the bottle in small quantities at once.... When the spot is observed where the maggots are, do not disturb them, but pour a little of the mixture upon the spot, as much as will wet the [hair] and the maggots. In a few minutes after the liquor it applied the maggots will all creep to the top of the [hair], and in a short time drop off dead. Check daily ... if any of the maggots remain ... touch them with a little more of the mixture.") [47]

- - - - -

July 18, 1863 | Sergeant Daniel H. Sheetz
Darkesville, Virginia | Co. K – 2nd Virginia Infantry

"I can not say that I am enjoying myself at all at this time. I am too much waried down from the march that we had in the yankee states ... it was the hardest times that we had since the war. I was in good hopes that the war would soon be over but it don't look much like it at this time." [48]

(ed: Darkesville, Virginia is now Inwood, West Virginia. It is only a few miles north of Winchester.)

- - - - -

July 19, 1863
Jefferson, North Carolina

Mr. James Wagg
Minister and Doctor

"My Dear John
I am going to try to write you a few line ... I can scarcely see from a suffusion of tears I have had to witness many gloomy Sabbath mornings you know; but this is one of the gloomiest of my life. I Just received intelegence yesterday that Samuel was killed at Gettysburge on the 2nd of this month and left to bleach probably unburied on the enemies soil he was shot in the breast, and lived but a few minutes. James Turner was by him when he was shot near a battery they were charging and I am told he gave him his pocket-book and sent some word home; ... the company was cut all to pieces ... When my feeling will permit and I learn the particulars I will write more oh! John have you forgotten us altogether that you write so seldom.
Affectionately
James Wagg" [49]

(ed: The 26th North Carolina Infantry sustained the highest rate of regimental casualties among all C. S. A. regiments engaged at Gettysburg. On July 1 on McPherson's Ridge they lost 14 color bearers. Some 75% of the regiment was killed, wounded or captured on July 1 and the survivors were used in the assault on Cemetery Ridge on July 3 and more men fell, including Capt. Samuel Wagg. In total the regiment lost 88 % of its men.) [50]

- - - - -

July 19, 1863
Darksville, Virginia

Surgeon Harvey Black
Hospital 2 ANV Corps

"My dear Wife –
I have just had a good camp dinner: poles & snaps, mutton, fried chicken, & Blackberry pie & Milk – and ... I ate heartily.... I have a respite from work at present....

This morning I went over to the Stonewall Brigade for the first time since the fight [Gettysburg] to see the remnant of the 4th Regt.... the whole regt now is but about 1/3 larger than was Col. Ronald's Company when it marched out of Blacksburg.

… I asked [Capt. Evans] where I could find his Company. He told me, and one of his men remarked they could nearly all get under one oil cloth. So with Capt. Bennett's Co. The former has 12, the latter 13 present….
Most affectionately
H Black" [51]

- - - - -

July 19, 1863 — Lt. Joshua K. Callaway
Chattanooga, Tennessee — Co. K – 28th Alabama Infantry

"My Dear Wife, …
We are still on short rations, but the meat that we have drawn lately has been so poor that I might say we are out of rations. But still we are doing finely. I can endure a great deal while I know you and the children are doing well. I sent out yesterday and bought half a gallon of milk for which I paid a dollar. It made me two meals. I could have bought butter milk for half that price. Today we will have some black berry pies for dinner….
Your affectionate Husband
JK" [52]

(ed: Joshua will get a furlough home in early August and return on August 22nd.)

- - - - -

July 20, 1863 — Private Benjamin Seaton
Near Chattanooga, Tennessee — Co. G – 10th Texas Infantry

"Monday 20th – on rigmental guard – it is a rumer in camp that the copperheads and aboolishion have fought in New York about the conscript law. They wold not leave home to fight if it had to be done they wold commence at home. They done a grate deal of damage before they were stoped and I hope they may do more before they quit." [53]

(ed: "The Federal Enrollment Act of March 3, 1863 became active in New York City on July 11 when the Provost Marshall drew the initial names to be drafted. The following day mobs gathered in the streets and began looting stores. Order was restored by July 18 with the arrival of Federal troops. Property damage was in the millions and over 1,000 people were killed or wounded.") [54]

- - - - -

July, 1863 Captain Samuel T. Foster
Chattanooga, Tennessee Co. H – 24th Texas Cavalry

"We hear that Vicksburg has fallen, and on the 10th Jackson Miss was attacked, and Charleston SC also, by land and by water and that Lee has fallen back, and the Yanks are advancing on this place with a view to going into Georgia and Alabama.

The Confederacy wants more men. Lee wants men. Bragg wants men. They are wanted everywhere, but where are they to come from –" [55]

- - - - -

July 20, 1863 Lt. Colonel James Williams
Fort Morgan, Alabama 21st Alabama Infantry

"Dear Lizzy:
… I wish you could have some of the fine fish which we get here; right fresh out of the water – for instance at dinner today we had – baked red fish – pompin – blue fish and trout – a flounder breakfast – all of them the very finest fish that swim the bay - … It is well that we get fish and crabs … for without them it would be sorry fare for us.
Williams" [56]

- - - - -

July 20, 1863 Mrs. Harriet Perry
Harrison County, Texas Farm wife

"My beloved Husband: Breakfast is just over, Mother is preparing Daniel with a load for Shreveport. he will carry bacon watermelons, butter fruite vegetables &c – while they are filling the wagons I thought I could write you a few lines – I wrote two long letters last week still you say you do not hear from me – I never miss a week without writing – never – and sometime twice ... Theophilus is such a promising little Babe. I would not have his mind impaired by medicine for the world. his tooth is through – I am very proud of it – he will be seven months old the 24th and has never seen his dear father but I hope will see him soon – Mattie [Sugar Lumpie] has a very bad cough and cold, so much so, she has fever nearly every night – was more unwell last night than usual.... I kept a candle burning all night as I was giving Theophilus quinine – she does very well in the day – I hope she will soon be well she is cutting more teeth - ... Your father sold one hundred bushels of wheat to Mr. Godwin at $2.75 per bushel, he will make between six & eight hundred bushels - ... I hope to be blessed with the sight of your sweet self soon – May your health continue good ... Thine forever
Harriet

... I wrote you of the death of your Mothers baby ... May God spare us to meet again ..." [57]

(ed: Little Theo has been having chills and while Harriet has been giving him some doses of quinine she is reluctant to give regular doses because she fears her personal usage has led to memory loss and that it would be even more harmful to children.)

- - - - -

July 20, 1863 Mrs. Martha Revis
Marshall, North Carolina Farm wife

"H. W. Revis:
Dear Husband: I seat myself to drop you a few lines to let you know that me and Sally is well as common, and I hope these few lines will come to hand

and find you well … I have no news to write to at this, only I am laying by my corn. I worked it all four times. My wheat is good; my oats is good. I haven't got my wheat stacked yet. My oats I have got a part of them cut, and Tom Hunter and John Roberts is cutting to-day. They will get them cut to-day.

I got the first letter yesterday … since you left. I got five from you yesterday; they all came together. This is the first one I have wrote, for I didn't know where to write you. You said you hadn't anything to eat. I wish you was here to get some beans for dinner. I have plenty to eat as yet. I haven't saw any of your pap's folks since you left home…. The people is all turning to Union here since the Yankees has got Vicksburg. I want you to come home as soon as you can after you get his letter. Jane Elkins is living with me yet. That is all I can think of, only I want you to come home the worst that I ever did. The conscripts is all at home yet, and I don't know what they will do with them. The folks is leaving here, and going North as fast as they can, so I will close.
Your wife, till death,
Martha Revis" [58]

(ed: Letters of distress from home were one of many reasons that weakened the resolve of a soldier to stay with his unit. As conditions in the Confederacy continue to deteriorate the situation for the families at home becomes ever more desperate creating a difficult situation for the soldier who must choose between his fellow soldiers and the needs of his family.)

July 20, 1863	Mr. Levin Perry
Harrison County, Texas	Farmer

"Theophilus, I am seated Harriet on one side and Nancy Greene on the other compelling me to write … I have just returned from Jonesville and seen the Proclamation of Genl Magruder calling upon the citizens without regard to age to come to the rescue of their wives and children … and also the request … to send in their negroes between the ages of Seventeen and forty five to work on the public works of Shreveport and Grand Ecore … I hardly believe the people will respond I tell you Theophilus the people will [not]

volunteer to fight any more, I mean those now at home, nor will they render any material voluntary assistance they seem absorbed in money making and in devising means of escape when the enemy approaches I am disgusted and ashamed …
Levin Perry" [59]

- - - - -

July 20, 1863	Sergeant W. W. Heartsill
Hamilton County, Tennessee	Co. F – 2nd Texas Cavalry

"Provisions are rather scarce and … are at exhoribitant prices; such as Coffee $5 per lb, Sugar $2 per lb, Soda $5 per lb, Potatoes $15 per bushel, Peaches $2 per dozen, Bacon $2 per pound, Onions $3 per dozen … Chickens $2 each and everything else in proportion." [60]

- - - - -

July 21, 1863	Mrs. Mary Watkins
Meherrin, Virginia	Farm wife

"My dear dear Husband
You can imagine how glad I was at receiving your letters last Friday, I had not heard from you in three weeks … Well baby is asleep again and I will resume my letter. Minnie is sitting on the floor by me … she says Mama must tell Papa Minnie loves him "heep o times." Emmie goes from the breakfast table out doors and I can hardly get her in again before night. She is very much sunburned but looks more healthy than Minnie … I rode Lizze Leigh over home yesterday and staid several hours … I rode with Mr. Anderson out in the plantation to see the crops. We have a splendid crop of corn now and if we could only have a little dry weather I should be sure of a fine crop. The hail and hot weather has injured the wheat … Mr A is having it hauled up to the grainery ready for threashing … He hadn't finished cutting oats and I didn't see any of the tobacco…. Sister Sue told me Sunday that Mr Anderson thought it was time for you to let him know whether you wanted him another year. He asks a very high salary but Mr. Redd and Bro. William

advise that you employ him again.... I reckon we have the best [corn] crop in the neighborhood now but if it continues to rain as it is doing now, ours will go like the rest.

So we were defeated at Gettysburg ..." [61]

(ed: An incomplete letter. The additional page or pages are missing.)

- - - - -

July 22, 1863 — Lt. Jesse P. Bates
Moulton Station, Mississippi — Co. G – 9th Texas Infantry

"My dear companion ... I am well but not very stout. We have rambled around about right smart since we come to Miss. We fell back to Jackson on the 7th of this month and we had some skirmish fighting and some charges. We had one Lieut. killed and one man badly and several slightly wounded in the Regt.... We are about 25 miles east of Brandon ... This army is low spirited and despondent, but I think the drooping spirits of the army will soon revive.... I have drawn some money since I wrote to you last on the 22nd of June.... that I could embrace my dear wife and kiss them sweet lips ... So farewell for this time
Jesse P Bates" [62]

- - - - -

July 22, 1863 — Major Smith Stansbury
St. George's, Bermuda — C. S. Ordnance Depot

"Lieut. Col. I. M. St John, Nitre and Mining Bureau
Colonel: Respectfully referring to your letter of 12th ultimo to the Chief of Ordnance [Col. Gorgas] in reference to shipping at least forty tons of lead and sixty tons of Saltpeter per month, and of accumulating reserves of these material.

... At present writing (after the loading of the *R E Lee*) we have on hand as follows –

- 1500 Pigs of Lead, 100 lbs. each
- No Saltpeter –" [63]

(ed: The R E Lee *was one of five blockade runners owned by the C. S. Ordnance Department. From their acquisition in 1862 through August 2, 1863 these ships made 50 trips without loss.)* [64]

- - - - -

July 23, 1863 — Miss. Kate Sperry
Winchester, Virginia — Nurse

"Ma and Pa will leave tomorrow [with the Confederate army]. Pa has bought a one-horse light covered wagon and a splendid strong horse – wants me to go – if Aunt Wardy only had someone to stay with her I would – but Maria [hired help] leaves for home in the morning and I'll have to keep house and cook." [65]

- - - - -

July 23, 1863 — Miss. Kate Cummings
Kingston, Georgia — Hospital Matron

"We arrived in Kingston, Georgia, last evening, and put up at one of the hotels … Dr. A[vent] called early this morning; he is post surgeon, a fine-looking old gentleman, and a man highly respected for his surgical abilities…. The first information we received from him was that he did not approve of ladies in hospitals; that was nothing new from a doctor, but we were a little taken aback to hear it said so bluntly. He then told us his principal objection was, that the accommodations in hospitals were not fit for ladies. We assured him … we were all good soldiers, and had been accustomed to hardships.

… He also told us that he wished us all to eat at the officers' table, with himself and the assistant surgeon, as he thought a table was not fit to eat at where there were no ladies. We did not object to that plan till we had given it a trial." [66]

(ed: Dr. Stout's hospitals serving the Army of Tennessee were located in Cleveland and Chattanooga, Tennessee; Ringgold, Rome, Dalton, Kingston, Cherokee Springs, Catoosa Springs, Tunnel Hill, Marietta, Newnan and of course Atlanta, Georgia. There was also a hospital for the Georgia militia in Milledgeville and prison hospitals in Macon and Andersonville, Georgia.) [67]

- - - - -

July 23, 1863
Chattanooga, Tennessee

Captain James P. Douglas
Douglas's Texas Artillery

"I thought of sending money home to pay debts, but everything has got so amazingly high that I can barely support myself on my wages. I am now saving no money, although my income is nearly 500 cts. per day." [68]

- - - - -

July 23, 1863
near Fort Fisher, North Carolina

Corporal W. T. McArthur
Anderson's Battery

"Mr. Neil Shaw
... My fare is bad for my quarters is a cold weather beaten tent. I get wet nearly every time it rains for it rains rite through you had as well been out ... in a low wet place. We are nearly surrounded by water and the mosquitoes is very bad.... Some of our boys had a rough time over at Bullhead Island last Sunday ... They went over to save the cargo of a steamer that was run ashore by the blockaders while trying to come in they saved a valuable cargo worth four hundred thousand dollars ..." [69]

- - - - -

July 25, 1863
Richmond, Virginia

Mr. John B. Jones
Clerk, War Department

"Advertisers in the papers offer $4000 for substitutes. One offers a farm in Hanover County, on the Central Railroad, of 230 acres for a substitute." [70]

- - - - -

July 26, 1863
Richmond, Virginia

Colonel Robert Kean
Confederate Bureau of War

"The Commissary General has written to tell General Lee that during the time he was in Pennsylvania, he was only able to get together here 500,000 pounds of meat, and to urge a reduction of the ration to one-fourth of a pound as it was last winter. This is a most alarming state of the supply question. God help this happy country!" [71]

- - - - -

July 26, 1863
Hugenot Springs Hospital, Virginia

Lt. Colonel Hillery Moseley
42nd Mississippi Infantry

"Hugenot Springs – situated in Powhatan, 17 miles from Richmond, and is approachable both by canal and R.R. three miles from the canal and six miles from Coal Field R.R. There are some beautiful farms on the lowland and in a high state of cultivation…. The location of the watery place is an undulating slope, studded with beautiful oak groves. The avenue in front of the building is very pretty and its shades cool and inviting. The wounded and invalid soldiers group about, indulging in various pastimes …

My foot for two days past has been painful and inflamed. This morning it gives me uneasiness for fear of erysipelas, the scourge of hospitals. This wet, damp atmosphere is highly favorable to its production, but as we leave tomorrow evening, I hope for better things.

The management of this hospital seems to be well arranged, and no doubt is conducted with the best ability the resources at command will admit…." [72]

(ed: Hillery had spent 2 days in Winchester and 5 days in Staunton before being transferred on to Richmond and then to Hugenot Springs. Hillery and Major Feeney are transferred to the home of a Mr. and Mrs. Ford in Cumberland County

to convalesce. In late August they return to Richmond and Hillery will be given a medical furlough to return to Mississippi.)

- - - - -

July 27, 1863
"Culpepper" Courthouse, Virginia

Private Charles W. Thomas
Co. B – 56th Virginia Infantry

"My Dear Wife,
... I am sorry to hear you ware so near bare footed. Try and swap you shoes for something you can ware. I dont want you to get bare footed ... I am bad off for clothes myself after losing my knapsack and cloths. I ant got but one suit and that I have on ... I ant got but $3.25. We haven't drawn any money in three months ... I am sorry to learn that such a destruction of crops by the freshes [freshet] ... your effectionate husband as ever – adieu. C. W. Thomas" [73]

(ed: Evidently a heavy rainstorm and perhaps the flooding of a stream running through their farm has caused major crop damage.)

- - - - -

July 27, 1863
"Back on Southern Soil"

1st Lt. W. R. Montgomery
3rd Bttn. Georgia Sharpshooters

"Dear Aunt Frank
My love to my Sweet Heart if you see her, or if you can find one for me. I am now forsaken. If you know any young lady that wants to marry as soon as I get home refer them to me & speak a word in my favor, as I am tired of waiting longer on the war & want some one to take care of me in my old age." [74]

- - - - -

July 28, 1863 Mr. Daniel Locklar
Laurinburg, Richmond Co N. C. Free Negro Farmer

"His Excellency the Governor
Sir – if your highness will condesend to reply to my feble Note, you will confer a great favor on me, and relieve me of my troubles.... I am a free man of Color, and has a large family to support, there is a man living near me, who is an Agent of the State Salt workes appointed by Worth, or is said to be, he took all we Colored men last winter to make Salt. he is now after us to make Barrels for the State Salt works. Comes at the dead hours of night and carries us off ... gives us one dollar and fifty Cents pr day ... I cannot support my family very well if I were left a home to work for my neighbors they pay me or sell provisions at the old price for my labor, this agent says he has the power by law ... but if there be no such law and this Agent taking this power within himself perhaps speculating on the labor of the free Colored men and our families suffering for bread, I am not willing to submit to such, please let me know if this Agent the power to use us as he does

DANIEL LOCKLAR" [75]

(ed: The governor replied, "He has no such authority.")

- - - - -

July 28, 1863 Mrs. Harriet Perry
Harrison County, Texas Farm wife

"My dear Husband: ... I write you a few lines to let you know how little Daughter is – she had no fever yesterday, last-night or to-day. I am giving her quinine, and I think she is better, she is gaining her appetite and seems to have more animation ... she is much reduced and very pale – There are several cases of chill and fever among the negroes ...

Your Father asked [Dr. Haywood] to look at Mattie yesterday, but she was improving and did not need medicine – he told me to give her blue mass rubarb last night if she had fever. she had none and I did not give it – he does not think she has worms, but I do she is a delicate little creature – Theophilus is well now, has one tooth and is very proud of it.... I hope you will come home ... I pray you will I want to see [you] more than I can tell – I live in hopes –" [76]

(ed: Blue Mass, sometimes called blue pills, is mercury mixed with chalk. Blue Mass was used to open the bowels and to treat fever. As with calomel, which is mercury chloride, the mercury content can cause death and an assortment of non fatal complications.)

- - - - -

July 29, 1863 | Miss. Kate Sperry
Winchester, Virginia | Nurse

"Our Post Office came in this afternoon about 2 o'clock – Charley Graves brought the mail in an Ambulance – fortunately he had a trunk belonging to a lady in this place – he stopped at the Hotel to put it out and saw the Yanks advancing – so he slipped off on a back road whilst a Battalion of Yankee Cavalry dashed down Main Street after *seven* of our men. The Yanks didn't shoot until they got out at the edge of town – then one of their Captains was killed ... I'm so thankful the mail escaped being captured." [77]

- - - - -

July 29, 1863 | Mrs. Judith McGuire
Richmond, Virginia | Nurse

"I was in Richmond this morning, and bought a calico dress, for which I gave $2.50 per yard, and considered it a bargain; the new importations have run up to $3.50 and $4 per yard. To what are we coming?" [78]

- - - - -

July 31, 1863 General James Slaughter
Mobile, Alabama

"In company with Admiral Buchanan and many officers of the C. S. Navy and Army, I witnessed her [the *Hunley's*] operations in the river and harbor of Mobile. I saw her pass under a large raft of lumber towing a torpedo behind her which destroyed the raft. She appeared three or four hundred yards beyond the raft and so far as I could judge she behaved as well under water as above it. I will add that I witnessed her experiments more than a dozen times with equal satisfaction." [79]

(ed: Built by a group of investors known as the Singer Submarine Corps, the submarine was built for an investment of $15,000 and construction was begun in April, 1863. She was built at the Park & Lyons Machine Shop in Mobile, Alabama and construction was overseen by William Alexander and James McClintock.) [80]

- - - - -

July 31, 1863 4th Sergeant Robert Elliott
Forest Station, Mississippi Co. E – 35th Alabama Infantry

"Feel pretty stout this morning … some of the Boys … buying things at exorbitant prices peaches sell at 50 cts & 100 doz watermelons although scarce sell at from five to seven dollars a peace …" [81]

- - - - -

July 31, 1863 Sergeant Henry M. Talley
David's Island, New York Co. G – 14th Virginia Infantry

"My Dear Mother, I take much pleasure in droping you a few lines to let you know I was wounded in the battle of Gettysburg. Also was taken prisoner. I was wounded in my right foot and my left ancle. I suffered a good deal at first." [82]

(ed: Henry was wounded on July 3, captured and sent to DeCamp General Hospital at David's Island. He is paroled/exchanged and is shown back with the 14th Virginia in March, 1864. Henry will be promoted to 2nd Lieutenant on April 16, 1864. He will be captured April 1, 1865 at Dinwiddie Court House, sent to Johnson's Island Prison, Ohio and will be released from prison on June 20, 1865 after taking the Oath of Allegiance.)

- - - - -

Raspberry Wine *Mackenzie's 5000 Receipts*

"Take of cold soft water, 6 gallons; cider, 4 do; raspberries, 6 do; any other fruit, 3 do. Ferment. Mix raw sugar, 18 or 20 lbs.; red tartar, in fine powder, 3 oz.; orange and lemon peel, 2 oz. dry, or 4 oz. fresh; then add brandy, 3 quarts. This will make 18 gallons.

Another – Gather the raspberries when ripe, husk them and bruise them; then strain them through a bag into jars or other vessels. Boil the juice and to every gallon put a pound of lump sugar. Now add whites of eggs and let the whole boil for 15 minutes; skimming it as the froth rises. When cool and settled, decant the liquor into a cask, adding yeast to make it ferment. When this has taken place, add a pint of white wine or half a pint of proof spirit to each gallon contained in the cask, and hang a bag in it containing an ounce of bruised mace. In three months, it kept in a cool place, it will be very excellent and delicious wine." [83]

- - - - -

August, 1863

Although President Lincoln is urging General Meade and the Army of the Potomac to pursue the defeated Army of Northern Virginia, there is no aggressive response. The Army of the Potomac has over 23,000 men killed, wounded and missing. While this is not as great, on a percentage basis, as the loss sustained by the Army of Northern Virginia, it still represents 26 percent of his forces. Some companies, regiments and brigades were impacted at rates far in excess of 26 percent. The 1st Minnesota Infantry Regiment and the 26th North Carolina Infantry Regiment are both virtually decimated as they sustain the highest casualty rates in the two armies.

In camps all over southern Maryland and northern Virginia, the two armies rest and recuperate knowing that the fighting season is not yet over.

In the Mobile River, a coal barge has been destroyed by a torpedo towed by a "submarine iron boat." The boat's inventors journey to Charleston, South Carolina, to discuss the weapon with General Beauregard as a possible means of sinking Union blockading ships and ironclads. The vessel is the *H. L. Hunley*.

In Charleston harbor the Union forces continue to shell Fort Sumter and Fort Wagner.

General Rosecrans is maneuvering his armies in an attempt to flank General Bragg and the Confederates out of the city of Chattanooga and force them into northwestern Georgia.

Following the capture of Vicksburg, General Grant proposes to take his army southward and capture Mobile, Alabama. This plan is rejected by the Federal War Department. Instead his army is broken up and sent to various other commands. The most successful general in the entire Union army is without a command. To add injury to insult, Grant is hurt when thrown from his horse in New Orleans.

The impact of the dual losses of Vicksburg and Gettysburg is being felt financially in the South. Confederate currency had been worth about 25 cents to the U. S. dollar in April. Despite the victory at Chancellorsville, it had slipped to about 14 cents in June and now in August it has fallen to slightly under 10 cents. The Confederacy is printing more and more money and the value continues to decline. Despite all the inflation there has been no adjustment in the salaries of the soldiers. A private gets $11 per month and the government, as many of the letters convey, is two or more months behind in their pay. A plug of chewing tobacco is $5, peaches are $3 a dozen, a watermelon costs $5 to $10 and chickens bring $2 apiece. The common soldier can hardly afford to either augment his own diet or send monies home to his family.

The *H. L. Hunley* capsizes and sinks in Charleston harbor. Only four of her nine crewmen escape the sinking submarine.

The blockade runners remain very successful and bring a steady stream of supplies into Wilmington, Charleston, Mobile and Galveston.

August, 1863

August 1, 1863
Winchester, Virginia

Miss. Kate Sperry
Nurse

"Syd and I managed to get in the Hospital this evening – I made and baked six loaves of nice bread – churned some butter and cooked dinner besides ... so I took some suppers to Syd's and my men. Syd made coffee – we took also some buttermilk and bread enough for ever so many – they all like cottage cheese, more familiarly known amongst the Dutch as "smearcase" – it's a change of diet for them.... Jenny came home today from Newton – brought me a calico dress at $1.00 per yard Confederate money – sells for three times that in Richmond – very pretty – got a beautiful bonnet also, grey silk with white and blue trimmings – cost about $20.00 and I had the strings – everything is awful high, but money (Confederate, or as Faulkner calls it, plasters off quinine bottles) is plentiful, so it's about the same." [1]

- - - - -

August 1, 1863
Mobile, Alabama

Admiral Franklin Buchanan
Naval Commandant – Mobile

"Flag Officer John Tucker
Naval Commandant – Charleston

Sir:

I yesterday witnessed the destruction of a lighter or coal flat in Mobile River by a torpedo which was placed under it by a submarine iron boat, the invention of Messrs Whitney and McClintock; Messrs Watson and Whitney visit Charleston for the purpose of consulting General Beauregard and yourself to ascertain whether you will try it, they will explain all its advantages, and if it can operate in smooth water where the current is not strong as was the case yesterday, I can recommend it to your favorable consideration; it can be propelled about four knots per hour, to judge from the experiment yesterday. I am fully satisfied it can be used successfully in blowing up one or more of the enemy's Iron Clads in your harbor.

Do me the favor to show this to Genl Beauregard with my regards.
Very Respectfully
Your Obt Servt
Franklin Buchanan
Admiral" [2]

- - - - -

August 1, 1863	Sergeant Benjamin F. Porter
Culpeper, Virginia	Co. E – 11th Alabama Infantry

"Camps 11th Alabama Regt. near Culpeper CH
Dear Ma & Sister I arrived in camps yesterday evening & was pleased to find two letters from you & one from Bro … I hope you have received all of my letters.

… I want you to …prey for me. I feel that your preyers are all around me & shealding me from harm. I am where all are sinful. I have but few to talk with who ever have a serious thought….

Your letters are dated as follows, 19th of July & the 6th of July & Brothers the 24th. He was well & at Chattanooga, Tenn.

Write soon, times are very gloomy. God bless & save us is my prey …
B. F. Porter" [3]

- - - - -

August 1, 1863
Orange C. H., Virginia

Private Samuel Pickens
Co. D – 5th Alabama Infantry

" ... After lying down & taking a good rest, Davy, Matt & I went out & got a bait of fine large black berries. Va abounds in black & dew berries & the largest I ever saw. They are a great treat to the soldiers &, as they make a change in diet, are beneficial to our health. We eat all the green apples we can get, too, & it is astonishing they don't make us sick...." [4]

- - - - -

August 2, 1863
"Culpepper" County

Sergeant John K. Beaton
Co. G – 9th Virginia Infantry

"Dear Ma & Sister
... I received your last letter the day before the fight at Gettysburg and have watched anxiously for an opportunity to answer it. I will make the effort now at last.

I was very much in hope we would pay you a visit when we were at Suffolk, but our object was to forage.... We are very anxious to get down that way again and have a chance at those negroes we hear are parading around town. We would soon make them wish they were back in the cornfields. Portsmouth received a fearful loss at the late battle in Pennsylvania.... Our regiment has suffered severely, we hope most of them are prisoners, but I fear to the contrary ... Our company sums up a loss of 34 men. I was struck and knocked down twice but was not seriously wounded. Thomas Owen was struck in the lower face on the left side, the ball coming out below the right shoulder blade. He can't possibly live, he was left at the hospital near Gettysburg. James Nash ... has lost his left leg.... I suppose you heard of the charge of our division.... we gained nothing ... I will send you a list of our wounded and missing ... Accept my love for yourself and Sarah.
John Beaton" [5]

- - - - -

August 2, 1863
Tatumville, Alabama

Miss. Ellen Gaddes
Hospital Volunteer

"To Mrs. B. A. G. Spears
I take up my pen to tell you very bad news. Your husband Henry Spears died at the Point Clear hospital on Wednesday night August 1. that evening I in company with some more ladies were in the hospital. I was talking to your husband and he asked me to write to you to say that he was sick, he said, "it will prepare her a little to hear of my death and will not be such a shock to her." ... It is very painful for me to tell you this bad news but as I promised him I thought that I had best do it. it will be some satisfaction for you to know that he was well attended to and all was done for him that could possibly be done. I can offer you no consolation, God alone can console you...." [6]

- - - - -

August 3, 1863
Little Rock, Arkansas

Captain Griffin Frost
Co. A – 2nd Missouri Infantry

" ... Board in Little Rock is from three to five dollars per day. Chewing tobacco five dollars per plug. Smoking [tobacco] eight dollars per lb Melons from one to two dollars apiece. Whiskey sixty dollars per gallon, everything else in proportion." [7]

- - - - -

August 3, 1863
St. George's, Bermuda

Major Smith Stansbury
C. S. Ordnance Depot

"John T. Bourne –
My Dear Sir - Please freight to *Banshee* as follows – 490 Pigs Lead, 25 Tons, 400 Cases Austrian Rifles, 50 [tons], 400 Boxes Ammunition, 25 [tons] 100 [tons]. There will be sixty tons of Lighter material which I will select and advise you." [8]

- - - - -

August 4, 1863
Richmond, Virginia

Mr. John B. Jones
Clerk, War Department

"Confederate notes are now given for gold at the rate of $12 or $15 for $1. Flour is $40 per barrel; bacon $1.75 per pound; ... Butter is selling at $3 per pound." [9]

- - - - -

August 6, 1863
Letterman Hospital, Gettysburg

Lt. Sanford Branch
Co. A – 8th Georgia Infantry

"Dear Mother,
I can write but few lines [as] Sergt. [Alexander K.] Wilson leaves in the morning early it is nearly dark now.

My wounds are nearly healed, fever gone, appetite excellent and if it was not for a discharge from the wound in my side I could walk all about. I am in good spirits & hope to see you soon.

Dear Mother God has indeed been very merciful. Do not worry yourself about me.
Your affect. son
Sanford" [10]

(ed: This is the first surviving letter in the collection since Sanford was wounded on July 2. Sanford has been shot through the left wrist [broken bone] and future letters will refer to his broken arm. The ball then passed through his ribs near the sternum, tore a tumbling path through his left lung, and exited beneath his left arm. In addition to the damage to his lung the bullet hit bone both entering and exiting. By late July, over 16,000 wounded have been evacuated from Gettysburg. Approximately 4,217 still remain at Camp Letterman, the consolidated hospital, on the Wolf farm, about 1 mile east of town on the York Pike.) [11]

- - - - -

August 6, 1863
Paris, Texas

Mrs. Margarette A. Harris
St. Clair Cty., Missouri refugee

"... We are living well this summer as we have plenty of vegetables melons and beef, also a little fruit." [12]

- - - - -

August 7, 1863
Fort Morgan, Alabama

Lt. Colonel James Williams
21st Alabama Infantry

"Dear Lizzy:
All females except laundresses are ordered away from the fort, and we are clearing the decks for action: ... I believe Admiral Farragut will find Ft. Morgan a refractory nut to crack when he has a mind to try it ...

I have heard that the Sub-marine is off for Charleston, I suppose Dixon went with it. – with favorable circumstances it will succeed, and I hope to hear a report of its success ...
Williams" [13]

(ed: James is referring to the submarine Hunley *which was built in Mobile and will attack and sink the U. S. S.* Housatonic *on February 17, 1864.)*

- - - - -

August 7, 1863
Meherrin, Virginia

Mrs. Mary Watkins
Farm wife

"My Darling Husband
... I wish so often that you could come home and get some peaches and vegetables and fatten up a little. I am so impatient for this war to end though I see no prospect of peace ... Do you reckon the war will last our lifetime?

I have taken a right bad cold this warm weather and have been so hoarse I could hardly speak.... Emmie and Minnie are both well and just as sunburnt as they can be. I am afraid you would not know Emmie she is so black. Minnie stays out just as much but her skin does not burn half as badly as Emmies.... Cousin John Knight spent the day with us Thursday. he said he promised you that he would come to see me and the children before he went back.... You wrote something about your wheat. Mr. George Redd I believe wants fifty bushels for seed. It is a right poor crop I am afraid, was late and took the rust. Mr Anderson says he will stay until the crops are secured and will try to get you another overseer.... Mama seems at a loss to know what to do about keeping Mr. Baker next year he asks $500 wages. Uncle Joe has engaged his for another year for $250 ...

Aug. 8th ... Oh I want to see you so bad. I have so much to talk to you about that I can't write. I am so glad that you write so often I ought to be ashamed of myself for not writing oftener, will try to do better hereafter.
Your own
Mary" [14]

(ed: Rust is a fungus that can attack several of the grain crops and cause great damage. "A parasitic fungi of the order Uredinales that are injurious to a wide variety of plants and are characterized by reddish or brownish spots on leaves, stems and other parts.") [15]

- - - - -

August 8, 1863 — Mr. Jacob R. Hildebrand
Augusta County, Virginia — Farmer

"There was a sale of cattle Horses and mules at Fishersville by some men from Clark county didn't sell anything but the cattle yearlings sold for $80 to $100 Gideon helped Wm S. Hanger to thrash quite a rain this P. M. Mr Stone came here to buy my Coffman place, offered me $8000 for 63 acres, Frank Myers asked him $10000 for 130 acres" [16]

(ed: Jacob maintained a wonderful diary and has some unique features to his writing style. Instead of using periods Jacob leaves a major gap. Sometimes he uses periods and other times he avoids them as you can note above with Wm S. Hanger and Mr Stone.)

- - - - -

August 8, 1863
Camp near Little Rock, Arkansas

Captain Griffin Frost
Co. A – 2nd Missouri Infantry

"Had a general review of Parsons's Brigade to-day. The soldiers made a splendid appearance, and marched well; but they are still deserting every night. There must be a change ... A few in the field cannot do it all, while the majority are at home taking the oath and scrambling to save their property. Who saves our property while we are offering our lives for the liberty of all?" [17]

(ed: In particular the soldiers from Missouri, Kentucky, Maryland (states totally under Union control) can desert from the Confederate forces and return to their home counties and take the Federal Oath of Allegiance. They are then done with the conflict and can return to their families and their occupations. In effect they have surrendered and sworn that they are loyal to the Union and will not take up arms against her or support the Confederate cause.)

- - - - -

August 8, 1863
Mobile, Alabama

Lt. George W. Gift
C. S. S. *Gaines*

"My Dear Ellen [Shackelford]
I have been employed for the past day or two in hoisting out of the water and sending away toward Charleston a very curious machine for destroying vessels, and which I certainly regard as the most important invention to us that could have been made. It is a submarine boat which is propelled with ease and rapidity underwater. But inasmuch as it will become in a very short time one of the great celebrities in the art of defense and attack on floating objects I will run the risk of inflicting a short description.

In the first place imagine a high pressure steam boiler, not quite round, say 4 feet in diameter in one way and 3 ½ feet the other – draw one end of the boiler down to a sharp wedge shaped point. On the bottom of the boat is riveted an iron keel weighing 4000 pounds. On top and opposite the keel is placed two man hole plates or hatches with heavy tops. They are just large enough for a man to go in and out. At one end is fitted a very neat little propeller 3 ½ feet in diameter worked by men sitting in the boat and turning the shaft by hand cranks. She also has a rudder and steering apparatus.

Embarked and under ordinary circumstances with men and ballast she floats about half way out of the water and resembles a whale. But when it is necessary to go underwater there are compartments into which water is allowed to flow, which causes the boat to sink to any required depth, the same being accurately indicated by a column of mercury.

Behind the boat at a distance of 100 to 150 feet is towed a plank and under that plank is attached a torpedo with say 100 pounds of powder. I saw them explode a vessel as an experiment. They approached to within about fifty yards from her keeping the man holes just above water. At that distance the submarine sank down and in a few minutes made her appearance on the other side of the vessel.

I consider it a perfect success! And in the hands of a bold man would be equal to the task of destroying every ironclad the enemy has off Morris Island [Charleston, S. C.] in a single night. It is perfectly safe and perfectly sure. She will be ready for service in Charleston by the 18th or 20th of this month." [18]

(ed: The problem with towing an explosive device became evident when they paused one night in the Charleston harbor and the torpedo came floating into the towing vessel and disaster was narrowly averted. They redesigned the delivery system by attaching the torpedo to a spar in front of the submarine. The spar would be driven into the hull of the victim, the submarine would back off leaving part of the spar and the torpedo attached to the enemy vessel, and a lanyard would pay out until it reached a predetermined distance and it would detonate the torpedo.)

- - - - -

August 8, 1863
Glade Springs, Virginia

Sergeant Robert Watson
Co. K – 7th Florida Infantry

"There is a revival going on in the Regt. and half of them are being converted.... The preacher is a regular "snorter" and can be heard for miles off yelling out Hell fire and brimstone which just suits the "Crackers." A good sensible preacher could not get along with them ..." [19]

- - - - -

August 9, 1863
Camp

Corporal Tally Simpson
Co. A – 3rd S. Carolina Infantry

"Dear Sister
... Genl Lee has seen fit to begin the furloughing system again. Two of every hundred are furloughed. They are chosen from those who have never been home since their enlistment. I having had one, it will be a long time before I can even get the privilege of drawing. Even then I stand a very poor chance, for I am always unfortunate of gaining anything by chance. Last winter when I was out of clothes and blankets and had to draw straws ... I ... came out the "little end of the horn." The furloughs are only 21 days long for South Carolinians. That will give them only about twelve days at home, a very short time.... Oh that this unholy war would be ended, and we be permitted to return to our loved ones at home! ...
Your affect bro
T. N. S." [20]

- - - - -

August 9, 1863
Fredericksburg, Virginia

Private William Corson
Co. G – 3rd Virginia Cavalry

"[Jennie] ... The once beautiful and flourishing city of F is for the most part in ruins and nearly deserted. What few of its inhabitants remain remind me of ... the dispersed builders of Babell ... I cannot see how the poor creatures subsist for everything in the way of provisions is exceedingly high and scarce.

A meal of victuals costs three dollars in town and mean whiskey is retailing at one dollar and a half per dose. I hope my regiment will not be kept here much longer, for if it is the men will all starve to death or get so poor and light that a hard wind will blow us all over the river in the Yankee lines. It is impossible to buy anything in twenty miles of this place and our rations is just three crackers and a greasy spot a day. Our horses look like graven images and are living on … the hope of a better day coming." [21]

- - - - -

August 10, 1863	Miss. Louisa Perry
Harrison County, Texas	Farm girl

"My dear Brother [Theophilus]
… Our darling sister Geneva died night before last of Deptheria. yesterday evening she was laid … by the side of her little brother Joe Willie of whom she talked so much while sick…. She asked for Mother one evening and said she was going to die, she was perfectly resigned…. the night before she died she told all Good bye…. Sister Harriet went over to Dr. Perry's this evening to get some medicine for Sugar Lumpy, she is looking right badly. Your children are both very sweet and loveable almost as much so as their father…. I hope it will not be long before you can procure a furlough to come home. Papa is going to send Kearney, Isam, & Anthony down to Shreveport Wednesday to work on the fortifications. I hope you & bro Hugh may live to come home when the war terminates.
May the God of battles shield you from danger is my fervent prayer.
Your devoted sister
Louisa" [22]

(ed: Martha (Sugar Lumpy) died on August 12 from unmentioned causes. Lt. Jesse Person, Harriet's brother, who served in Co. E of the 1st North Carolina Cavalry was killed at Gettysburg on July 3, 1863. Harriet will not know until she receives the news from her sister Tempie in a letter dated November 14, 1863. Theophilus's brother, Hugh, is wounded at Gettysburg and will survive. Word of Hugh and his condition is also delayed in reaching Texas. Theophilus will get his furlough and spend late August and early September with the family. He departs to return and falls ill and is forced to return to Harrison County, Texas to recover.)

(ed: Diptheria is an acute contagious disease caused by infection with the bacillus Cornebacterium diphtheriae. It is characterized by the formation of false membrances in the throat and other air passages causing difficult breathing, high fever, and weakness.) [23]

- - - - -

August 12, 1863
Cargo Manifest

Venus
Charles Muney – Master

"365 tons from St. George's Bermuda to Nassau

600 cases rifles, 300 boxes cartridges, 1 puncheon rum (100 gallons)." [24]

- - - - -

August 12, 1863
Richmond, Virginia

Cadet Hubbard Minor
Confederate Naval Academy

"... when I got on board of the *Patrick Henry* it was quite late & I now am a little disappointed but I hope [everything] will be all right soon. I sleep tonight in a hammock." [25]

(ed: Hubbard is a brand new cadet at the Confederate Naval Academy in Richmond and has just reported aboard the training ship.)

- - - - -

August 12, 1863
near Orange Court House, Virginia

Private Louis Leon
Co. C – 1st N. Carolina Infantry

"We had a very severe storm to-day which killed two men and hurt several of our brigade. It tore up trees and played smash in general." [26]

- - - - -

August 13, 1863
Camp

Corporal Tally Simpson
Co. A – 3rd S. Carolina Infantry

"My dear Aunt
… Preaching is going on regularly. Every morning at 9 o'clock one of the regimental chaplains holds forth in a place convenient for the whole brigade. Mr C is my favorite. He is an excellent man and an excellent preacher and is bound to do a good deal of good in his present field of action. The Rev Dr Stiles of Geo[rgia], the great army revivalist, has preached for us twice. He is a very able man and preached two elegant sermons….

There is no news from the Northern army. They are lying on the other side of the river, recruiting and perhaps waiting for reinforcements….

I would like to know what you are all doing at this very moment. Eating water melons and cantaloupes perhaps. Oh how I would like to be there to enjoy them with you….

Your ever aff nephew
T. N. Simpson" [27]

(ed: The Rev. Joseph C. Stiles, D. D. was one of the most able and respected Presbyterian ministers and evangelists of the time. Despite being 70 years of age, at the start of the war, he tirelessly worked the camps of the Southern armies during the war.) [28]

- - - - -

August 13, 1863
Orange Courthouse, Virginia

Sergeamt Benjamin F. Porter
Co. E – 11th Alabama Infantry

"Dear Ma …
There has been two sermons a day for several days in this Regt., one baptist, one methodist minister. Indead there is a glorious work going on among the soldiers. Two of my company has joined the Baptist, Wall & Ward. They have gon to receive Baptism…. Ma, I no you prey for me.
Benj. F. Porter" [29]

- - - - -

August 13, 1863 Miss. Kate Cummings
Cherokee Springs, Georgia Hospital Matron

"The hospital covers about thirty acres of ground, abound in mineral springs, and in nice shady nooks.

We visited the wards; there are only three, although there are accommodations for five hundred patients; they are composed of tents which are tastefully arranged. Each ward is separate, having a wide street in the center, shaded by magnificent trees.

At present the hospital is filled with patients, a few of whom are sick enough to be confined to their beds; they are mostly chronic cases, sent here for the benefit of the water....

As this has been a watering-place, there are quite a number of small wooden houses on it ... Each ward has one connected with it ... One is a linen and ironing-room, of which a man has charge; besides, there is a woman who does the mending and part of the ironing.

The patients and attendants have their washing and ironing done in the hospital. I wonder what "*head-quarters*" would say if this were known. It seems strange that in one hospital can be done what is unlawful in another.

... There is also a fine bakery, and a convalescent kitchen, in which are large boilers for cooking ... We next visited the kitchen, where the diet for the very sick is prepared; in which are four stoves and as many cooks, besides a head one ... There are no less than two hundred and fifty patients fed every day from this kitchen....

General Bragg is in this hospital sick. He has his head-quarters ... here. Mrs. Bragg is with the general." [30]

(ed: Kate noted in her August 12 entry, "We have always made a rule of wearing the simplest kind of dress, as we think any other kind sadly out of place in the hospital; calico or homespun is the only dress fit to wear, but to get the former is a rare treat.")

- - - - -

August 14, 1863
Orange Court House, Virginia

Corporal Benjamin Freeman
Co. K – 44th N. Carolina Infantry

"Dear Farther
I this morning take the opportunity … to let you know that I am well … I received your letter day before yesterday and was glad to here from you all and that you all was well … This evening I wish I was at home so I can eat Water Mellons and Apples and Peaches. I have not see but [few] ripe Peaches this year. I have not seen a Water Mellon this year
all of the boys are well Mr. Stark is complaining of Disentry it is very bad here now … We got plenty of rations to eat now…. I am glad to here your corn looks so good … Give my love to all the Children … you must excuse bad writing but I am writing in a hurry. Write soon Direct you letters to Richmond Va
Co K 44th Regt NCT Corpl B H Freeman" [31]

- - - - -

August 15, 1863
near Orange Court House, Virginia

Private Bryant Folsom
Co. C – 26th Georgia Infantry

"… suppose you would like to know what we had to eat … we had some cold beaf and we hashed it up … we had some warm biiscuits and some cold ones … and I will tel you … for breakfast we had a oven of beef stewed and sorty baked together and we had fine chance of gravy … and buiscuits … a verey good breadkfast …" [32]

- - - - -

August 15, 1863	Mrs. Margarette A. Harris
Paris, Texas	St. Clair Cty., Missouri refugee

"I must confess that you are very definite as to the time that you will come to Texas … "This fall, winter, spring or sometime."; think you ought to come this fall … Oh that this war would end …" [33]

- - - - -

August 16, 1863	Lt. Colonel James Williams
Fort Morgan, Alabama	21st Alabama Infantry

"Dear Lizzy:
It is Sunday morning, the rain is pouring down aslant in torrents. A soldier who has managed to be caught in it … is rushing for the quarters as if he expected to save his clothes from a wetting, but a plunge in the bay wouldn't wet him more than he is now …

The *Vivian* & *Lizzy Davis* got out safely this week. The first may make the trip, but it seems the height of absurdity to send out such a snail as the *Davis* to run the blockade – if she goes through safely we may well say the race is not to the swift.
Williams" [34]

(ed: The Alice Vivian *was captured coming out of Mobile Bay on August 16. She was a converted wooden, side wheeled Alabama river packet. She was placed into service in June and had made one successful round-trip to Havana. The* Lizzie Davis *also had a short career as she was captured on a return trip from Havana on September 16. She was also a wooden side wheeler 115' in length, 60' shorter than* Alice Vivian.*)* [35]

- - - - -

August 16, 1863
Richmond, Virginia

Mr. John B. Jones
Clerk, War Department

"My tomatoes are maturing slowly, but there will be an abundance, saving me $10 per week for ten weeks." [36]

- - - - -

Bon Secours Bay, Alabama

Salt Manufacturing

A major Salt work was in the Bon Secours Bay on the east shore of Mobile Bay. The works consisted of "55 furnaces, averaging 18 pans or pots each, making a total of near 1000 ... The whole works covering an area of a square mile ... [and] averaging 2000 bushels of salt per day." [37]

- - - - -

August 17, 1863
Brandon, Mississippi

Sergeant Elijah Y. Fleming
Wood's Mississippi Cavalry

"Dear Dicie
... Your letter informed me that you are still on foot. I was much surprised to hear it. I had no idea you would keep up a week after I left....I have never seen as many flies as there are about camp. At this time, one cannot sleep or read with any satisfaction.... I will be glad when winter comes on their account. Do you all ever have any peach and apple pies? How often I wished for some since I left. We get some peaches occasionally....

You said you were needing $25. I will send it to you the first chance that offers.... Remember me to the little ones often.
... with much love
E Y Fleming" [38]

(ed: Mary was about to deliver their third child when Elijah departed to return to his cavalry unit. He is very surprised that she is still moving around. In fact, the

baby was born on August 17th while Elijah was writing this letter. Dicie is taken from Mary's middle name "Ledecia.")

- - - - -

Late August
Chester, Pennsylvania

Private Joseph P. Bashaw
Co. I – 7th Tennessee Infantry

"We had the very best treatment, fed well, furnished clean underwear once a week, and were required to bathe when we changed clothing.... They kept us about six weeks, then sent us back to "Dixie." I got a [3 month] furlough until exchanged ... I had gotten completely well and went back to the Army some time in early winter." [39]

- - - - -

August 17, 1863
St. George's, Bermuda

Major Smith Stansbury
C. S. Ordnance Depot

"Mr. J T Bourne
Sir: Please load the Steamer *Ella & Annie* at Mrs. Todd's Wharf with. – 500 Cases Austrian Rifles, 480 Boxes Austrian Ammunition, 20 Carboys Nitric Acid, 10 Carboys Sulphuric Acid, 10 Carboys Muriatic Acid, 1 Case Gum Shellac, 5 Case Surgical Instruments, 50 Cases Saddlery, Emery, 10 Kegs Horse Shoes." [40]

(ed: A carboy is a large glass bottle, usually encased in a protective basket or crate. Carboys are used to hold and ship various corrosive liquids.) [41]

- - - - -

August 17, 1863
Richmond, Virginia

Cadet Hubbard Minor
Confederate Naval Academy

"Studied Hard all day long & will in a day or two catch up with the class for which I am now studying. This morning went in and had a nice swim & also got a single Drawer cut large enough to [fit] the few clothes I have & put most of them together with [my] smoking Tobacco which I find it quite difficult to keep under lock & key. We have it a great deal worse on board than I expected & some times I wish I were still in the army ..." [42]

- - - - -

August 18, 1863
Hanover Academy Hospital
20 miles from Richmond, Virginia

Captain Richard Watkins
Co. K – 3rd Virginia Cavalry

"Darling
Where do you reckon I am? At Hanover Academy Hospital, and a patient. Not very sick just too unwell to do duty.... I was taken with a violent cold about the same time that you were. Was obliged to report sick for two or three days when I improved so much that I again took charge of the company. The cold returned upon me accompanied with severe headaches and some fever.... the cold still hangs on ... applied to Surgeon Leigh to be sent to Farmville Hospital as others had been heretofore. He said that it has lately been forbidden and that the order of Genl Lee now were that the cavalry sick should all be sent this place and the infantry to Staunton that I could not even be sent to Richmond. Accordingly I came here and am happy to inform you that it is decidedly the most comfortable & apparently best regulated Confederate Hospital that I have ever seen. Everything neat & clean & well arranged & the meals very nicely prepared indeed with the best bread and the freshest coolest water I ever saw in a Hospital. The Academy is a large frame building two stories surrounded by many little cabins ... Some distance from the main building are two single story oblong buildings which were formerly used as debating Halls for the students. These two constitute the officers Ward and from the appearance of the patients you would not judge that there was a sick man among them. All looking as well and cheerful & well content as any men I ever saw. I do not believe there is a sick man among them at all....
Yr own
Richard" [43]

(ed: Richard was transferred to Farmville General and released to recuperate at home with Mary and his family. He checked in with the hospital periodically. Richard was able to spend two weeks with Mary, Emmie, Minnie and his new daughter, Mary P.)

- - - - -

August 19, 1863 Lt. Jesse P. Bates
Near Morton, Mississippi Co. G – 9th Texas Infantry

"My dear wife, … I am well at present … I have not received any letter from you … since the 24th of Feb and I have certainly sent you 12 or 15 since that time…. The whole army appears to be in fine health … We have had an abundance of rain lately and everything that can grow is doing fine…. I expect to send this to you by Capt. Wm. A. Wortham as he has been discharged by reason of disability….

The price of vegetables and produce are very high at present. I saw a watermelon to day was $18.00 and now while I write I hear $20.00 was asked for one. Mutton is $1.00 per pound and flour sells at $1.00 per pound and peaches and apples get as hy as $1.50 to $2.00 to $3.00 per doz…. May God bless you and keep you from harm is my prayer. So farewell for present.
Jesse P Bates" [44]

- - - - -

August 19, 1863 *Phantom*
Cargo Manifest S. G. Porter – Master

"266 tons from St. George's, Bermuda to St. John, N. B.

130 pieces pig iron, 402 cases cartridges, 20 cases steel, 100 ingots tin, 501 boxes sheet tin, 284 pigs lead, 100 bundles sheet iron, 97 cases rifles, 45 bales bagging." [45]

- - - - -

August 19, 1863
Macon, Georgia

Macon Daily Telegraph

$25 REWARD

"Ranaway on Friday, the 14th instant, A NEGRO WOMAN, by the name of Rachel, about 24 years old, of copper color, has been sick with typhoid fever, and seems to be laboring under some debility from its effects. She is doubtless endeavoring to make her way to Columbus, Georgia or Opelika, Alabama where she came from. She has some children at the latter place. The above reward will be paid for her delivery to me or J. B. Smith & Co., Macon.

F. W. JOHNSON" [46]

- - - - -

August 20, 1863
Orange County, Virginia

Private Charles W. Thomas
Co. B – 56th Virginia Infantry

"Dear Wife; I want you to send me some socks and my flannel Shirts and a piece of soap and a par of pants … put me a apple in the bundle too…. You must let me no how your cow are getting along. How much milk she gives and if your calf is likely or not…. Adieu, I am as ever your husband C W Thomas" [47]

- - - - -

August 20, 1863
Augusta County, Virginia

Mr. Jacob L. Hildebrand
Farmer

"The day has been set apart by President Davis as a day of fasting & humiliation & prayer It was observed by the Menonite church. The first thought that struck me this morning when I awoke was the comprehensibility of God, he who has been from all eternity, who has had no beginning of days he who never was created but is the creator of all things If we think back millions of years to find out his beginning, we are still as far from the beginning at is still Eternity he has neither beginnings of days nor End of Life Today old man Wheeler was buryed his age 72 years 6 months & 27 days" [48]

(ed: Bishop Samuel Coffman of the Middle District of the Virginia Mennonite Conference was critical of such worship since it involved the government. The Hildebrand Mennonite Church observed the day thereby continuing a running controversy with Bishop Coffman that began in January of this year.) [49]

- - - - -

Undated – Late August | Private Joshua M. Dickson
8 miles east of Ripley, Mississippi | Co. G – 21st Tennessee Infantry

"Aug, 1863 I was captured 8 miles east of Ripley, Miss … sent to Johnston Island … We suffered very much there from hunger. For breakfast had one cup of tea and a very small slice of bread. Dinner one table spoon full of beans and one cup of tea without bread, if you got any supper you had to save part of your dinner. Some of the prisoners ate rats to keep from starving, one day a fine fat dog came into camp – it was drawn, cooked and eaten." [50]

(ed: Johnson's Island Prison is on the shore of Lake Erie just west of Sandusky, Ohio. Johnson's Island was an "officer's prison" so it is odd that Private Dickson would be sent to this prison.)

- - - - -

August 21, 1863 | Mr. John T. Bourne
St. George's, Bermuda | C. S. Commercial Agent

"Ed. Lawrence & Co., Liverpool
Gentlemen: - I have the pleasure of sending you acct. of Disbursement sh. *Banshee* amt. to L734.95 and have to advise drafts on you to that amount.

The *Milicent* [for Liverpool] will leave early next week with *Banshee's* cotton and please effect insurance.

I am happy to inform you that the *R E Lee* arrived here a day or two ago and reports that the *Banshee* arrived in safe after a passage of 4 days. The charges on reshipment of cotton will follow cargo." [51]

- - - - -

August 21, 1863
Enroute to Knoxville

Sergeant Robert Watson
Co. K – 7th Florida Infantry

"I slept on top of the [railroad] car as there was no room inside. I spread my blanket and Alfred Lowe and I lay on it and covered with his. I put my cartridge box under my head for a pillow. During the night I awoke and found that my blanket and cartridge box was gone and Alfred's hat also. The car shook so much I could not get to sleep any more for I was afraid of being shook off." [52]

- - - - -

August 22, 1863
Sulphur Springs, North Carolina

Mrs. Cornelia Henry
Farm wife

"I finished Pinck's shirt after dinner & helped Harrie make cider. He got the press up & it done finely. We made a fine chance. Mr. Peake left this morning for Greenville, Tenn. He is going to buy salt. He will be back in a week or so. I have heard nothing from Mr. Henry since he left. Wish I could hear something of him. Uncle Sam & others killed a beef this evening. A very nice young beef. We have had some watermellons this week. They were not very good." [53]

- - - - -

August 22, 1863
Charleston, South Carolina

Miss. Emma Holmes
Resident

" … He [General Gillmore on Morris Island] has turned his guns against a city filled with old men, women, children and hospitals. I think I must have woke about three o'clock. Mr. Bull called out soon after to Rosa to listen to the shelling. It was a most peculiar fearful sound – the sharp scream or whiz through the air, and they sounded exactly as if coming over the house.

I was startled and much excited, but not frightened, but it produced a very solemn feeling. I lay with the window partly open every moment expecting a shell might burst and kill me. I must have lain thus a least three quarters of an hour, when Rosa and Becca came down to my room so thoroughly scared they did not know what to do. I had never seen or heard of Rosa's being scared before, but this time she acknowledged she was so scared that her strength had utterly failed her, every limb ached, and she thought if she remained she would have fever.

She declared she could not move while the shelling was going on, for she was afraid to go upstairs. Her feeling had been similar to mine. She said she did not feel fit to die, yet every moment expected death … " [54]

(ed: Emma and her two sisters gathered a few basic possessions and fled to Columbia on the 23rd to seek shelter with relatives.)

- - - - -

August 22, 1863 — Corporal Benjamin Freeman
Camp near Orange CH, Virginia — Co. K – 44th N. Carolina Infantry

"Dear Farther
… your [letter] on the 19th … found me well except my bowels, it is the cuss of all of now – I never saw the like of it in my life … I have not seen but two or three Water Mellons this Somer I saw one of them Sell this morning at 5 dollars abot the size of my head Apples about the size of Walnut 1.00 a dozen. Irash potatoes 12 and 16 dollars a bushel Onions 25 cents a head Chickens little larger than a Partridge 1 1-2 to 2 1-2 dollar apiece. There is a great many sick in the Regiment our Company had 16 yesterday on the Sick list I think and the same this morning. There is 5 or 6 in my tent complaining … I was glad to hear your corn looks so well I should like to be at home to eat some Water melons. I don't expect to get a chance to come home soon … Our Band

of Music has come from Richmond now we have music in our Regiment now They practice every day I will come to a close by saying write soon and direct your letters to Richmond
Corpl B H Freeman to W H Freeman Louisburg Franklin County" [55]

- - - - -

August 22, 1863
Canton, Mississippi

Major James C. Bates
9th Texas Cavalry

"My Dear Ma:
… I got up this morning minus a pocket book & near seven hundred dollars in sach[el], and my finest horse. I am satisfied a scoundrel who deserted took my horse, but ca'nt tell where my money went – several pocket books were stolen. Ten men from my old Co are missing this morning … " [56]

- - - - -

August 23, 1863
Forsyth County, North Carolina

Mrs. Temperance Tise
Farm wife

"To Your Exelency, Z B Vance
Sir, Beliving you to be a true friend to the Soldiers their wives and Mothers … I being a Widdow and a Mother of a Soldier, I earnestly beg of you a favor … My Husband Died a few months ago and the Conscription Act has taken my only Son and only help from me – I further more declare that my Son in plain words is not a man and he is not able to stand the hardships of war … I beg that you will permit my Son William R Tise To return home and if others are needing to fill his place, that you will take those extortioners who are extortioning on the verry lives of the poor Soldiers wives and widowed Mothers. I will mention one Cavine Hine who is public tanner in Salem – I went to him a day or two ago … barefooted and tried to get enough leather to make me a pair of shoes no he said … I asked then if I could not get enough to half sole a pair of shoes – no I could not … I know he has got leather, but none for poor Soldiers wives and widows. This man I think Gov is a very suitable man to take my sons place in the army … I will mention another instance …

a poor crippled soldier who had been fighting for this same Cavine Hine, and who had one arm and one leg shot off went to this man to get leather enough to make straps for a wooden stump … and Hines charged the poor crippled Soldier $2.75 Saying he would drop five cents because he was a Soldier. My son is in the 10 eng N C Regiment What I have told you in regard to my Son is true … Please write to me as soon as possible whether there is any chance of my Son's getting to come home and if you will let him off Yo will Please write to Col Pool or Capt Cogdell as the case may require
So nomore from your obedient
Servent
Temperance Tise" [57]

- - - - -

August 23, 1863
Richmond, Virginia

Colonel Robert Kean
Confederate Bureau of War

"The part of the Confederacy we still hold is in the shape of a boot, of which middle Virginia, North Carolina, South Carolina, and Georgia to the Gulf is the leg and Alabama and part of Mississippi the foot; besides this, the Trans-Mississippi. Nearly half the whole area is in the hands of the enemy, or outside of our lines. We have never substantially recovered any territory once lost, have never retaken any important strategic point once occupied. I do not regard Louisiana as yet recovered, nor Winchester [Virginia] as constituting an exception. Galveston comes nearest to it. The signal scouts below report that yellow fever has appeared at Norfolk and Portsmouth, also in the enemy's camp in Yorktown; that the latter has been removed to Newport News. An epidemic like that of 1857 might do us a good deal of good all along the coast." [58]

(ed: Yellow Fever, or Yellow Jack, is an acute infectious disease of subtropical areas caused by a filterable virus transmitted by the mosquito. The disease is characterized by jaundice and dark-colored vomit resulting from internal hemorrhages.) [59]

- - - - -

August 23, 1863
Orange Court House, Virginia.

Private Marion H. Fitzpatrick
Co. K – 45th Georgia Infantry

"Dear Amanda,
... Cout I wish you to send me some sewing thread. I have used all that black you gave me and the white ball, of which I have a good deal yet, is too coarse for any of the needles I have now. Also a little red pepper, not much, for I shall loose it. Do not send any clothes. I have as many as I can take care of. I patch my clothes and darn my socks regular and they last more than twice as long by it. I also wash them regular now and can wash as clean and nice as anybody. We draw soap and I bought 50 cts worth so I have a good supply now... May God bless you. Write soon and write a long letter. Pray for me.
Your husband,
M. H. Fitzpatrick" [60]

(ed: Cout is Marion's private nickname for Amanda. Perhaps it is supposed to be "coot" which is a small aquatic bird.)

- - - - -

August 23, 1863
Washington, D. C.

Miss. Kate Sperry
Winchester resident

"Will go back to Baltimore tomorrow – it's too hot and dusty here – never saw such a place for dust and nigger soldiers – beg their pardon – *unbleached regiments, Ethiopian Brigades* – they are flourishing. All the merchants here in favour of South – too hot to go to church today – haven't even been to Capitol – the dome is almost completed – in fact only wants the statue of *Goddess Liberty* to render it *charming*." [61]

(ed: Kate has gotten a pass and gone to visit relatives in Baltimore and Washington City in hopes of gaining some monies, left to her grandmother, to assist with the desperate financial situation in Winchester. The money is tied up in the estate which has not been administered. Kate returned to Winchester in early September.) [62]

- - - - -

August 26, 1863
St. George's, Bermuda

Mr. John T. Bourne
C. S. Commercial Agent

"Jn. B. Lafette Esq., Nassau
Dear Sir: - … The steamer *Elizabeth* arrived safely, landed her cotton … Str. *Eugenie* arrived in port yesterday with 400 bales cotton. – Str. *Spaulding* at Charleston, *Cornubia, Venus, Gibraltar, Advance* at Wilmington." [63]

- - - - -

August 26, 1863
Richmond, Virginia

Mrs. Judith McGuire
Nurse

"A week ago I was called to Camp Jackson to nurse … the hospital is very extensive and in beautiful order. It is under … Surgeon Hancock …. [Today] I heard a Methodist chaplain preach to several hundred soldiers." [64]

- - - - -

August 27, 1863
Orange Courthouse, Virginia

Sergeant Benjamin F. Porter
Co. E – 11th Alabama Infantry

"Dear Ma … I will not fail to state a few incidences of Desertion in our army, none though in my Regt. All as far as I am able to learn was caused by ill treatment from officers or by letters of discouragement from their relations at home. O, what a thought. God forbid that any of our friends should express sutch sentiments as would caus our brave soldiers to quit the fielde at so criical a moment as this. Almost every one who has been shot for desertion, say that their parents was the final caus of thir desertion.

I hope I will not heare of no more … Ma, do not let any one see what I have saide about desertion. I feare it will make them uneasy.

Ma, … I was baptized on the 21st inst. by the chaplin of our Regt. Lut Atchison was baptized the same time. I thank god I have been able to over come this cross…. Every serious thought, every prayer, I saw my duty but failed to obey. Some 35 or 40 have joined the church, both Baptist & Methodists.

… Prey for us …
B. F. Porter" [65]

- - - - -

August 29, 1863
Augusta County, Virginia

Mr. Jacob R. Hildebrand
Farmer

"Quite a rain last night Gideon & others Wyers cave on a pleasure Excursion spread the most of our flax, sugar is worth $200 per lb coffee $5 lb flour $40 per barrel cotton yarn from $20 to $25 per bunch cotton cloth $2.00 per yd chickens are worth $2.00 apiece Brandy $5 per pint." [66]

- - - - -

August 29, 1863
Camp Texas, Louisiana

Captain Elijah P. Petty
Co. F – 17th Texas Infantry

"My Dear Wife
… I sent you by Col Jones a lot of peach seeds. They are from the finest peaches I have ever seen in Texas and as fine I believe as I have ever seen anywhere. The peaches were as large as my fist and perfectly luscious – please plant them with care away from other seed. Keep the seed of the free stone separated from the others. The reason is the seeds in part belongs to another man who will want some of the young trees … I also here in send you some tame indigo seed. It grows finely here and will do so I suppose with you … C. S. money here rates at 15 to 1 gold & is growing worse daily … I was paid up to 1st Sept 4 months making $520 [sent $450 home]…. Kisses & love to all.
Your truly
E P Petty" [67]

- - - - -

August, 1863 Blockade Runners Arriving in Wilmington, North Carolina

Ship	Date	From
"*Margaret & Jessie*	August 8	Nassau
General Beauregard	August 8	Nassau
Hansa	August 8	Nassau
Arabian	August 11	Nassau
Banshee I	August 12	Bermuda
Venus	August 16	Bermuda
Eugenie	August 17	Bermuda
Mary Ann	August 18	Bermuda
Cornubia	August 18	Bermuda
Advance	August 19	Bermuda
Flora II	August 22	Bermuda
Gibraltar (Sumter)	August 23	Bermuda
Phantom	August 23	Bermuda
Elizabeth (Atlantic)	August 26	Bermuda" [68]

(ed: "All dates are approximate based on newspaper accounts, consul reports and port records. The names in parenthesis refer to the vessel's name when it first ran the blockade.")

- - - - -

August 29, 1863
Orange, Texas

Private J. N. Scott
Co. H – 20th Texas Infantry

"To Capt Edmond Turner
Sir I desire to put in a substitute and pray that I be allowed to do so.
... About the first of May I was taken with severe pains in my legs ... which completely prostrated me about the 22nd of May ... I have been unable to perform duty for 70 days and therein the certificate of the Surgeon that I had Rheumatism ... am utterly incapable of performing a long or forced march.... I have a large and helpless family consisting of a wife and ten children and

nineteen negroes ... my oldest son near 18 years old will join the army as soon as I confirm him an outfit for cavalry and when he is gone there will be no one left capable of attending to the business of the place. I am or have been acting as agent for my Mother and Mother in law both widows ... " [69]

(ed: The application and his substitute were approved and accepted. As manpower needs became more desperate in 1864 he was called back into the service. In 1864 and 1865 he was stationed at Fort Magruder in Galveston, Texas, as part of the garrison.)

- - - - -

August 29, 1863 — Lt. Charles Hasker
Fort Johnson, Charleston, S. Carolina — *H. L. Hunley*

"I was anxious to see how the boat worked and volunteered as one of the crew. We were lying astern of the steamer *Etowah*, near Fort Johnson, in Charleston Harbor. Lieutenant Payne, who had charge got fowled in the manhole by the hawser and in trying to clear himself got his foot on the lever which controlled the fins. He had just previously given the order to go ahead. The boat made a dive while the manholes were open and filled rapidly. Payne got out of the forward hole and two others out of the aft hole. Six of us went down with the boat. I had to get over the bar which connected the fins and through the [forward] manhole. This I did by forcing myself through the column of water which was rapidly filling the boat. The manhole plate came down on my back, but I worked my way out until my left leg was caught by the plate, pressing the calf of my leg in two. Held in this manner I was carried to the bottom in 42 feet of water. When the boat touched bottom I felt the pressure relax. Stooping down I took hold of the manhole plate, drew out my wounded limb, and swam to the surface. Five men were drowned on this occasion. I was the only man that went to the bottom with the 'Fish Boat' and came up to tell the tale." [70]

(ed: Initially Mr. James McClintock, one of the designers of the H. L. Hunley, *captained the boat. Military authorities deemed him too cautious and replaced McClintock and his civilian crew with a C. S. Naval crew. They were not as familiar with the operational characteristics of the boat.)*

- - - - -

August 29, 1863 — Mrs. Catherine Edmondston
Halifax County, North Carolina — Farm wife

"The [Raleigh] *Standard* newspaper does its best to induce them to penetrate the heart of N C by its advocacy of reconstruction, its abuse of Mr Davis, its insisting that the masses in the country are sick of war, & ready for peace on any terms, complaining, grumbling, and abusing everything & everybody generally in the Southern Confederacy. I wish the people of Raleigh would fling the types and presses into the streets & take Holden the Editor … & send [him] into the enemy's lines …

Holden, a miserable illegitimate son of a worthless woman, to presume to dictate laws or public opinion to the gentlemen of North Carolina. Such assurance!" [71]

- - - - -

August 30, 1863 — Mrs. Mary Edmondson
Phillips County, Arkansas — Farm wife

"My letter commenced the 11th has not found a messenger to Little Rock yet…. We hear rumors of fighting on the White River … more Federal reinforcements. Alas, our poor little army will be swallowed up…. There is another rumor that Lee has defeated Meade … but the reading of Federal papers distresses me in their tone of confidence, cruelty, and contempt." [72]

- - - - -

August 31, 1863 — Mr. Samuel Robbins
Shugulak, Mississippi — Refugee from St. Louis

"Dear Son
I have just received a letter from home by way of Havanna. They are all well and undisturbed. Em is enjoying herself in Kentucky. I am going to

Columbus, Miss. this morning to spend a week or ten days … I have not had but one letter from you since I saw you at Mobile. Did you get my letters … Let me know …" [73]

- - - - -

Piles [Hemorrhoids] *Mackenzie's 5000 Receipts*

"A pain in the fundament [anus] when going to stool; on examination small tumours are perceived to project beyond its verge. They are of two kinds, the blind and bleeding. They may also be internal and external.

Treatment – A diet of rye mush and milk, strictly adhered to for a length of time, will very frequently cure the disease. If they project, are swelled, and painful, apply twenty or thirty leeches to them, and cold applications. The common gall ointment is a very soothing application. Balsam copaiva, in doses sufficiently large to purge freely, is also highly recommended. A radical cure, however, is only to be sought for in the knife or ligature, for which apply to a surgeon. If the pain is very great, laudanum may be taken to ease it." [74]

- - - - -

September, 1863

Union forces capture the Arkansas cities of Fort Smith on the 1st and Little Rock on the 10th.

Russian warships, on a tour of friendship, visit the cities of New York and San Francisco.

Confederate forces in Charleston, South Carolina, abandon Fort Wagner on the 6th and, on the night of the 8th, repulse another Union night attack on Fort Sumter.

General Burnside and his Union forces occupy Knoxville, Tennessee, on the 4th and on the 9th they capture the garrison protecting the Cumberland Gap. A key Confederate rail connection running from southwestern Virginia into Tennessee is severed.

On September 9th General Longstreet and the divisions of Hood and McLaws are pulled from Confederate lines in northern Virginia and transferred by rail to northwestern Georgia. The plan is to give General Bragg and the Army of Tennessee additional manpower to administer a damaging blow to the Union army under General Rosecrans. This is the first strategic use of railroads to transfer troops between theatres of operation to gain a tactical advantage.

On the 15th President Abraham Lincoln is granted the power to suspend Habeas Corpus anywhere in the United States when he deems it necessary. Congress is yielding an extraordinary power to the President and removing a fundamental pillar of freedom from the citizens.

The *Raleigh Standard, Richmond Examiner* and *Richmond Whig* are all publishing daily anti-Jefferson Davis articles and editorials. These newspapers, and several others, seem determined to undermine the young Confederacy and demoralize the citizenry with their writings. Despite their constant anti-government rhetoric, Jefferson Davis and the Confederate government never restrain the freedom of the press. This same right does not exist in the United States. Anti-Lincoln newspapers quickly discover that freedom of the press has vanished even before Habeas Corpus is suspended.

At Chickamauga Creek in northwestern Georgia one of the five bloodiest battles of the war rages on the 19th and 20th of the month. The addition of Longstreet's men is critical; they spearhead the breakthrough on the 20th. Half of the Union army is routed and flees in total disarray toward Chattanooga. General Thomas forms the rest of the army in a horseshoe shaped defensive line on Snodgrass Hill and holds his ground against repeated assaults. During the night he withdraws his command toward Chattanooga. His actions save the Union army from what could have been total destruction. The cost is terrible for both sides. The Union loses 11,413 killed or wounded and the attacking Confederates lose 16,986 killed or wounded. The defeated Union army has 4,800 men captured.

On the 24th General Hooker is sent west from northern Virginia with the 11th and 12th Corps to bolster the defenses of the Union around Chattanooga.

Private John Jackman, of the 9th Kentucky Infantry, writing from near Chattanooga on the 28th sees, *"a train of 160 ambulances coming out of Chattanooga under a flag of truce, for the Federal wounded that had been left on the field.* Long wagon trains with Confederate wounded are also departing the battlefield toward the rail depot at Ringgold, Georgia, for transportation to the hospitals in Atlanta.

September, 1863

September 1, 1863
Richmond, Virginia

Colonel Robert Kean
Confederate Bureau of War

"The *Examiner* and the *Whig* in their persistent malice towards the President do only less harm than the Raleigh *Standard.* By the way, the followers of the latter in North Carolina are throwing off all disguises and have begun to hold "Union" meetings in some of the western counties. What the *Examiner* and *Whig* propose to themselves as the good to be produced by stirring up opposition, distrust, and hatred towards the President, I can not imagine. I am far from being a universal admirer of the President … but I see no conceivable end but harm from such attack and such a policy." [1]

(ed: As Colonel Kean mentions, these three papers, and several others, were very anti-Davis and anti-government. However, not once during the entire life of the Confederacy was the freedom of the press ever restrained. This was not the case north of the Mason-Dixon line.)

- - - - -

September 1, 1863
Phillips County, Arkansas

Mrs. Mary Edmondson
Farm Wife

" … Have made Albert a pair of pants … I walked down to Will's yesterday … had a kid [lamb] killed – took half.… We have had lovely fall weather this last week of August, but today the thermostat is at 80. I have [been] trying to persuade Jake and Davy to get up the grass in the garden … and making a turnip patch … but they are set against as useless … they [C. S. government] are pressing the few men [negroes] left in the country … and women for nurses.…" [2]

- - - - -

September 2, 1863
Sulphur Springs, North Carolina

Mrs. Cornelia Henry
Farm wife

"I spent the day at Mr. A. B. Jones. Went to see Matilda Morris as she is sick, had a miscarriage last Wednesday. It was dead. She is doing finely. They had some fine watermellons. I enjoyed the day finely. I rode John & took Rose behind me to attend to Gus. He was no trouble. I think I shall go again soon to see Mrs. Moore & Mrs. Alexander." [3]

- - - - -

September 2, 1863
Richmond, Virginia

Cadet Hubbard Minor
Confederate Naval Academy

"Succeeded in having my teeth fixed & returned to the ship & went steadily to work, I have still one tooth to plug for which it will cost me 12 dollars & this will make 37 dollars in all for fixing My teeth. Tomorrow I will go at ten oclock & have the above job done …" [4]

- - - - -

September 3, 1863
Vernon, Mississippi

Major James C. Bates
9th Texas Cavalry

"Dear Will [brother]
… The commissioners for the exchange of prisoners meet again shortly, but I think it hardly probable that they will come to an understanding. The difficulty is … that Lincoln insists on negroes being recognized and treated as, prisoners of war, and that when captured they shall be exchanged for white men. This will never be submitted to … & the exchange of prisoners will therefore be at an end. Once [we] quit exchanging and it will not be long before no prisoners are taken … " [5]

(ed: The Dix-Hill Cartel had been the guideline for prisoner exchange since July, 1862. Now, if the CSA decides that they will not exchange Negroe POWs for Confederate POWs they will be "cutting off their nose to spite their face." The Confederacy needs manpower and eliminating returning prisoners as a source for troop replacement would be very foolish.)

(ed: In a 9-12 letter to his mother it was noted that "32 of my old Co & 53 from the Regt." have deserted.)

- - - - -

September 4, 1863 | Corporal Tally Simpson
Camp | Co. A – 3rd S. Carolina Infantry

"My dear Sister
... There is no news in these quarters.... We had a large muskmelon today for lunch. It cost five dollars. We settled our mess account the other day, and for the past six weeks, perhaps seven or eight, our account for things bought for the mess ran up to one hundred and seven dollars.

... Tell Hester and Aunt Judy I want to see them very badly and they must send me something to eat. I am powerful "grubbish" for a mess of something from home....
Your affect bro
T. N. Simpson

There is no probable chance of getting a furlough. There are so many in the regiment who have never been home that we who have stand very poor chances indeed." [6]

(ed: This is the final letter from Tally. He dies on September 20th at Chickamauga during the attack on Snodgrass Hill. On September 22, 1863, Rev. John M. Carlisle sends a letter to Richard F. Simpson with news of Tally's death and details regarding where his body is buried.)

- - - - -

September 4, 1863
Union, Virginia

Reverend Samuel Houston
Presbyterian Minister

"Paid $16 for just putting single soles on two pairs of gaiters for Mary and Helen. Vile extortion practiced all over the land." [7]

- - - - -

September 4, 1863
near Charleston, Tennessee

Sergeant Robert Watson
Co. K – 7th Florida Infantry

"After breakfast I went in swimming and washed my under clothes and kept my pants and shirt on until they were dry, then put my under clothes on and washed the others ..." [8]

- - - - -

September 4, 1863
Camp

Lt. William M. Haselden
Co. G – 15th S. Carolina Infantry

SPECIAL REQUISITION

"Special Requisition for Co G in the 15th Regt SC Vol

1 one shirt @ 2.5d; five pr drawers @ 2.50. I certify that his requisition is necessary to supply existing wants in Co.

W. M. Haselden Lieut Cmdg Co G 15th SCV

Received of Captain ___ ___ Middleton AQM 15th Regt SCV the above requisition in full.

W. M. Haselden, Lieut Cmdg Co G 15th SC Regt

Sept 4, 1863" [9]

- - - - -

September 5, 1863
Waller's Tavern, Virginia

Private Alfred O. Atkinson
Co. G – Cobb's Legion

"Dear Brothers Polk, Eugene and Everett,
… We never have any news in camp … nor much of anything else but dirt…. Gen. Lee is letting some men go home on furlough but it looks like I can't get off. If I do we will make the old rabbits and possums "get up dust." … It would make you laugh to see how we live here. You see two or three hundred men all living under a few old blankets and cloths spread up … with nothing to eat but a little musty flour and some meal and bacon or poor beef …

I guess you have had plenty of peaches and watermelons and other fruit. I have not had any fruit in about two years. I tell you I want to come home mighty bad to help you eat peaches … but Genl Lee thinks a soldier has no business going home.

We are encamped near a river which is a good place to fish but the men are not allowed to go out of camp without getting a Pass which is a good deal of trouble so we don't go often.
Write soon.

Your brother
Alfred O Atkinson" [10]

- - - - -

September 6, 1863
Orange C. H., Virginia

Private Samuel Pickens
Co. D – 5th Alabama Infantry

"I rode with Tom Moore this eveng, to a millpond 1 ½ ms. fr. Camp and witnessed for the 1st time the process of baptizing by immersion. Mr. Curry [of the] Color Corp. wh[o] was ordained as Baptist minister today at Orange C. H. immersed 16 men." [11]

(ed: On September 2nd Samuel had noted, "There is a religious revival going on all thro' out the army … & the soldiers seem to take more interest in the preaching & prayer meetings held every night & on Sundays … ")

- - - - -

September 8, 1863 Private Robert C. Dunlap
Demopolis, Alabama Landis Missouri Light Artillery

"Price of articles in Demopolis. Shoes per pair $10 to $75. Boots $75 to 100, socks $1.50 to 2.00. Hats $20 to 50, small silk hand chief $10 to 15, Sweet potatoes per bu $4 to $6. Beef per lb from .50 to $1.00 Bacon $2 to 5, Butter .50 to $2.00 Soda $5. Black pepper $5. Sugar $2 to 4, & Tea $15, per lb." [12]

- - - - -

September 10, 1863 Private Marion H. Fitzpatrick
Near Orange Court House, Va. Co. K – 45th Georgia Infantry

"Dear Amanda,
… I am sorry to hear that you suffered so much with toothache. I hope you will be rid of it since you had your tooth pulled out…. I am sorry you can get no shoes. I do not know how to tell you to manage but you must have some, no matter what price." [13]

- - - - -

September 10, 1863 D. S. T.
Mobile Advertiser & Register 3rd Alabama Infantry

"My Dear Mother: …
It is truly gratifying to see the progress of religion in this army; revivals are going on at this time. We have a new Chaplain to our regiment, he is from Tuskegee, Ala. We have preaching and prayer meetings regularly every night. Nearly the whole brigade attends, and hundred go up nightly to be prayed for, and many are being converted. A "Christian Association" has been formed, and Gen. Battle is President – a large number have already joined from our regiment. On Tuesday last I attended preaching at a country church, about five miles from camp; the church was crowded with soldiers and citizens, among them a number of ladies - … the congregation were singing a good

old hymn, nearly half of the soldiers who were present went up to be prayed for….
Your affectionate son," [14]

(ed: A local family has given the editor their son's letter and it was printed in the October 1, 1863 edition. He removed the soldier's name and just used initials. Since there are few grammatical and punctuation errors in this letter, and others printed by the various papers, we must assume the editors "corrected" the text. A check of the roster of 3rd Alabama reveals Corporal David S. Taylor as the only soldier with the initials D.S.T. He served in Company K and was a candidate for promotion to 2nd Lieutenant in the fall of 1863.)

- - - - -

September 11, 1863 — Mr. Jacob R. Hildebrand
Augusta County, Virginia — Farmer

" … Mrs. Jno Harman sent here & got 18 chickens at $1.25 cents a piece Thos. P. Wilson was here to asseys my property I have to pay the tenth of wheat, Rye, oats, hay, fodder etc" [15]

(ed: In April, 1863 legislation passed the Confederate Congress establishing a 10% tithe or tax in kind on grains and also hogs. Government collection points were established under the control of the Quartermaster General. Mr. Wilson, as a representative of the government, is determining the 10% on the Hildebrand farm.) [16]

- - - - -

September 11, 1863 — Lt. Sanford Branch
Camp Letterman, Gettysburg — Co. A – 8th Georgia Infantry

"Dear Mother
I have been expecting to hear from you the last week but have been disappointed. do write as often as you can … My health continues to improve slowly. Our treatment here is excellent the fare for a sick man is very good, but if I could

only get some good Homeny & Rice I think I could fatten on it.... Remember me in your prayers dear Mother I feel as if that will do more good than all the medicine in the world.
Your affect. Son
Sanford" [17]

(ed: In July the U. S. Sanitary Commission had issued a plea for assistance to help care for the more than 21,000 wounded at Gettysburg. Women from as far away as Baltimore and New York flocked to Gettysburg to provide food, clothing, and, most importantly, care and nursing for the Confederate and Union wounded. Without the support of these volunteers several thousand of these wounded would have no doubt perished.) [18]

- - - - -

September 12, 1863
Orange C. H., Virginia

Captain C. L. G______
Co ___ - 2nd Georgia Battalion

"My Friends: ...
There has nothing of interest occurred to break the dull monotony of camp life, since I last wrote.... Our pickets on the Rappahannock are on very friendly terms with Meade's conscripts and substitutes; they exchange papers, and give tobacco for coffee, etc., etc. The army is still recruiting, and is now in fine fighting trim. We get full rations now, which is beef, flour and salt, and sometimes rice, sugar and peas.... Our Quartermaster, also, has a good supply of clothing now on hand, and, while in camp here, we have determined to play the gentleman a while, and put on a *white* shirt at least *every two weeks.* The boys are in fine health and spirits. A. P. Hill's corps was reviewed yesterday by Gen. Lee. It was a grand sight; and while Uncle Bob was reviewing us, we were reviewing the fair damsels of Orange who came out to witness the grand sight." [19]

- - - - -

September 13, 1863
Fredericksburg, Virginia

Captain Richard Watkins
Co. K – 3rd Virginia Cavalry

"My Darling Mary
I reached camp on Wednesday and found all well ...

Monday Morning Sep 14th – This morning rode to Fredericksburg and for the sum of eighty dollars purchased six good coats and three blankets for our negroes. If Nelly will wash them thoroughly I reckon you will find them worth the money at any rate you will have less sewing & cutting & weaving to do. If another opportunity present itself soon will try to get some more blankets. These are clothes picked up by poor people from the battlefields and I buy them the more willingly because the people need the money. At the same time they are well worth what I have paid....
Your own
Richard" [20]

(ed: The winter coats were collected from the Union dead from the December, 1862 battle and blankets could be from then or from the battles around Fredericksburg in May, 1863.)

- - - - -

September 15, 1863
Mechlenburg County, Virginia

Mrs. Mary R. Thomas
Teacher and Farm Wife

"Rehoboth

My Dear Husband ... I was very glad to learn that your health was improving ... Hope you received $10 by letter from me ... and also $5 ... your father sent you. I beg you to excuse me for not sending your peaches ... I have heard you were gone to Tennessee but I hope it is not so.... I am very glad to hear that you are seeking religion. May the Lord be with you ... I shall never forget you in my feeble efforts of prayer ... I must close as it is nearly time to go to books. I have 22 scholars today. I remain ever your affectionate wife.
Mary R. Thomas" [21]

(ed: Mary taught school at the Rehoboth Methodist Church earning some additional monies to supplement what the farm could provide. In a September 23 note Mary added that, "Dr. Rose paid me $60 Saturday. I have sent $40 to Brodnax to get meat. I have got a pair of shoes at last.... I got a barrel of flour ... at $30 on Sunday.... the children join in love to you.")

- - - - -

September 17, 1863 Mrs. Mary Watkins
Meherrin, Virginia Farm wife

"My dear precious Husband
... Mama is busy as she can drying fruit and pickling and making cider and vinegar. She got $100 for that little keg of pickled peaches that she sent down last week. The last two barrels of peaches brought only $20 apiece....

Minnie is learning a new accomplishment ... She mounts Lizzie Lee and walks off with her as fearlessly as I could. Emmie looks on almost ready to cry and says Mama please make Minnie get down she will fall. But Minnie just laughs and says get up behind me sister. I don't believe the child knows what fear is and I am afraid she will get killed some of these days. I saw her yesterday go up behind Lizzie Lee and stroke her legs and she will stand up in the saddle just as quick as any way.... Please try to get some more blankets if you have an opportunity. They are badly needed [by the negroes this winter]. Did you leave any money in Farmville or any where to pay taxes?
Your loving
Mary" [22]

(ed: Inflation is growing rapidly. It now takes $10 Confederate to equal $1 U. S.)

- - - - -

September 17, 1863
Lafayette County, Arkansas

Captain Theophilus Perry
Co. F – 28th Texas Cavalry

"Dear Harriet: I feel better today, and am up. I was quite sick yesterday, and lay in bed most all day…. I lay upon my bed close to the window looking out every minute for papa carriage with you and the baby…. Above all things I desire to see you once more. Every thing is lonely without you…. I am afraid that the baby will have a serious spell. He is delicate, and subject to colds. Give him brandy toddies freely whenever there are appearances of cold…. I shall leave here Saturday I think. I think that I will take more calomel to night. My Liver and spleen have caused me some pain. The calomel I have taken has not acted well. I have very little appetite…. Since I have been here I have eat almost nothing. I have drunk several glasses of Butter-milk … I relish the Butter milk very much…. I can drink it and feel refreshed when the very thought of water is sickening. I wrote a letter to our Adjutant, stating the cause of my absence beyond my furlough….

… God have mercy upon me, and save me to unite with you …
Theophilus Perry" [23]

(ed: Calomel is Mercurous Chloride. When used as a purgative calomel is normally a white, tasteless compound. Calomel can be a powder or a paste and can be used both internally and externally. Sometimes massive necrosis and tissue loss occurred with excessive dosages, this is known as "mercurial gangrene," and results in disfiguring and disabling injuries. "Given in large doses and for extended period only the strongest patients survived the treatment. Gunn's New Family Physician, 1872, recommended doses of 5 to 10 grams (320-640 milligrams) taken at night. In 1984 the smallest dosage of mercury chloride reported to cause death was 500 milligrams.") [24]

- - - - -

September 19, 1863
Chickamauga, Georgia

Private John D. Bryant
Co. A – 44th Tennessee Infantry

" …then we brought on the battle of Chickamauga, which I was captured on the first days of battle. I had my left hand shot … I was captured in the little field near a spring – I had got lost from the rest and the Yank had me cut off from the rest. They kep us all night near the battle lines. They taken us to Chatanooga … " [25]

(ed: Private Bryant was shipped to Camp Douglas in Chicago, Illinois and would be a prisoner there until the summer of 1865.)

- - - - -

September 19, 1863
Camp near Orange CH, Virginia

Corporal Benjamin Freeman
Co. F – 44th N. Carolina Infantry

"Dear Farther
… I am glad to here that you had finished you Foder and your Peas … Green Peas are selling at 2 Dollars a quart here I would like to have some to eat but I cannot give that price for them … I have been up ever since 2 oclock las night cooking my ration for to day. I will write you a letter and then I will take a nap. This morning I [requisitioned] for a Blanket, Jacket, Over Coat Pants, Socks, Shirt, and Shoes. I will get them in a few days. I have drawn a new knapsack since I left home … Pa I want you to have my boots fixed up for the Winter. I will send for them … We had a tramendious rain yesterday The folk have not pull much foder here yet The boys are tolerably well some few are sick When you write Back direct you letter to … Co K 44th Regt. NC Troops Cerklands Brigade Heath Division AP Hills Corps" [26]

(ed: Benjamin had a furlough home in late May and returned to his unit in mid-June. Gen. W. W. Kirkland was assigned command of the brigade in August. The brigade remained in Gen. Henry Heth's Division.)

- - - - -

September 19, 1863
Chickamauga Creek, Georgia

Private Milton L. Wheeler
Co. A – 33rd Alabama Infantry

" … we hurried to the Chickamauga Creek at Thedfords Ford and after taking off our shoes, socks, pants and drawers waded through it and put on our clothes. Then about sunset formed in line of battle and advanced across a field coming to a worn rail fence … we soon encountered the Federal line … who checked us at first but gave way. Then we pursued them in the dark, routing them …" [27]

- - - - -

September 19, 1863
Chickamauga, Georgia

Reverend John G. Richards
10th South Carolina Infantry

"[Tonight] everything is just as calm the moonshines just as serenely as if there had been no carnage today & the dead and wounded were not thickly strewn around us O God have mercy upon us & be with us on the coming morrow! Have Mercy upon our poor wounded men!! …" [28]

(ed: Reverend Richards was Presbyterian and had requested service with South Carolina troops in the Army of Tennessee.)

- - - - -

September 19, 1863
Phillips County, Arkansas

Mrs. Mary Edmondson
Farm wife

"We sent our remaining wheat to mill last week by our hitherto faithful Davy. He brought back 200 pounds of flour…. Lucy, Davy, Jake, Mahala, and Henry all the black family we now have. Poor Lucy came back from her sojour with the Federals naked and sick – just four weeks ago and has not been able to work … we have ministered to her and [she] looks like living now…. " [29]

- - - - -

September 19, 1863
Cargo Manifest

Phantom
S. G. Porter – Master

"266 tons from St. George's, Bermuda to Nassau

9 cases whiskey, 2 cases gin, 1 case wine, 2 Blakely guns, 50 cases leather, 50 cases Austrian rifles, 135 barrels pork, 150 barrels gunpowder, 1 case merchandise." [30]

- - - - -

September 20 & 21, 1863
Chickamauga, Georgia

Private Benjamin Seaton
Co. G – 10th Texas Infantry

"Sunday 20th – another hard days battle and late in the eaving drove them out of ther brestworks and they run to the four winds of the earth and we captered a large number of them and thar loss heavy.

Monday 21st – in camp today. I went over the battlefield and found a grate many dead Yankees and a good many of ours. At dark we took up the line of march and went som 10 miles and camped fer the night. The calvery hard fight on the rode to Chattanooga and took a good many prisners and drove them [Yankees] back to Chattanooga wher thay are fortifying as hard as they can." [31]

- - - - -

September 21, 1863
Chickamauga, Georgia

Private Milton L. Wheeler
Co. A – 33rd Alabama Infantry

"The morning of the 21st, details usually of their friends, buried our Confederate dead, either singly where they fell, or putting two or more under the ground together, each wrapped in his blanket with his hat over his face." [32]

- - - - -

September 21, 1863
Chickamauga, Georgia

Private William L. Morelock
Co. E – 2nd Tennessee Cavalry

"Was in Battle of Chickamauga … captured … staid in prison two years, starved and frozen, weighed only 70 lbs. when released … at Camp Morton, Indianapolis." [33]

- - - - -

September 21, 1863
Chickamauga, Georgia

Reverend John G. Richards
10th South Carolina Infantry

"Rode over the battle field – Scene terrible – 3 P.M. Visited the Yankee hospitals which have fallen into our hand – Slaughter terrible – Many begged me for help – Could but feel greatly for them." [34]

(ed: Rev. Richards has notes in the margins of wounded men he saw, probably from his service in the hospitals: Wm. Kirkland, Co A, 19th SC, both thighs; C Randall, Co A, 19th SC, back; James Brogden, Co B, 19th SC, both thighs; James Morrison, Co _, 19th SC, thigh & side. He even lists under "Strangers" soldiers from the 4th Texas, 19th Louisiana & 15th SC. He noted that Wm Kirkland was left at Manigos [Manigault's] Hospital near Ledford Ford.)

- - - - -

September 22, 1863
Rapidan Station, Virginia

Sergeant Benjamin F. Porter
Co. E – 11th Alabama Infantry

"Dear Sister, …
We have sent one Corps of men from this army to the west to see if they could whip the Yanks. They do nothing but advance to the reare. They almost dishearten us in Va. We hear too of Deserters by the score in the pine woods of Alabama. This is redicalus a shame to the nation. I wish they wer in Yankeydom where they belong.

… I receive a letter from Mr. Smith. He was well & braging on his little wife. She is a methodist.
B. F. Porter" [35]

(ed: Benjamin is expressing the disgust that the men in the Army of Northern Virginia have for their counterparts serving under General Bragg in the Army of Tennessee. General Longstreet has taken two divisions, two thirds of his Corps,

to join General Bragg and hopefully overpower the Union army under General Rosecrans. The battle at Chickamauga was the result.)

- - - - -

September 22, 1863
Johnson's Island Prison, Ohio

2nd Lt. James H. Wentworth
Co. D – 5th Florida Infantry

"This is a much better prison than Fort Delaware. It is a large enclosure of about 16 acres fenced in with plank about 20 feet high, around the top of which is a parapet for the sentinels … There is 13 large two story frame houses inside of this pen for our quarters and we get tolerable good rations here, but not quite enough of bread …" [36]

(ed: James was transferred by steamer to Philadelphia on September 18th. From there they traveled west by rail through Harrisburg and Pittsburgh and arrived on the shores of Lake Erie on September 22nd.)

- - - - -

Undated
Chickamauga, Georgia

Captain Samuel J. Frazier
Co. D – 19th Tennessee Infantry

"shot in windpipe at Chickamauga … Sent to Johnson Island. Shot rats with a cross bow and fried them … hungry often … scant rations." [37]

(ed: Samuel will be released from prison on June 11, 1865 after taking the Oath of Allegiance. He will be 25 years of age and will have spent most of the last 21 months in prison, 19 of those months at Johnson's Island.)

- - - - -

September 22, 1863
Chickamauga, Georgia

Private Milton L. Wheeler
Co. A – 33rd Alabama Infantry

"Some men on each side in their excitement had failed to remove their ramrods after reloading and had shot them away, sticking them in trees or saplings … some twenty feet high or more, and all were usually bent…. Details of men with wagons policed the battle field gathering abandoned guns, accoutrements, taking the harness off dead horses, and other war stores scattered about." [38]

- - - - -

September 22, 1863
Chickamauga Creek, Georgia

Lt. Joshua K. Callaway
Co. K – 28th Alabama Infantry

"My Dear Love,
Through the amazing mercy of God I am alive … I have just passed through the terrible ordeal of a hard battle, and strange to say, I am untouched, although we were in a few yards of their line … fighting like tigers; had fought them about forty steps for an hour and a half another time. We have routed them and run them off. They are … leaving as hard as they can….

It is now 9 o'clock and we leave in the morning at 3. Continue your prayers for me, the struggle may not be over yet….
Your Affectionate husband
J K Callaway" [39]

(ed: Chickamauga was one of the five bloodiest battles of the entire war. Manigault's Brigade was in the thick of the fight. General Manigault's post battle report indicated his brigade was 2025 strong and lost 540 killed, severely wounded & mortally wounded; 69 slightly wounded and 47 captured for a total loss of 656 men. The Brigade was composed of the 24th, 28th &34th Alabama and the 10th & 19th South Carolina.)

- - - - -

September 22, 1863
Charleston, South Carolina

Lt. John A. Payne
C. S. Navy

"**Confederate War Department,**

To Joseph Poulnot **Dr.**

For 5 Coffins @ $15	$ 75.00
For Transportation to Mariners Graveyard	$ 20.00
For Interment of 5 seaman from torpedo boat @ $6	$ 30.00
For Drayage of coffins to R.R. Wharf	$ 10.00
	$ 135.00

I certify that the above is correct. The amount is large but the body[ies] had been under water and required large coffins.

John A. Payne
Lieut. C. S. Navy

Approved for One Hundred thirty five Dollars __________ Cents. Ordered to be paid by Paymaster Henry Myers, Confederate Navy.

[ ] Commanding Naval Station

Received Sept. 26, 1863 from Henry Myers Paymaster, Confederate Navy, the sum of One Hundred thirty five Dollars, ________ Cents, in full of the above bill.

Joseph Poulnet" [40]

(ed: As the five sailors from the submarine H. L. Hunley *are being buried, Mr. Horace Hunley is making arrangements for the cleaning and repair of the boat.)* [41]

- - - - -

Late September, 1863
Camp Douglas, Illinois

Private Abraham Gredig
Kain's Tennessee Artillery

"I was captured and taken to Camp Douglas. Hd chronic diareah for six months while there. Signed a parole of exchange in Mar. 65 and some 500 of prisoners left for Hampton Rhodes [Virginia] for exchange but we were all stoped at Point Lookout Prison [Maryland] and were left there till the war closed. Our feed at Point Lookout was miserable. At Camp Douglas it was fair ..." [42]

- - - - -

September 23, 1863
Sevier County, Arkansas

Captain Griffin Frost
Co. A – 2nd Missouri Infantry

"We are camping in Sevier County, Ark., forty-five miles from Texas ... the salt works are not far from here, and doing a flourishing business, some fifteen or twenty furnaces in operation, each furnace boiling twenty or thirty kettles, turning out about thirty-five bushels of salt per day. The woods are full of muscadines, large and sweet, the finest I ever saw. This fruit is one of the principal products of Arkansas, and very justly prized." [43]

(ed: Muscadine is a woody vine bearing a musky grape used to make wine.) [44]

- - - - -

September, 1863
Wilmington, North Carolina

Dr. John Milton Worth
State Salt Commissioner

"After the loss of earlier salt works in Currituck Sound and Morehead City, Dr. Worth selected a location 8 miles from Wilmington and some 20 miles from the forts that protected the entrance to the Cape Fear River. Production was at 250 bushels daily when a yellow fever epidemic in late 1862 almost entirely suspended production. In the fall of 1863 chills, fever, malaria and other diseases hampered the effectiveness of the workforce. Dr. Worth had to continually raise the price of the salt as his 1863 cost of provisions and materials encountered enormous advances. In September he charged six dollars a bushel, in November seven dollars and in December nine dollars. Throughout 1863 he battled with the military authorities who constantly impressed his horse teams, wagons, boats and workers for military purposes." [45]

- - - - -

September, 1863
Eastern North Carolina
Cape Fear District

Surgeon John H. Kinyoun
66th North Carolina Infantry

"Register of Sick and Wounded of 66th North Carolina Regiment

Name	Rank	Regt	Company	Disease
M. Vickers	Priv	66	A	Intermittent Fever
W. Woods	Priv	66	A	Anemia
S. Chisenhall	Priv	66	A	Bronchitis Acute
T. Gray	Priv	66	E	Diarrhea
M. Nelson	Priv	66	E	Diarrhea
T. M. Ross	Priv	66	E	Bronchitis
Cyrus Strickland	Priv	66	E	Bronchitis
F. Dupree	Priv	66	E	Poisoned Arm
M. Batchelor	Priv	66	B	Tetanus
G. Collins	Priv	66	B	Diarrhea
J. B. Cook	Priv	66	B	Psoriasis
J. Stiles	Priv	66	B	Furunculus
B. Wester	Priv	66	B	Intermittent Fever
G. E. Matthews	Priv	66	B	Rubiola – Furloughed Home" [46]

(ed: These are the final 14 names in Dr. Kinyoun's ledger of soldiers reporting for "sick call" during the month of September. A total of 115 came through with a wide variety of ailments. Intermittent Fever is often associated with malaria and Furunculus refers to a boil in the skin. The 66th North Carolina was officially

mustered into duty in the first week of October but the majority of the troops had been in Camp during the month of September.)

- - - - -

Undated	Lt. Pressley N. Conner
Near Chickamauga, Georgia	Co. K – 9th Tennessee Infantry

" ... in the battle of Chickamauga ... I was wounded by reason of which I was never able for field duty again. After being wounded stayed in the field hospital 10 or 12 days, very poor medical attention, not much to eat, transferred to Atlanta ... received good attention there, except contracted gangrene in wound and made it hard to recover, was transferred to Macon, Ga. into a hospital.... discharged." [47]

- - - - -

Undated	Private Jesse H. Green
Near Chickamauga, Georgia	Co. A – 19th Tennessee Infantry

"At the Chickamauga fight Billie Ham and I were brought a piece of old cornpone and our stomachs were so weak we couldn't eat it ..." [48]

- - - - -

September 24, 1863	3rd Corporal Milton Barrett
Near Chattanooga, Tennessee	Co. E – 3rd Battalion
	Georgia Sharpshooters

"Dear Brother and sister I seit my self behind a bluff to pertect me from the Yankee bums that have bin a whirling a round us in grand stile this morning.

i have bin on the front line two days a poping a way. on last tuesday even[ing] we had a hard crurmish [skirmish] had several kild and wounded.... i can not tel what our genereals aim to do … the Yankees is advancen. i must lay down my pen and go to shooting.

September the 25th we had a lively time last night. we had a heavy crurmishing for three hours. we drove ther crurmishinges in and kill sevrel. we had non kild a few wounde. everything is quite this morning. our line of Battle have move back a bout one mile and ar a fortifying. we still hold the lines that we first establish.… Bragg is not the genral that Lee is and the western army cant fight like the virginia army. if Genral Lee was hear he would have had the yankees drove out of Tennesee.

… i am a ever your loving Brother
Milton Barrett" [49]

(Longstreet's men headed toward Richmond, from the Rapidan line, on September 9th. The divisions of Hood and McLaws were placed on trains in Richmond to travel via North Carolina, South Carolina and Atlanta to reinforce Bragg's Army of Tennessee in northwestern Georgia. "The 843 mile trip took seven days and ten hours over sixteen different railroad lines of varying gauges." Longstreet's men spearhead the Confederate breakthrough at Chickamauga on September 20th. The brigades of Wofford and Jenkins arrived after the battle was over.) [50]

- - - - -

September 24, 1863 — Mr. Jacob R. Hildebrand
Augusta County, Virginia — Farmer

"Went to Waynesboro for my salt got 90 lbs paid $8.10 cents for it got 105 lbs for Gabriel 105 lbs for J. G. Henne Capt E Bateman went to his company, Elick bo't Gid's three sheep at $91.66 cts." [51]

- - - - -

September 26, 1863
Chattanooga, Tennessee

Sergeant George W. Bradley
Co. E – 2nd S. Carolina Rifles

"My dear companion,
It is with much pleasure to me, to drop you a few lines to inform you that this leaves me in fine health for present.

… we give them [Yanks] one of the worst thrashings last Saturday and Sunday that ever any set of men got. I know it was the 19th and 20th of September.

I do not know how many was killed though they was a great many on either side. They were more of them killen than our men. We attack about five thousand prisoners and forty-five guns [cannons] and run them some ten or fifteen miles before we stayed for the night … We have come up with them at a town called Chattanooga in Tennessee. The battle was fought in … Georgia near Ringold Station … I think we have them in such a close place … we have his supply lines cut off so he can't do much here … There is some firing on the line now….

So nothing more at present time. I remain as ever, your husband until death. Write as soon as this comes to hand and give my love and best respects to all … G W Bradley" [52]

- - - - -

September 26, 1863

Captain Elijah P. Petty
Co. F – 17th Texas Infantry

"#40 Special Requisition

(40) Forty Pr Shoes
(13) Thirteen Hats
(8) Eight Pr Pants
(30) Thirty Pr Drawers
(32) Thirty-Two Shirts
(1) One Jacket

I certify That the above requisition is correct and that the articles specified are absolutely requisite for the public service rendered so by the following circumstances.

E. P. Petty, Capt. Co F
17 Texas Regt. Infantry

Capt. D. D. Rosborough, AQM, Confederate States Army will issue the articles specified in the above requisition.

Col. R. T. P. Allen,
Commanding

Received in full the 26 Sept 1863 of D. D. Rosborough, AQM, Confederate States Army the articles above specified.

E. P. Petty Co F
17 Tex" [53]

- - - - -

September 27, 1863 Private Marion H. Fitzpatrick
Orange Court House, Virginia Co. K – 45th Georgia Infantry

"Dear Amanda,
... Orders were issued for all to stay in Camps but there was no use talking. A large Chinese sugar cane patch was soon discovered a short distance up the river on the Yankee side. A foot log was also discovered to cross on and the result can better be imagined than told. A fine roasting ear patch was also discovered near at hand and the final result the next morning was about two thirds of the Comp[any] was gentlemanly sick, your humble servant among the sickest. But it being only a belley ache it soon wore off. Among the other good things we found were pumpkins which we cook and eat at all stages ... They eat splendid ..." [54]

- - - - -

September 27, 1863
Camp near Chattanooga, Tennessee

Private T. M. Woods
Co. K – 16th Alabama Infantry

"Dear Father,
... if you come up to see us I want you to fetch me 2 pair of pants, 2 shirts, 2 pair drawers, two or three pair of socks and my jeans coat and vest. I would like to have my big blanket as nights are getting cool." [55]

- - - - -

September 28, 1863
near Chattanooga, Tennessee

Private John Jackman
Co. B – 9th Kentucky Infantry

"Went to the wagon train – 7 miles to the rear – and changed linen after taking a bath in the "River of Death." The ablution was quite necessary, for I had been in dirt for sometime past. At noon returned, and saw a train of 160 ambulances coming out of Chattanooga under flag of truce, for the Federal wounded that had been left on the field." [56]

(ed: The "River of Death" is the Chickamauga and the ambulances are enroute to the Chickamauga battlefield to collect wounded Union soldiers.)

- - - - -

September 29, 1863
Rapidan Station, Virginia

Sergeant Benjamin F. Porter
Co. E – 11th Alabama Infantry

"Miss Jane ... Sister, I hear of Mosely bying Negroes. It looks strange to me that some are starving & others getting rich. I fear that they do fail to do there duty to there country, to there God or they would not have money to spare of the purchase of negroes....

Winter is approaching the weather is very cold & we generally are very badly clad. A greate many of us have no blankets at all. I am doing very well except for shoes. I am sorry to hear that corn & wheat is so high it is the same or worse here too. I have not heard from Bro. in a long time…. "[57]

- - - - -

September 29 & 30, 1863 Mrs. Cornelia Henry
Sulphur Springs, North Carolina Farm wife

"… Made some molasses today. Mr. Henry went to Asheville today. The militia has gone into camps at Reems Creek camp ground. 'Tis a great pity the the men have to leave home at this season [harvest] of the year. It will cause them to lose their wheat crop & molasses too for the cane will soon spoil if not made up on account of frost.

Wednesday 30th – I sewed a little today. Mr. Henry went to Asheville today. Nothing new. Made some molasses today. Cloudy & warm…. I am up at the furnace where they boil every night till the molasses gets done. My old teeth have been hurting me some. They are decaying very fast. I will soon have none to ache."[58]

(ed: In a September 24th letter, from Governor Vance, Mr. Henry has been appointed Captain of a North Carolina home guard cavalry company for defense of the mountain region of western North Carolina.)

- - - - -

September 30, 1863 Mr. John B. Jones
Richmond, Virginia Clerk, War Department

"… prices for medicines in the Confederate States, I select the following: Quinine, per oz., $100; calomel, $20; blue mass, $20; Opium, $100; … borax, $14; oil of bergamot, per lb., $100 …

Boots are selling in this city at $100 per pair."[59]

(ed: bergamot is a small pear shaped fruit whose rind bears an aromatic oil used in perfumes.)[60]

- - - - -

Preserving Potatoes *Mackenzie's 5000 Receipts*

"Large quantities may be cured at once, by putting them into a basket as large as the vessel containing the boiling water will admit, and then just dipping them a minute or two at the utmost. The germ, which is so near to the skin, is thus killed, without injuring the potatoe; and in this way several tons might be cured in a few hours. They should then be dried in a warm oven, and laid up in sacks or casks, secure from the frost, in a dry place." [61]

- - - - -

October, 1863

In Virginia the armies of General Lee and General Meade jockey back and forth along the Rapidan River. Neither side seems very interested in bringing on an engagement. On October 14th at Bristoe Station near Manassas, General A. P. Hill makes an ill-advised assault on Union positions and is repulsed with heavy losses.

General Hooker takes his two corps and captures Bridgeport, Alabama, in an effort to relieve some of the pressure on the Union forces trapped in Chattanooga. On October 17th General Grant is given overall command of the Union armies of the Tennessee, the Cumberland, and the Ohio. General Thomas replaces General Rosecrans as commander of the Army of the Tennessee.

General Grant arrives in Chattanooga on October 23rd and determines to open a supply line across the Tennessee River at Brown's Ferry. The current supply line involves a difficult and inadequate mountain route that is not capable of providing adequate supplies of provisions and munitions to the army. On the 28th the pontoon bridge is in place and supplies are reaching the city. The potential for starvation and lack of supply causing the abandonment of Chattanooga has been removed.

On October 25th Confederate forces are defeated at Pine Bluff, Arkansas, and withdraw below the Red River. This effectively places half of Arkansas under Union control.

As October closes, a map of the Confederacy shows the northern third of Virginia, virtually all of Tennessee, all of Kentucky, all of Missouri, half of Arkansas, the city of New Orleans and surrounding areas of southern Louisiana plus the Mississippi River under Union control. The Confederacy is reduced to less than nine and a half states. The loss of the Mississippi River cuts off Texas, Louisiana and the southern part of Arkansas from the rest of the Confederacy.

The bleak early winds of winter do not carry many reasons for optimism in the Confederacy.

October, 1863

October 1, 1863
Chattanooga, Tennessee

Sergeant Robert Watson
Co. K – 7th Florida Infantry

" … stopped raining at midnight when we stripped off and dried our clothes by the fire. All hands as hungry as wolves and nothing to eat." [1]

- - - - -

Early October, 1863
Chickamauga Field Hospitals, Georgia

Miss. Kate Cummings
Hospital Matron

" … I took my seat by the [ambulance] driver…. We were to lead one of those long dreary looking trains, of which I have seen so many.

There were two men with us; one was wounded in the jaw, and had the erysipelas very badly; the other had one of his legs broken, which was nicely fixed in a splint. The latter I expected to suffer very much from the jolting, but he seemed to suffer little compared to the other.

I thought I had seen the worst our men had to endure, but this ride proved I was mistaken. I never saw such roads in my life; the rain had been heavy and made deep ruts in it. We had to pass two or three fords, in which the water was so high that it nearly came into our wagon. We came to one which had a wagon stuck fast in it, and blocking up the way; our driver and some others had to unharness their mules and get it out of the mire before we could proceed. All this was very trying to the wounded, and the wonder to me is how they could live after such a ride, for it was really harrowing." [2]

- - - - -

October 3, 1863 — Cadet Hubbard Minor
Richmond, Virginia — Confederate Naval Academy

" … will go on watch again today from 12 to 4 & then shall go uptown was paid off Also on this day & the Ammt I recd is not sufficient to pay my mess bill I hope this evening … to have a good game of billiards." [3]

- - - - -

October 4, 1863 — Captain Elijah P. Petty
Bayou Rouge, Louisiana — Co. F – 17th Texas Infantry

"Dear Wife
… The boys have just found & cut a bee tree and I stopped to eat some honey. It was a tremendous sycamore and there was a good deal of honey. Oh we soldiers have a fine time. We have as much sugar cane as we can eat and find that is quite healthy as well as palateable. We are living finely new potatoes in great abundance…. if I can get potatoes I dont want corn bread. We have beef, some times mutton, corn Bread, some times flour, sugar, molasses, sugar cane, Sweet potatoes etc…. God bless & protect you all.
E P Petty" [4]

- - - - -

October 4, 1863 — Colonel Robert Kean
Richmond, Virginia — Confederate Bureau of War

"My salary of $3000 goes about as far as $300 would do in ordinary times … The consequence is that with an income from all sources of at least $6000 and a good deal of help from my father-in-law, my family is reduced to two meals a day (since last May) and they are of the most plain and economical scale. Wood for fuel is $38 per cord, butter $4 per pound, coal $1.25 per bushel, calico $4.50 a yard." [5]

- - - - -

October 5, 1863
Camp near Chattanooga, Tennessee

Private Stephen Barnett
Co. F – 19th Georgia Infantry

"When this you see remember me"

"My dear Sister [Fannie],
... I am in good health ... and [hope this] find you enjoying the same ...

I must tell you something about the Battle of Chickamauga. It commenced the 18th of September and ended the 19th. I was in it all but thank goodness I never got touched. It was a horrible sight to see... We routed them and drove them to Chattanooga. We had one man killed and 8 wounded. H. H Forest was killed, James Hous wounded severely through the hand, J I Melton run over by a horse, Joe Houston slightly on the head, Bill Milligan through the leg severely, Bill Moore in the breast severely, Sargeant M. Marshall in the back severely, Robert Sparks on the head slightly and Sargeant B L Walker on the thigh slightly. 4 killed in the regiment and 27 wounded ...

I want you and Lizzie to send me 2 prs. of socks ... and a pr. of pants ... I would like to see all of you if I could ... Goodby
Stephen Barnett" [6]

(ed: Stephen will be killed at the Battle of Atlanta on July 22, 1864.)

- - - - -

October 5, 1863
Augusta County, Virginia

Mr. Jacob R. Hildebrand
Farmer

"Monday – Grinding cane & boiling molassis. Mrs. Jno Harman bought 10 turkeys of me at $6.4 per head & 2 barrels of simlons at $12 per barrel amounting to $88 alltogether" [7]

- - - - -

October, 1863
Chimborazo Hospital
Richmond, Virginia

Private Charles W. Thomas
Co. B – 56th Virginia Infantry

"My Dear Wife ... We have twenty two of our regiment here in a small room ... I dont get nothing to ate here but some of the poorest beef you ever saw boiled and ... a few Irish potatoes and a very small piece of light bread is our fare ... I dont entend to dy here ... Give my love to all ...
CWT" [8]

(ed: Charles will serve another 18 months in the Army of Northern Virginia and will be captured on April 6, 1865 near Farmville, Virginia just 3 days before the surrender at Appomattox. He will be sent to Point Lookout Prison in Maryland where he will contract pneumonia and die on April 26, 1865. Charles is buried in grave #1572 of the Point Lookout Confederate Cemetery.)

- - - - -

October 5, 1863
near Canton, Mississippi

4th Sergeant Robert Elliott
Co. E – 35th Alabama Infantry

"... we all were very glad to see come into camp Mr Giles from home who had come down to see his son & he brought me a letter clothes Tabaco paper & envelopes & some nice sweet cakes & some of the largest apples that I have ever seen ... was sorry to hear that my little daughter Kate had been sick with the fever but is better now ..." [9]

(ed: Mr. Giles departed on the 14th and carried letters from many of the Co. E soldiers back to their loved ones at home.)

- - - - -

Undated
Abbeyville, South Carolina

Mrs. Alice Ball Duvall
Refugee from Virginia

"… [We] would dig up the meat house floors, put the earth in a big pot of water and boil it, leave it over night and in the morning there would be a thick crust of salt on top of the pot, the dirt all settling to the bottom." [10]

- - - - -

October 6, 1863
Ringgold, Georgia

Miss. Kate Cummings
Hospital Matron

" … found that the rail track had been finished to Ringgold; so we passed on to that place. As I was familiar with it, I went to the nearest building, which had been the Bragg Hospital…. Wounded men, wrapped in their blankets were lying on the balcony. I went into a room which was filled with others in the same state; some of whom were suffering for want of water….

… I went down to the main hospital, where I was introduced to the surgeon in charge, Dr Ushery [Ussery]. He gave me bandages to roll; … rolled bandages all afternoon, and could scarcely supply the demand. The surgeons were getting the wounded ready to send off on the train….

I took the blackberry wine which Dr. Divine had given me and put it in a bucket of water, which made a nice drink…. I went down and waited on the men; I never saw any thing relished as much as it was. When we came to Mississippians and told them it was from Mississippi, they relished it still more." [11]

- - - - -

October 6, 1863
Sulphur Springs, North Carolina

Mrs. Cornelia Henry
Farm wife

"I made a shirt today. They killed a hog this morning, very nice. We were out of lard, why we killed it…. Nothing new going on. Corn is selling at seven dollars a bu. & wheat at ten dollars, sugar three." [12]

- - - - -

Early October, 1863
Chattanooga, Tennessee

Private M. L. Wheeler
Co. A – 33rd Alabama Infantry

"We drew no soap now, but on still bright days undressed, then boiled our shirts, drawers, and cotton socks. We washed our wollen socks sent us from home, scalded them, after which we dried all in the sunshine … and got into them again." [13]

(ed: They would wear their pants and shoes while boiling the above clothes to clean them and to kill the lice. Then when the boiled clothes were dry they would wash and boil their pants while standing around with shirts, drawers, socks and shoes on.)

- - - - -

October 7, 1863
Paris, France

Mr. C. J. McRae
C.S.A. Loan Agent – Europe

In a report to the Confederate government Mr. McRae included the below listing of recent purchases by Major Huse from Messrs. S. Isaac Campbell & Co.:

"30,000	jackets @ $3.30	$ 99,000
30,000	pants @ $2.96	88,000
30,000	great coats @ $7	210,000
60,000	shirts @ 52 cents	31,200
60,000	drawers @ 62 cents	37,200
60,000	socks @ 26 cents	15,000
30,000	shoes @ $2.14	64,200
30,000	blankets @ $1.80	54,000" [14]

- - - - -

October 8, 1863
Richmond, Virginia

Colonel Robert Kean
Confederate Bureau of War

"The secret arrangements which have been made for burning steamboats on the Mississippi river are working pretty well. Nineteen have been wholly destroyed and many more injured. One method is to fire into them from the shore with a small two pound shell filled with a phosphoric liquid which burns in spite of water. The gun weighs only 240 pounds and is carried on horseback. A Captain [John C.] McKay is in charge of the enterprise." [15]

- - - - -

October 10, 1863
Chattanooga, Tennessee

Private John Jackman
Co. B – 9th Kentucky Infantry

"All quiet this morning, when we had reveille at 2, and the troops kept under arms, fearing an advance. To-day "Jeff" rode around the lines, and was generally loudly cheered. When he and Bragg, with other general officers, passed our lines, our boys stood very respectfully on the works, but not a man opened his mouth." [16]

(ed: "The silence of the Kentuckians was not aimed at him [President Davis]. Their antipathy for Bragg had by this time become almost a religion.")

- - - - -

October 11, 1863
Greensboro, North Carolina

Mr. Carter Coupland
Riverboatman

"My dear Brother –
Your last & much prized letter came to hand some time ago & I should have answered it sooner but for my being taken sick. I was quite sick for two weeks in Mobile with Typhoid Fever & it left me so weak & debilitated that I determined Mother and Cousin Tiff a short visit in hopes the change might do me good – I am improving & will soon return to work again. They don't seem to think that the Boat can run unless I am about – I was truly sorry

to learn of your bad health & you have my heartfelt sympathy in all your afflictions – Oh that it was in my power to relieve the sufferings & hardships of your dear little children – brother get them away from Wmsbg if it be possible – I do not know that any suggestions of mine would aid you, but will leave that to the better judgement of yourself & Mother – I think your plan of renting a cottage on the R Rd is a good one; I will do all in my power to help you along, and you must not hesitate to call on me – for you are as welcome as I am – I have been here two days & will remain 4 or 5 more – I am in hopes by that time to be strong enough to go to work –
… Write soon – Yr Aff Bro – Carter" [17]

(ed: To get away from Yankee controlled Williamsburg, Virginia, his brother will move to Richmond in 1864 and rent accommodations near the railroad. Carter is recovering his health at the home of Cousin Tiff in Greensboro where his mother is also a guest.)

- - - - -

October 11, 1863 — Mrs. Cornelia Henry
Sulphur Springs, North Carolina — Farm wife

"This has been a long day…. since dinner I have washed three of the children & put clean clothes on them. They went off with Henderson before dinner & did not return till after we were done our dinner…. We had sweet potatoes & turnip salad for dinner & several other things. I got a few sweet potatoes Saturday. They have done no good this year at all. Neither have our turnips. It has been so very dry. Corn is hurt, some by the frost & badly by dry weather…." [18]

- - - - -

October 12, 1863 — Mr. Jacob R. Hildebrand
Augusta County, Virginia — Farmer

"Monday – I have very much concerned about my son Benjamin as he has one blanket to sleep under & the nights are getting cold but the army is moving

& there is no chance to get it, as the authoritys Refuse to grant passes from Gordonsville to the army   my son Benjamin was elected 2nd Lieutenant in Company A, 52nd Reg Va Volunteers" [19]

- - - - -

October 12, 1863 Private Grant Taylor
Demopolis, Alabama Co. G – 40th Alabama Infantry

"Dear wife and children,
… There is a great revival going on here and has been for several week. There is preaching every night and from 50 to 100 mourners. They say that 190 have joined the different denominations. 9 were baptized into the Baptist denomination yesterday. Oh how touching it is to see strong men come up with tears streaming down their manly cheeks and tell that they have found the Lord precious to their souls. May the good Lord carry on his good work until every soldier shal be converted.

… believe me your loving husband …
Grant" [20]

- - - - -

October 13, 1863 Lt. Jesse P. Bates
Camp near Meridian, Mississippi Co. G – 9th Texas Infantry

"Dear companion … I have not heard from you yet, not since the date of Feb. 24th. I have almost lost all hope of getting any more letters from you…. James Hooten is going to start home this evening and he will carry this to you for me and I will send two hundred $200 dollars by him. I am sorry to tell you that A. L. Hamilton was killed in the late battle of Chicamauga.

I was sick last week. I had the dipthery in my jaw and throat.

… Tell Frank and Sarah to be good children and help Ma … Send me a letter ever chance you get … I send you the token of my unchanging love …
Jesse P Bates" [21]

- - - - -

October 13, 1863
Camp near Rome, Georgia

Private Joseph T. Dunlap
Co. B –Wilcoxon Regiment

"Dear Ma:
I received a letter today from Mit and was glad to hear that you are well…. I haven't got the box that Pa sent by Capt. Bray. He said somebody stole it at Rome. I am very sorry that it was lost. Mr. Gilliespie said there was a suit of clothes in it for me. I received the box of provisions you send me … I found a pair of pants one pair of drawers and two pairs of sox. I am glad you sent me a pair of boots for my old shoes was busted.

We drill twice a day … We get from eight to ten ears of corn at a feed … We pull our corn ourselves…. It has been raining for two days…. Mr. Gillespie says that it is reported that we are in Bragg's Army. We are not in Bragg's Army.

… Ma I want you to make an overcoat for me, for I need one very badly. I want you all to answer this as soon as you receive this. Your affectionate son,
Joseph" [22]

(ed: It appears that the Wilcoxon Regiment is probably part of the Home Guard. Confederate enlistment records show that at age 17, when Joseph was subject to Confederate conscription in 1864, he enlisted in Company A, 4th Regiment of Georgia Reserve Infantry. Joseph rose to the rank of 4th Sergeant. Company A was assigned to guard duty at Andersonville Prison during Joseph's service.)

- - - - -

October 14, 1863
Chattanooga, Tennessee

Captain James P. Douglas
Douglas's Texas Artillery

"The President is on a visit here. He rode around our lines yesterday. The troops seemed much rejoiced and cheered loudly as he passed. He was very polite, raising his hat to every squad of soldiers he passed. He is a much finer looking man than I expected ..." [23]

- - - - -

Occupations at Enlistment

Gauley-Mercer Artillery

"farmer	35	carpenter	1
farm laborer	27	printer	1
laborer	2	real estate appraiser	1
blacksmith	2	merchant	1
teacher	2	potter	1
miller	2	attorney	1
		student	1" [24]

(ed: Occupations were shown on 77 of the 104 enlistment cards for the soldiers who served in the Gauley-Mercer Light Artillery.)

- - - - -

October 15, 1863
Charleston, South Carolina

General P. G. T. Beauregard
General Commanding

"Lieutenant Dixon made repeated descents in the harbor of Charleston, diving under the navy receiving ship which lay at anchor there. But one day when he was absent from the city, Mr. Hunley, unfortunately, wishing to handle the boat himself, made the attempt. It was readily submerged, but did not rise again to the surface, and all on board perished . ." [25]

(ed: The submarine was found in 9 fathoms of water by Angus Smith and his salvage crew. He began to proceed with operations to raise the boat.)

- - - - -

October 15, 1863
Camp Morton, Indiana

Private Archelaus M. Hughes
Co. G – 9th Tennessee Infantry

"I was captured by the Federals the 15th of October 1863 and sent to Federal prison, Camp Morton at Indianapolis, Indiana. I had pneumonia, erysipelas and mumps all at the same time … I became so ill … that the prison authorities wired my father at Columbus [Tennessee] that I would not live. He immediately took the first train to Indianapolis … the doctors told him that if he could get me out of there I had a chance to live. He obtained the certificates from the doctor to that effect and immediately left for Washington … it so happened that Andrew Johnson who was then Military Governor of Tennessee was there, and he and my father went together to the White House to see Mr. Lincoln. Mr. Lincoln took the application and wrote on the back of it this order … "I direct the release of this young man as a 'boon' to Governor Johnson." After my release I was along time recovering from the effects of the illness and just about the time I recovered I took inflammatory rheumatism and was in bed for three months…." [26]

- - - - -

Undated
with The Army of Tennessee

Dr. Deering J. Roberts
Surgeon – 20th Tennessee Infantry

"My experience was that of the average Regimental Surgeon with a regiment that was in the fore front of all engagements of the Army of Tenn. under Bragg … I had all essential medicines, never any want of chloroform, aspirin, morphine & quinine. My medical books from my own library weighed more than my medicine chest; and a pocket case and amputating case made by Geo. Tieman, the best instrument maker in the world … were my personal property …" [27]

(ed: Dr. Deering Roberts, for 40 years, was the proprietor and editor of Southern Practitioner *a monthly medical publication that was published by the* Surgical Journal.*)*

(ed: The George Tiemann Company, of New York City, was a highly regarded manufacturer of surgical equipment and they sold a variety of types of surgical cases and kits.)

- - - - -

October 16, 1863
Phillips County, Arkansas

Mrs. Mary Edmondson
Farm wife

"The day was made memorable by our having seen Captain Moore and Lieut Price from Bragg's army, bringing us news from Brother John, from whom we had not heard from in many months, and from Paul, his son, whom we were not aware had escaped alive from Vicksburg. Also from our son, William, from who we had not heard since January, and whose fate through all the fighting in and on the Mississippi we were ignorant … they were all well." [28]

- - - - -

October 17, 1863
Fort Morgan, Alabama

Lt. Colonel James Williams
21st Alabama Infantry

"Dear Lizzy:
By the boat I will send a barrell of oysters and some palmetto marked in your name care of Mrs. Turner.

If I can find a good man – I will also send you a bottle of fine brandy which is part of a lot presented to me by the Captain of the "blockade" steamer *Isabella* – dont get drunk with Mrs Parrot and Mrs Turner now or I will never give you a sample of the next lot I am fortunate enough to receive.
Williams" [29]

(ed: In an October 20 letter James wrote, "I have heard of the loss of the Submarine – I telegraphed to know if Dixon is safe and hear that he was not with it." This was the second sinking of the submarine and 9 sailors lost their lives, including Mr. Hunley, the inventor and designer. Lt. Dixon will resume command when they raise the boat.)

- - - - -

October 17, 1863
Camp Letterman, Gettysburg

Lt. Sanford Branch
Co. A – 8th Georgia Infantry

"Dear Brother,

I have just a half an hour before dinner and dont think I can spend it more profitably than by leting you hear from me. My wound continues to improve but I have had a tedious time of it 75 days without getting off my back. If I live I never want to go near a hospital again. I am perfectly disgusted with hospital life, a day seems like a week. Hoping to meet you and our dear Mother soon. With love to all.
I am your affect Brother, Sanford W. Branch" [30]

(ed: In other recent letters Sanford has noted that he is still discharging material from his chest wound. In a September 30th note to his Mother he mentioned that he was "up walking today for the first time.")

- - - - -

October 18, 1863
Harrison County, Texas

Mrs. Harriet Perry
Farm wife

"My dear Sallie & Tempie: Four months have passed away and I have not heard a word from you – I am all anxiety – sometimes I think I cannot bear the silence. I send this by a man who is going to try to cross the river [Mississippi] … Theophilus … did not know how to eat and I did not give milk enough for him and I thought he would starve before he would eat … but he has learned how now and loves it … he loves to suck *all* the time – he is nearly 10 months old and as smart as he can be … I told Mother & Pap all about the death of my darling little Mattie It was my first great sorrow … Mother Perry has lost her two youngest children and next to the oldest one. Aunt Octavia … has lost her only child a little boy 7 years old – all buried here, five little new made graves …

I am nearly crazy to hear from my Brothers. if either one killed or wounded…. Mr. Perry started back to the army about a month ago and was taken sick on the way and was sick a week we sent for him and brought him back home – he is well now, but weak and not able I think to return yet but he will start in the morning – I am miserable. I will not see him again for a year under the most favorable circumstances – he was gone thirteen months before he got a furlough … Give my love to Mother & Pap & every one of the children … I am still living with Mr. Perrys folks … I love them very much…. I am coming just as soon as the war closes Mr. Perry says and I know I shall – affectionately your Sister Harriet" [31]

(ed: Theophilus executed a brief will leaving all of "my property of every description consisting of negroes notes and accounts unto my wife Harriet Eliza Perry." Between his sickness and the hazards of military life he wanted to make sure his affairs were in order.)

- - - - -

October 20, 1863	Mr. Jacob R. Hildebrand
Near Culpeper, Virginia	Farmer

"The boys say that we lost about 100 killed and 500 wounded at the fight near bristow station & that we took about 2000 prisoners today   I turned my hilda mare loose to graze, she strayed off & I have not been able to find her, I think she was taken by some Soldier   when I was looking for her I met a man on horseback who discribed her & said that she was up the Road at some cavelry camp, but I am now satisfied that he sent me on the wrong track & that he knew where she was   the Division moved up about 3 miles near Brandy Station & there went into camp" [32]

- - - - -

October 20, 1863	Mr. John B. Jones
Richmond, Virginia	Clerk, War Department

"I saw flour sell at auction to-day for $61 per barrel…. It is the result of the depreciation of a redundant currency, and not of an ascertained scarcity." [33]

- - - - -

October 20, 1863
Gordonsville, Virginia

Private Felix Miller
Co. H – 48th N. Carolina Infantry

"My Dear Wife
… I came to this place on the 16 and we could not pass and we are still hear yet. I want you to do the best you can for there is hard times hear. You can gather for your self whin possoms is 5 five dollars apeace and chickens is twenty You no how it is if you can manage to git Levi in to anything to keep him out of this war try to do so … I hope to the Lord we will meat again rite soon …" [34]

(ed: Their son, Levi, must be nearing draft age and Felix is suggesting that perhaps she, with the help of friends, can get him a job in an exempt occupation.)

- - - - -

October 20 & 21, 1863
Chattanooga, Tennessee

Sergeant Robert Watson
Co. K – 7th Florida Infantry

"I reported sick this morning and the doctor gave me 2 powders and rubbed my breast with croton oil. Drew 2 days ration of flour. Cold all night.
Oct 21 – Sick this morning. Took a blue pill about ½ size of a pigeon's egg and rubbed my breast with croton oil … sick all night, violent pains in breast, head and bowel and severe cough." [35]

(ed: Croton oil is a violently cathartic oil normally used as a laxative. The blue pill is blue mass. Subsequent journal entries noted blisters on his chest from the croton oil. Who knows what the content or the purpose of the powders might have been? Robert was back to normal duties in November.)

- - - - -

October 21, 1863
Chattanooga – Camp Wagon Train

Lt. Joshua K. Callaway
Co. K – 28th Alabama Infantry

"My Dear Wife, …
I am having a gay time. I am chief cook and bottle washer. No one has control over me. And I command all the cooks from the whole Brigade. And when the commissaries want a detail, or want my cooks to do anything out of their line, they have to ask me. Although some of them are as big as Majors…. I sit in my tent out of the rain … walk round and see the cooks once or twice a day. I pay what all officers do for rations: 85 cts. a pound for bacon, 20 for beef, 12 ½ for flour, 4 for meal, .35 for salt and .25 for rice. About $25 a month, and then my tobacco writing papers pens, ink, envelopes and other foolishness, takes about all my wages. But I think I will send you a few hundred after awhile.

… Oh, how I wish I was home with you …
Your loving
J K Callaway" [36]

(ed: Eight days before, on the 13th, Joshua wrote, "I am sick! I am sick of our separation! Sick of war! And I am sick anyhow. I had a dumb little chill yesterday … I am afraid I am going to be sick sure enough.")

- - - - -

October 22, 1863
Macon City, Missouri

Captain Griffin Frost
Co. A – 2nd Missouri Infantry

" … arrived at Macon City … We were taken to Head Quarters, and from thence to prison…. It is certainly the filthiest place I ever saw; floor covered with dirty, lousy straw, windows all open; one old broken stove … with one camp kettle, a little tin bucket and a frying pan to be used for cooking for forty men … " [37]

(ed: Griffin ranks the conditions here worse than the prison ship he took from Ft. Delaware to City Point, Virginia, worse than Fort Delaware, and worse than Gratiot. He is hoping to be sent from Macon to Gratiot. On October 23rd they are told that they are being transferred to Gratiot Prison in St. Louis and Griffin is "highly agreeable.")

- - - - -

October 23, 1863 Mrs. Mary Watkins
Meherrin, Virginia Farm wife

"My Precious Husband
... went over home last week and walked all over the cornfield with Mr Anderson and then back home ... I think the fattening hogs are improving, they are very young most of them but I reckon we can make out meat enough.... I think I shall have some sorghum planted next year for molasses. Some [neighbors] made 150 gallons of molasses from one acre of sorghum and I think it would be better for the negroes not to have as much meat.... Mr A is gathering corn and sowing wheat.

Poor Mr Pollard died last Sunday of inflammation of the stomach ... He will be right much missed ... He has done nearly all the shoemaking since the war commenced. Poor Mrs Pollard is left with nine children (oldest just sixteen) and is expecting another. Isn't she to be pitied? Mama ... is afraid her mind will become unbalanced ...

... Oh dear how I wish this cruel war was over.... Must wash the baby now.
Good bye
Your own
Mary" [38]

- - - - -

October 23, 1863 *Macon Daily Telegraph*
Macon, Georgia

RAGS RAGS RAGS

"The Undersigned respectfully asks all persons in Macon and vicinity having any linen or cotton rags white or colored, to send them to his store, where the highest market price will be paid for them in goods or cash as may be desired. Old baggin and rope, or stained cotton will also be received on same terms.... All readers of the Macon Daily Telegraph are specially invited to interest themselves in sending in their rags &c as money will not purchase printing paper at any price. I shall collect them specifically for the Telegraph and stand ready always to pay cash or sell goods at lowest prices for rags.

T. W. FREEMAN
Wholesale & Retail Grocer
Cherry Street below Telegraph Building" [39]

- - - - -

October 24, 1863 — 1st Lt. W. R. Montgomery
Near Chattanooga, Tennessee — 3rd Bttn. Georgia Sharpshooters

"My Dear Aunt Frank
... We have no tents yet, so we have to make out as best we can be stretching our blankets. So you see when it is cold & raining too we need our blankets to cover with. I am awful tired of Gen Brag & this part of the country & am too anxious to be again in "Old Va" under Gen Lee." [40]

(ed: William is part of the two divisions of men General Longstreet took west to join General Bragg and the Army of Tennessee in their victory at Chickamauga and the Siege of Chattanooga. They will soon be departing to head toward Knoxville to attempt to wrest that area from Union control.)

- - - - -

October 25, 1863 — Captain Richard Watkins
Culpeper, Virginia — Co. K – 3rd Virginia Cavalry

"My Darling
Henry & Josh Ewing are going after fresh horses and I write to let you know that I am well ... A great many horses played out on our last campaign and nearly one half of my company will have to get fresh ones. Some are talking about going into infantry the price of horses is so high. And I fear that unless

our horses are better fed many will be compelled to change their branch of service. Old John Wesley still keeps up though considerably reduced … " [41]

(ed: The Confederate government has come up with a solution to the problem of starving horses. They will now require the men to all keep two horses in the field. This will reduce trips home for new mounts. 2nd Lt. Archer Haskins will not be allowed to go home for a fresh mount unless he brings 2 horses back to camp. Richard will note to Mary in a letter on November 11th, "Archer is in a great bother. He does not want to keep two horses starving at a time …" Only a government bureaucrat could hatch such an idea.)

- - - - -

Late October, 1863 — John Kell – Exec. Officer
Straits of Sunda, Sumatra — C. S. Cruiser *Alabama*

"As we drew near the Straits of Sundra we fell in with several ships and chased and boarded three English and one Dutch ship. A day or two later, while we were giving chase to two English ships, a third ship hove in sight. It was too American to be allowed to elude us. We fired across the bow, and the flag of the United States went up, our first prize in East Indies Waters. She was the *Amanda*, from Boston; cargo, sugar and hemp. The papers were not satisfactory, so we burned her, after taking necessary articles for our ship. We soon came to anchor … a mile or two from Sumatra, where we hoped to procure the fresh food needed for the good health of our crew, for we had been a long time at sea." [42]

- - - - -

October 26, 1863 — Mr. John T. Bourne
St. George's, Bermuda — C. S. Commerical Agent

"John White Esq., London
Dear Sir: - I have the pleasure to inform you of the safe arrival this day of the str. *Advance* from Wilmington.

The cargo consists of Five Hundred Bales of Cotton which I would suggest you insure against fire while now in the course of reshipment….

News – *Venus* lost on Wilmington coast. No further progress by the enemy on Charleston." [43]

- - - - -

October 27, 1863	Private J. H. Armstrong
Shreveport, Louisiana	Co. F – 14th Texas Infantry

"My Dear Martha,
I received yours of 18th inst[ant] day before yesterday … I wrote to Mother & Mary on yesterday evening not knowing when I would leave here … the fortifying is still going forward slowly. There is more negroes coming in every day … Tell Billy to be a good little boy and learn all he can. Tell Junius to feed the little pigs and raise a heap of big hogs before I get home. Tell Charley & Sammy that I will come home so soon as I can. You will soon contract the habit of managing your business and will get along finely…. I would like to know how you fix up the Confederate tax. When you get the wagon fixed you must also let me know….

I will now close, be of good cheer, my confidence is in God and I verily believe that I will return.
Your husband
J H Armstrong" [44]

(ed: James enlisted, at age 42, on September 18, 1863. Martha is just beginning to adjust to being the farm manager and making all the decisions regarding farm work, repairs, tax payments and a myriad of other items.)

- - - - -

October 28, 1863 Mrs. Catherine Edmondston
Halifax County, North Carolina Farm wife

"Yesterday Mr E went out Deer Hunting & the party was so fortunate that he brought me home a fine fat haunch as his portion of the spoils....

Besides the romance of the thing, the reminiscences of Robin Hood & Friar Tuck it awakens, the addition to my larder is a consideration with beef at 50 cts and Turkeys $10 a piece, & we with nine in family." [45]

- - - - -

October 28, 1863 Miss. Ellen Gaddes
Mobile, Alabama Hospital volunteer

"Mrs. B. A. Spears
I received your letter of the 20th [September] three weeks after date. I should have answered it sooner but I wished to find out all I could about your husband before I wrote.... a great affliction [has] befallen our family since I last wrote you, you may have heard about the submarine boat that sank with eight men on her, in Charleston Harbor. one of them was my Stepfather, since his death we have hardly been fit for anything.... I will write to you about your business. I applied to the steward of the hospital to find if your husband had left anything, he directed me to the ward steward ... he told me that there was nothing left, I told him I knew that he left a pocket book ... I know that he did have a pocket book because he wanted some one to take care of it for him. I had advised him to give it to one of the matrons ... they all deny having it .... I am very sorry that I cannot do something to help you ... Give my love to all your little ones ...

Mobile is about thirty five miles from Point Clear where the hospital is situated. our summer residence is there, we always live here in winter. I went across to Point Clear on purpose to attend to your business. I am very sorry that I did not succeed any better ... my best wishes for your welfare ... I remain your sincere friend." [46]

- - - - -

October 28, 1863 Mrs. Judith McGuire
Richmond, Virginia Nurse

"A merino dress cost $150, long cloth $5.50 per yard, fine cotton stockings $6 per pair, handkerchiefs … $5.00…. Carpets are not to be found – they are too large to run the blockade … " [47]

- - - - -

October 28, 1863 Mr. John B. Jones
Richmond, Virginia Clerk, War Department

"We have some 13,000 prisoners here, hungry; for there is not sufficient meat for them." [48]

- - - - -

October 29, 1863 Private William H. Arial
Camp near Chattanooga, Tennessee Co. D – Hampton Legion

"Dear Friend [Mrs. Margaret Bradley],
By your request I will drop you a few lines witch I am very sorrow to State that George [Sgt. Geo. W. Bradley, Co. E, 2nd S. C. Rifles] breath his last breth last night between 12 and one o'clock. We had a very hard fite he was shot through the bodie at the comenssment…. I don't know how many is cill and wound in that company. His capt was wound in hip but not dangerous. I don't know how many cill and wound in this company I belong to…. Do not grieve for your husband for his spirit is now in that happy land where there is no more worees and sorrow…. I know that it will be awful news to you but you mus bare it with all the patien that you can … I now nothing more but remain as ever your most affectnite friend.
Wm H. Ariail" [49]

(ed: Confederate service records spell his name Arial but he signed this letter Ariail.)

- - - - -

October 29, 1863
W of Camden, Arkansas

Dr. William McPheeters
Price's Division

"Went with Maj. Cabell after breakfast to Mr. Blake's to see Dr. Clark and get provisions. Brought back 2 turkeys, 6 chickens, and 4 lbs butter – turkeys $5 for the two, chickens $5, and butter $4. Rode back in drizzling rain. Dr. Cunningham and Col. Taylor dined with us on a fine turkey. Read and smoked at night." [50]

- - - - -

October 29, 1863
"Rappahanock" River, Virginia

Private Marion H. Fitzpatrick
Co. K – 45th Georgia Infantry

"Dear Amanda,
... I am writing with ink of my own make which is simply polk berries squeezed out. I want you to put a little coppera in your next letter for me to put in it. They say it will turn it black and make it more indelible...." [51]

- - - - -

October 30, 1863
Brandy Station, Virginia

Dr. Thomas F. Wood
HQ – 3rd N. Carolina Infantry

"Dear Pa,
Capt. R. F. Langdon, AQM of this Regt., leaves tomorrow for Raleigh for clothing for officers and men. He will probably remain until the next arrival of a steamer; if so I will be able to buy a pr. of blankets, $10., one of shoes or boots at $___; cloth at $10 per yard, overcoats $40., shirts $8. or $10. per pair and other things ... Also I am nearly threadbare, I will have to keep the cloth; but ... you can divide the other things between you. I am entitled to one each only. It does not amount to much but I thought if you wanted them I could secure them for you....
Affectionatley your son,
Thomas F." [52]

- - - - -

October 31, 1863
Camp Letterman
Gettysburg, Pennsylvania

Lt. Sanford Branch
Co. A – 8th Georgia Infantry

"Dear Mother
This will probablly be the last letter you will receive from this place, as I will be sent to Balt. next week. I am very anxious to get there as it is very cold now and I don't improve as fast in a tent as I would in a house. Thank God I am still improveing and just as home sick as it is possible to be. I hear there is a chance of exchanging being resumed. again hope it may be so, as I have no ideas of spending the winter in a Fort. much prefer the Sunny South, but I may not be allowed a preference. Love to all. Good bye.
Your affect. Son
Sanford W. Branch" [53]

(ed: Sanford has been hoping for almost a month to get a transfer to West Building Hospital in Baltimore. The splint has finally come off his arm. He will arrive by train in Baltimore on November 4th. The West Building Hospital is in a converted cotton warehouse "on Concord Street near Union Dock.") [54]

- - - - -

October 31, 1863
Camp near Kelly's Ford, Virginia

Private Lawrence E. Day
Co. D – 3rd Alabama Infantry

"My Very Dear Sister,
Your kind epistle of the 23rd inst. arrived … I would liked to have been there when you had so much fish to eat. I could eat my share of them … There is some talk of us all going home next May when our term of enlistment expires … I don't think we will have any more fighting until next spring…. as soon as we get in winter quarters … you must send me a little box … be sure to put a bottle of brandy and you will oblige your bro …
Your brother, Lawrence Day" [55]

- - - - -

Milk Fever *Mackenzie's 5000 Receipts*

"This fever usually arises about the third or fourth day after delivery. The symptoms are pain and distention of the breasts, shooting frequently toward the arm-pit. Sometimes the breasts become hard, hot and inflamed. It generally continues a day or two, and ends spontaneously by copious sweats, or a large quantity of pale urine.

Remedies – If it should prove violent, especially in young women ... we should abate the inflammation by bleeding; this, however, is rarely necessary. But, in every constitution, the body must be kept open by gentle cooling laxatives or clysters. The breasts should be often drawn either by the child, or, if the mother does not design to give suck, by some proper person. If the breasts are hard, very turgid, or inflamed, emollient fomentations ought to be applied to them. The common poultice of bread and milk, with the addition of a little oil, may be used on this occasion, and warm milk, or a decoction of elderflowers, for a fomentation." [56]

- - - - -

November, 1863

Union forces capture the Texas cities of Brownsville on the 6th and Corpus Christi on the 16th.

General Bragg detaches General Longstreet to attempt to retake Knoxville, Tennessee, from the forces of Union General Burnside.

In Charleston, South Carolina, the *H. L Hunley* is raised from the bottom of the harbor. Lt. Dixon returns to Charleston and is recruiting a new crew.

On November 19th a new cemetery is dedicated in Gettysburg, Pennsylvania. The principal speaker at the dedication is the renowned orator Edward Everett. After his lengthy talk, President Abraham Lincoln gives a brief 300 word address. The President's remarks are ridiculed and Mr. Everett is praised. In a matter of weeks not a word of Mr. Everett's talk will be remembered and the simple magic of Lincoln's prose will become etched into our minds, "*Four score and seven years ago our fathers brought forth on this continent a new nation …*"

In northern Virginia General Meade and the Army of the Potomac try to surprise General Lee in a quick thrust across the Rapidan River. Lee meets him in prepared defensive positions near the Wilderness. Meade withdraws back across the Rapidan and begins moving his army into winter quarters. The Mine Run Campaign and major action by the armies in Virginia is concluded for 1863.

General Grant has massed armies under Generals Hooker, Thomas and Sherman and is ready to attempt to break the Confederate siege of Chattanooga. On the 24th Hooker's troops assault and literally climb Lookout Mountain and gain control of the heights on the morning of the 25th. At mid-afternoon on the 25th the troops of General Thomas take the Confederate rifle pits at the base of Missionary Ridge and then, without orders, continue the attack right up the steep slopes of the ridge and break the center of the Confederate line. General Bragg, with his center broken and in retreat, withdraws his army into northwestern Georgia. General Grant has broken the siege of Chattanooga, defeated Bragg's army and returned south central Tennessee to Union control.

General Bragg has squandered the tremendous advantage he gained with his victory at Chickamauga. The staggering loss of life by his soldiers on that Georgia battlefield, just 60 days ago, has been in vain.

Letters between soldiers and their families at home tell a tale of rising inflation, food scarcity, disease and hardship. The soldiers are moving into winter quarters and requesting boxes of provisions from home. The fighting is basically over for 1863.

November, 1863

November 1, 1863
West Point, Georgia

Private Grant Taylor
Co. G – 40th Ala. Infantry

"Beloved wife & children,
These few lines leave me in good health though considerable jaded for the want of sleep not having lain down in the last 2 nights to sleep. I wrote you a few lines Wednesday [28th] stated that we should start for Chattanooga Tenn. the next day. We did so. Took the cars at 12 o'clock M and arrived in Selma that evening. Staid there till 12 the next day. Took steamboat there and landed in Montgomery yesterday morning at daylight. Staid there until last night 12 o'clock. Took the cars and landed here one hour ago. Where we will stay till this evening. Then we will take cars to Atlanta.

... I gave $5 per quire for paper in Selma. Steel pens are generally 25 cent apiece. In Montgomery pork is $1.50, beef $1.00, butter $3.50 and honey $2 and flour 50 cents per pound. Common pocket knives are $15. What are we coming to Potatoes are about $8 per bushel.

Malinda, a broad strip of country is lengthening out between us. Oh shall I ever see my sweet home and family again? ...
Your ever loving,
Grant" [1]

- - - - -

November 3, 1863
"Chatanooga," Tennessee

3rd Corporal Milton Barrett
Co. E – Third Battalion
Georgia Sharpshooters

"Dear Brother and sister,
... The water hear does not a gree with me and I have had the direar [diarrhea] every scence i have bin hear and it have reduce me down rite smarte. Lawrence is pestered with the same. i saw him this morning. he was a giting rite fat before he took the Direar....

We have had a bounance [abundance] of rain have wash a way some of our railroad bridges, makes it very difacult to git supplyes. hear in fack our rashings have bin of a infery [inferior] kind every scence we have bin heare, mostley corn meal and it damage and our beef not very good and I dout haveing that long.

... Tha is but a few fur lows give now and tha in espechel cases. i think i will git one this winter if i dont git well perty soon. i am going to make a effort for a fur low for i dont believe i will git wel whil i have to drink this blue lime stone water. Tha is a grate meany it serves like it dose me.

... i will close hopeing thes lines may find you all well.... i remain your loving
Brother
Milton Barrett" [2]

- - - - -

November 3, 1863
Newnan, Georgia

Miss. Kate Cummings
Hospital Matron

"In looking over letters received from a friend in Mobile, I was a little astonished at an assertion in one about the planters. It seems they will not sell produce unless at an exorbitant price, and many will take nothing in return but gold and silver. If this is really the case, which I have no reason to doubt, I am at a loss to understand how they can be so blinded. Are they not aware that we are blockaded, and can only procure food from them; and do they not also know, if the enemy succeed – which they assuredly will, if the planters and others act as they are now doing – that they will be ruined, as well as every body else? Heaven help the country! I am getting sick at heart with seeing men from whom we expected so much acting as they are now doing. I wonder if they expect men to fight for them and their property, if they leave their wives and children to starve?" [3]

- - - - -

November 4, 1863
Cargo Manifest

Cornubia
Richard H. Gayle – Master

"588 tons from St. George's, Bermuda to Nassau

58 cases bacon, 3 cases bacon, 19 hogsheads bacon, 3 cases cartridge paper, 1 case blankets, 12 bales, 1 case, 15 cases caps, 36 pigs lead, 300 sacks saltpeter, 64 cases rifles, 4 quarter casks brandy." [4]

- - - - -

November 5, 1863
Richmond, Virginia

Colonel Robert Kean
Confederate Bureau of War

"How in the midst of a war, requiring the expenditure of $600,000,000 per annum … is the change to be made from one currency in the hands of the people to another, without producing starvation in the interval before prices would readjust themselves … ? Even if the existing circulation were swept out of existence, any new one … would rapidly depreciate to the present rate of Confederate money. It remains therefore to base the new issue on property specifically pledged for its redemption. For this, the property must belong to the Government.

The following appears to me to be the only adequate measure: to lay a tax of such a percent of all the taxable property of the country as will raise $600,000,000, payable in money, bonds, cotton, tobacco, wheat, corn, flour, forage, meat, negroes, and perhaps real estate.... By allowing a certain latitude of choice to the taxpayer as to the subject in which to make payment the burden would be lightened." [5]

(ed: The seventh and final issue of Confederate currency will be issued in February of 1864 and once again they try to remove earlier currencies, similar to methods tried on issue six, and again they fail. In the process, inflation continues to run rampant and the Confederate dollar will become virtually worthless.)

- - - - -

November 5, 1863	Mrs. Mary Watkins
Meherrin, Virginia	Farm wife

"My dear Husband
... Mr Anderson [overseer] took me the usual rounds to the grainery, cornhouse, hog pen, smoke house, dairy and garden. He was filling the corn house from the grainery where he has been drying it out. They had gathered 240 barrels ... and not more than half done. Finished sowing wheat this morning. We have had fine weather for sowing wheat and drying our corn. Mr A has ... twenty nine and a half stacks of fodder. The hogs are really improving right fast.... Mr. Anderson has all of that back square of the garden that we used to have in potatoes full of cabbages ... he told me he had thirteen hundred heads of cabbage in that square ... think we might sell some ...

I am going to send you two pair of flannel drawers by Henry Ewing. I reckon they will be very comfortable this winter. Aunt Jane is going to send a flannel shirt to Cousin Willie of the Nottoway Troop by him too....
Your own
Mary" [6]

- - - - -

November 5, 1863 Mrs. Malinda Taylor
Pickens County, Alabama Farm wife

"Dear husband,
With pleasure I am seated to pen you a few lines. We are all well hoping you are in good health. I supose you have left Demopolous and gon to Chattanuga. I heard yesterday they ware fighting thare.... I have not got but the 2 letter from you yet....

I have the childrens winter clothes ready for the loom, 25 yds. It is now daylight. I have been witing by firelight. I must quit and get breakfast....

Grant, I have been very lonesum since you went off but am getting over that now. I expect to send this by James Williams as he is here now.... Write evry chance you have and I will do so two.

You can write on the other side of this leaf. Nothing more, only I remain yours, as ever,
Malinda" [7]

- - - - -

November 5, 1863 Lt. Colonel Hillery Moseley
Panola County, Mississippi 42nd Mississippi Infantry

"Columbus Miss Nov 5 1863

Hon. Jas. A. Seddon
Secretary of War Confederate States of America

Dear Sir, Believing that I shall not be able for duty for several months on account of a wound suffered at the Battle of Gettysburg and having been elected a Member of the Legislative body of Mississippi. I think it due to the Regiment of which I am now the Senior Officer and to the interest of the Service that I make a tender of my Resignation.

And respectfully Tender you my Resignation as Lt. Col of the 42nd Missippi Regiment To take affect immediately.

Respt your Obdt Servt.
H Moseley

Post Officer
Panola
Miss" [8]

(ed: This resignation is really a formality. The wound to his foot renders him unfit for further duty as an infantry officer. His resignation is accepted and Hillery receives his medical discharge on December 18, 1863.)

- - - - -

November 6, 1863
Near Lookout Mountain, Tennessee

Sergeant Archie Livingston
Co. G – 3rd Florida Infantry

"Dear Enoch:
Feeling something in the spirit of writing, have thought I would send you this scroll…. We often wish that a Lee, Beauregard, Johnston or Longstreet was in command of this army. Whether they would accomplish more than Genl Bragg has is a matter that is to be tried. H[owever] is a known fact that the troops of his command … and it is thought by many that the victory was not so complete as it might have been if the battle of Chickamauga had been fought & won by other of those generals. – The President seems yet to sustain Genl Bragg and pronounces him competent …

… There is much talk in camp with reference to re-enlistments. The Florida troops say they are going home in May, anyhow in August – 3 years from the date of original enlistment. As for me I am a soldier for the war, but would prefer service in Florida or else where than Tenn or Miss. I committed a blunder when I enlisted in the 3rd and only did so to please Father & Mother, who seemed very desirous that I should follow Albert & Theodore…. " [9]

- - - - -

November 6, 1863 Mrs. Cornelia Henry
Sulphur Springs, North Carolina Farm wife

"Harrie went to Asheville today, heard nothing of Mr. Henry. Betsy got the cloth out today, 10 ½ yds. I sent Henderson to Mrs. Rutherford's for the soap she has been making, got 32 lbs. That was Wednesday. Pinck went along. On Thursday, Henderson went to Cook's & got my shoes. Tom Cook is to come this week & finish making shoes as Harrie got some leather in Asheville last Tuesday. Henderson has had a very sore heel, the oxen tramped on it. It is better now." [10]

- - - - -

November 7, 1863 Sergeant John K. Beaton
Near Winton, North Carolina Co. G – 9th Virginia Infantry

"Dear Sister
I have not received a letter from you in a very long time.... I received the bundle you sent for which I am very much obliged. I tried to see Mrs. Flemming at Kinston ... I saw her children they have been very sick with agere and fever but are getting better ... I have just seen a letter from Lt. Lewis of our company. He is a prisoner at Johnson's Island....

I would like very much to stay near Petersburg a while. I heard two very able sermons last week. I went to Mr. Wheelwrights church he looks like the same as ever and I think preaches better.

We are treated very well by the people of Carolina ... they sold us vegetables very cheap and in fact gave us all they could spare. They knew we had had a very hard time and tried to make our stay with them as pleasant as possible....
Accept my love for yourselves.
JKB" [11]

- - - - -

November 8, 1863
Steamer *Senator*
Near Selma, Alabama

Mr. Carter Coupland
Riverboatman

"My dear Mother

This is a beautiful Sunday morning & while I am nearing Selma with 450 troops, I can imagine your [______] household preparing for church – I am well & doing well – have no right to complain, but oh! I am sick & tired of the life I am leading! I think there is a better day in store for me yet – Last week I received a letter from Harriet – she was in James City [County, Virginia]. had not been able to see her Mother, but hope to do so in a few days.... said she intended writing to you in a few days – Her letter was a month reaching me – I keep as warm as a toast under cover of your nice Yarn Shirts – many, many thanks for them - ! Give my aff love to Cousin Tiff & the children – Aunt Sally Uncle Tom &c – not time to day more –
Your Aff Son
Carter" [12]

- - - - -

November 8, 1863
Gordo, Alabama

Mrs. Evalina Skelton
Farm wife

"Dear Husband
... I am suffering right bad with my breast and Sary Ann and the baby is both bad off with cold.... We have got our potatoes dug and we made a fine chance of them. We made fifty or sixty bushells and I wish you was here to help us eat them ... I let the pork hogs eat out the peas and yesterday evening I had them put in the pen.... Abel, I have had the good luck to draw fifty six pounds of salt ... and I got enough sole leather to make Julius and Tommy a pair of shoes and half sole mine.... I will send you what clothes you wrote for the very first chance I get ... your affectionate wife Evalina ..." [13]

- - - - -

November 9 & 10, 1863
Augusta County, Virginia

Mr. Jacob R. Hildebrand
Farmer

"Took tenth of my fodder to Staunton weight 1150 pounds Took 10th of my hay to Staunton tax in kind 1600 pounds" [14]

- - - - -

November 9, 1863
"Rappidan River", Virginia

Private Bryant Folsom
Co. C – 26th Georgia Infantry

" … I am not well at this time tho I dont think every thing mutch is the matter with mee only the diarrhae." [15]

- - - - -

November 9, 1863
Moton's Ford, Virginia

Private George Davis
Co. K – 30th N. C. Infantry

"Ma
I will write a few hurried lines this morning … I am sorry to have to tell you that Weldon is a prisoner, and twenty one members of his co.… Most of his men who escaped are of the opinion that Weldon was wounded …

Our army, I reckon, is nearly by this time on this side of the Rappidan. The last we heard from A. P. Hill he was at Brandy Station …

I have never been so put up for something to eat in my life as I have been for the last two or three days. We have just drawn some bread and beef. We drew five biscuits and a piece of beef two inches square Saturday morning and we drew nothing else until this morning (Monday) but I am well and have some rations left. I do hope we get something from home soon. I would like you to make me a pr of gloves and sent me two prs of socks.… write soon
Your affectionate son, George" [16]

(ed: Weldon was wounded in the lower right leg at Kelly's Ford on November 7. He was treated at the Union Third Corps Hospital and forwarded to Douglas Hospital in Washington, D.C. His lower leg was fractured and gangrene had set in. The leg was amputated, above the knee, on the lower 1/3 of the femur on November 9. Weldon died of tetanus on November 22 and was buried in the hospital cemetery on November 25.)

(ed: Tetanus is an acute, often fatal disease caused by a bacillus, Clostridium tetani, *that generally enters the body through wounds, characterized by rigidity and spasmodic contractions of the voluntary muscles.)* [17]

- - - - -

November 9, 1863 — Salvage Contract
Charleston, South Carolina — Submarine *H. L. Hunley*

"General:
The undersigned referees appointed to ascertain the salvage due Messrs. Smith and Broadfoot (divers) for raising the "submarine Torpedo Boat" sunk off Fort Johnson, in consideration of the difficulties in raising said boat – i.e. Depth of water, number of days employed and loss of submarine armor and from the best information we can obtain that the said boat could not be replaced for less than twenty-seven thousand five hundred ($27,500) dollars, therefore we do award to Messrs. Smith and Broadfoot (divers) the sum of thirteen thousand seven hundred + fifty ($13,750) dollars, being 50 percent of the salvage of the boat." [18]

(ed: The Confederate Government reduced this payment to $7000 citing the fact that Confederate naval ships, tools, equipment and manpower were used to assist Messrs. Smith and Broadfoot in raising the submarine.)

- - - - -

November 11, 1863
Chattanooga, Tennessee

Private John Jackman
Co. B – 9th Kentucky Infantry

"Johnnie G[reen] and I commenced building us a house to-day, tearing down an old out house in the country for this purpose. All the boys are busy as beaver building cabins for winter…. " [19]

- - - - -

November 12, 1863
Gratiot Prison, St. Louis, Missouri

Captain Griffin Frost
Co. A – 2nd Missouri Infantry

"Received a box from home. Every prisoner knows how to interpret that. What a sensation it produces in our mess … "chicken fixens" – fresh butter, baked chickens, nice biscuits, apples, apple butter, dried peaches and so on. A letter came with the box, of course, but the Provost ain't done hunting for contraband in that yet. All right – will be good when it comes…. " [20]

- - - - -

November 13, 1863
Newnan, Georgia

Miss. Kate Cummings
Hospital Matron

"Our wounded are doing badly; gangrene in its worst form has broken out among them. Those whom we thought were almost well are now suffering severely. A wound which a few days ago was not size of a silver dime is now eight or ten inches in diameter.

The surgeons are doing all in their power to stop its progress. Nearly every man in the room … there is very little laughing among them now … it is a most painful disease … We can not tempt them to eat, and we have little sweet milk, and that is the cry with them all…. It is distressing to go into the wards for I hear but the one cry – milk!" [21]

- - - - -

November 13, 1863
Richmond, Virginia

Mrs. Judith McGuire
Clerk – Commissary Department

"My appointment to a clerkship in the Commissary Department has been received, with a salary of $125 per month…. [my] duties are those of accountants." [22]

(ed: Judith has moved to Richmond and is renting rooms for $60 per month. She was unable to afford the Richmond rent with her pay as a nurse and took the train in from her rented home in Ashland on a varied commuting schedule.)

- - - - -

November 13, 1863
Richmond, Virginia

Mr. John B. Jones
Clerk, War Department

"Flour at $110 per barrel…. Bacon, hoground, $2.75 to $3 … butter $3.75." [23]

- - - - -

November 14, 1863
Louisburg, North Carolina

Miss. Mary T. Person
Farm girl

"My dear sister Harriet:
It has been so long since you red'd a letter from home, and so many *sad sad* changes have taken place I hardly know how to begin. Two of our dear Brothers have been taken from us – Jesse and Tom. Jesse was instantly killed the 3rd of July in the battle of Gettysburg, Pa…. when shot with a pistol ball just above the left eye. he was taken from the field … and carried a short distance to the hospital and expired in a few minutes … He was buried the next morning in a Presbyterian church yard near Hunterstown, Pa…. Tom … [was] wounded in the fight at Bristol Station [Bristoe Station, Virginia] the wound in the upper part of the left lung – the ball passing entirely through passing out under the left shoulder. He was carried to Warrenton Va living only six days afterwards – and died at four o'clock Tuesday, the morning of the 20th…. We rec'd your letter informing us of dear little Mattie's death – it

is so sad and all of the circumstances connected with it – I felt so much for you but … she is resting quietly in Heavan. We always anticipated so much pleasure in hope of seeing her but it was all in vain. Give a thousand kisses to sweet little Theophilus … Cousin Hugh was a great sufferer with his wound – but he gets around very well now on his crutches….

Pap Mother and every one join me in love to you with many kind regards to Brother T … I remain your fond and aff.
Sister
Tempie" [24]

(ed: This is a letter to Harriet Perry of Marshall, Texas.)

- - - - -

November, 1863
Eastern North Carolina
Cape Fear District

Surgeon John H. Kinyoun
66th North Carolina Infantry

"Register Sick and Wounded of the 66th North Carolina Infantry

Name	Rank	Regt	Company	Disease
John Capps	priv	66	K	Catarrh - Sent Hosp #4 Wilmington
Thomas Couch	priv	66	A	Intermittent Fever
T. H. Kearney	Lt.	66	D	Rhumatism – Home 30 day furlough
Rufus Batcheler	priv	66	B	Pneumonia – Sent to Gen. Hosp. #4
J. R.Braswell	priv	66	B	Lumbago – Sent to Gen. Hosp. #4
J. Holland	Lt.	66	C	Remitans
R. Weaver	priv	66	G	Chronic Dysentery – Hosp. #4
O. Mobley	priv	66	C	Typhoid – Sent to Gen. Hosp. #4
S. Chisenhall	priv	66	A	Chronic Diarrhea" [25]

(ed: In November 170 soldiers reported to sick call. Listed above are a few about mid-month in the ledger. The numbers continued to increase with close confinement, bad diet, exposure, and poor sanitation. From September, 1863 through the end

of the war more than 2900 men would be recorded in Dr. Kinyoun's ledger. That is almost 3 times for each soldier based on the initial strength of the 66th North Carolina. It is obviously much higher when you factor in the losses due to death, woundings, capture, desertions, details for other duties, discharges and all the other instances that reduced the effective manpower of the regiment.)

- - - - -

November 15, 1863
"On the side of Look-out Mountain,"
Tennessee

Private Grant Taylor
Co. G – 40th Alabama Infantry

"Beloved wife and children,
... We are faring badly for something to eat. I had no meat for 5 days until last night. We drew 2 days rations of beef and I could have eaten it all at 2 meals and not have had enough. And we do not get near bread enough. I hear of desertions daily and in fact I do not see how men can expect to keep an army together on such fare for we all know they could give us bread plenty.

... There is no fighting going on here except occasionally a shell from one side or the other. I have not seen a hog nor cow since I came to Tenn. except some that came from Ga. on the cars and there is no chance to buy anything to eat.

What is the reason that Ki will not let you have any leather. Tell him that he must let me have enough to make me a pair of shoes with that upper leather that I let him have ... The rocks here are very severe on shoes. I do not believe these I have will last longer than Christmas.... Many [of the soldiers] are nearly or quite barefooted now.

... Farewell for the present my dearest,
Grant" [26]

- - - - -

November 16, 1863
Athens, Tennessee

Private George W. Alexander
Co. E – 9th Tennessee Cavalry

" ... captured 276 Head of fine Beeves was detailed to drive them to Bragg army the Battle of Missionary ridge occured on Nov 26th confederated defeated retreated to Dalton, GA. I drove the cattle there." [27]

- - - - -

November 16, 1863
Camp near Meridian, Mississippi

Lt. Jesse P. Bates
Co. G – 9th Texas Infantry

"Dear wife, ... I am well at this time.... I returned to my command from Ellisville the day before yesterday ...

Our neighbor boys are all well except Loflen. He is absent at a hospital. We are preparing to build houses to winter in as we expect to stay here all winter...

I am going to try to get a furlough in a short time ... If there was another officer in our Company present for duty, there would be no problem ... but the order granting furloughs requires that there be two officers left with the Company....

My love, I have fared well ... I have plenty to eat ... I hope that I will be home by the first of Jan.... So farewell for present.
Jesse P Bates" [28]

(ed: Jesse will get a furlough in early 1864 and he will write home to Susan on March 21, 1864 from Nachitoches, Louisiana that he is "trying to cross the Red River & head on E to Miss Riv." He was able to cross the Mississippi on March 29 and then headed on eastward to rejoin his command. Jesse will be killed at Altoona, Georgia on October 5, 1864.)

- - - - -

November 16, 1863 *Wytheville Dispatch*
Wytheville, Virginia

"Wytheville Female College
VIRGINIA
This institution was opened on the tenth day of September
TERMS FOR SESSION OF TEN WOMEN

Board, washing and fuel	$ 450.00
Tuition in regular course	60.00
Tuition in music	90.00
Tuition in vocalization	80.00
Tuition in French	40.00

Each boarder will be required to furnish six pounds of tallow candles, … Each day scholar will be charged $5.00 extra for fuel, pens and ink. Farmers from this vicinity will be expected to furnish produce for a part, at least, of the amount of the charges.

W. D. ROEDEL. Principal" [29]

(ed: The publishing offices of the "Dispatch" were moved to Hillsville, Virginia at the end of 1863 due to the increasing frequency of Union cavalry raids into the Wytheville and Saltville areas attempting to destroy the railroads, and disrupt production at the lead mines and salt mines. The 1864 and 1865 issues were printed in Hillsville and the paper published without interruption during the entire conflict.)

- - - - -

November 17, 1863 Captain Griffin Frost
Gratiot Prison, St. Louis, Missouri Co. A – 2nd Missouri Infantry

"… a singular circumstance occurred at the hospital last night. Two men – one Confederate, the other a Federal, died and were laid out side by side. This morning when the dead room was entered, the body of the Federal was found to be terribly mutilated by the rats, while his neighbor … undisturbed. What cause could produce the difference? Most probably the nature of the disease or the medicine employed; but the curious fact has been the occasion of a good many queer remarks …" [30]

- - - - -

November 19, 1863
West Building Hospital, Baltimore

Lt. Sanford Branch
Co. A – 8th Georgia Infantry

"Dear Mother
... I am improving very rapidly, for the last week have been up nearly all day. A piece of bone cam from my lung wound this morning making No. 40. I am geting home sick. when confined to bed I was more contented than now. We continue to hope for exchange however, although there appears to be but poor prospects at present. There are but 2 officers left here now from Georgia. Lt. Newell of Millidgeville & myself. Love to all
Your affect.son
Sanford W. Branch" [31]

(ed: Sanford's odyssey of prison camps is about to begin. In March, 1864 he is sent to Ft. McHenry in Baltimore, in June to Ft. Delaware Prison on Pea Patch Island in Delaware, in August to Port Royal, South Carolina on a prison ship, in September he is at Morris Island Prison in Charleston, South Carolina and in October he is in Fort Pulaski Prison in Savannah, Georgia. The final prison is just a few miles from his home. He will finally be exchanged in December of 1864. Sanford survived 18 months in Union hospitals and prisons.) [32]

- - - - -

November 19, 1863
Camp near "Orage C. H., Va"

Private Bryant Folsom
Co. C – 26th Georgia Infantry

"My Dear Wife ... I have no nuse that would be interesting to rite ... times appears to bee quiet & we are facing winter quarters some of the boys has got their huts done ... we got the honey and wine last night & we had a fine time with our wine we have not eat our honey yet we had Irish potatoes for supper and cabbage for breakfast ... I will come to A close for this time as I have got to wash my clothes ..." [33]

(ed: In a November 15th note to his wife Nancy he wrote, "I have sold one pair of my pants for 25 dollars to Lieut N. B. Rodgers ..." He had one good pair that would get him through the winter and it was too heavy to carry extra clothing while marching.)

- - - - -

November 20, 1863 Mrs. Cornelia Henry
Sulphur Springs, North Carolina Farm wife

"The mail brought me no letter from Mr. Henry. I was sadly disappointed.... I began a cloak for Pinck but did not finish it today as there was tax giving in day. I paid 73.31$ tax today to Joshua Roberts as Harrie did it for me. I gave 75$ yesterday for two bu. of salt. Dear salt.... " [34]

(ed: On Wednesday, October 25th, Cornelia notes, "We have paid 60 bu. of tithe corn & one load of hay.")

- - - - -

November 22, 1863 Mr. John B. Jones
Richmond, Virginia Clerk, War Department

"Every night robberies of poultry, salt meats and even cows and hogs are occurring. Many are desperate." [35]

- - - - -

November, 21, 1863 Sergeant Benjamin F. Porter
Rapidan Station, Virginia Co. E – 11th Alabama Infantry

"Dear Sister ... my health is very good indeed. The Co. also enjoy excelent health. Not a man out of 21 has reported sick for more than a month. We have built a termporary winter quarters. We are comfortably fixed for the winter. We have good little Bunks with chimneys to them & from two to six men in a Bunk. The Bunk is from eight to twelve feet long & seven wide from seven to ten high. The tops cover with tents, the cracks daubed with mud.

… As Boots are so high you need not trouble youself about them. I thought you could have a coarce pare made at a reduced price. As for shoes, I now have a good pare of English shoes ishued to us by the government. I will not need but very little clothing as I can get it from the confed mutch cheaper than there. Though you may send me one pare pants, gloves, & socks …

… Paper I know is very scarce sutch paper as I am writing on is worth three dollars per quire. I have sent two dollars worth of stamps in one letter, five dollars in the second & an olde paper with two or three sheets of paper & envelops…. I will send you more paper soon….

Let me have the latest account of the Deserters.

I deem it useless to say anything about my Va. Miss. She is all right.
B. F. Porter" [36]

- - - - -

November 22, 1863
Magnolia, North Carolina

Captain A. B. Mulligan
Co. B – 5th S. Carolina Cavalry

(No 32)

"Requisition for Forage for Public Horses in the service of Mulligans Company 5th Regiment of S. C. Cav C.S. Army for 9 days commencing the 22nd of Nov 1863 and ending on the 30th day of November 1863, at Kernersville, NC

Date 1863	Mules	Total Animals	Days	Number Rations	Pounds Corn	Pounds Fodder	Total Corn	Total Fodder
22 Nov	4	4	9	36	12	14	432	504

I certify, on honor, that the above requisition is correct and just: and that I have now in service the number of animals for which forage is requested, and that forage has not been received for any part of the time specified.

A B Mulligan
Capt Co B 5th SC Cavalry

Received at Magnolia, NC the 22nd of November, 1863 of Capt M. K. Crenshaw, QM C. S. Army 432 pounds of corn and five hundred and four pounds of fodder in full of above requisition.

A B Mulligan
Capt Co B 5th SC Cavalry" [37]

- - - - -

Undated
Near Chattanooga, Tennessee

Private Robert L. Bowden
3rd Tennessee Infantry

"we were poorely cloathed and fed wee would draw rations for one day I could eat it all at one meal trust faith in providence for next meal. for want of beading bitter coald weather wee would build a big fire sit around telling yarns until fire burn down the ground then dig it up and … spread one blanket on the ground all but one of the men lye down then blankets over them then he would pile some tops over them then they would let him root up in the middle." [38]

(ed: Tops is a slang term for pine boughs. The ground would be warmed by the coals and the men would all be covered with the rest of the blankets and pine boughs.)

- - - - -

November 23, 1863
Chickamauga, Georgia

Adjutant Charles V. Thompson
Co. H – 13th Tennessee Infantry

"Dear Uncle
… Our Army is tolerably well clothed – except in shoes & socks and while I am speaking of socks – What would be the chance to buy three or four

hundred pairs in your country & if they could be bought what would they cost. Please write me soon about this … I do not wish to buy to sell again. I only want to buy for the men of my regt…." [39]

- - - - -

November 24 to 26, 1863
Augusta County, Virginia

Mr. Jacob R. Hildebrand
Farmer

"Bro Gabriel intended to butcher his hogs but the Rain disappointed him, I am quite unwell today I think I am threatened with fever Wednesday – Gabriel butchered his 5 hogs average weight about 200 Thursday – We killed our hogs 6 in number Whole weight 699 pounds" [40]

- - - - -

November 24, 1863
Steamer *Reindeer*
Near Selma, Alabama

Mr. Carter Coupland
Riverboatman

"My dear Mother –
I have received your last letter – of Nov 12th. Have not time to answer now, only drop these few lines in a great hurry to let you know I am very well – Capt Baldwin has sold the *Senator* & we are running the *Reindeer*. She is one of the nicest boats on the River – just as fine as they ever make them! I wish you could come & take a trip to Mobile with me. We leave Mobile on our regular day Friday & Selma every Tuesday Morning. John Marshall is at Mrs Jayses & doing very well, he was severly wounded, but is recovering fast – was up last trip & moving about in the house – I will write in a few days –
Yr Aff Son
Carter Coupland

We heard they are fighting
Sure the mischief at Chatanooga
No particulars as yet – I hope
Bragg will move them -!" [41]

- - - - -

November 24, 1863 Corporal Benjamin Freeman
Camp near Orange CH, Virginia Co. K – 44th N. Carolina Infantry

"Dear Farther and Mother
I this morning take the opportunity of writing you a few lines to let you know that I am well and getting on tolerably well except a boil on my Belly but it will be well in a day or two … Thos B Jones has come back … I thought he was going to bring me a box of vituals. I herd from him several times when he was at home and evry time he was Drunk and I expect you was afraid to send any thing by him for fear he would loose it … I though a heap of Thos. but I cant think much of him now … Give my love to all of the neighbors Write me word how you Hogs are getting on fatning Polk [pork] selling very high also corn and Wheat. Tell Lucy to take care of her little Pigs … " [42]

- - - - -

November 24, 1863 Sergeant Richard M. Jordan
Charleston, South Carolina Co. E – 6th Georgia Infantry

"Dear Mat
… I have also received the box sent me. The hat was lost. The chicken & pies were spoiled … the balance were all saved. Ned Weaver is coming home in a few days. You must send me another [box] by him …
We are just about to compleat our houses. If we sta here this winter we will have a fine time eating oysters." [43]

- - - - -

Late November, 1863 Private M. L. Morrison
"Chicamauga Creek," Georgia Co. I – 26 Tennessee Infantry

"While I saw Gen Bragg often, I remember him best as sitting upon his horse at the ford of Chicamauga Creek watching the infantry wade through the cold water on our retreat from Missionary Ridge. Most of the boys did not take off their shoes, but some of us knowing the bad effect on our feet of marching in wet shoes, sat down and removed both shoes and socks, taking time, also to replace them on the other side of the Creek. We halfway expected Gen Bragg to rebuke us for the delay, but he did not." [44]

- - - - -

November 27, 1863 Private William J. Bowers
Camp near Wiet, Mississippi Co. E – Waul's Texas Legion

"Dear Cousin,
… We have orders to cook up 6 days rations to start in the morning. Bragg has had another fight … The report is that Bragg had to fall back though the slaughter of the Yankees was dreadful. We have not heard any of the particulars.

I sometimes think the war will close this winter and then I think we will be blessed if it closes when Lincoln's time is out. I have been blessed so far with good health with the exception of the spell I had last spring…. Yours most truely. Goodbye
W J Bower" [45]

- - - - -

November 27, 1863 2nd Lt. George D. Buswell
Wilderness Tavern, Virginia Co. H – 33rd Virginia Infantry

"Today I am 21 years old & it appears that my birthday is not to pass unnoticed. As we were marching toward the Wilderness Tavern our rear was fired on, which caused us considerable surprise. We formed a line & about 4:30 pm engaged a force of the enemy. The fighting continued until darkness closed the scene when we moved on. Co. "H" had but one man wounded, Franklin Rothgeb in shoulder…. " [46]

- - - - -

November, 1863 Blockade Runners Departing Wilmington, North Carolina

Ship	Date	Bound To
"Fannie	Nov. 3	Nassau
Hansa	Nov. 10	Nassau
Beatrice	Nov. 11	Nassau
Antonica (Herald)	Nov. 11	Nassau
Gibraltar (Sumter)	Nov. 11	Bermuda
Syren	Nov. 13	Nassau
Flora II	Nov. 14	Bermuda
Dee	Nov. 14	Bermuda
Don	Nov. 14	Nassau
Spunkie	Nov. 17	Nassau
Scotia II	Nov. 17	Nassau
Advance	Nov. 19	Nassau
Lucy	Nov. 27	Nassau
General Beauregard	Nov. 28	Nassau" [47]

(ed: "Blockade runners will supply 60% of the Confederacy's arms, 30% of the lead for their bullets, ingredients for 75% of the gunpowder, virtually all the paper for cartridges and the majority of cloth and leather for uniform and accoutrements." A new nation, virtually devoid of any manufacturing capacity, believed that they could import all of their needs for waging war against an industrialized opponent and export cotton, rice and tobacco to fund the effort.) [48]

- - - - -

November 28, 1863
Marietta, Georgia

Private Grant Taylor
Co. G – 40th Alabama Infantry

"Dear Malinda,
… I am well except a sprained ankle. I am in the Academy Hospital at this place. I came here yesterday evening.

… As we started [the retreat from Lookout Mountain] I slipped and sprained my ankle badly. The Regt was engaged the next day on Missionary Ridge …

our company lost one man killed John Turnupseed and 3 wounded and 8 prisoners and one missing….

… I think I shall be able to go back to my Regt in a week. It is nearly dark I must quit. May God bless you all…. From your loving
Grant" [49]

- - - - -

Late November, 1863
Blountsville, Tennessee

Private Joseph P. Thomas
Co. E – 15th Virginia Infantry

" … we started on a march toward Knoxville … on the 27th of November, a cold, frosty morning, about sunrise, we forded the Holston River the water being up to my arms…. Some days after my shoes gave out and I marched over frozen ground for two or three days before I got another pair." [50]

- - - - -

November 30, 1863
Newnan, Georgia

Miss. Kate Cummings
Hospital Matron

"One of the coldest days I have experienced in a long time. The water froze in the buckets and pitchers in our rooms. My heart sickens when I think of the sufferings of our men. I have been told that many of them have scarcely enough clothes to cover them, and neither shoes or stockings. We have had many come here in this plight. This makes me feel perfectly miserable; I wish I could forget it." [51]

- - - - -

To Salt Hams

Mackenzie's 5000 Receipts

"For three hams, pound and mix together, half a peck of salt, half an ounce of salt prunells, three ounces of salt-petre, and four pounds of course salt; rub the hams well with this, and lay what is to spare over them, let them lie three days, then hang them up. Take the pickle in which the hams were, put water enough to cover the hams with more common salt, till it will bear an egg, then boil and skim it well, put it in the salting tub, and the next morning put it to the hams; keep them down the same as pickling pork; in a fortnight take them out of the liquor, rub them well with the brine, and hang them up to dry.

To dry salt beef and pork – Lay the meat on a table or in a tub with a double bottom, that the brine may drain off as fast as it forms, rub the salt well in, and be careful to apply it to every niche; afterwards put it into either of the above utensils, when it must be frequently turned; after the brine has ceased running, it must be quite buried in salt, and kept closely packed. Meat which has had the bones taken out is the best for salting. In some places the salted meat is pressed by heavy weights or a screw, to extract the moisture sooner." [52]

- - - - -

December, 1863

The armies are building their winter camps. Diarrhea and dysentery soon become a major concern with the combination of poor diet, improper sanitation and contaminated water.

There is stalemate on the Virginia front, regrouping from defeat in northwestern Georgia, and minor activity in Florida, along the Gulf Coast and in the Trans-Mississippi. On December 1st General Bragg resigns as commander of the Army of Tennessee and is transferred to Richmond to assume the duties of military advisor to President Davis. On the 16th General Joseph Johnston is assigned to command the Army of Tennessee and begins the job of restoring discipline and rebuilding morale.

Christmas letters echo hopes for peace and an end to war.

Salt is difficult to find and, when found, the price is exorbitant. Winter is the time for butchering hogs and smoking meat for the upcoming year. Poor crops have led to fewer hogs and therefore less meat is available for the coming year. The difficulty in finding salt makes the situation worse.

Perhaps wondering if she will ever get married, Miss. Emily Robbins of St. Louis writes on the 29th, "*if the war continues in a year or two there will not be many masculines left.*" Her humor, unfortunately, is not far from the truth.

As the year closes Private Benjamin Seaton of the 10th Texas Infantry, writing from Pine Ridge, Georgia, notes, *"O that his war wold end and let peace raign again."*

December, 1863

December 2, 1863
Academy Hospital
Marietta, Georgia

Private Grant Taylor
Co. G – 40th Alabama Infantry

"Beloved wife & children,
... I am well except a sprained ankle and I hope you and the dear children are in the best of health....
Be sure to attend to my shoes and send them the first safe opportunity.

This is the finest watered country I ever saw. Close together all around the side of the mountain are springs of the finest water and even on top of the mountain are some very fine springs... Marietta is a nice place 20 miles north of Atlanta and in good times it has the appearance of being a right business place.
Grant" [1]

(ed: In a December 6 letter, still at the Academy Hospital, Grant notes, "My Brigade is 2 miles south of Dalton, Ga. They have received orders to build winter quarters. Gen Bragg has been relieved from command by his own request. General Hardee is temporarially in command.")

- - - - -

December 2, 1863
Richmond, Virginia

S. P. Moore
C. S. Surgeon General

"War Department
Surgeon General's Office
Medical directors of hospitals will instruct surgeons in charge of hospitals not to use coffee as an article of diet for the sick in consequence of the very

limited supply, it is essential that it be used solely for its medicinal effects as a stimulant." [2]

- - - - -

December 2, 1863
Sulphur Springs, North Carolina

Mrs. Cornelia Henry
Farm wife

"Mr. Stevens was over today, seems to think Boston had no hand in the hog stealing. Betsey cut out the cloth for Mr. Henry's shirts yesterday. I began one today. Fannie is rendering up the tallow today & moulded some candles. A fine lot of tallow out of the two beeves. A pleasant day after the morning." [3]

(ed: On December 8th Cornelia noted, "got 7 lbs. of sugar & paid 21.00, three$ pr. lb. & got 1 paper of needles & paid 1.50, a paper of pins 1.25 & one card of agate buttons for 4.50. I really think speculators will ship us sooner than the yanks.")

- - - - -

December 3, 1863
Halifax County, North Carolina

Mrs. Catherine Edmondston
Farm wife

"Very busy dying warp for Mr E's & my own clothes. So we have come to it & are to wear our own homespun! In fact I find that almost all articles of prime necessity except salt, iron, & paper can be produced at home by us...." [4]

- - - - -

December 4, 1863
Orange CH, Virginia

Private Blackwood Benson
Co. B - 1st S. Carolina Infantry

"Dear Bro [Barry]:
... You want to know my 'earthly possessions and the condition they are in! – One hat in tolerable order, one overcoat, 2 pieces of carpet (one good, one burnt) 2 pieces of tent fly (both burnt, one patched) 2 pairs of shoes (one good, one bad); 1 knapsack; 1 worn haversack; 4 shirts; 1 drawers; 1 pants; 1

cup; 1 fork; 2 halves of a Yankee canteen for plates; and that's about all except for my gun and harness. Lice are not very plentiful because we all wage a war on exterminating them … When you come bring as much soap as you conveniently can…. Bring some pounded red pepper … needles and thread. This is the only pen and ink in the company … B. K. B." [5]

(ed: Barry had been wounded in May. His recovery, most of which was accomplished on furlough at home, was completed in early December. Barry boarded a train in Augusta, Georgia on December 2nd and reached Orange Court House on December 6th.)

- - - - -

December 4, 1863 — Sergeant Oliver C. Hamilton
Orange Court House, Virginia — Co. H – 38th N. Carolina Infantry

"Dear Father:
… You may now fix to come out here if you want to come and bring me a big box of something to eat, though I have no money to satisfy you for your trouble &c. If you can you may bring a jug of molasses, a large ball of butter, some eggs if you have them, potatoes, onions, sausages &c. Bring a good big box of such good substantial victuals as you think best …" [6]

- - - - -

December 5, 1863 — Mrs. Mary Watkins
Meherrin, Virginia — Farm wife

"My dear Husband
Did you know it had been two weeks tomorrow … since I received a letter from you….

Mama had her pork killed this week and has just got through with tying up lard, smoking sausage meat &c. &c. I expect to have a hog killing next week if it turns cold enough … Mr. Redd thought I had better have all my meat brought over here [to Mama's] … be safer … Mr. Baker made a very

short crop of corn this year and Mama took thirty three bushels of ours in payment for the seed wheat and oats that she had let us have. Mr. Redd sold the remainder in the grainery at $51 per barrel. I don't reckon there will be more than fifty or sixty barrels though after the Government corn is taken out.... They have come for Mr Redd's papers and I want to send this along with them. Good bye from your loving
Mary" [7]

(ed: Mary sold 114 barrels at $51 per barrel generating $5814. In a December 14 letter to Richard she notes, "would almost get you out of debt if people would take Confederate money wouldn't it?" In mid-December Mary butchered 12 hogs that averaged 90 lbs. This is half the amount of hams and sausages they put up in 1861.)

- - - - -

Candle Making – Undated
near Centerville, Virginia

Miss. Josephine Ross
Farm girl

"Our lights at night were from tallow candles. Some candles were made in moulds that held a dozen and other candles were made by the dripping process. My grandmother, with whom I lived several years, preferred the drip candles. They were not so smoothe but could be made more quickly. Farmers killed beeves [and hogs] and from the fat made tallow that was suitable for making candles. Cold days were selected for moulding candles as the hot tallow could cool rapidly when the mould was set out of doors or the hot tallow cooled rapidly if drip candles were being made. The candle wick could be gotten at the country store." [8]

- - - - -

December 5, 1863
Dalton, Georgia

Lt. W. F. Aycock
Co. K – 28th Alabama Infantry

"Mrs J. K. Callaway,
It now falls to my unhappy lot to write you a short letter letting you know what has become of your much beloved and Devoted Husband Lieut. Joshua K.

Callaway who fell in the battle of Missionary Ridge, mortally wounded while rallying his Company he was shot through the Bowels with a Miney Ball. We picked him up, started off the field with him when he asked us to lay him down and let him die. We laid him down…. [He] left some clothing; also some bed clothing … 1 jacket 2 shirts … there is nothing in the satchel … I want you to write me as soon as you get this letter and let me know what disposition to make of these things … I can sell [the bedding] and send you the money….

The Company and officers deeply sympathize with you in his loss but what is your and our loss is his Eternal gain." [9]

- - - - -

December 6, 1863 Mrs. Harriet Perry
Harrison County, Texas Farm wife

"My dear Husband:
Your Father and Mother speak of going to Marshall in the morning. There is no Post office at Jonesville and we have to send all the letters to Marshall. I … will try to send you a letter by every courier.

… I have cut out twelve garments for the negroes and made eight – I have bought a pair of cards [cotton cards] gave $40 for them – I get much more cotton spun now … I am more content when at work busily … Kearney died last Friday at Shreveport of Pneumonia. he had just had measles previous to that – Daniel says there have been a great many deaths among the negroes – he got back Sat. morning. he got thirty dollars a bushel for all the apples he carried … your Mother is going to have plain cloth spun for the Government. she … has engaged to weave 120 yards before Christmas….

I hope you reached the Army safe with all your baggage…. Theophilus & I miss you very much and wish for you every night and morning…. We send you a thousand kisses and embraces – May God preserve your health and spare your life is the heartfelt prayer of
Your devoted wife
Harriet" [10]

- - - - -

December 6, 1863
Bayou Fordouche, Louisiana

Captain Elijah P. Petty
Co. F – 17th Texas Infantry

"My Dear Wife
... just heard that Corpus Christi Texas has been taken by the feds.... The trade with Brownsville is gone. The salt works are gone I fear. The sugar crop is light – I cant send you any from here because I cant get transport for it. Every thing will now be higher & scarcer. Money will be more depreciated so you had better without delay lay in salt, sugar, molasses, clothing, etc ... If you have any gold or silver cling to it ..." [11]

- - - - -

December 6, 1863
Richmond, Virginia

Mrs. Judith McGuire
Clerk – Commissary Department

"... we just received from our relatives in the country some fine Irish and sweet potatoes, cabbages, butter and sages, chines, and a ham.... these things are very acceptable as potatoes are twelve dollars per bushel, pork and bacon two dollars and fifty cents per pound ... How are the poor to live?" [12]

(ed: A chine is a cut of meat containing the backbone. It would probably be mainly used in making soups.) [13]

- - - - -

December, 1863
Pt. Lookout Prison, Maryland

Private Jordan W. Grant
Co. G – 9th Virginia Infantry

"I am very sorry to have to write to you in this manner ... I am sick with chronic Diarhhoea have had it five months. [I am] a mere skeleton am unable to help myself, there is no medicine here that does me any good ... They say

I can not last this winter. The only alternative is for you all to send me the proper medicine or come on here after me … " [14]

(ed: This is a final letter to his mother. Jordan was captured at Gettysburg and sent to Point Lookout. The water and sanitary conditions were terrible. In fact, Point Lookout had the second highest prison death rate of all the Union prison camps. Private Grant died on January 1, 1864.)

- - - - -

December 8, 1863
Camp on the "Fourdoche"
8 miles from Mississippi

Captain Theophilus Perry
Co. F – 28th Texas Cavalry

"Dear Harriet: I left the wagon yard in the Atchafalaya, 12 miles from here last sunday evening. Last night it blowed up cold from the North and rained considerably. I was in a tent … and fared right well, though it misted in enough to damped the top Blanket….

… Sugar is scarce here. The cold weather has ruined the new crop, or cut it off very short. I think that you can sell the tobacco I brought of Mr. English for five dollars a pound in Shreveport. It will sell for ten in the spring…. Sugar is good speculation at fifty cents. Don't laugh at my tobacco speculation. I will make several hundred dollars on it…. I am in good health and doing well….
My love to all. Farewell
Your Husband Theophilus Perry" [15]

- - - - -

December 8, 1863
Wellington, Georgia

Mr. Steve Prior
Farmer

"Dear Brother
… Went to Mr Sayers sale – Everything sold high – Corn brought 5 dollars and 50 cents per bushel – So You see a soldiers pay will buy 2 bushels of corn a month –

The cattle grabbers are in Madison now. The most of the people are killing up their cattle now. This morning I started to shoot two of ours but Ma came out and thought that she had such a poor chance that she would risk them taking them…. Ma sent you some biscuits, a cake and a baked ham by Mr Mangold – Did you receive them - … the family joins in love to you –

Your Bud Steve" [16]

(ed: The "cattle grabbers" are the government conscription agents.)

- - - - -

December 10, 1863 Mrs. Mary Edmondson
Phillips County, Arkansas Farm wife

"All our efforts to procure salt have failed thus far. Our hogs are eating up our small supply of corn fast. What shall we do?" [17]

- - - - -

December 12, 1863 Mrs. Harriet Perry
Harrison County, Texas Farm wife

"My dear Husband:
We are all well. I am writing again on the Sabbath…. The measles are spreading … I have put another bag of Asofeatida around the neck of Theophilus – I do not wish for him to have it while teething if I can prevent it. he is well & lively. his bowels have been a little disordered but it did not seem to hurt him much. he has two more teeth nearly through – I have a great quantity of milk for him – he can say "Titty" right plain, and calls for it whenever he wants and "pats a cake" & can do a great many little pretty tricks – he is so much company for me… " [18]

(ed: Asofoetida is also called "devil's dung." It is a resin derived from the roots of plants from the genus Ferula, of the parsley family, and has a bitter taste and an unpleasant and somewhat obnoxious odor. It is an antiflatulent and an antispasmodic. There are "claims for it being used to cure bronchitis and even hysteria.") [19]

- - - - -

Undated | 4th Sergeant Benjamin T. Powell
Co. G – 60th Georgia Infantry

"The scarcity of food was felt very much among the men in the army. Most of them suffered from chronic dysentery. Pneumonia was prevalent among the ranks during winter brought on from exposure. Many of the men died from exposure and lack of proper medical attention." [20]

- - - - -

Undated
Charleston, South Carolina

Lt. William Alexander
C. S. submarine *H. L. Hunley*

"Detail on the loss of the *H. L .Hunley* in October, 1863:

The position in which the boat was found on the bottom of the river, the condition of the apparatus discovered after it was raised and pumped out, and the position of the bodies in the boat, furnished a full explanation of her loss. The boat, when found, was lying on the bottom at an angle of about 35 degrees, the bow deep in the mud. The bolting-down bolts of each cover had been removed. When the hatch covers were lifted considerable air and gas escaped. Captain Hunley's body was forward, with his head in the forward hatchway, his right hand on top of his head (he had been trying, it would seem, to raise the hatch cover). In his left hand was a candle that had never been lighted, the sea-cock on the forward end, or *Hunley's* ballast tank, was wide open, the cock-wrench not on the plug, but lying on the bottom of the boat. Mr. Park's body was found with his head in the after hatchway, his right hand above his head. He also had been trying to raise the hatch cover, but the pressure was too great. The sea-cock to his tank was properly closed, and the tank was nearly empty. The other bodies were floating in the water. Hunley and Parks were undoubtedly asphyxiated, the other drowned. The bolts that had held the iron keel ballast had been partly turned, but not sufficient to release it.

In the light of these conditions, we can easily depict before our minds, and almost readily explain, what took place in the boat during the moments immediately following its submergence. Captain Hunley's practice with the boat had made him quite familiar and expert in handling her, and this familiarity produced at this time forgetfulness. It was found in practice to be easier on the crew to come to the surface by giving the pumps a few strokes and ejecting some of the water ballast, then by the momentum of the boat operating on the elevated fins. At this time the boat was under way, lighted through the dead-lights in the hatchways. He partly turned the fins to go down, but thought, no doubt, that he needed more ballast and opened his sea cock. Immediately the boat was in total darkness. He then undertook to light the candle. While trying to do this the tank quietly flooded, and under great pressure the boat sank very fast and soon overflowed, and the first intimation they would have of anything being wrong was the water rising fast, but noiselessly, about their feet in the bottom of the boat. They tried to release the iron keel ballast, but did not turn the keys quite far enough, therefore failed. The water soon forced the air to the top of the boat and into the hatchways, where captains Hunley and Parks were found. Parks had pumped his ballast tank dry, and no doubt Captain Hunley had exhausted himself on his pump, but he had forgotten that he had not closed his sea cock." [21]

(ed: Lt. Alexander was part of the Mobile team that was involved with the submarine from the beginning. He was part of her crew and served as first officer in late 1863 and early 1864. Lt. Alexander determined his above findings based on his personal knowledge of the submarine and the condition of the boat and the crew members when she was salvaged. His findings were published in the New Orleans Picayune *on June 29, 1902.)*

- - - - -

December 13, 1863	*Coquette*
Cargo Manifest	R. R. Carter – Master

"391 tons from St. George's, Bermuda to Nassau

45 barrels pork, 256 barrels pork, 4 casks insulators, 3 casks telegraph wire, 60 bundles telegraph wire, 14 cases railroad caps, 300 sacks saltpeter, 100 pigs lead, 30 barrels pork, 2 cases woolens, 2 packages, 8 cases steel." [22]

- - - - -

December 14, 1863	Mrs. Catherine Edmondston
Halifax County, North Carolina	Farm wife

"Prices are almost fabulous now … in Richmond Corn meal was $18 a bu…. in Danville $750 for a barrel of sugar." [23]

- - - - -

"Wartime Fate of the Men of
Companies A & D – 16th Georgia Infantry

Circumstance	Number of Men	%
Killed	35	12.9
Died of Disease	59	21.8
Wounded	30	11.1
Captured	61	22.5
Captured Died in Prison	11	4.1
Died (unspecified)	11	4.1
AWOL	9	3.3
Discharged Disability	16	5.9
Surrendered at Appomattox	20	7.4
No Record	19	7.0" [24]

(ed: Some of these numbers overlap, but of the 270 men who served in these two infantry companies only 20 were present to surrender at Appomattox. 35 were killed in battle, 59 died of disease in camps and hospitals and another 11 in prison, and 11 more are listed as dead from unspecified causes. Some of that final 11 could have been from the 30 wounded men. 116 of 270 died, 16 were disabled, and several probably brought home chronic disease or a wound that killed them in the next couple of years. Madison County probably lost half of the men that they sent to war with the 16th Georgia Infantry.)

- - - - -

December 14, 1863 — Private John Jackman
Dalton, Georgia — Co. B – 9th Kentucky Infantry

"Johnnie G. and I have again commenced internal, or rather external, improvements. We built a chimney to our fly to-day.

Dec. 15th – We have concluded to build a house for winter, and have been cutting and hauling pine logs for the purpose, to-day. The troops had four pounds of sweet potatoes issued to-day in lieu of bread. "Hard up Ike", who had been over to the cavalry camp, says they are worse off. He says the "spurred" gentry are cutting down old trees, and robbing the wood-peckers of their winter stores of acorns, to the great discomfiture of the red-headed foresters. He says he saw an old wood-pecker expostulate in vain with a cavalryman, to leave his stores alone." [25]

- - - - -

December 14, 1863 — Private George T. Johnston
Enroute home on furlough — Co. F – 60th Alabama Infantry

"… I was wounded at Bean Station … and had my wound dressed by a surgeon in the 41st Alabama … was furloughed for forty days and started home staid all day in Petersburg … At Petersburg I drew clothing for I was nearly naked & barefooted besides…. passed through [Weldon] in the night Raleigh is a miserable hole Columbia is a beautiful city …" [26]

- - - - -

December 15, 1863 *Macon Daily Telegraph*
Macon, Georgia

A GANG OF 101 NEGROES
-by-
JOHN B. HABERSHAM & CO.
Geo. W. Wylly, Auctioneer

"On Tuesday, the 15th December, in front of the Court House, Macon, Ga., will be sold a very prime gang of 101 Negroes. The families will be sold together. There are several likely single negroes in the gang that will be sold singly. Terms cash.

Immediately after the sale of negroes, at 10 a.m.,
1 Bay Mare, 4 years old broke to saddle
1 Carriage with double harness
1 Buggy
1 Jersey Wagon
10 shares Macon & Brunswick R. R. stock" 27

- - - - -

December 15, 1863 Private Samuel Pickens
20 miles north of Orange C. H. Co. D – 5th Alabama Infantry

"Jack Wynne, Hausman & I took a wash in creek, mountain run, this evening. Water very cold. Before war would never have thought of doing such a thing as bathing in creek in middle Decr.... " [28]

- - - - -

December 15, 1863
Near Taylorsville, Virginia

1st Lt. John D. Camper
Co. D – 11th Virginia Infantry

"Major
I would most respectfully ask leave of absence for twenty days to visit my home in Botetourt County, Va. The grounds upon which I base this application are that my mother, with a numerous family of children, mostly daughters, is improvided for the winter and there being no one at home who can attend to this it is necessary that I should be there. In addition to this I desire to finish settling up the estate of my father, lately deceased.
John D. Camper
1st Lt, Co D, 11th Va Infty" [29]

(ed: On December 16th Captain James (Company), Colonel Otey (Regiment) and General Terry (Brigade) approve the leave request of Lt. Camper. John has two younger brothers, Private Thomas J. Camper and Private Newton Camper, who are also members of Co. D of the 11th Virginia.)

- - - - -

December 15, 1863
Macon, Georgia

Macon Daily Telegraph

DESERTED - $30 REWARD

"C. S. Arsenal, Macon, Ga.
Dec. 10, 1863

On or about the 1st of December, 1863, Edward T. Howe a detailed conscript employed at the Arsenal as machinist. Said Howe is of low stature, light hair, brown eyes, and speaks in a very low tone.
The above reward will be paid for his apprehension.

Richard Cuyler
Lieut. Co Com'g" [30]

- - - - -

December 18, 1863 Mrs. Harriet Perry
Harrison County, Texas Farm wife

"My dearest Companion:
... The weather has been extremely cold nearly all the time since you left – for three or four days past it has been freezing all day, does not thaw at all & is pinchy cold. I shiver for you many & many times – Theophilus & I can scarcely keep warm in our bed by a good little fire – I know not how you get along ... We killed 22 hogs at the Todd place yesterday. Aunt Betsy is busy over her lard today ...

I wish you a happy Christmas – Think of me & I will of you all the time – My heart will be sad sad.

I have written three times I hope you will get all the letters.... Good-bye my sweetest best beloved – May God spare you is my prayer
Harriet" [31]

- - - - -

December 19, 1863 Private J. H. Armstrong
Bayou De Glaze, Louisiana Co. F – 14th Texas Infantry

"My Dear Martha, ... Our regiment was on picket duty [on 29th Nov.] and were not allowed to have a fire, we did not have all of our bedding and that night I suffered, we have had as cold weather for the last 3 days as they ever have in this climate ... I have never told you that the long moss grows here on nearly every tree and from 2 to 3 feet long and we can get enough in half an hour to make a layer 3 or 4 inches thick under us, it is great help to the soldiers.... If you can rent the bottom land for 150 bushels of corn or $100 in money you had better do it.... You said you had sold some flour, I would not sell any more. You will not need the money and you might need the flour.... Ther getting considerable of sweet potatoes ... everything enormously high here ... tobacco $4 to $5 per plug, soap $1 per pound, honey in comb $1 per

pound … flour cannot be bought at all … Pray that this foolish & wicked war may soon pass away …
Your husband
J H Armstrong" [32]

- - - - -

December 20, 1863
Bayou De Glaze, Louisiana

Captain Theophilus Perry
Co. F – 28th Texas Cavalry

"Dear Harriet: … We are about 5 miles west of Simsport…. We are engaged in fortifying on this Bayou … The work is heavy and on a large scale. I hear that it will take nine weeks to complete … I am troubled with Constipation again. It attacked me last night. I am better this Evening…. I have chicken to eat. They cost one dollar a piece.

I have received your letter of the 6 Dec enclosing Hughs. It fills me with pleasure to hear that you and the baby are in good health. I am in hopes that Hugh will come home this Winter….
Farewell. Farewell
Your Husband Theophilus Perry" [33]

(ed: Hugh had been wounded in the leg at Gettysburg and the wound developed gangrene. Hugh has been recuperating at the Person and Perry farms in North Carolina and Theophilus hopes that Hugh can soon make the journey to Texas.)

- - - - -

December 21, 1863
Oxford, Mississippi

Private William J. Bowers
Co. E – Waul's Texas Legion

"Miss Mattie J Nunn

Dear Cousin, … We drew for furloughs yesterday and William [Mattie's brother] drew one and he expect to come home. I know that you will be glad to see him….

John [another brother] captured a fine animal. He was offered $800.00 for her.... Your letter of the 23 of September came to hand a few days since and brought the tidings that you were all well ... You have but little idea of the horrors of war ... Evils so many and so great that the heart sinks in contemplating it. Millions in property has been consumed and millions in debt have been accumulated to oppress the rising generation ... Many thousands ... have perished in battle or by disease ... and other thousands have been maimed ... The land is filled with widows and orphans.... Where shall we look for help? I shall put my trust in the Lord ... So, I will close. Forgive all mistakes. So farewell.
William J Bowers" [34]

- - - - -

December 24, 1863 Mrs. Mary Watkins
Meherrin, Virginia Farm wife

"Linden. Dec 24th 1863

"Tis the night before Christmas and all through the house not a creature was stirring, not even a mouse" except one.

My darling Husband
It seems a very long time since I heard from you ... [thought] perhaps you would drop in from [winter quarters]. Willie Dupuy dispelled that illusion this morning with the information that the 3rd Regt was in pursuit of Averill ... Emmie and Minnie hung up their stockings before going to bed and I have just filled them with apples, ground peas [peanuts] some candy ... and some cakes Mrs Baker sent them. Our negro men have been over to get pay for their corn and get their overcoats. They made eighteen barrels of corn this year. [from the servant gardens]
Dec 25th Little Mary waked up last night and would not go back to sleep again until I went to bed with her so I could not finish my letter. She and Minnie both sleep with me. Minnie sleeps at the foot to keep my foots warm she says

and she is a regular little stove.... You never saw children more delighted than Emmie and Minnie were at finding their stockings full Christmas morning ... Emmie was rather expecting a china doll but I told her the Yankees would not let Santa Claus get such things nowadays.... I asked [Minnie] how she got so black [with soot] she said she had been looking up the chimney to see if Santa Claus was up there now....

... I can't help thinking about you shivering in a cold rain and can hardly enjoy a good fire when I think that you are perhaps suffering with cold.

We are all well here. Little Mary has one tooth ... I want to send this letter to the Depot now. Good bye for the present. Hope too see you at home soon as you get here ... begin to think about your going back.
Your own
Mary" [35]

(ed: Reverend Clement Moore had composed "The Night Before Christmas" for his children in 1822. It was officially published in Manhatten, N. Y. in 1844 and caught on rapidly throughout the United States as is evidenced by Mary quoting from it 19 years later.) [36]

- - - - -

December 24, 1863 — Dr. Thomas F. Wood
Culpeper, Virginia — HQ – 3rd N. Carolina Infantry

"Dear Pa & Ma,

... Capt. Langdon arrived in good time with his clothes etc. I am obliged to you for the bundle. It contained what I wanted and things that could not be bought here. I succeeded yesterday in procuring some drawers, pants, jackets & blankets from the QM Dept. so that I am well prepared for the coming Winter. I will send the jackets home.... All these things sell very cheap and are a great accommodation to the officers. We can wear our course clothes around camp, and in this way cheat the extortioners out of their high prices for uniforms....

A Merry Christmas to you All!!
Affectionately your son
Thomas F." [37]

- - - - -

December 24, 1863
Jones Landing, Virginia

Mr. George R. Wood
Barge boatman

"I was getting a load of wood at Jones Landing opposite Varina in Christmas week on the 24th. It was snowing hard and Henry, my man, asked for the musket to kill a wild goose; there were [many] flying around and feeding in a wheat field. He was gone about an hour; when he returned [he had] a fat wild goose for our Christmas dinner." [38]

- - - - -

Undated
Camp Morton, Indiana

Private Melmon M. Butts
Maury Artillery

"My treatment at Camp Morton bad. No wholesome food – expose to cold weather some froze to death – went hungry and about half starved – had lice and mites which was very troublesome." [39]

- - - - -

December 25, 1863
Augusta County, Virginia

Mr. Jacob R. Hildebrand
Farmer

"This is Christmas day there are maney who were alive one year ago who are now in their graves maney of whom died of disease others were killed in battle & were denied buriel, in this most unrightous & desolating war & we don't know what God has laid up in store in the Impenetrable council of his wisdom for us, yet we must say that he has been our help in times past & is our hope in years to come, there were two Deacons ordained in the Menonite church today" [40]

- - - - -

December 25, 1863
Gratiot Prison, St. Louis, Missouri

Captain Griffin Frost
Co. A – 2nd Missouri Infantry

" … Friday was Christmas Day – I arose and answered roll call, then breakfast – pickled pork, bread and coffee … a pickled pork dinner … after dinner a fellow prisoner sent me a pear … a most acceptable Christmas gift … Fine fruits are not so plentiful in Gratiot…. went to the lamp room, brought in our lamp, pulled out the table, and played cards till time to go to bed, and thus ended Christmas day 1863 in the officer's quarters, Gratiot street Military Prison, St Louis, Mo." [41]

- - - - -

December 25, 1863
Camp in N. W. Georgia

Private Robert C. Dunlap
Landis Missouri Light Artillery

"Christmas & the weather is as mild as autumn in my own native State [Missouri]. On guard & I cannot enjoy myself & christmas as well as I might if off of duty. However it only gave me a better appetite for my dinner, which was a most magnificent one to have been gotten up in camp – to say nothing of oysters in abundance between meals. Our table was spread with roasted turkey with dressing, pork, potatoes buscuit butter, stewed fruit &c. &c. Our dinner & christmas tricks cost each one in the mess about $20. Every thing bears an extravagant price especially where ever the army goes." [42]

- - - - -

December 25, 1863
Rapidan Station, Virginia

Sergeant Benjamin F. Porter
Co. E – 11th Alabama Infantry

"Esteemed Sister … This has been a very dul Christmas to me. Though some of my commrids appeare to enjoy themselves finely….

… 500 men from the Brigade [Wilcox] had gon to Orange C. H. to rob some sutler stores. One man was sent from our Company in a squad to bring them back, but too late. They had done all they wanted … Every man he saw was loaded with something. He captured a fine mutton, tobacco, cakes, apples, pinders, etc in abundance so I had a bate of cakes & mutton as he was a mess mate of mine. There was about 8 or 10 large tents filled with everything good … Property of all description belonging to sutlers was destroyed….

I don't know when I will ever get to come home….

B. F. Porter" [43]

- - - - -

December 25, 1863 Mrs. Mary Edmondson
Phillips County, Arkansas Farm wife

"Christmas Day. The children were made happy by having their stockings filled last night in a manner mysterious to them … Albert suspected that the benevolent Kriss Kringle lived at home with us, Lou's faith was entire." [44]

- - - - -

December 25, 1863 4th Sergeant Robert Elliott
Canton, Mississippi Co. E – 35th Alabama Infantry

"Well this is Christmas day it has roled around again & we are still in the army & away from home & our dear ones at home we miss all the good things that we were used to at home but out here we cant expect to have such all I do hope that it may be the last one that we will spend out here … Sgt Spotswood ariving from Mobile with a great many little tricks for us of Tobaco, letter paper & alot of good papers for us to read & we were all glad to see him it is right cold & is very cloudy … " [45]

- - - - -

December 25, 1863
Dalton, Georgia

Private James M. Morey
Co. D – 32nd Tennessee Infantry

"Christmas dinner consisted of first course corn bread and beef tripe fried in tallow. 2nd course rice pudding made by your humble servant … all well, and in fine spirits." [46]

- - - - -

December 26, 1863
Dalton, Georgia

Sergeant Archie Livingston
Co. G – 3rd Florida Infantry

"My dear Sister:
… Christmas passed off very much like any other day, … Cousin john and I indulged in a drink of *warm whiskey punch.* Directly after roll call on that morning I was called for at this cabin where we drank to the health of our family at home … Dear sister it is almost impossible to believe that men would remain in service under circumstances so trying. Rations are cut down to a mite so scanty that it appears inadequate for a rightful sustenance. Corn meal & 3/4th pound green beef with an occasional ration of flour and sometimes a sprinkling of sugar and rice, is about what our troops are getting in the army…. This very day a little box came from Theodore & his friend Wilson as a Christmas present which was highly valuable in camps….

Our Regt has nearly completed winter quarters. I am in a very good shanty with two good friends, Sergt Rye & Warren McLeod. We have chimneys and comfortable bunks, and upon the whole find our new cabin dry warm & comfortable….

… The messages of the *two* Presidents do not offer much grounds for hope of peace….
Affectionately your brother
A Livingston" [47]

- - - - -

December 28, 1863
Dalton, Georgia

Captain Thomas Key
Key's Arkansas Light Artillery

"I called upon General Cleburne and I had scarcely seated myself when he introduced a conversation upon the propriety of bringing into the military service, and at once beginning to drill, 300,000 negroes! He remarked that this was not his idea alone, but that it represented the views of General Hindman, Colonel Govan, General Polk, General Hardee, and General Breckinridge ... The question at once arose as to whether these slaves brought into the field should have their freedom. Would they not fight better under the pledge that at the expiration of the War they should be free? Genl. Cleburne boldly assumed the grounds that not only those called into the field should have their freedom but that their wives and children should have the same guarantee ... Cleburne ... argued that ... 1864 would find us as near exhausted [for man power]. He assumed the position that Confederate acceptance of the Emancipation Act would turn it to our advantage whereas the Lincoln Government was now using it to injure us...." [48]

(ed: General Cleburne is correct in his prediction that manpower to replenish the Confederate armies would basically vanish in 1864. The draft age is lowered to 17 in 1864 and even taken further in 1865 [16-55] but those measures can not produce the required replacement manpower. The merits of his concept are debated till the end of the Confederacy.)

- - - - -

December 28, 1863
near Dalton, Georgia

Private Grant Taylor
Co. G – 40th Alabama Infantry

"Beloved wife & children,
... I am well except cold and sore throat....

Well Malinda I did not think I ever would send to you for something to eat. But if you can spare some 15 or 20 pounds of meat and have a plenty left to do you and the children, I want you to send it by Ide. Also a good pone of light cornbread. Tell Mother to send me a few of her big potatoes if they are not all gone. Send me some Sausage … and some butter but do not send anything if you think you will be scarce….

We drew 4 days rations of beef and we can eat it up at 2 meals and we only draw meal enough for 2 small meals a day … On Christmas day 7 of us paid $13.50 for pork enough for 2 small meals. So you see we are living bully. On Christmas morning they gave us a small dram [of whisky] apiece, but I sold mine for one dollar and bought meat with it….
Goodbye for the present,
Grant" [49]

- - - - -

December 29, 1863 Private Benjamin Seaton
Pine Ridge, Georgia Co. G – 10th Texas Infantry

"I was detailed as ordance guard. All of the command are comferetable situated in ther cabins and it is hoped ther peace may not be disturbed untell the winter is over and spring set in as everthing is quiet in front. Thar is no military news to be had while both armays remain in ther present position.

The present year is about to close and will close leaving many a widow and orphan to moan the loss of the brave hoo have fallen on the battlefields to rise no more – O that this war wold end and let peace raign again." [50]

- - - - -

December 29, 1863 Private Samuel Pickens
6 miles from Orange C. H. Co. D – 5th Alabama Infantry

"On guard to day. There's another order from Gen Lee now – granting 4 men furloughs to every 100 present for duty & as our Rgt. nos. 400 we can furl. 16 at once. 8 are now gone home, so 8 more will leave now. The order in addition to this allows an extra furl. to every Co. that has 50 arms bearing men present. Cos. H & [. .] have that no; - so there will be 10 more furloughs fr. the Regt." [51]

- - - - -

December 29, 1863 Miss. Emily Robbins
St. Louis, Missouri Resident

"My darling Ed –
… Oh! how we did miss you both Christmas. You know it is the first Christmas Pa has been from home…. everybody is getting married … I believe I will get married too – no I wont either…. if this war continues in a year or two there will not be many masculines left …

Your loving sister" [52]

- - - - -

December 30, 1863 Corporal Benjamin Freeman
In camp Orange CH, Virginia Co. F – 44th N. Carolina Infantry

"Dear Farther, Mother, Sisters
… I received your letter that you wrote the 24th and I got it the 28th I was glad to here from home and here you all were well. We had a dull Christmust here I worked all day Christmust building me a house to live in I have a nice house with a chimny … it is the mudiest times I have seen here. There has been a good deal of rain … They are giving 3 furloughs for evry 50 men for duty … Pa you must come and bring me Christmust … it will cost you about 15 to 17 dollars to come and same to go back … They say We will draw Sugar and Coffee and drid frute to day - … I have not eatin a pice of corn Bread since I cant say when. We have Loden Bread or Biscuts evry day … we have the best mess in the company no cursing going in our tent…. I send my love to all … I will close.
Benj H Freeman" [53]

- - - - -

December 30, 1863
Newnan, Georgia

Miss. Kate Cummings
Hospital Matron

"Lincoln has again refused to exchange prisoners. I do think this is the cruelest act of which he has been guilty, not only to us, but his own men. He is fully aware that we can scarcely get enough of the necessaries of life to feed our own men; and how can he expect us to feed his. Human lives are nothing to him; all the prisoners we have might die of starvation, and I do not expect they would cost him thought, as all he had to do is to issue a call for so many more thousands to be offered up on his altars of sacrifice. How long will the people of the North submit to this …" [54]

- - - - -

December 30, 1863
W of Camden, Arkansas

Dr. William McPheeters
Sterling Price's Division

"The surgeons of this division have recently formed themselves into an Army Medical Association for the purposes of mutual improvement while we are in permanent encampment to which they have done me the honor of electing me President. Today the Association held its second meeting … quite interesting … Three papers on the peculiarities of intermittent fever … There was a general exchange of ideas…. The subject of the next meeting is pneumonia…." [55]

- - - - -

December 30, 1863
Halifax County, North Carolina

Mrs. Catherine Edmondston
Farm wife

"Went out on horseback with Mr Edmondston to Hascosea on the 30th to attend to putting up the years provisions of pork – a beautiful day – He finished his labors in time to take me [on] a long walk, a real tramp over the farm, showing me his improvements both accomplished & intended…. we were awakened at daylight with heavy rain, rain which continued incessantly the whole day [31st] … It seemed as tho the year was going out in tears of sorrow and misery…." [56]

- - - - -

December 31, 1863
Richmond, Virginia

Mr. John B. Jones
Clerk, War Department

"Yesterday the Senate passed the following bill, it having previously passed the House: *A Bill to be entitled An Act to put an end to the exemption from military service of those who have heretofore furnished substitutes."* [57]

- - - - -

Catarrh, or cold

Mackenzie's 5000 Receipts

"A dull pain in the head, swelling and redness in the eyes, the effusion of a thin acrid mucus from the nose, hoarseness, cough, fever, &c.

Treatment – If the symptoms be violent, bleed and give twenty drops of hartshorn in half a pint of warm vinegar whey. Hoarhound and boneset tea, taken in large quantities, are very useful. The patient should be confined to his bed, and be freely purged. If there is great pain in the breast, apply a blister to it. To ease the cough take 2 teaspoonsful of No. 1 every 15 minutes, or till relief is obtained.

The influenza is nothing more than an aggravated state of catarrh, and is to be cured by the same remedies.... Neglected colds lay the foundation of diseases that every year send thousands to the grave.

No. 1 Cough Mixture: Paregoric, half an ounce; syrup of quills, 1 oz; antimonial wine, 2 drachms; water, six ounces." [58]

- - - - -

Postscript

Many of the closing letters of 1863 pray for peace and an end to the war. The realities and the horrors of war have reached every county in the Confederacy and have touched every family. In his December 21st letter Private William Bowers sadly noted, "*The land is filled with widows and orphans ...*"

Bleak prospects face the Confederacy and her citizens as 1863 draws to a close.

I found two key differences between the letters, diaries and journals quoted in *Mama, I Am Yet Still Alive* and *No Soap, No Pay, Diarrhea, Dysentery & Desertion*. First, the humor, satire, and jesting are much more prevalent in the 1863 writings. Secondly, the volume of prison camp correspondence is much greater in 1864-65 for the simple reason that the exchange of prisoners was drastically reduced and was totally discontinued for a significant portion of the final 16 months.

The great common denominator in both books is the impact of disease both in the armies and at home. In the 1860's virtually every disease could be fatal. Germ theory is ten years away and acceptance by the medical community of this new theory is even further away. Some doctors are still practicing bloodletting to purge the body of "bad blood." Doctors have chloroform, ether, and morphine for use in surgery and pain management. Quinine and the smallpox vaccination are available to combat malaria and smallpox.

Beyond that, all of the major medicines use some combination of mercury, opium, turpentine, pine resin, whisky, or chalk among their key ingredients. People faced life with a more fatalistic outlook. They had large families not only to work the farm but also because a significant number of the children would never reach adulthood.

Through it all is the magic of their writing. I have been collecting their 'voices' for more than ten years and I continue to be amazed and awestruck by the simplicity and power of their words. Quite frankly, there are Pulitzer Prize winning authors who have never written a line to equal *"I washed my old shirt and draws yestady. My old pant is verry nasty and my ass is out and these is all I have got …"*

I am honored to help them tell their story.

Acknowledgements

The letters, diaries and journals in the archives of the Mary Walpole Brewer Library at the United Daughters of the Confederacy Memorial Building in Richmond, Virginia were an unexplored treasure waiting to be mined. I thank Mary M. Williams, Chairman of the Memorial Building Board of Trustees, for permission to transcribe, edit and quote selections from their archives. Additionally I would like to thank Mary Valentino, Hilda Bradberry and Betty Luck for their support and assistance during my many research trips to their facility.

Proofreading remains a thankless task. It is impossible to catch all the errors and the project seems to be never ending. I have personally proofed the text so often that I overlook the same mistake multiple times. My wife Jan, of course, is my major proofreader and also my major source of support and encouragement. I am forever grateful. My sincere thanks to my primary proofreading team of Chuck Redding, Bobbe Redding, George Barnett, Martha Barnett, Paul Huelskamp and Joli Huelskamp. Your sharp eyes and critical suggestions were instrumental in the successful completion of the project.

To the members of the James City Cavalry Camp #2095, of the Sons of Confederate Veterans, my thanks for your help proofreading the text. I would like to specifically thank Tom Banks, Bill and Wendy Blizzard, Fred Boelt, Joel

Goodwin, William and Betty Harrison, Ken Parsons, Paula Raines, Ed Truslow, Sherron Ware and Don Woolridge for all of your notes and suggestions.

Thank you to Amelia Barnett (www.luckybugdesigns.com), my graphics wizard, for her cover design. Amelia also designs the bookmarks I provide when I am at booksignings and book talks.

My final words of appreciation go to the writers of these remarkable documents and to their descendants who saved them. Thank you to a wide variety of editors and family members who have published these documents or have donated them to libraries for safekeeping. One hundred of these writers are published here for the first time because their descendants realized the value of their words and took the necessary steps to insure that their 'voices' were not lost to our collective history.

Notes

Introduction

1. All quotes by soldiers and civilians will be documented when their monthly quote appears in the appropriate chapter. Thomas (1-14); Blount (2-1); Edmondson (12-10); Sikes (5-1) and Harris (5-10).

January

1. *Wytheville Dispatch,* January 13, 1863, page 2. From the microfilm files of the Library of Virginia - Richmond, Virginia. (Hereafter cited as *Wytheville Dispatch*).
2. The Diary of Robert D. Smith, Manuscript Collection of the United Daughters of the Confederacy, 328 North Boulevard, Richmond, Virginia – by date (future collections from the UDC will just note UDC.)
3. *Tennessee Civil War Veterans Questionaire,* Easley, S. C., 1985, p.1027. (Hereafter cited as TCWVET?) [Harris].
4. The W. E. Preston Diary & Others, UDC. (Hereafter cited as Preston Diary).
5. Nimrod Newton Nash Letters, UDC. (Hereafter cited as Nash Letters).
6. Edmondston, Catherine; *Journal of a Secesh Lady - The Diary of Catherine Ann Devereux Edmondston 1860-1866,* Beth Crabtree & James Patton, editors, Raleigh, 1979, by date. (Hereafter cited as Halifax County)
7. The Journal of Mr. R. S. Norton of Rome, Georgia, UDC. (Hereafter cited as Norton Journal).

8. *10th Virginia Infantry,* Terrance Murphy, Lynchburg, 1989, p.62.
9. Henry S. Figures Letter, Private collection of Henry Kidd, Petersburg, Virginia.
10. *Southern Historical Society Papers.* Richmond, 1876-1959, 52 volumes, *Detailed Minutia of a Soldiers Life,* Carlton McCarthy, Vol. 2, #3, Sept., 1876. (Hereafter cited as SHSP).
11. TNCWVET?, p. 1334, [Larmer].
12. Preston Diary, UDC.
13. Lowe, Jeffrey & Hodges, Sam – editors, *Letters to Amanda – The Civil War Letters of Marion Hill Fitzpatrick, Army of Northern Virginia,* Macon, 1998, by date. (Hereafter cited as Dear Amanda).
14. Exemption Application for Mr. G. W. Rhodes, UDC.
15. The William Charles Letters, UDC.
16. Harwell, Richard B., editor, *Kate: The Journal of a Confederate Nurse,* Baton Rouge, 1998, by date. (Hereafter cited as Cummings).
17. ibid, p. 82.
18. TNCWVET?, p. 164 [Acuff].
19. Russell, Richard and Clinard, Karen L., editors, *Fear in North Carolina – The Civil War Journals and Letters of the Henry Family,* Asheville, 2008, by date. (Hereafter cited as Fear).
20. Davis, William C., *Diary of a Confederate Soldier – John S. Jackman of the Orphan Brigade,* Columbia, 1990, by date. (Hereafter cited as Jackman).
21. The Diary of Robert D. Smith, UDC, by date.
22. Petty, Elijah; *Journey to Pleasant Hill,* Norman Brown, ed., San Antonio, 1982, by date. (Hereafter cited as Journey).
23. Blomquist, Ann K. and Taylor, Robert A., editors, *This Cruel War – The Civil War Letters of Grant and Malinda Taylor, 1862-1865,* Macon, 2000, by date. (Hereafter cited as Taylor).
24. Halifax County, by date.
25. Frost, Griffin; *Camp & Prison Journal,* Iowa City, 1994, by date. (Hereafter cited as Frost).
26. Morton, Oren F.; *A History of Monroe County, West Virginia,* Staunton, Va., 1916, reprinted 1998 by the Greenbrier Historical Society, p. 177. (Hereafter cited as Monroe County).
27. Norton Journal, UDC.
28. The Edward C. Robbins Letter, UDC, by date. (Hereafter cited as Robbins).

29. Journey, by date.
30. Heartsill, W. W., *1400 & 91 Days in the Confederate Army*, edited by Bell I Wiley, Jackson, 1953, by date (Hereafter cited as Heartsill).
31. James Carmichael Letters, UDC.
32. DeVinne, Pamela – editor, *American Heritage Dictionery,* Boston, 1976, p. 1310. (Hereafter cited as AHD).
33. Ordnance Receipt – 3rd Louisiana Infantry; Compiled Service Record – Confederate; Micro Copy 320, Roll 121; United Daughters of the Confederacy, 328 N. Boulevard, Richmond, Virginia. (hereafter shown as CSA Records – UDC).
34. J. W. Calton Letters, UDC. (Hereafter cited as Calton Letters).
35. *The Wytheville Dispatch*, January 9, 1863, page 3.
36. Hubbs, G. Ward, editor – *Voices from Company D – Diaries by the Greensboro Guard, Fifth Alabama Infantry Regiment, Army of Northern Virginia,* Athens, 2003, by date. (Hereafter cited as Company D).
37. Company D, by date.
38. Fear, by date.
39. Koonce, Donald – editor, *Doctor to the Front – The Recollections of Confederate Surgeon Thomas Fanning Wood, 1861-1865,* Knoxville, 2000, p. 67. (Hereafter cited as Dr. Wood).
40. Ibid., p.207.
41. TNCWVET?, p.1462. [McLarrin].
42. Jones, John B., *A Rebel War Clerk's Diary at the Confederate States Capital*, 2 volumes, Philadelphia, 1866, by date. (Hereafter cited as RWCD).
43. Simpson, Harold B., editor - *The Bugle Softly Blows – The Confederate Diary of Benjamin M. Seaton,* Waco, 1965, by date. (Hereafter cited as Seaton).
44. Brown, Norman D., editor – *One of Cleburne's Command – The Civil War Reminiscences and Diary of Capt. Samuel T. Foster, Granbury's Texas Brigade, CSA,* Austin, 1980, p. 22-24. (Hereafter cited as Foster).
45. Ibid., p. 23-39.
46. Heartsill, by date.
47. Toalson, Jeff – editor, *Send Me a Pair of Old Boots & Kiss My Little Girls – The Civil War Letters of Richard and Mary Watkins, 1861-1865,* Bloomington, 2009, by date (Hereafter cited as Boots & Kisses).

48. Joiner, G., Joiner, M., & Cardin, C. editors – *No Pardons to Ask, No Apologies to Make – The Journal of William H. King, Gray's 28th Louisiana Infantry Regiment*, Knoxville, 2006, by date. (Hereafter cited as King).
49. Baird, R. L. Sr. & Wright, H. S., editors – *Write Soon and Often – Treasured Letters of a Civil War Wife, Mary Pearson Thomas of Mechlenburg County, Virginia,* Mechlenburg, 2005, by date (Hereafter cited as Thomas).
50. Diary of Robert Inge Elliott – Co. E – 35th Alabama Infantry, UDC, Richmond, Virginia, by date. (Hereafter cited as Elliott).
51. RWCD, by date.
52. Everson, Guy R. & Simpson, Edward W., editors – *Far, far from home – The Wartime Letters of Dick and Tally Simpson, 3rd South Carolina Volunteers,* New York, 1994, by date. (Hereafter cited as Tally).
53. Johansson, Jane M. – editor, *Widows by the Thousand – The Civil War Letters of Theophilus and Harriet Perry 1862 -1864*, Fayetteville, 2000, by date. (Hereafter cited as Widows 1000).
54. RWCD, by date.
55. The Bryant Folsom Letters, UDC.
56. Cutrer, Thomas & Parrish, Michael – editors, *Brothers in Gray – The Civil War Letters of the Pierson Family*, Baton Rouge, 1997, by date. (Hereafter cited as Brothers in Gray).
57. Yearns, W. B. and Barrett, J. G. editors, *North Carolina Civil War Documentary,* Chapel Hill, 2002, p. 185. (Hereafter cited as NCCWDOC).
58. Frost, by date.
59. *The War of the Rebellion; a Compilation of the Official Records of the Union and Confederate Armies,* Series IV, Vol. 2, p. 382 (Hereafter cited as O. R.).
60. Swank, Col. Walbrook D., editor - *Confederate Letters and Diaries 1861-1865*, Shippensburg, 1992, p. 78-79. (Hereafter cited as Swank). (Pvt. Shelton letter).
61. Vandiver, Frank – editor, *Confederate Blockade Running Through Bermuda 1861-1865,* Austin, 1947, p. 110. (Hereafter cited as Blockade Running).
62. Lehr, Suzanne, editor - *As The Mockingbird Sang – The Civil War Diary of Pvt. Robert Caldwell Dunlap, C.S.A.*, Mansfield, 2005, by date. (Hereafter cited as Dunlap).

63. Douglas, Lucia R. editor – *Douglas's Texas Battery CSA*, Waco, 1966, by date (Hereafter cited as Douglas).
64. Tally, by date.
65. *10th Virginia Infantry*, Terrance Murphy, Lynchburg, 1989, p.61.
66. Journey, by date.
67. Andrae, Christian, editor. *Kate Sperry's Diary 1861-1866,* published in *Virginia Country's Civil War,* Vol. 1, 1983, Middleburg, by date. (Hereafter cited as Sperry).
68. Heartsill, by date.
69. Wise, Stephen R., *Lifeline of the Confederacy – Blockade Running During the Civil War,* Columbia, 1991, p.133. (Hereafter cited as Lifeline).
70. Widows 1000, by date.
71. Noah B. Feagin Letter, UDC.
72. Mackenzie, Dr., editor – *Mackenzie's Five Thousand Receipts in all the Useful and Domestic Arts: constituting A Complete Practical Library,* Pittsburgh, 1853, p. 230. (Hereafter cited as Mackenzie's 5000).

February

1. Kate T. Blount Letters, UDC, (Hereafter cited as Blount Letters).
2. Hallock, Judy L., *The Civil War Letters of Joshua K. Callaway*, Athens, 1997, by date. (Hereafter cited as Callaway).
3. Mrs. Eli Duvall Experiences in the Civil War, UDC, p. 14-15. (Hereafter cited as Duvall).
4. Cummings, by date.
5. O. R., Series IV, Vol. 2, p. 382-384.
6. Leon, L., *Diary of a Tar Hell Confederate Soldier*, Charlotte, 1913, by date. (Hereafter cited as Leon).
7. Fear, by date.
8. Halifax County, by date.
9. Heartsill, by date.
10. Widows 1000, by date & p. 277.
11. Lonn, Ella. *Salt As A Factor In The Confederacy,* Tuscaloosa, 1965, p. 13-17. (Hereafter cited as Salt).
12. Taylor, by date.
13. Monroe County, p. 177.

14. TNCWVET?, p. 203. [Allen].
15. Cummings, by date.
16. The Wade Letters, Personal collection of Jean Keating, Williamsburg, Virginia.
17. TNCWVET?, p. 1511-13. [Matthews]
18. The Foreman Family Letters, UDC.
19. William J. Bowers Letters, UDC, (Hereafter cited as Bowers Letters).
20. Frost, by date.
21. Heller, J. Roderick III and Heller, Carolynn A., editors - *The Confederacy Is on Her Way Up the Spout – Letters to South Carolina 1861-1864,* Athens, 1992, p. 90-91. (Hereafter cited as Barrett).
22. *Wytheville Dispatch, Friday, Vol. 2, #6, page 4.*
23. Taylor, by date.
24. McGuire, Judith W. *Diary of a Southern Refugee*, Richmond, 1889, by date. (Hereafter cited as McGuire).
25. *Wytheville Dispatch, February 13th, page 2.*
26. Norton Journal, UDC.
27. Fear, by date.
28. Younger, Edward, editor - *Inside the Confederate Government – The Diary of Robert Garlick Hill Kean,* Westport, 1957, by date. (Hereafter cited as Kean).
29. E. W. Jones Letters, UDC.
30. AHD, p. 178.
31. The Diary of William Ross Stillwell, UDC.
32. Widows 1000, by date.
33. TNCWVET?, p. 1409, [McAlister].
34. Brothers in Gray, by date.
35. Mary Cheek Letter, UDC.
36. O. R., Series IV, Vol. 2, p. 404-405.
37. RWCD, by date.
38. Sgt. Levin Gayles Diary – Personal collection of Ellen Goodwin, Suffolk Virginia.
39. Journey, by date.
40. Boots & Kisses, by date.
41. Brothers in Gray, by date.

42. Schroeder, Glenna. *Confederate Hospitals on the Move,* Columbia, 1994, p. 17-33 & p. 134.
43. Bowers Letters.
44. *The Georgia Historical Quarterly,* Vol LXXIX, Spring 1995, Number 1, Savannah, *A Profile of Two Madison County Companies,* David G. Smith, p. 172 & 177. (Hereafter cited as Madison County).
45. Halifax County, by date.
46. The John W. Robinson (Robison) Letters, UDC, by date. (Hereafter cited as Robison).
47. Williams, Ellen – editor – *Prey for Us All – The war letters of Benjamin Franklin Porter, 11th Alabama,* Mobile, 2006, by date. (Hereafter cited as Prey).
48. Cummings, by date.
49. ibid, p. 92.
50. Boots & Kisses, by date.
51. Brown, Susan W., editor - *The Wagg Family of Ashe County, N. C. Correspondence 1858 – 1885,* Roanoke, 1991, by date. (Hereafter cited as Wagg).
52. Jesse P. Bates Letters, UDC. (Hereafter cited as Bates Letters).
53. Widows 1000, p. 104-105.
54. Wagg, by date.
55. Carter, Rosalie editor, *Capt. Tod Carter of the Confederate States Army,* Franklin, 1975, p. 22-23.
56. Tally, by date.
57. Leon, by date.
58. NCCWDOC, p. 97-99.
59. Ibid., p. 193-194.
60. Ibid., p.135 & 139.
61. Elliott, by date.
62. Heartsill, by date.
63. Mackenzie's 5000, p. 404.

March

1. Michael Hambrick Letters, UDC.
2. Alvin Dempsey Letters, UDC.
3. Styple, William B. – editor, *Writing & Fighting from the Army of Northern Virginia – A Collection of Confederate Soldier Correspondence,* Kearny, 2003, by date. (Hereafter cited as Writing – ANV).

4. Frost, by date.
5. Robison, by date.
6. The Diary of William Ross Stillwell, UDC.
7. Journey, by date.
8. Dear Amanda, by date.
9. George W. Bradley Letters, UDC. (Hereafter cited as Bradley).
10. O. R., Series IV, Vol. 2, p. 421.
11. Wagg, by date.
12. Robison, by date.
13. Kean, by date.
14. Widows 1000, by date.
15. Frost, by date.
16. Cummings, by date.
17. AHD, p. 129.
18. The Charles Palmer Letter Book, UDC.
19. The Joseph A. Rogers Letters, UDC, by date.
20. Barrett, p. 91-92.
21. RWCD, by date.
22. Madison County, p. 173-176.
23. Markham, Jerald H., *The Botetourt Artillery,* Lynchburg, 1986, p.74.
24. The Francis McCutcheon Letters, UDC.
25. Calton Letters.
26. Dear Amanda, by date.
27. AHD, p. 822.
28. The Diary of Capt. John W. Taylor, UDC.
29. Prey, by date.
30. Callaway, by date.
31. George Crosby Letters, UDC, p. 7.
32. Brothers in Gray, by date.
33. Mial Howard Gammon Letters, UDC.
34. *Wytheville Dispatch,* March 17th, page 3.
35. King, by date.
36. The Lt. George D. Buswell Papers, private collection of Jean Buswell Sutton, Mulberry, Indiana. by date. {Hereafter cited as Buswell).
37. Carter Coupland letters, Dorsey-Coupland Papers, 39.1 D73, Folder 4, Special Collections Research Center of the E. G. Swem Library, College of

William & Mary, Williamsburg, Virginia. (Hereafter cited as Coupland Papers).

38. Boots & Kisses, by date.
39. Kean, by date.
40. RWDC, by date.
41. Nash Letters, UDC.
42. Kell, John McIntosh: *Recollections of a Naval Life – Executive Officer of the Sumter and Alabama,* Washington, 1900, p. 215. (Hereafter cited as Kell).
43. Slabaugh, Arlie R., *Confederate States Paper Money,*Iola, 2000, p. 59-64.
44. Sgt. John K Beaton Letters – Personal collection of Ellen Godwin, Suffolk, Virginia (Hereafter cited as Sgt. Beaton Letters).
45. The Issac J. Meadows Letters, UDC.
46. Widows 1000, by date.
47. James T. Drake Letters, UDC.
48. *The Confederate Records of the State of Georgia,* Candler, Allan D. – compiler, volume 2, p. 437-429, New York, 1972. (Hereafter cited as Georgia Records).
49. Dunlap, by date.
50. The Diary of R. A. Hardaway, UDC, page 1.
51. Georgia Records, p. 396-399.
52. Bates Letters.
53. Boots & Kisses, by date.
54. AHD, p. 1380 & p. 247.
55. Halifax County, by date.
56. Tally, by date.
57. RWCD, by date.
58. Mackenzie's 5000, p. 273.

April

1. Widows 1000, p. 116-118.
2. McMullen, Glenn – editor, *A Surgeon with Stonewall Jackson – The Civil War Letters of Dr. Harvey Black,* Baltimore, 1995, by date. (Hereafter cited as Dr. Black).
3. Ibid., p. 45-46.

4. OR., Series IV, Vol. 2, p. 467.
5. Halifax County, by date.
6. Nash Letters, UDC.
7. The Harris Letters, UDC.
8. Frost, by date.
9. Company D, by date.
10. Mackenzie's 5000, p. 217
11. McGuire, by date.
12. Corson, Blake W. Jr., editor, *My Dear Jennie – A Collection of Love Letters from a Confederate Soldier ...* , Richmond, 1982, by date. (Hereafter cited as Corson).
13. Dr. Wood, p. 68.
14. Widows 1000, by date.
15. Boots & Kisses, by date.
16. Elliott, by date.
17. RWCD, by date.
18. Georgia Records, p. 440.
19. Callaway, by date.
20. Bates Letters.
21. The James Lewis Letters, UDC.
22. Tally, by date.
23. Widows 1000, by date.
24. Kean, by date.
25. Elliott, by date.
26. Thomas, by date.
27. Halifax County, by date.
28. RWCD, by date.
29. Blount Letters.
30. Barrett, p. 93 & 96.
31. ibid, p. 137-138.
32. OR, Series IV, Vol. 2, p. 484.
33. Montgomery, George F., editor - *Georgia Sharpshooter – The Civil War Diary & Letters of William Rhadamanthus Montgomery,* Macon, 1997, p. 80. (Hereafter cited as Georgia Sharpshooter)
34. McGuire, by date.
35. The Hardin Family Letters, UDC.

36. Journey, by date.
37. John C. Allen Letters. UDC.
38. J. T. Forrest Letter, UDC.
39. Dear Amanda, by date.
40. Mackenzie's 5000, p. 207
41. The James Lewis Letters, UDC.
42. The Charles Segler Letters, UDC.
43. Fear, by date.
44. Taylor, by date.
45. Company D, by date.
46. C______, T. F. Letter, UDC.
47. Cutrer, Thomas – editor, *Longstreet's Aide – The Civil War Letters of Major Thomas J. Goree,* Charlottesville, 1995, by date. (Hereafter cited as Goree).
48. Boots & Kisses, by date.
49. ibid, p. 187-189.
50. AHD, p. 399.
51. Taylor, by date.
52. Jackman, by date.
53. Frost, by date.
54. Tally, by date.
55. Buswell, by date.
56. Fear, by date.
57. Brothers in Gray, by date.
58. Sgt. Beaton Letters, by date.
59. *Civil War Times Illustrated,* Gettysburg, April – 1985, Vol. 24, #2, p. 26, Carnes, F. G., editor – *We Can Hold Our Ground – Calvin Smith's Diary.* (Hereafter cited as Lt. C. Smith).
60. Frost, by date.
61. Wagg, by date.
62. NCCWDOC, p. 223.
63. Sperry, by date.
64. Michael Hambrick Letters, UDC.
65. Mackenzie's 5000, p. 209.

May

1. The Jordan Family Letters, UDC. (Miss. Elizabeth Sikes).
2. David Champion Memoirs, UDC, by date. (Hereafter cited as Champion Memoirs).
3. TNCWVET?, p. 1475, [Maiden].
4. Bowers Letters.
5. Swank, p. 82 (Pvt. Shelton letter).
6. Kean, by date.
7. Sgt. Levin Gayles Diary – Personal collection of Ellen Goodwin, Suffolk, Virginia.
8. Memories of Leroy W. Cox, p. 15, UDC.
9. Company D, by date.
10. Tally, by date.
11. Elliott, by date.
12. Company D, by date.
13. Nancy Porter Letters & Notebook, UDC.
14. Dr. Wood, p.76-79.
15. Writing – ANV, by date. (Sgt. M. D. Martin)
16. Buswell, by date.
17. Fear, by date.
18. Taylor, by date.
19. Sperry, by date.
20. *Wytheville Dispatch,* May 9th, page 3.
21. Wagg, by date.
22. *10th Virginia Infantry,* Terrance Murphy, Lynchburg, 1989, p. 71.
23. The Harris Letters, UDC.
24. Boots & Kisses, by date.
25. The J. N. & Susan E. Scott Letters, UDC.
26. Swank, p. 53-63. (Sgt. William McCoy)
27. Journey, by date.
28. ibid., p. 245.
29. Fear, by date.
30. Boots & Kisses, p. 194.
31. Wright, Stuart T., editor - *The Confederate Letters of Benjamin H. Freeman,* Hicksville, 1974, by date. (Hereafter cited as Freeman).

32. Davis Letters, UDC.
33. Lt. C. Smith, p. 27.
34. Molineux, Will – editor, *A Young Virginia Boatman Navigates the Civil War – The Journals of George Randolph Wood,* Charlottesville, 2010, p. 73.
35. *Macon Daily Telegraph,* page 2.
36. Corson, by date.
37. TNCWVET?, p. 670. [Dennis]
38. Crosby Letters, UDC.
39. Pitcock, Cythia – editor, *I Acted from Principle – The Civil War Diary of Dr. William M. McPheeters, Confederate Surgeon in the Trans-Mississippi,* Fayettteville, 2002, by date. (Hereafter cited as McPheeters).
40. Cummings, by date.
41. Fear, by date.
42. Dunlap, by date.
43. RWCD, by date.
44. TNCWVET?, p. 427. [Butts]
45. Prey, by date.
46. Compiled Service Records – Confederate – Alabama – Micro Copy 311, Roll 206 in the files of the United Daughters of the Confederacy, Richmond, Virginia.
47. Prey, by date.
48. Sperry, by date.
49. TNCWVET?, p. 1040. [Hassell]
50. Lowe, Richard – editor, *A Texas Cavalry Officer's Civil War – The Diary & Letters of James C. Bates,* Baton Rouge, 1999, p. 251. (Hereafter cited as 9th Texas).
51. Buswell, by date.
52. Hoehling, A. A., *Vicksburg – 47 Days of Siege*, Mechanicsburg, 1996. p/ 40-41. (Hereafter cited as 47 Days).
53. Robbins, by date.
54. Widows 1000, by date.
55. Writing – ANV, by date. (Captain A. J. McBride)
56. Tally, by date.
57. TNCWVET?, p1834, (Rice).
58. 47 Days, p. 49.
59. Douglas, by date.

60. Jackman, by date.
61. Lt. C. Smith, p. 30.
62. The Cornelius Sharp Letters, UDC.
63. Kean, by date.
64. Norton Journal, by date, UDC.
65. The Bryant Folsom Letters, UDC.
66. NCCWDOC, p. 149.
67. Ibid, p. 149 & 151.
68. 47 Days, p. 75.
69. James M. Amos Letters. UDC.
70. John D. A. Brown Letters, Private collection of Henry Kidd, Petersburg, Virginia.
71. Mackenzie's 5000, p. 54.

June

1. RWCD, by date.
2. Jackman, by date.
3. Buswell, by date.
4. The Bryant Folsom Letters, UDC.
5. Bates Letters.
6. Salt, p. 52-53.
7. Barrett, p. 88-89.
8. Davis Letters, UDC. (hereafter cited as Davis Letters).
9. Blockade Running, p. 112.
10. Fear, by date.
11. Boots & Kisses, by date.
12. TNCWVET?, p. 1398, [Lucy].
13. Nash Letters, UDC.
14. Tally, by date.
15. 47 Days, p. 127.
16. Wagg, by date.
17. Dr. Wood, p. 89.
18. John D. A. Brown Letters, Private collection of Henry Kidd, Petersburg, Virginia.
19. Elliott, by date.

20. Joslyn, Mauriel Phillips, editor - *Charlotte's Boys – Civil War Letters of the Branch Family of Savannah,* Berryville, 1996, by date. (Hereafter cited as Charlotte).
21. Sperry, by date.
22. NCCWDOC, p. 191.
23. Buswell, by date.
24. Sperry, by date.
25. NCCWDOC, p. 139-140.
26. Halifax County, by date.
27. UDC Magazine, Richmond, Virginia, Vol. XXIV #10, October, 1961, p. 22.
28. Dunlap, by date.
29. Charlotte, by date.
30. Company D, by date.
31. Cummings, by date.
32. Mackenzie 5000, p. 215 and AHD, p. 464.
33. The Diary of Vicksburg, 1863 by J. H. Pepper, UDC, by date.
34. Fear, by date.
35. Kell, p. 220 – 221.
36. Robison, by date.
37. Dunlap, by date.
38. Prey, by date.
39. Callaway, by date.
40. 47 Days, p. 198-199.
41. 47 Days, p. 201.
42. Nash Letters, UDC.
43. Barrett, p. 98-100.
44. RWCD, by date.
45. Dunlap, by date.
46. AHD, p. 432.
47. Buswell, by date.
48. 47 Days, p. 221.
49. The Diary of Vicksburg, 1863 by J. H. Pepper, UDC, by date.
50. Diary of William R. McCrary, UDC.
51. Thomas, by date.
52. Tally, by date.

53. Company D, by date
54. NCCWDOC, p. 252-253.
55. TNCWVET?, p. 867. (Funk)
56. Charlotte, by date.
57. Ibid., p. 159-162.
58. Tally, by date.
59. Dr. Wood, p. 102.
60. Hezekia L. Hamilton Letters, UDC.
61. Private Newton L. Camper, *A Short Sketch of the Fincastle Rifles,* E. A. Luster, editor, Fincastle, 1979, p. 13.
62. Mackenzie's 5000, p. 400.

July

1. Foote, Shelby – *The Civil War a Narrative,* New York, 1962, Vol. 2, p. 636-637.
2. Campbell, Thomas R., editor – *Southern Service on Land and Sea – The Wartime Journal of Robert Watson CSA/CSN,* Knowville, 2002, by date. (Hereafter cited as Watson).
3. Company D, by date.
4. Journal of Lt. Colonel Hillery Moseley – Personal collection of Audrey Hoitsma, Williamsburg, Virginia. Typed transcription, p. 3. (Hereafter cited as Moseley).
5. *The Confederate Soldier in the Civil War,* editors of Fairfax Press, New York, undate, p. 379-380.
6. Sgt. Levin Gayles Diary – Personal collection of Ellen Goodwin, Suffolk, Virginia.
7. TNCWVET?, p. 282. (Bashaw)
8. TNCWVET?, p. 304. (Blakely)
9. Champion Memoirs, by date.
10. Buswell, by date.
11. McGuire, by date.
12. Dunlap, by date.
13. Leon, by date.
14. Folmar, John K., editor - *From That Terrible Field – The Civil War Letters of James M. Williams,* Tuscaloosa, 1981, by date (hereafter cited as Williams).

15. *The Daily Citizen,* July 4, 1863 final "wallpaper edition." Personal collection of Jeff Toalson, Williamsburg, Virginia.
16. Nezbeth, Linda B., editor, *Recollections of a Private – William Preston Holland, Co. G - 11th Virginia Infantry,* Rocky Mount, 2009, p.17.
17. Boots & Kisses, by date.
18. Moseley, p. 4.
19. Norton Journal, by date, UDC.
20. TNCWVET?, p. 282. {Bashaw]
21. Capt. McPherson POW Parole; CSA Records – UDC; Micro Copy 331, Roll 174.
22. TNCWVET?, p. 193. [Alexander]
23. Williams, by date.
24. Fear, by date.
25. Frost, by date.
26. Davis Letters, UDC, Richmond, Virginia.
27. The Diary of James H. Wentworth, Co. D, 5th Florida, UDC.
28. NCCWDOC, p. 143-144.
29. McPheeters, by date.
30. Widows 1000, by date.
31. Prey, by date.
32. Williams, by date.
33. Watson, by date.
34. Company D, by date.
35. Blockader Running, p. 73.
36. Ibid., p. xxxii.
37. Leon, by date.
38. Nash Letters, UDC.
39. W. K. Hadaway Letters, UDC.
40. Tally, by date.
41. Widows 1000, by date.
42. Jackman, by date.
43. RWCD, by date.
44. Heartsill, by date.
45. *Macon Daily Telegraph,July 17th, page 2.*
46. I. Norval Baker Diary, UDC.
47. Mackenzie's 5000, p. 276.

48. *2nd Virginia Infantry,* Dennis Frye, Lynchburg, 1984, p. 55.
49. Wagg, by date.
50. *The Confederate Soldier in the Civil War,* editors of Fairfax Press, New York, undated, p. 379.
51. Dr. Black, by date.
52. Callaway, by date.
53. Seaton, by date.
54. Ibid., p. 84.
55. Foster, p. 48 -49.
56. Williams, by date.
57. Widows 1000, by date.
58. NCCWDOC, p. 97.
59. Widows 1000, by date.
60. Heartsill, by date.
61. Boots & Kisses, by date.
62. Bates Letters.
63. Blockade Running, p. 75.
64. Ibid., p. xxxii.
65. Sperry, by date.
66. Cummings, by date.
67. ibid, p. xv.
68. Douglas, by date.
69. The Laughlin & John Shaw Letters, UDC.
70. RWCD, by date.
71. Kean, by date.
72. Moseley, p. 6-7.
73. Thomas, by date.
74. Georgia Sharpshooter, p.90.
75. NCCWDOC, p. 252.
76. Widows 1000, by date.
77. Sperry, by date.
78. McGuire, by date.
79. Ragan, Mark K., *The Hunley*, Orangeburg, 2005, p. 36-37. A postwar letter from General Slaughter describing the test of 7/31/63. (hereafter cited as Hunley).
80. Hunley, p. 30 & 31.

81. Elliott, by date.
82. *14th Virginia Infantry,* Timothy Parrish, Lynchburg, 1995, p. 43 & 143.
83. Mackenzie's 5000, p. 125.

August

1. Sperry, by date.
2. Hunley, p. 38.
3. Prey, by date.
4. Company D, by date.
5. Sgt. Beaton Letters, by date.
6. Ellen Gaddes Letters, UDC.
7. Frost, by date.
8. Blockade Running, p. 77.
9. RWCD, by date.
10. Charlotte, by date.
11. Ibid., p. 160, 166-167.
12. The Harris Letters, UDC.
13. Williams, by date.
14. Boots & Kisses, by date.
15. AHD, p. 1079.
16. Hildebrand, John R., editor - *A Mennonite Journal, 1862-1865*, Shippensburg, 1996, by date. (Hereafter cited as Hildebrand).
17. Frost, by date.
18. Hunley, p. 42-43.
19. Watson, by date.
20. Tally, by date.
21. Corson, by date.
22. Widows 1000, by date.
23. AHD, p. 399.
24. Blockade Running, p. 116
25. Minor, Hubbard, Jr. – *I Am Getting A Good Education: Diary by a Cadet at the Confederate Naval Academy*, published in *Civil War Time Illustrated*, Vol. XIII, No. 7, November 1974, Gettysburg, p24-32. (Hereafter cited as Cadet Minor).
26. Leon, by date.

27. Tally, by date.
28. Ibid., p. 273-274.
29. Prey, by date.
30. Cummings, by date.
31. Freeman, by date.
32. The Bryant Folsom Letters, UDC.
33. The Harris Letters, UDC.
34. Williams, by date.
35. Lifeline, p. 265, 268, 287, 309.
36. RWCD, by date.
37. Williams, postscript after August 16th letter; ORN 21: 631-38.
38. Elijah Fleming Letters, UDC.
39. TNCWVET?, p. 282 (Bashaw)
40. Blockade Running, p. 85.
41. AHD, p. 239.
42. Cadet Minor, by date.
43. Boots & Kisses, by date.
44. Bates Letters.
45. Blockade Running, p. 117.
46. *Macon Daily Telegraph,* August 19th, page 2.
47. Thomas, by date.
48. Hildebrand, by date.
49. Hildebrand, p. 14.
50. TNCWVET?, p. 688 [Dickson]
51. Blockade Running, p. 42.
52. Watson, by date.
53. Fear, by date.
54. Hunley, p. 61.
55. Freeman, by date.
56. 9th Texas, p. 266.
57. NCCWDOC, p. 144-145.
58. Kean, by date.
59. AHD, p. 1400.
60. Dear Amanda, by date.
61. Sperry, by date.
62. Ibid, p.64 – 66.

63. Blockade Running, p. 42.
64. McGuire, by date.
65. Prey, by date.
66. Hildebrand, by date.
67. Journey, by date.
68. Lifeline, p. 233 – 235.
69. The J. N. & Susan E. Scott Letters, UDC.
70. Hunley, p. 70.
71. Halifax County, by date.
72. Diary of Mrs. Mary Edmondson 1863-1864, UDC. (Hereafter cited as Edmondson).
73. Robbins, by date.
74. Mackenzie's 5000, p. 219.

September

1. Kean, by date.
2. Edmondson, by date
3. Fear, by date.
4. Cadet Minor, by date.
5. 9th Texas, p.270.
6. Tally, by date.
7. Monroe County, p. 177.
8. Watson, by date.
9. Compiled Service Records – Confederate, United Daughters of the Confederacy, Richmond, Virginia, Micro-copy 267, Roll 280.
10. Marcellus & Alfred Atkinson Letters. UDC.
11. Company D, by date.
12. Dunlap, by date.
13. Dear Amanda, by date.
14. Writers – ANV, by date. (D. S. T. – 3rd Alabama)
15. Hildebrand, by date.
16. Hildebrand, p. 15.
17. Charlotte, by date.
18. Ibid., p. 166-167.
19. Writers – ANV, by date. (Capt. C. L. G___, 2nd Georgia)

20. Boots & Kisses, by date.
21. Thomas, by date.
22. Boots & Kisses, by date.
23. Widows 1000, by date.
24. Schaadt, Mark. *Civil War Medicine,* Qunicy, 1998, p. 83; Heimlich, J. *What Your Doctor Won't Tell You,* New York, 1990, p. 54.
25. TNCWVET?, p. 416 [Bryant]
26. Freeman, by date.
27. Preston Diary [Wheeler], by date.
28. The Diary of Reverend John Gardiner Richards, UDC, by date. (Hereafter cited as Rev. Richards).
29. Edmondson, by date.
30. Blockade Running, p. 118.
31. Seaton, by date.
32. Preston Diary [Wheeler], by date.
33. TNCWVET?, p. 1578. [Morelock]
34. Rev. Richards, by date.
35. Prey, by date.
36. The Diary of James H. Wentworth, Co. D – 5th Florida, UDC.
37. TNCWVET?, p. 851, [Frazier].
38. Preston Diary [Wheeler], by date.
39. Callaway, by date.
40. Hunley, p. 86-87.
41. ibid., p. 127.
42. TNCWVET?, p. 949 [Gredig].
43. Frost, by date.
44. AHD, p. 823.
45. Salt, p. 97-99.
46. Houts, Joseph K. Jr. – editor, *A Darkness Ablaze – The Civil War Medical Diary … of Dr. John Hendricks Kinyoun, 66th North Carolina Infantry Regiment,* St. Joseph, 2005, p. 146-147. (Hereafter cited as Surgeon Kinyoun).
47. TNCWVET?, p. 546 [Connor].
48. TNCWVET?, p.950-951 [Green].
49. Barrett, p. 107-108.
50. ibid., p. 106.

51. Hildebrand, by date.
52. Bradley Letters.
53. Compiled Service Records – Confederate, United Daughters of the Confederacy, Richmond, Va., Micro Copy 323, Roll 389.
54. Dear Amanda, by date.
55. Letters from Co K, UDC.
56. Jackman, by date.
57. Prey, by date.
58. Fear, by date.
59. RWCD, by date
60. AHD, p. 172.
61. Mackenzie's 5000, p. 394.

October

1. Watson, by date.
2. Cummings, by date.
3. Cadet Minor, by date.
4. Journey, by date.
5. Kean, by date.
6. Stephen Barnett Letters, UDC.
7. Hildebrand, by date.
8. Thomas, by date.
9. Elliott, by date.
10. Duvall, p. 15.
11. Cummings, by date.
12. Fear, by date.
13. Preston Diary [Wheeler], by date.
14. OR., Series IV, Vol. 2, p. 986.
15. Kean, by date.
16. Jackman, p. 91.
17. Coupland Papers.
18. Fear, by date.
19. Hildebrand, by date.
20. Taylor, by date.
21. Bates Letters.

22. Joseph T. Dunlap Letters, UDC.
23. Douglas, by date.
24. West, Michael, *The Gauley-Mercer Artillery,* Lynchburg, 1991, p. 111.
25. Hunley, p. 95-97.
26. TNCWVET?, p. 1177, [Hughes].
27. TNCWVET?, p. 1855, [Roberts].
28. Edmondson, by date.
29. Williams, by date.
30. Charlotte, by date.
31. Widows 1000, by date.
32. Hildebrand, by date.
33. RWCD, by date.
34. The Felix Miller Letters, UDC.
35. Watson, by date.
36. Callaway, by date.
37. Frost, by date.
38. Boots & Kisses, by date.
39. *Macon Daily Telegraph,* October 23rd, page 2.
40. Georgia Sharpshooter, p.96.
41. Boots & Kisses, by date.
42. Kell, p. 233.
43. Blockade Running, p. 49.
44. Harvey Armstrong Letters, UDC.
45. Halifax County, by date.
46. Ellen Gaddes Letters, UDC.
47. McGuire, by date.
48. RWCD, by date.
49. Bradley Letters.
50. McPheeters, by date.
51. Dear Amanda, by date.
52. Dr. Wood, p. 121.
53. Charlotte, by date.
54. Ibid., p.182.
55. Day Letters, UDC.
56. Mackenzie's 5000, p. 245.

November

1. Taylor, by date.
2. Barrett, p. 110-111.
3. Cummings, by date.
4. Blockade Running, p. 121.
5. Kean, by date.
6. Boots & Kisses, by date.
7. Taylor, by date.
8. Lt. Col. Hillery Moseley records, CSA Records, UDC; Micro Copy 269, roll #396.
9. *North and South,* Tollhouse, CA., April, 2003, Vol. 6 #3, p. 78 -79, "Letters of Archie Livingston, 3rd Florida Infantry," John M. Coski, editor, (Hereafter cited as Livingston).
10. Fear, by date.
11. Sgt. Beaton Letters, by date.
12. Coupland Papers.
13. The Abel Skelton Letters, UDC.
14. Hildebrand, by date.
15. Bryant Folsom Letters, UDC.
16. Davis Letters.
17. AHD, p.1257.
18. Hunley, p. 118.
19. Jackman, by date.
20. Frost, by date.
21. Cummings, by date.
22. McGuire, by date.
23. RWCD, by date.
24. Widows 1000, by date.
25. Surgeon Kinyoun, p. 157 – 158.
26. Taylor, by date.
27. TNCWVET?, p. 186 [Alexander].
28. Bates Letters.
29. *Wytheville Dispatch,* November 16th, page 3.
30. Frost, by date.
31. Charlotte, by date.

32. Ibid., p. 185-218.
33. Bryant Folsom Letters, UDC.
34. Fear, by date.
35. RWCD, by date.
36. Prey, by date.
37. Forage Requisition – 5th S. C. Cavalry; CSA Records – UDC; Micro Copy 267, Roll 36.
38. TNCWVET?, p. 361 [Bowden]
39. The Charles Thompson Letter, UDC.
40. Hildebrand, by date.
41. Coupland Papers.
42. Freeman, by date.
43. The Jordan Family Letters, UDC.
44. TNCWVET?, p. 1594. [Morrison]
45. Bowers Letters.
46. Buswell, by date.
47. Lifeline, p. 244 – 245.
48. Lifeline, p. 7 – 8.
49. Taylor, by date.
50. *15th Virginia Infantry,* Louis Manarin, Lynchburg, 1990, p. 51
51. Cummings, by date.
52. Mackenzie's 5000, p. 186.

December

1. Taylor, by date.
2. O. R., Series IV, Vol. 2, p. 1021.
3. Fear, by date.
4. Halifax County, by date
5. Benson, Susan – editor; *Berry Benson's Civil War Book,* Athens, 1992, p. 51.
6. Oliver C. Hamilton Letters, UDC.
7. Boots & Kisses, by date.
8. Ross, Josephine (Neel), *Memories of the Civil War*, dictated to Lake Ross Neel in July, 1943, p. 4. Document typed on onionskin. Personal collection of Jeff Toalson, editor.

9. Callaway, by date.
10. Widows 1000, by date.
11. Journey, by date.
12. McGuire, by date.
13. AHD, p. 266.
14. *9th Virginia Infantry,* Benjamin Trask, Lynchburg, 1984, p. 29.
15. Widows 1000, by date.
16. The Felix Prior Letters, UDC, by date.
17. Edmondson, by date.
18. Widows 1000, by date.
19. Widows 1000, p. 293.
20. TNCWVET?, p. 1760. [Powell]
21. Hunley, p. 104-105.
22. Blockade Running, p. 122.
23. Halifax County, by date.
24. Madison County, p. 178.
25. Jackman, by date.
26. Diary of George T. Johnston, UDC.
27. *Macon Daily Telegraph,* December 15th, page 2.
28. Company D, by date.
29. Leave Request – 11th Virginia Infantry; CSA Service Records – UDC; Micro Copy 324, Roll 500.
30. *Macon Daily Telegraph,*December 15th, page 2.
31. Widows 1000, by date.
32. Harvey Armstrong Letters, UDC.
33. Widows 1000, by date.
34. Bowers Letters.
35. Boots & Kisses, by date.
36. Marshall, Nancy H.; *The Night Before Christmas, A Descriptive Bibliography …,* New Castle, 2002, p. xx-xxiv.
37. Dr. Wood, p. 132-133.
38. Molineux, Will – editor, *A Young Virginia Boatman Navigates the Civil War – The Journals of George Randolph Wood,* Charlottesville, 2010, p. 89.
39. TNCWVET?, p. 428 [Butts]
40. Hildebrand, by date.

41. Frost, by date.
42. Dunlap, by date.
43. Prey, by date.
44. Edmondson, by date.
45. Elliott, by date.
46. TNCWVET?, p. 1580. [Morey]
47. Livingston, p. 79.
48. Cate, W. A. – editor, *Two Soldiers – The Campaign Diaries of Thomas J. Key & Robert J. Campbell,* Chapel Hill, 1938, p. 16-17.
49. Taylor, by date.
50. Seaton, by date.
51. Company D, by date.
52. Robbins, by date.
53. Freeman, by date.
54. Cummings, by date.
55. McPheeters, by date.
56. Halifax County, by date.
57. RWCD, by date.
58. Mackenzie's 5000, p. 205

Sources

Manuscripts:

The Mary Walpole Brewer Library, United Daughters of the Confederacy, Richmond, Virginia:

The John C. Allen Letters
The James M. Amos Letters
The Harvey Armstrong Letters
The Marcellus & Alfred Atkinson Letters
The I. Norval Baker Diary
The Stephen Barnett Letters
The Jesse P. Bates Letters
The Kate T. Blount Letters
The William J. Bowers Letters
The George W. Bradley Letters
The T. F. C______ Letters
The J. W. Calton Letters
The James Carmichael Letters
The David Champion Memoirs
The William Charles Letters
The Mary Cheek Letters
The Memories of Leroy W. Cox
The George Crosby Letters

The Weldon E. Davis Letters
The Lawrence E. Day Letters
The Alvin Dempsey Letters
The James T. Drake Letters
The Joseph T. Dunlap Letters
Mrs. Eli Duvall Experiences in the Civil War
The Diary of Mrs. Mary Edmondson
The Diary of 4th Sgt. R. I. Elliott – Co. E – 35th Alabama Infantry
The Noah B. Feagin Letter
The Elijah Fleming Letters
The Bryant Folsom Letters
The Foreman Family Letters
The J. T. Forrest Letter
The Ellen Gaddes Letters
The M. H. Gammon Letters
The W. K. Hadaway Letters
The Michael Hambrick Letters
The Hazekia L. Hamilton Letters
The Diary of R. A. Hardaway
The Hardin Family Letters
The Harris Letters
The Diary of George T. Johnston
The E. W. Jones Letters
The Jordan Family Letters
The James Lewis Letters
The Diary of William R. McCrary
The Francis McCutcheon Letter
The Isaac J. Meadows Letters
The Felix Miller Letters
The Nimrod Newton Nash Letters
The Journal of Mr. R. S. Norton of Rome, Georgia
The Charles Palmer Letter Book
Diary of Vicksburg, 1863 by J. H. Pepper
The Nancy C. Wallace Porter Notebook
The W. E. Preston Diary & Others
The Felix W. Prior Letters

The G. W. Rhodes Exemption Application
The Diary of Rev. John Gardiner Richards
The Edward C. (Ned) Robbins Letters
The John W. Robinson (Robison) Letters
The Joseph A. Rogers Letters
The J. N. & Susan E. Scott Letters
The Charles Segler Letters
The Cornelius Sharp Letters
The Laughlin & John Shaw Letters
The Abel Skelton Letters
The Diary of Robert D. Smith
The Diary of William Stillwell
The Diary of Capt. John W. Taylor
The Diary of James A. Wentworth, Co. D – 5th Florida
Letters from Company K (Pvt. T. M. Woods – 16th Alabama Infantry)

The Earl Gregg Swem Library Manuscripts Department, College of William & Mary, Williamsburg, Virginia:

The Dorsey-Coupland Papers

Newspapers:

The Atlanta Southern Confederacy – Atlanta, Georgia
The Chattanooga Daily Rebel – Chattanooga, Tennessee
The Daily Citizen – Vicksburg, Mississippi
The Greensboro Patriot – Greensboro, North Carolina
The Macon Daily Telegraph – Macon, Georgia
The Mobile Advertiser & Register – Mobile, Alabama
The Wytheville Dispatch – Wytheville, Virginia

Private Collections – Individuals:

Ellen Goodwin of Suffolk, Virginia:
The Letters of Sgt. John Beaton
The Diary of Sgt. Levin Gayle

Audrey Hoitsma of Williamsburg, Virginia:
The Journal of Lt. Colonel Hillery Moseley
Jean Keating of Williamsburg, Virginia:
The Wade Letters
Henry Kidd of Petersburg, Virginia:
The John D. A. Brown Letters
The Letter of 1st Sgt. Henry S. Figures of the 4th Alabama Infantry
Jean Buswell Sutton of Mulberry, Indiana:
The Lt. George D. Buswell Papers
Jeff Toalson of Williamsburg, Virginia:
Memories of the Civil War by Josephine Ross of Monroe County, Virginia
The Daily Citizen (The Final Wallpaper Edition), July 4, 1863.

Personal Reminiscences, Diarys and Journals:

Andrae, Christian – editor, *Kate Sperry's Diary 1861-1865, (*published in *Virginia Country's Civil War),* Middleburg, 1983.

Baird, R. L. Sr. & Wright H. S., editors – *Write Soon and Often – Treasured Letters of a Civil War Wife, Mary Pearson Thomas of Mechlenburg County, Virginia,* Mechlenburg, 2005.

Blomquist, Ann K. & Taylor Robert A., editors, *This Cruel War – The Civil War Letters of Grant and Malinda Taylor, 1862-1865,* Macon, 2000.

Brown, Norman – editor, *Journey to Pleasant Hill – The Civil War Letters of Captain Elijah P. Petty,* San Antonio, 1982.

Brown, Norman – editor, *One of Cleburne's Command – The Civil War Reminiscences and Diary of Capt. Samuel T. Foster, Granbury's Texas Brigade, CSA,* Austin, 1980

Brown, Susan W., editor – *The Wagg Family of Ashe County, N. C. Correspondence 1858 – 1885,* Roanoke, 1991.

Carnes, F. G., editor – *We Can Hold Our Ground – Calvin Smith's Diary, (Civil War Times Illustrated),* Gettysburg, April, 1985.

Carter, Rosalie – editor, *Capt. Tod Carter of the Confederate States Army,* Franklin, 1975.

Cate, W. A., editor – *Two Soldiers – The Campaign Diaries of Thomas J. Key & Robert J. Campbell,* Chapel Hill, 1938.

Corson, Blake W. Jr., editor – *My Dear Jennie – A Collection of Love Letters from a Confederate Soldier,* Richmond, 1982.

Coski, John M., editor – *The Letters of Archie Livingston – 3rd Florida Infantry, (North & South),* Tollhouse, April, 2003.

Crabtree, Beth & Patton, James – editors, *Journal of a Secesh Lady – The Diary of Catherine Ann Devereux Edmondston 1860-1866,* Raleigh, 1979.

Cutrer, Thomas & Parrish, Michael – editors, *Brothers in Gray – The Civil War Letters of the Pierson Family,* Baton Rouge, 1997.

Cutrer, Thomas – editor, *Longstreet's Aide – The Civil War Letters of Major Thomas J. Goree,* Charlottesville, 1995.

Davis, William C., editor – *Diary of a Confederate Soldier – John S. Jackman of the Orphan Brigade,* Columbia, 1990.

Douglas, Lucas R., editor – *Douglas's Texas Battery CSA,* Waco, 1966.

Everson, Guy R. & Simpson, Edward W., editors – *Far, far from home – The Wartime Letters of Dick & Tally Simpson, 3rd South Carolina Volunteers,* New York, 1994.

Folmar, John K., editor – *From That Terrible Field – The Civil War Letters of James M. Williams,* Tuscaloose, 1981.

Frost, Griffin – *Camp and Prison Journal,* Iowa City, 1994.

Hallock, Judy L., editor – *The Civil War Letters of Joshua K. Callaway,* Athens, 1997.

Harwell, Richard B., editor – *Kate: The Journal of a Confederate Nurse,* Baton Rouge, 1998.

Heller, J. Roderick III & Heller, Carolynn A., editors – *The Confederacy Is on Her Way Up the Spout – Letters to South Carolina 1861-1864,* Athens, 1992.

Hildebrand, John R., editor – *A Mennonite Journal, 1862-1865,* Shippensburg, 1996.

Houts, Joseph K. Jr., editor – *A Darkness Ablaze – The Civil War Medical Diary ... of Dr. John Hendricks Kinyoun, 66th North Carolina Infantry Regiment,* St. Joseph, 2005.

Hubbs, G. Ward, editor – *Voices from Company D – Diaries of the Greensboro Guard, Fifth Alabama Infantry Regiment, Army of Northern Virginia,* Athens, 2003.

Johansson, Jane M., editor – *Widows by the Thousand – The Civil War Letters of Theophilus and Harriet Perry, 1862-1864,* Fayetteville, 2000.

Joiner, G., Joiner, M. & Cardin, C., editors – *No Pardons to Ask, No Apologies to Make – The Journal of William H. King, Gray's 28th Louisiana Infantry Regiment,* Knoxville, 2006.

Jones, John B., *A Rebel War Clerk's Diary at the Confederate States Capital,* 2 volumes, Philadelphia, 1866.

Joslyn, Mauriel Phillips – editor, *Charlotte's Boys – The Civil War Letters of the Branch Family of Savannah,* Berryville, 1996.

Kell, John McIntosh, *Recollections of a Naval Life – Executive Officer of the Sumter and Alabama,* Washington, 1900.

Koonce, Donald, editor – *Doctor to the Front – The Recollections of Confederate Surgeon Thomas Fanning Wood, 1861-1865,* Knoxville, 2000.

Lehr, Suzanne – editor, *The Mockingbird Sang – The Civil War Letters of Private Robert Caldwell Dunlap, C.S.A.,* Mansfield, 2005.

Leon, L., *Diary of a Tar Heel Confederate Soldier,* Charlotte, 1913.

Lowe, Jeffrey & Hodges, Sam – editors, *Letters to Amanda – The Civil War Letters of Marion Hill Fitzpatrick, Army of Northern Virginia,* Macon, 1998.

Lowe, Richard – editor, *A Texas Cavalry Officer's Civil War – The Diary & Letters of James C. Bates,* Baton Rouge, 1999.

Luster, E. A., editor – *Private Newton Camper - A Short Sketch of the Fincastle Rifles,* Fincastle, 1979.

McGuire, Judith W., *Diary of a Southern Refugee,* Richmond, 1889.

McMullen, Glenn – editor, *A Surgeon with Stonewall Jackson – The Civil War Letters of Dr. Harvey Black,* Baltimore, 1995.

Minor, Hubbard, Jr., *I Am Getting a Good Education: Diary by a Cadet at the Confederate Naval Academy, (Civil War Times Illustrated),* Gettysburg, November, 1974.

Molineux, Will – editor, *A Young Virginia Boatman Navigates the Civil War – The Journals of George Randolph Wood,* Charlottesville, 2010.

Montgomery, George F., editor – *Georgia Sharpshooter – The Civil War Diary & Letters of William Rhadamanthus Montgomery,* Macon, 1997.

Nesbeth, Linda B., editor – *Recollections of a Private – William Preston Holland, Co. G – 11th Virginia Infantry,* Rocky Mount, 2009.

Pitcock, Cynthia – editor, *I Acted from Principle – The Civil War Diary of Dr. William M. McPheeters, Confederate Surgeon in the Trans-Mississippi,* Fayetteville, 2002.

Russell, Richard & Clinard, Karen L., editors – *Fear in North Carolina – The Civil War Journals and Letters of the Henry Family,* Ashville, 2008.

Simpson, Harold B., editor – *The Bugle Softly Blows – The Confederate Diary of Benjamin M. Seaton,* Waco, 1965.

Styple, William B., editor – *Writing & Fighting from the Army of Northern Virginia – A Collection of Confederate Soldier Correspondence,* Kearny, 2003.

Swank, Col. Walbrook D., editor – *Confederate Letters & Diaries 1861-1865,* Shippensburg, 1992.

Toalson, Jeff – editor, *Send Me a Pair of Old Boots & Kiss My Little Girls – The Civil War Letters of Richard and Mary Watkins, 1861-1865,* Bloomington, 2009.

Vandiver, Frank – editor, *Confederate Blockade Running Through Bermuda 1861-1865,* Austin, 1947.

Wiley, Bell I., editor – *1400 & 91 Days in the Confederate Army – The Journals of W. W. Heartsill,* Jackson, 1953.

Williams, Ellen – editor, *Prey for Us All – The War Letters of Benjamin Franklin Porter, 11th Alabama,* Mobile, 2006.

Wright, Stuart T., editor – *The Confederate Letters of Benjamin H. Freeman,* Hicksville, 1974.

Yearns, W. B. & Barrett, J. G., editors – *North Carolina Civil War Documentary,* Chapel Hill, 2002.

Younger, Edward – editor, *Inside the Confederate Government – The Diary of Robert Garlick Hill Kean,* Westport, 1957.

Regimental and Units Histories:

Frye, Dennis - *2nd Virginia Infantry,* Lynchburg, 1984.

Manarin, Louis -*13th Virginia Infantry,* Lynchburg, 1990.

Markham, Jerald H. – *The Botetourt Artillery,* Lynchburg, 1986.

Murphy, Terrance - *10th Virginia Infantry,* Lynchburg, 1989.

Parrish, Timothry - *14th Virginia Infantry,* Lynchburg, 1995.

Trask, Benjamin – *9th Virginia Infantry,* Lynchburg, 1984.

West, Michael – *Gauley-Mercer Artillery,* Lynchburg, 1991.

Other Primary Sources:

Battle and Leaders of the Civil War, 4 volumes, New York, 1956.

Confederate Records – Georgia, 5 volumes, Atlanta, 1910.

Foote, Shelby – *The Civil War – A Narrative,* 3 Volumes, New York, 1963.

Hoehling, A. A., *Vicksburg – 47 Days of Siege,* Mechanicsburg, 1996.

Lonn, Ella – *Salt As A Factor in the Confederacy,* Tuscaloosa, 1965.

Mackenzie, Dr., editor – *Mackenzie's Five Thousand Receipts in all the Useful and Domestic Arts: constituting A Complete Practical Library,* Pittsburg, 1853.

Morton, Oren F.; *A History of Monroe County, West Virginia,* Staunton, 1998.

Ragan, Mark K., *The Hunley,* Orangeburg, 2005.

Schaadt, Mark. *Civil War Medicine,* Quincy, 1998.

Schroeder, Glenna. *Confederate Hospitals on the Move,* Columbia, 1994.

Slabaugh, Arlie R., *Confederate States Paper Money,* Iola, 2000.

Southern Historical Society Papers, Richmond, 52 volumes, 1876-1959.

Tennessee Civil War Veterans Questionaire, Easley, S. C., 5 volumes, 1985.

The Confederate Soldier in the Civil War, editors of Fairfax Press, New York, undated.

The Georgia Historical Quarterly, Savannah, Vol LXXIX, Spring 1995.

The Roster of Confederate Soldiers, 1861-1865, 16 volumes, Wilmington, 1996.

Wise, Stephen R., *Lifeline of the Confederacy – Blockade Running During the Civil War,* Columbia, 1991.

Index

I have created three parts to the index: Biographical, Command and General Event. The biographical records the name of the individual along with the dates where his or her quotes appear. Therefore 4-25 means the quote will be found on April 25th. Should you see 4 -5, 25, 30 it would mean that there are three quotes in April from this person on the 5th, 25th and 30th. Command will list units, vessels, military department etc. and will list the name of the person or persons from that command in the book. For example the 11th Virginia Infantry lists Private Newton Camper, Lt. John Camper and Private William Holland. You then refer to those individuals for a listing of dates where their quotes are utilized. These first two indexes should provide easy access between soldiers and their commands. The general event index will be the more standard subject index but will still use the same date/name system versus page numbers.

BIOGRAPHICAL:

COMMAND:

Artillery:

Cavalry:

3rd South Carolina – Mulligan, A.

3rd Tennessee – Allen, W.
7th Tennessee – Rice, C.
9th Tennessee – Alexander, G.
9th Tennessee Battalion – Matthews, W.
11th Tennessee – McAlister, R.
24th Tennessee – Foster, S.
59th Mtd. Tennessee Battalion – Hardin, M.

2nd Texas – Heartsill, W. W.
9th Texas – Bates, J.
28th Texas – Perry, T.

3rd Virginia – Corson, W.; Watkins, R.
18th Virginia – Baker, I. N.
25th Virginia – Larmer, E.
27th Virginia Battalion – Wade, D.

Infantry:

3rd Alabama – Taylor, D.; Day, L.
4th Alabama – Figures, H.
5th Alabama – Corwin, J.; Pickens, S.
11th Alabama – Porter, B.
15th Alabama – Feagin, N.
16th Alabama – Woods, T.
21st Alabama – Williams, J.
28th Alabama – Callaway, J.; Aycock, W.
30th Alabama – Alexander, W.
33rd Alabama – Preston, W.; Wheeler, M.
35th Alabama – Elliott, R.
40th Alabama – Taylor, G.; Foreman, N.
42nd Alabama – Drake, J.
60th Alabama – Johnson, G.

3rd Florida – Livingston, A.
5th Florida – Wentworth, J.
7th Florida – Watson, R.

Cobb's Legion – Atkinson, A.
Wilcoxen Regiment (Home Guard) – Dunlap, J.
1st Georgia Sharpshooters – Montgomery, W.
1st Georgia – Forrest, J.
2nd Georgia Battalion – G., C. L.
2nd Georgia – Martin, M.
3rd Battalion Georgia Sharpshooters – Barrett, M.; Montgomery, W.
8th Georgia – Soldier Jim; Branch, S.
9th Georgia – Callaway, J.
10th Georgia Battalion – Hambrick, M.; Culpepper, W.
10th Georgia – McBride, A.
13th Georgia – Allen, J.
14th Georgia – Champion, D.
16th Georgia – 3-11; 12-14
18th Georgia – Barrett, M.; Mauldin, L.
19th Georgia – Barnett, S.
24th Georgia – Hadaway, W.
26th Georgia – Folsom, B.
30th Georgia – Hamilton, H.
45th Georgia – Fitzpatrick, M.
53rd Georgia – Stillwell, W.

56th Georgia – Gammon, M.
60th Georgia – Powell, B.

9th Kentucky – Jackman, J.

3rd Louisiana – Pierson, D.
9th Louisiana – Pierson, R.
28th Louisiana – King, W.

13th Mississippi – Nash, N.; Ross, F.
42nd Mississippi – Moseley, H.
43rd Mississippi – McCrary, W.

Price's Division – McPheeters, W.
2nd Missouri – Frost, G.

1st North Carolina – Leon, L.
3rd North Carolina – Wood, T.
21st North Carolina – Amos, J.
26th North Carolina – Wagg, S.
30th North Carolina – Davis, G.; Davis, W.
38th North Carolina – Hamilton, O.
44th North Carolina – Freeman, B.
46th North Carolina – Brown, J. D. A.
48th North Carolina – Miller, F.
49th North Carolina – Johnson, A.
51st North Carolina – Goddin, O.
56th North Carolina – Calton, J.
66th North Carolina – Kinyoun, J.

Hampton Legion – Arial, W.
1st South Carolina – Benson, Blackwood
2nd South Carolina Rifles – Bradley, G.
3rd South Carolina – Simpson, T.
10th South Carolina – Richards, J.
14th South Carolina – Blakely, H.
15th South Carolina – Haselden, W.

2nd Tennessee – Smith, R. D.
3rd Tennessee – Lucy, W.; Bowden, R.
7th Tennessee – Bashaw, J.
8th Tennessee – Harris, T.
9th Tennessee – Conner, P.; Hughes, A.
13th Tennessee – Thompson, C.
19th Tennessee – McLarrin, W.; Frazier, S.; Green, J.
20th Tennessee – Carter, T.; Robert, D.
21st Tennessee – Dickson, J.
26th Tennessee – Acuff, S.; Morrison, M.
28th Tennessee – Rogers, J.
31st Tennessee – Smith, C.
32nd Tennessee – Morey, J.
43rd Tennessee – Dennis, J.; Funk, J.
44th Tennessee – Bryant, J.
50th Tennessee – Hassell, E.
59th Tennessee – Crosby, G.

Waul's Texas Legion – Bowers, W.
4th Texas – Sharp, E.
9th Texas – Bates, J.
10th Texas – Seaton, B.
14th Texas – Armstrong, J.
17th Texas – Petty, E.
20th Texas – Scott, J.

Miscellaneous Departments & Commands:

Naval Commands:

GENERAL SUBJECT INDEX:

Artillery:

Battles:

Cost of Goods & Services:

Desertion:

Disease, Maladies & Pests:

Draft Exemption – See "Conscription"

Farmlife:

Mail:

Manufacturing:

Medicine & Medical Practices:

Money & Currency:

Naval Activity:

Politics:

Prison Camps:

Railroads:

Religion:

Salt:

Soldiers – Clothing:

Soldiers – Conditions of the March:

Soldiers – Rations:

Soldiers - Weapons & Ordnance:

Taxes:

Union Occupation: